KU-485-808

ESSAYS IN PHILOSOPHICAL PSYCHOLOGY

ESSAYS IN PHILOSOPHICAL PSYCHOLOGY

EDITED BY

DONALD F. GUSTAFSON

MACMILLAN
LONDON · MELBOURNE
1967

First published in the United States of America 1964
First published in Great Britain 1967

MACMILLAN AND COMPANY LIMITED
Little Essex Street London WC2
also Bombay Calcutta Madras Melbourne

THE MACMILLAN COMPANY OF CANADA LIMITED
70 Bond Street Toronto 2

ST MARTIN'S PRESS INC
175 Fifth Avenue New York NY 10010

Printed in Great Britain by
Fletcher & Son Ltd, Norwich

CONTENTS

Preface	ix
A PLEA FOR EXCUSES, J. L. Austin	1
INTENTION, G. E. M. Anscombe	30
VOLITION, G. N. A. Vesey	41
ACTION, A. I. Melden	58
EMOTIONS, Errol Bedford	77
PRETENDING, J. L. Austin	99
IMAGINATION, Gilbert Ryle	117
IMAGINATION, J. M. Shorter	154
REMEMBERING, B. S. Benjamin	171
PLEASURE, Gilbert Ryle	195
THE CONCEPT OF HEED, U. T. Place	206
THE LOGIC OF PLEASURE, Terence Penelhum	227
SLEEPING AND WAKING, Margaret Macdonald	248
THE CONCEPT OF DREAMING, Norman Malcolm	265
DREAMING, D. F. Pears	277
THE CRITERIA FOR A PSYCHO-ANALYTIC INTERPRETATION, B. A. Farrell	299
PERSONAL IDENTITY AND INDIVIDUATION, B. A. O. Williams	324
ONE'S KNOWLEDGE OF OTHER MINDS, A. J. Ayer	346
KNOWLEDGE OF OTHER MINDS, Norman Malcolm	365
PERSONS, P. F. Strawson	377
Bibliography	404

ACKNOWLEDGMENTS

The kindness of authors and publishers who gave permission for the inclusion of material in this book is gratefully acknowledged.

"A Plea for Excuses," by J. L. Austin; "Intention," by G. E. M. Anscombe; "Emotions," by Errol Bedford; and "Personal Identity and Individuation," by B. A. O. Williams are reprinted with the permission of the Aristotelian Society (A. A. Kassman, Honorary Secretary and Editor) from *Proceedings of the Aristotelian Society* (LVII, 1956–57); also by permission of the Aristotelian Society, from the *Supplementary Volume*: "Pretending," by J. L. Austin (XXXII, 1958); "The Criteria for a Psycho-analytic Interpretation," by B. A. Farrell (XXXVI, 1962); and "Pleasure," by Gilbert Ryle (XXVIII, 1954).

"The Concept of Heed" is reprinted from *The British Journal of Psychology* (XLV, no. 4, 1954) by permission of the editor and U. T. Place.

"Knowledge of Other Minds" is reprinted from *The Journal of Philosophy* (LV, 1958) by permission of the editor and Norman Malcolm.

"Remembering," by B. S. Benjamin (LXV, 1956); "Professor Norman Malcolm: Dreaming," by D. F. Pears (LXX, 1961); and "Imagination," by J. M. Shorter (LXI, 1952) are reprinted from *Mind*, by permission of the editor and the authors. Also reprinted from *Mind*, by permission of the editor and Bedford College, University of London, is "Sleeping and Waking," by Margaret Macdonald (LXII, 1953).

"Action" is reprinted from *The Philosophical Review* (LXV, no. 4, 1956), by permission of the editor and A. I. Melden.

"Volition" is reprinted from *Philosophy* (XXXVI, no. 138, 1961), by permission of the editor and G. N. A. Vesey.

"The Logic of Pleasure" is reprinted from *Philosophy and Phenomenological Research* (XVII, 1956–57), by permission of the editor and Terence Penelhum.

"Persons" is reprinted with the permission of P. F. Strawson and the University of Minnesota Press from *Minnesota Studies in the Philosophy of Science*, Vol. II, Concepts, Theories, and the Mind-Body Problem, edited by Herbert Feigl, Michael Scriven, and Grover Maxwell. University of Minnesota Press, Minneapolis. Copyright 1958 by the University of Minnesota.

"One's Knowledge of Other Minds" is reprinted from *Philosophical Essays*, by A. J. Ayer (1954), by permission of the author, St. Martin's Press, New York, and Macmillan & Company Ltd., London.

"The Concept of Dreaming" is reprinted from *Dreaming*, by Norman Malcolm (1959), with the permission of The Humanities Press, Inc., New York, and Routledge & Kegan Paul Ltd., London.

"Imagination" by Gilbert Ryle, is reprinted from his book *The Concept of Mind* (London, 1949; New York, 1950) by permission of Barnes & Noble, Inc., New York, and Hutchinson & Company Ltd., London.

PREFACE

The fact that much of the important philosophy of the twentieth century has been published in the various philosophical journals is largely responsible for the appearance of collections of readings on various philosophical topics. Much of recent philosophy is also being taught from the professional journals. This is especially true of types of analytic philosophy. Because philosophy of mind or philosophical psychology has become increasingly important in the twentieth century, it would be useful to have under one cover some of the articles and selections from books which have furthered philosophical investigations of this type.

Perhaps most philosophers, both teachers and students, would agree to the need for such a collection, although I am sure that few would agree on its precise makeup. But at least it can be claimed for these papers that students of philosophy will find them necessary for an understanding of the way current philosophers are likely to deal with questions of the nature and powers of the mind.

Limiting a collection to twenty essays when the addition of one or two more might add to its value does, I recognize, seem arbitrary. I am confident that the addition of one more essay would increase the value of the whole, just as the addition of but ten more would make it all but perfect. Yet the conditions of publication, length, cost, and availability of material impose their limitations; I hope this is the best that could be done. A bibliography is included to make further reference easier. It covers mainly the years 1945 to the present; its length and diversity indicate the richness of material from which this collection was made.

As the bibliography indicates, philosophical psychology is at present a lively area of philosophic interest. The present articles and selections from books are either responsible for a good deal of this interest, or they are examples of the fruits of it. Some of them were selected because they set out an initial problem that is also treated elsewhere in the volume. Thus Bedford's "Emotions," Ryle's "Imagination" and "Pleasure," Macdonald's "Dreaming and Waking," Malcolm's "The Concept of Dreaming," and Ayer's "One's Knowledge of Other Minds," raise important issues and propose views that are also treated by Austin, Shorter, Benjamin, Pears, Place, Penelhum, and Strawson. Other articles were chosen because, of those available, each represents either the best explanation of one solution to a given problem or the best discussion of similar issues. The essays by Austin, Anscombe, Vesey, Melden, and Bedford are all relevant to discussions of action. And the articles by Williams, Ayer, and Strawson, plus Malcolm's second paper, form a section on the concept of a person and the problem of our knowledge of other minds. Page references to other selections in this volume are in brackets.

I should like to thank the various authors and the editors of philosophical journals for their permission to reprint their material here. Very slight changes, mainly to correct misprints, have been made in "Volition," by G. N. A. Vesey, "Emotions," by Errol Bedford, "The Concept of Heed," by U. T. Place, and "Personal Identity and Individuation," by B. A. O. Williams. The bibliography is due to Mr. John Gordon Burke.

A PLEA FOR EXCUSES

J. L. Austin

The subject of this paper, *Excuses,* is one not to be treated, but only to be introduced, within such limits. It is, or might be, the name of a whole branch, even a ramiculated branch, of philosophy, or at least of one fashion of philosophy. I shall try, therefore, first to state *what* the subject is, *why* it is worth studying, and *how* it may be studied, all this at a regrettably lofty level: and then I shall illustrate, in more congenial but desultory detail, some of the methods to be used, together with their limitations, and some of the unexpected results to be expected and lessons to be learned. Much, of course, of the amusement, and of the instruction, comes in drawing the coverts of the microglot, in hounding down the minutiae, and to this I can do no more here than incite you. But I owe it to the subject to say, that it has long afforded me what philosophy is so often thought, and made, barren of—the fun of discovery, the pleasures of co-operation, and the satisfaction of reaching agreement.

What, then, is the subject? I am here using the word "excuses" *for a title*, but it would be unwise to freeze too fast to this one noun and its partner verb: indeed for some time I used to use "extenuation" instead. Still, on the whole "excuses" is probably the most central and embracing term in the field, although this includes others of importance—"plea", "de-

John L. Austin (1911–60) was White's Professor of Moral Philosophy at Oxford University and a Fellow of Corpus Christi College. Three volumes of his lectures and articles—*Philosophical Papers* (Oxford, 1961), *Sense and Sensibilia* (Oxford, 1962), and *How to Do Things with Words* (Oxford, 1962)—have been published since his death.

fence", "justification" and so on. When, then, do we "excuse" conduct, our own or somebody else's? When are "excuses" proffered?

In general, the situation is one where someone is *accused* of having done something, or (if that will keep it any cleaner) where someone is *said* to have done something which is bad, wrong, inept, unwelcome, or in some other of the numerous possible ways untoward. Thereupon he, or someone on his behalf, will try to defend his conduct or to get him out of it.

One way of going about this is to admit flatly that he, X, did do that very thing, A, but to argue that it was a good thing, or the right or sensible thing, or a permissible thing to do, either in general or at least in the special circumstances of the occasion. To take this line is to *justify* the action, to give reasons for doing it: not to say, to brazen it out, to glory in it, or the like.

A different way of going about it is to admit that it wasn't a good thing to have done, but to argue that it is not quite fair or correct to say *baldly* "X did A". We may say it isn't fair just to say X did it; perhaps he was under somebody's influence, or was nudged. Or, it isn't fair to say baldly he *did* A; it may have been partly accidental, or an unintentional slip. Or, it isn't fair to say he did simply A—he was really doing something quite different and A was only incidental, or he was looking at the whole thing quite differently. Naturally these arguments can be combined or overlap or run into each other.

In the one defence, briefly, we accept responsibility but deny that it was bad: in the other, we admit that it was bad but don't accept full, or even any, responsibility.

By and large, justifications can be kept distinct from excuses, and I shall not be so anxious to talk about them because they have enjoyed more than their fair share of philosophical attention. But the two certainly can be confused, and can *seem* to go very near to each other, even if they do not perhaps actually do so. You dropped the tea-tray: Certainly, but an emotional storm was about to break out: or, Yes, but there was a wasp. In each case the defence, very soundly, insists on a fuller description of the event in its context; but the first is a justification, the second an excuse.

Again, if the objection is to the use of such a dyslogistic verb as "murdered", this may be on the ground that the killing was done in battle (justification) or on the gound that it was only accidental if reckless (excuse). It is arguable that we do not use the terms justification and excuse as carefully as we might; a miscellany of even less clear terms, such as "extenuation", "palliation", "mitigation", hovers uneasily between partial justification and partial excuse; and when we plead, say, provocation, there is genuine uncertainty or ambiguity as to what we mean–is *he* partly responsible, because he roused a violent impulse or passion in me, so that it wasn't truly or merely me acting "of my own accord" (excuse)? Or is it rather that, he having done me such injury, I was entitled to retaliate (justification)? Such doubts merely make it the more urgent to clear up the usage of these various terms. But that the defences I have for convenience labelled "justification" and "excuse" are in principle distinct can scarcely be doubted.

This then is the sort of situation we have to consider under "excuses". I will only further point out how very wide a field it covers. We have of course to bring in the opposite numbers of excuses–the expressions that *aggravate*, such as "deliberately", "on purpose" and so on, if only for the reason that an excuse often takes the form of a rebuttal of one of these. But we have also to bring in a large number of expressions which at first blush look not so much like excuses as like accusations–"clumsiness", "tactlessness", "thoughtlessness" and the like. Because it has always to be remembered that few excuses get us out of it *completely*: the average excuse, in a poor situation, gets us only out of the fire into the frying pan–but still, of course, any frying pan in a fire. If I have broken your dish or your romance, maybe the best defence I can find will be clumsiness.

Why, if this is what "excuses" are, should we trouble to investigate them? It might be thought reason enough that their production has always bulked so large among human activities. But to moral philosophy in particular a study of them will contribute in special ways, both positively towards the development of a cautious, latter-day version of conduct, and negatively towards the correction of older and hastier theories.

In ethics we study, I suppose, the good and the bad, the right and the wrong, and this must be for the most part in some connexion with conduct or the doing of actions. Yet before we consider what actions are good or bad, right or wrong, it is proper to consider first what is meant by, and what not, and what is included under, and what not, the expression "doing an action" or "doing something". These are expressions still too little examined on their own account and merits, just as the general notion of "saying something" is still too lightly passed over in logic. There is indeed a vague and comforting idea in the background that, after all, in the last analysis, doing an action must come down to the making of physical movements with parts of the body; but this is about as true as that saying something must, in the last analysis, come down to making movements of the tongue.

The beginning of sense, not to say wisdom, is to realise that "doing an action", as used in philosophy,[1] is a highly abstract expression—it is a stand-in used in the place of any (or almost any?) verb with a personal subject, in the same sort of way that "thing" is a stand-in for any (or when we remember, almost any) noun substantive, and "quality" a stand-in for the adjective. Nobody, to be sure, relies on such dummies quite implicitly quite indefinitely. Yet notoriously it is possible to arrive at, or to derive the idea for, an over-simplified metaphysics from the obsession with "things" and their "qualities". In a similar way, less commonly recognised even in these semi-sophisticated times, we fall for the myth of the verb. We treat the expression "doing an action" no longer as a stand-in for a verb with a personal subject, as which it has no doubt some uses, and might have more if the range of verbs were not left unspecified, but as a self-explanatory, ground-level description, one which brings adequately into the open the essential features of everything that comes, by simple inspection, under it. We scarcely notice even the most patent exceptions or difficulties (is to think something, or to say something, or to try to do something, to do

[1] This use has little to do with the more down-to-earth occurrences of "action" in ordinary speech.

an action?), any more than we fret, in the *ivresse des grandes profondeurs,* as to whether flames are things or events. So we come easily to think of our behaviour over any time, and of a life as a whole, as consisting in doing now action A, next action B, then action C, and so on, just as elsewhere we come to think of the world as consisting of this, that and the other substance or material thing, each with its properties. All "actions" are, as actions (meaning what?), equal, composing a quarrel with striking a match, winning a war with sneezing: worse still, we assimilate them one and all to the supposedly most obvious and easy cases, such as posting letters or moving fingers, just as we assimilate all "things" to horses or beds.

If we are to continue to use this expression in sober philosophy, we need to ask such questions as: Is to sneeze to do an action? Or is to breathe, or to see, or to checkmate, or each one of countless others? In short, for what range of verbs, as used on what occasions, is "doing an action" a stand-in? What have they in common, and what do those excluded severally lack? Again we need to ask how we decide what is the correct name for "the" action that somebody did —and what, indeed, are the rules for the use of "the" action, "an" action, "one" action, a "part" or "phase" of an action and the like. Further, we need to realise that even the "simplest" named actions are not so simple—certainly are not the mere makings of physical movements, and to ask what more, then, comes in (intentions? conventions?) and what does not (motives?), and what is the detail of the complicated internal machinery we use in "acting"—the receipt of intelligence, the appreciation of the situation, the invocation of principles, the planning, the control of execution and the rest.

In two main ways the study of excuses can throw light on these fundamental matters. First, to examine excuses is to examine cases where there has been some abnormality or failure: and as so often, the abnormal will throw light on the normal, will help us to penetrate the blinding veil of ease and obviousness that hides the mechanisms of the natural successful act. It rapidly becomes plain that the breakdowns signalised by the various excuses are of radically different kinds, affecting different parts or stages of the machinery, which the excuses consequently pick out and sort out for us. Further, it emerges that not *every* slip-up occurs in connexion with *every*thing that could be called an "action", that not every excuse is apt with every verb—far indeed from it: and this provides us with one means of introducing some classification into the vast miscellany of "actions". If we classify them according to the particular selection of breakdowns to which each is liable, this should assign them their places in some family group or groups of actions, or in some model of the machinery of acting.

In this sort of way, the philosophical study of conduct can get off to a positive fresh start. But by the way, and more negatively, a number of traditional cruces or mistakes in this field can be resolved or removed. First among these comes the problem of Freedom. While it has been the tradition to present this as the "positive" term requiring elucidation, there is little doubt that to say we acted "freely" (in the philosopher's use, which is only faintly related to the everyday use) is to say only that we acted *not* un-freely, in one or another of the many heterogeneous ways of so acting (under duress, or what not). Like "real", "free" is only used to rule out the suggestion of some or all of its recognised antitheses. As "truth" is not a name for a characteristic of assertions, so "freedom" is not a name for a characteristic of actions, but the name of a dimension in which actions are assessed. In examining all the ways in which each action may not be "free", *i.e.*, the cases in which it will not do to say simply "X did A", we may hope to dispose of the problem of Freedom. Aristotle has often been chidden for talking about excuses or pleas and overlooking "the real problem": in my own case, it was when I began to see the injustice of this charge that I first became interested in excuses.

There is much to be said for the view that, philosophical tradition apart, Responsibility would be a better candidate for the rôle here assigned to Freedom. If ordinary language is to be our guide, it is to evade responsibility, or full responsibility, that we most often make excuses, and I have used the word myself in this way above. But in fact "responsibility" too seems not really apt in all cases: I do not exactly evade responsibility when I plead clumsiness or tactlessness, nor, often, when I plead that I only did it unwillingly or reluctantly, and still less if I plead that I had in the circumstances no choice: here I was constrained and have an excuse (or justification), yet may accept responsibility. It may be, then, that at least two key terms, Freedom and Responsibility, are needed: the relation between them is not clear, and it may be hoped that the investigation of excuses will contribute towards its clarification.[2]

So much, then, for ways in which the study of excuses may throw light on ethics. But there are also reasons why it is an attractive subject methodologically, at least if we are to proceed from "ordinary language", that is, by examining *what we should say when*, and so why and what we should mean by it. Perhaps this method, at least as *one* philosophical method, scarcely requires justification at present—too evidently, there is gold in them thar hills: more opportune would be a warning about the care and thoroughness needed if it is not to fall into disrepute. I will, however, justify it very briefly.

First, words are our tools, and, as a minimum, we should use clean tools: we should know what we mean and what we do not, and we must forearm ourselves against the traps that language sets us. Secondly, words are not (except in their own little corner) facts or things: we need therefore to prise them off the world, to hold them apart from and against it, so that we can realise their inadequacies and arbitrarinesses, and can re-look at the world without blinkers. Thirdly, and more hopefully, our common stock of words embodies all the distinctions men have found worth drawing, and the connexions they have found worth marking, in the lifetimes of many generations: these surely are likely to be more numer-

[2] Another well-flogged horse in these same stakes is Blame. At least two things seem confused together under this term. Sometimes when I blame X for doing A, say for breaking the vase, it is a question simply or mainly of my disapproval of A, breaking the vase, which unquestionably X did: but sometimes it is, rather, a question simply or mainly of how far I think X responsible for A, which unquestionably was bad. Hence if somebody says he blames me for something, I may answer by giving a *justification*, so that he will cease to disapprove of what I did, or else by giving an *excuse*, so that he will cease to hold me, at least entirely and in every way, responsible for doing it.

ous, more sound, since they have stood up to the long test of the survival of the fittest, and more subtle, at least in all ordinary and reasonably practical matters, than any that you or I are likely to think up in our armchairs of an afternoon—the most favoured alternative method.

In view of the prevalence of the slogan "ordinary language", and of such names as "linguistic" or "analytic" philosophy or "the analysis of language", one thing needs specially emphasising to counter misunderstandings. When we examine what we should say when, what words we should use in what situations, we are looking again not *merely* at words (or "meanings", whatever they may be) but also at the realities we use the words to talk about: we are using a sharpened awareness of words to sharpen our perception of, though not as the final arbiter of, the phenomena. For this reason I think it might be better to use, for this way of doing philosophy, some less misleading name than those given above—for instance, "linguistic phenomenology", only that is rather a mouthful.

Using, then, such a method, it is plainly preferable to investigate a field where ordinary language is rich and subtle, as it is in the pressingly practical matter of Excuses, but certainly is not in the matter, say, of Time. At the same time we should prefer a field which is not too much trodden into bogs or tracks by traditional philosophy, for in that case even "ordinary" language will often have become infected with the jargon of extinct theories, and our own prejudices too, as the upholders or imbibers of theoretical views, will be too readily, and often insensibly, engaged. Here too, Excuses form an admirable topic; we can discuss at least clumsiness, or absence of mind, or inconsiderateness, even spontaneousness, without remembering what Kant thought, and so progress by degrees even to discussing deliberation without for once remembering Aristotle or self-control without Plato. Granted that our subject is, as already claimed for it, neighbouring, analogous or germane in some way to some notorious centre of philosophical trouble, then, with these two further requirements satisfied, we should be certain of what we are after: a good site for *field work* in philosophy. Here at last we should be able to unfreeze, to loosen up and get going on agreeing about discoveries, however small, and on agreeing about how to reach agreement.[3] How much it is to be wished that similar field work will soon be undertaken in, say, aesthetics; if only we could forget for a while about the beautiful and get down instead to the dainty and the dumpy.

There are, I know, or are supposed to be, snags in "linguistic" philosophy, which those not very familiar with it find, sometimes not without glee or relief, daunting. But with snags, as with nettles, the thing to do is to grasp them—and to climb above them. I will mention two in particular, over which the study of excuses may help to encourage us. The first is the snag of Loose (or Divergent or Alternative) Usage; and the second the crux of the Last Word. Do we all say the same, and only the same, things in the same situations? Don't usages differ? And, Why should what we all ordinarily say be the only or the best or final way of putting it? Why should it even be true?

Well, people's usages do vary, and we do talk loosely, and we do say different things apparently indifferently. But first, not nearly as much as one would think. When we come down to cases, it transpires in the very great majority that what we had thought was our wanting to say different things of and in *the same* situation was really not so—we had simply imagined the situation *slightly* differently: which is all too easy to do, because of course no situation (and we are dealing with *imagined* situations) is ever "completely" described. The more we imagine the situation in detail, with a background of story—and it is worth employing the most idiosyncratic or, sometimes, boring means to stimulate and to discipline our wretched imaginations—the less we find we disagree about what we should say. Nevertheless, *sometimes* we do ultimately disagree: sometimes we must allow a usage to be, though appalling, yet actual; sometimes we should genuinely use either or both of two different descriptions. But why should this daunt us? All that is happening is entirely explicable. If our usages disagree, then you use "X" where I use "Y", or more probably (and more intriguingly) your conceptual system is different from mine, though very likely it is at least

[3] All of which was seen and claimed by Socrates, when he first betook himself to the way of Words.

equally consistent and serviceable: in short, we can find *why* we disagree—you choose to classify in one way, I in another. If the usage is loose, we can understand the temptation that leads to it, and the distinctions that it blurs: if there are "alternative" descriptions, then the situation can be described or can be "structured" in two ways, or perhaps it is one where, for current purposes, the two alternatives come down to the same. A disagreement as to what we should say is not to be shied off, but to be pounced upon: for the explanation of it can hardly fail to be illuminating. If we light on an electron that rotates the wrong way, that is a discovery, a portent to be followed up, not a reason for chucking physics: and by the same token, a genuinely loose or eccentric talker is a rare specimen to be prized.

As practice in learning to handle this bogey, in learning the essential *rubrics*, we could scarcely hope for a more promising exercise than the study of excuses. Here, surely, is just the sort of situation where people will say "almost anything", because they are so flurried, or so anxious to get off. "It was a mistake", "It was an accident"—how readily these can *appear* indifferent, and even be used together. Yet, a story or two, and everybody will not merely agree that they are completely different, but even discover for himself what the difference is and what each means.[4]

Then, for the Last Word. Certainly ordinary language has no claim to be the last word, if there is such a thing. It embodies, indeed, something better than the metaphysics of the Stone Age, namely, as was said, the inherited experience and acumen of many generations of men. But then, that acumen has been concentrated primarily upon the practical business of life. If a distinction works well for practical purposes in

[4] You have a donkey, so have I, and they graze in the same field. The day comes when I conceive a dislike for mine. I go to shoot it, draw a bead on it, fire: the brute falls in its tracks. I inspect the victim, and find to my horror that it is *your* donkey. I appear on your doorstep with the remains and say—what? "I say, old sport, I'm awfully sorry, etc., I've shot your donkey *by accident*"? Or *"by mistake"*? Then again, I go to shoot my donkey as before, draw a bead on it, fire—but as I do so, the beasts move, and to my horror yours falls. Again the scene on the doorstep—what do I say? "By mistake"? Or "by accident"?

ordinary life (no mean feat, for even ordinary life is full of hard cases), then there is sure to be something in it, it will not mark nothing: yet this is likely enough to be not the best way of arranging things if our interests are more extensive or intellectual than the ordinary. And again, that experience has been derived only from the sources available to ordinary men throughout most of civilised history: it has not been fed from the resources of the microscope and its successors. And it must be added too, that superstition and error and fantasy of all kinds do become incorporated in ordinary language and even sometimes stand up to the survival test (only, when they do, why should we not detect it?). Certainly, then, ordinary language is *not* the last word: in principle it can everywhere be supplemented and improved upon and superseded. Only remember, it *is* the *first* word.[5]

For this problem too the field of Excuses is a fruitful one. Here is matter both contentious and practically important for everybody, so that ordinary language is on its toes: yet also, on its back it has long had a bigger flea to bite it, in the shape of the Law, and both again have lately attracted the attentions of yet another, and at least a healthily growing, flea, in the shape of psychology. In the law a constant stream of actual cases, more novel and more tortuous than the mere imagination could contrive, are brought up *for decision*—that is, formulae for docketing them must somehow be found. Hence it is necessary first to be careful with, but also to be brutal with, to torture, to fake and to override, ordinary language: we cannot here evade or forget the whole affair. (In ordinary life we dismiss the puzzles that crop up about time, but we cannot do that indefinitely in physics.) Psychology likewise produces novel cases, but it also produces new methods for bringing phenomena under observation and study: moreover, unlike the law, it has an unbiased interest in the totality of them and is unpressed for decision. Hence its own special and constant need to supplement, to revise and to supersede the classifications of both ordinary life and the law. We have, then, ample material for practice in learn-

[5] And forget, for once and for a while, that other curious question "Is it true?". May we?

ing to handle the bogey of the Last Word, however it should be handled.

Suppose, then, that we set out to investigate excuses, what are the methods and resources initially available? Our object is to imagine the varieties of situation in which we make excuses, and to examine the expressions used in making them. If we have a lively imagination, together perhaps with an ample experience of dereliction, we shall go far, only we need system: I do not know how many of you keep a list of the kinds of fool you make of yourselves. It is advisable to use systematic aids, of which there would appear to be three at least. I list them here in order of availability to the layman.

First we may use the dictionary—quite a concise one will do, but the use must be *thorough*. Two methods suggest themselves, both a little tedious, but repaying. One is to read the book through, listing all the words that seem relevant; this does not take as long as many suppose. The other is to start with a widish selection of obviously relevant terms, and to consult the dictionary under each: it will be found that, in the explanations of the various meanings of each, a surprising number of other terms occur, which are germane though of course not often synonymous. We then look up each of *these*, bringing in more for our bag from the "definitions" given in each case; and when we have continued for a little, it will generally be found that the family circle begins to close, until ultimately it is complete and we come only upon repetitions. This method has the advantage of grouping the terms into convenient clusters—but of course a good deal will depend upon the comprehensiveness of our initial selection.

Working the dictionary, it is interesting to find that a high percentage of the terms connected with excuses prove to be *adverbs*, a type of word which has not enjoyed so large a share of the philosophical limelight as the noun, substantive or adjective, and the verb: this is natural because, as was said, the tenor of so many excuses is that I did it but only *in a way*, not just flatly like that—*i.e.*, the verb needs modifying. Besides adverbs, however, there are other words of all kinds, including numerous abstract nouns, "misconception," "accident," "purpose" and the like, and a few verbs too, which often hold key positions for the grouping of excuses into classes at a high level ("couldn't help", "didn't mean to", "didn't realise", or again "intend" and "attempt"). In connexion with the nouns another neglected class of words is prominent, namely, prepositions. Not merely does it matter considerably which preposition, often of several, is being used with a given substantive, but further the prepositions deserve study on their own account. For the question suggests itself, Why are the nouns in one group governed by "under", in another by "on", in yet another by "by" or "through" or "from" or "for" or "with", and so on? It will be disappointing if there prove to be no good reasons for such groupings.

Our second source-book will naturally be the law. This will provide us with an immense miscellany of untoward cases, and also with a useful list of recognised pleas, together with a good deal of acute analysis of both. No one who tries this resource will long be in doubt, I think, that the common law, and in particular the law of tort, is the richest storehouse; crime and contract contribute some special additions of their own, but tort is altogether more comprehensive and more flexible. But even here, and still more with so old and hardened a branch of the law as crime, much caution is needed with the arguments of counsel and the dicta or decisions of judges: acute though these are, it has always to be remembered that, in legal cases—

(1) there is the overriding requirement that a decision be reached, and a relatively black or white decision—guilty or not guilty—for the plaintiff or for the defendant;

(2) there is the general requirement that the charge or action and the pleadings be brought under one or another of the heads and procedures that have come in the course of history to be accepted by the Courts. These, though fairly numerous, are still few and stereotyped in comparison with the accusations and defences of daily life. Moreover contentions of many kinds are beneath the law, as too trivial, or outside it, as too purely moral,—for example, inconsiderateness;

(3) there is the general requirement that we argue

from and abide by precedents. The value of this in the law is unquestionable, but it can certainly lead to distortions of ordinary beliefs and expressions.

For such reasons as these, obviously closely connected and stemming from the nature and function of the law, practising lawyers and jurists are by no means so careful as they might be to give to our ordinary expressions their ordinary meanings and applications. There is special pleading and evasion, stretching and strait-jacketing, besides the invention of technical terms, or technical senses for common terms. Nevertheless, it is a perpetual and salutary surprise to discover how much is to be learned from the law; and it is to be added that if a distinction drawn is a sound one, even though not yet recognised in law, a lawyer can be relied upon to take note of it, for it may be dangerous not to–if he does not, his opponent may.

Finally, the third source-book is psychology, with which I include such studies as anthropology and animal behaviour. Here I speak with even more trepidation than about the Law. But this at least is clear, that some varieties of behaviour, some ways of acting or explanations of the doing of actions, are here noticed and classified which have not been observed or named by ordinary men and hallowed by ordinary language, though perhaps they often might have been so if they had been of more practical importance. There is real danger in contempt for the "jargon" of psychology, at least when it sets out to supplement, and at least sometimes when it sets out to supplant, the language of ordinary life.

With these sources, and with the aid of the imagination, it will go hard if we cannot arrive at the meanings of large numbers of expressions and at the understanding and classification of large numbers of "actions". Then we shall comprehend clearly much that, before, we only made use of *ad hoc*. Definition, I would add, explanatory definition, should stand high among our aims: it is not enough to show how clever we are by showing how obscure everything is. Clarity, too, I know, has been said to be not enough: but perhaps it will be time to go into that when we are within measurable distance of achieving clarity on some matter.

So much for the cackle. It remains to make a few remarks, not, I am afraid, in any very coherent order, about the types of significant result to be obtained and the more general lessons to be learned from the study of Excuses.

(1) *No modification without aberration.*—When it is stated that X did A, there is a temptation to suppose that given some, indeed perhaps *any*, expression modifying the verb we shall be entitled to insert either it or its opposite or negation in our statement: that is, we shall be entitled to ask, typically, "Did X do A Mly or not Mly?" (*e.g.*, "Did X murder Y voluntarily or involuntarily?"), and to answer one or the other. Or as a minimum it is supposed that if X did A there must be at least *one* modifying expression that we could, justifiably and informatively, insert with the verb. In the great majority of cases of the use of the great majority of verbs ("murder" perhaps is not one of the majority) such suppositions are quite unjustified. The natural economy of language dictates that for the *standard* case covered by any normal verb,—not, perhaps, a verb of omen such as "murder," but a verb like "eat" or "kick" or "croquet"—no modifying expression is required or even permissible. Only if we do the action named in some *special* way or circumstances, different from those in which such an act is naturally done (and of course both the normal and the abnormal differ according to what verb in particular is in question) is a modifying expression called for, or even in order. I sit in my chair, in the usual way—I am not in a daze or influenced by threats or the like: here, it will not do to say either that I sat in it intentionally or that I did not sit in it intentionally,[6] nor yet that I sat in it automatically or from habit or what you will. It is bedtime, I am alone, I yawn: but I do not yawn involuntarily (or voluntarily!), nor yet deliberately. To yawn in any such peculiar way is just not to just yawn.

(2) *Limitation of application.*—Expressions modifying verbs, typically adverbs, have limited ranges of application. That is, given any adverb of excuse, such as "unwittingly" or "spontaneously" or "impulsively", it will not be found that it

[6] Caveat or hedge: of course we can say "I did *not* sit in it 'intentionally' " as a way simply of repudiating the suggestion that I sat in it intentionally.

makes good sense to attach it to any and every verb of "action" in any and every context: indeed, it will often apply only to a comparatively narrow range of such verbs. Something in the lad's upturned face appealed to him, he threw a brick at it—"spontaneously"? The interest then is to discover why some actions can be excused in a particular way but not others, particularly perhaps the latter.[7] This will largely elucidate the meaning of the excuse, and at the same time will illuminate the characteristics typical of the group of "actions" it picks out: very often too it will throw light on some detail of the machinery of "action" in general (see (4)), or on our standards of acceptable conduct (see (5)). It is specially important in the case of some of the terms most favoured by philosophers or jurists to realise that at least in ordinary speech (disregarding back-seepage of jargon) they are not used so universally or so dichotomistically. For example, take "voluntarily" and "involuntarily": we may join the army or make a gift voluntarily, we may hiccough or make a small gesture involuntarily, and the more we consider further actions which we might naturally be said to do in either of these ways, the more circumscribed and unlike each other do the two classes become, until we even doubt whether there is *any* verb with which both adverbs are equally in place. Perhaps there are some such; but at least sometimes when we may think we have found one it is an illusion, an apparent exception that really does prove the rule. I can perhaps "break a cup" voluntarily, *if* that is done, say, as an act of self-impoverishment: and I can perhaps break another involuntarily, *if*, say, I make an involuntary movement which breaks it. Here, plainly, the two acts described each as "breaking a cup" are really very different, and the one is similar to acts typical of the "voluntary" class, the other to acts typical of the "involuntary" class.

(3) *The importance of Negations and Opposites.*—"Voluntarily" and "involuntarily," then, are not opposed in the obvious sort of way that they are made to be in philosophy or jurisprudence. The "opposite", or rather "opposites", of "vol-

[7] For we are sometimes not so good at observing what we *can't* say as what we can, yet the first is pretty regularly the more revealing.

untarily" might be "under constraint" of some sort, duress or obligation or influence[8]: the opposite of "involuntarily" might be "deliberately" or "on purpose" or the like. Such divergences in opposites indicate that "voluntarily" and "involuntarily," in spite of their apparent connexion, are fish from very different kettles. In general, it will pay us to take nothing for granted or as obvious about negations and opposites. It does not pay to assume that a word must have an opposite, or one opposite, whether it is a "positive" word like "wilfully" or a "negative" word like "inadvertently." Rather, we should be asking ourselves such questions as why there is no use for the adverb "advertently." For above all it will not do to assume that the "positive" word must be around to wear the trousers; commonly enough the "negative" (looking) word marks the (positive) abnormality, while the "positive" word, *if* it exists, merely serves to rule out the suggestion of that abnormality. It is natural enough, in view of what was said in (1) above, for the "positive" word not to be found at all in some cases. I do an act A_1 (say, crush a snail) *inadvertently* if, in the course of executing by means of movements of my bodily parts some other act A_2 (say, in walking down the public path) I fail to exercise such meticulous supervision over the courses of those movements as would have been needed to ensure that they did not bring about the untoward event (here, the impact on the snail).[9] By claiming that A_1 was inadvertent we place it, where we imply it belongs, on this special level, in a class of incidental happenings which must occur in the doing of any physical act. To lift the act out of this class, we need and possess the expression "not . . .

[8] But remember, when I sign a cheque in the normal way, I do *not* do so *either* "voluntarily" *or* "under constraint."

[9] Or analogously: I do an act A_1 (say, divulge my age, or imply you are a liar), *inadvertently* if, in the course of executing by the use of some medium of communication some other act A_2 (say, reminiscing about my war service) I fail to exercise such meticulous supervision over the choice and arrangement of the signs as would have been needed to ensure that. . . . It is interesting to note how such adverbs lead parallel lives, one in connexion with physical actions ("doing") and the other in connexion with acts of communication ("saying"), or sometimes also in connexion with acts of "thinking" ("inadvertently assumed").

inadvertently": "advertently," if used for this purpose, would suggest that, if the act was not done inadvertently, then it must have been done noticing what I was doing, which is far from necessarily the case (e.g., if I did it absent-mindedly), or at least that there is *something* in common to the ways of doing all acts not done inadvertently, which is not the case. Again, there is no use for "advertently" at the *same* level as "inadvertently": in passing the butter I do not knock over the cream-jug, though I do (inadvertently) knock over the teacup—yet I do not by-pass the cream-jug *advertently*: for at this level, below supervision in detail, *anything* that we do is, if you like, inadvertent, though we only call it so, and indeed only call it something we have done, if there is something untoward about it.

A further point of interest in studying so-called "negative" terms is the manner of their formation. Why are the words in one group formed with *un-* or *in-*, those in another with *-less* ("aimless," "reckless," "heedless," etc.), and those in another with *mis-* ("mistake," "misconception," "misjudgment," etc.)? Why care*less*ly but *in*attentively? Perhaps care and attention, so often linked, are rather different. Here are remunerative exercises.

(4) *The machinery of action.*—Not merely do adverbial expressions pick out classes of actions, they also pick out the internal detail of the machinery of doing actions, or the departments into which the business of doing actions is organised. There is for example the stage at which we have actually to *carry out* some action upon which we embark—perhaps we have to make certain bodily movements or to make a speech. In the course of actually *doing* these things (getting weaving) we have to pay (some) attention to what we are doing and to take (some) care to guard against (likely) dangers: we may need to use judgment or tact: we must exercise sufficient control over our bodily parts: and so on. Inattention, carelessness, errors of judgment, tactlessness, clumsiness, all these and others are ills (with attendant excuses) which affect one specific stage in the machinery of action, the *executive* stage, the stage where we *muff* it. But there are many other departments in the business too, each of which is to be traced and mapped through its cluster of

appropriate verbs and adverbs. Obviously there are departments of intelligence and planning, of decision and resolve, and so on: but I shall mention one in particular, too often overlooked, where troubles and excuses abound. It happens to us, in military life, to be in receipt of excellent intelligence, to be also in self-conscious possession of excellent principles (the five golden rules for winning victories), and yet to hit upon a plan of action which leads to disaster. One way in which this can happen is through failure at the stage of *appreciation* of the situation, that is at the stage where we are required to cast our excellent intelligence into such a form, under such heads and with such weights attached, that our equally excellent principles can be brought to bear on it properly, in a way to yield the right answer.[10] So too in real, or rather civilian, life, in moral or practical affairs, we can know the facts and yet look at them mistakenly or perversely, or not fully realise or appreciate something, or even be under a total misconception. Many expressions of excuse indicate failure at this particularly tricky stage: even thoughtlessness, inconsiderateness, lack of imagination, are perhaps less matters of failure in intelligence or planning than might be supposed, and more matters of failure to appreciate the situation. A course of E. M. Forster and we see things differently: yet perhaps we know no more and are no cleverer.

(5) *Standards of the unacceptable.*—It is characteristic of excuses to be "unacceptable": given, I suppose, almost any excuse, there will be cases of such a kind or of such gravity that "we will not accept" it. It is interesting to detect the standards and codes we thus invoke. The extent of the supervision we exercise over the execution of any act can never be quite unlimited, and usually is expected to fall within fairly definite limits ("due care and attention") in the case of acts of some general kind, though of course we set very different limits in different cases. We may plead that we trod on the snail inadvertently: but not on a baby—you ought to look where you're putting your great feet. Of course it *was*

[10] We know all about how to do quadratics: we know all the needful facts about pipes, cisterns, hours and plumbers: yet we reach the answer "3¾ men." We have failed to cast our facts correctly into mathematical form.

(*really*), if you like, inadvertence: but that word constitutes a plea, which isn't going to be allowed, because of standards. And if you try it on, you will be subscribing to such dreadful standards that your last state will be worse than your first. Or again, we set different standards, and will accept different excuses, in the case of acts which are rule-governed, like spelling, and which we are expected absolutely to get right, from those we set and accept for less stereotyped actions: a wrong spelling may be a slip, but hardly an accident, a winged beater may be an accident, but hardly a slip.

(6) *Combination, dissociation and complication.*—A belief in opposites and dichotomies encourages, among other things, a blindness to the combinations and dissociations of adverbs that are possible, even to such obvious facts as that we can act at once on impulse and intentionally, or that we can do an action intentionally yet for all that not deliberately, still less on purpose. We walk along the cliff, and I feel a sudden impulse to push you over, which I promptly do: I acted on impulse, yet I certainly intended to push you over, and may even have devised a little ruse to achieve it: yet even then I did not act deliberately, for I did not (stop to) ask myself whether to do it or not.

It is worth bearing in mind, too, the general rule that we must not expect to find simple labels for complicated cases. If a mistake results in an accident, it will not do to ask whether "it" was an accident or a mistake, or to demand some briefer description of "it." Here the natural economy of language operates: if the words already available for simple cases suffice in combination to describe a complicated case, there will be need for special reasons before a special new word is invented for the complication. Besides, however well-equipped our language, it can never be forearmed against all possible cases that may arise and call for description: fact is richer than diction.

(7) *Regina* v. *Finney.*—Often the complexity and difficulty of a case is considerable. I will quote the case of *Regina* v. *Finney:*[11]

[11] A somewhat distressing favourite in the class that Hart used to conduct with me in the years soon after the war. The italics are mine.

Shrewsbury Assizes. 1874. 12 Cox 625.

Prisoner was indicted for the manslaughter of Thomas Watkins.

The Prisoner was an attendant at a lunatic asylum. Being in charge of a lunatic, who was bathing, he turned on hot water into the bath, and thereby scalded him to death. The facts appeared to be truly set forth in the statement of the prisoner made before the committing magistrate, as follows: "I had bathed Watkins, and had loosed the bath out. *I intended putting in a clean bath,* and asked Watkins if he would get out. At this time *my attention was drawn* to the next bath by the new attendant, who was asking me a question; and *my attention was taken from the bath* where Watkins was. I put my hand down to turn water on in the bath where Thomas Watkins was. *I did not intend to turn the hot water,* and *I made a mistake in the tap. I did not know what I had done until* I heard Thomas Watkins shout out; and *I did not find my mistake out till* I saw the steam from the water. You cannot get water in this bath when they are drawing water at the other bath; but at other times it shoots out like a water gun when the other baths are not in use. . . ."

(It was proved that the lunatic had such possession of his faculties as would enable him to understand what was said to him, and to get out of the bath.)

A. *Young* (for Prisoner). The death *resulted from accident.* There was no such *culpable negligence* on the part of the prisoner as will support this indictment. A *culpable mistake,* or some degree of *culpable negligence,* causing death, will not support a charge of manslaughter; unless the *negligence* be so gross as to be *reckless.* (R. v. *Noakes.*)

Lush, F. To render a person liable for *neglect of duty* there must be such a degree of culpability as to amount to *gross negligence* on his part. If you accept the prisoner's own statement, you find no such amount of *negligence* as would come within this definition. It is not every little *trip or mistake* that will make a man so liable. It was the duty of the attendant not to let hot water into the bath while the patient was therein. According to the prisoner's own account, *he did not believe that* he was letting the hot water in while the deceased remained there. The lunatic was, we have heard, a man capable of getting out by himself and of understanding what was said to him. He was told to get out. A new attendant who had come on this day, was at an adjoining bath and he *took off the prisoner's attention*. Now, if the prisoner, knowing that the man was in the bath, had turned on the tap, and turned on the hot instead of the cold water, I should have said there was gross negligence; for he ought to have looked to see. But from his own account he had told the deceased to get out, and *thought he had got out*. If you think that indicates gross *carelessness*, then you should find the prisoner guilty of manslaughter. But if you think it *inadvertence* not amounting to culpability—*i.e.*, what is properly termed an *accident*—then the prisoner is not liable.

Verdict, Not guilty.

In this case there are two morals that I will point:

(8 ff.) Both counsel and judge make very free use of a large number of terms of excuse, using several as though they were, and even stating them to be, indifferent or equivalent when they are not, and presenting as alternatives those that are not.

(11) It is constantly difficult to be sure *what* act it is that counsel or judge is suggesting might be qualified by what expression of excuse.

The learned judge's concluding direction is a paradigm of these faults.[12] Finney, by contrast, stands out as an evident master of the Queen's English. He is explicit as to each of his acts and states, mental and physical: he uses different, and the correct, adverbs in connexion with each: and he makes no attempt to boil down.

(8) *Small distinctions, and big too.*—It should go without

[12] Not but what he probably manages to convey his meaning somehow or other. Judges seem to acquire a knack of conveying meaning, and even carrying conviction, through the use of a pithy Anglo-Saxon which sometimes has literally no meaning at all. Wishing to distinguish the case of shooting at a post in the belief that it was an enemy, as *not* an "attempt," from the case of picking an empty pocket in the belief that money was in it, which *is* an "attempt," the judge explains that in shooting at the post "the man is never on the thing at all."

saying that terms of excuse are not equivalent, and that it matters which we use: we need to distinguish inadvertence not merely from (save the mark) such things as mistake and accident, but from such nearer neighbours as, say, aberration and absence of mind. By imagining cases with vividness and fullness we should be able to decide in which precise terms to describe, say, Miss Plimsoll's action in writing, so carefully, "DAIRY" on her fine new book: we should be able to distinguish between sheer, mere, pure and simple mistake or inadvertence. Yet unfortunately, at least when in the grip of thought, we fail not merely at these stiffer hurdles. We equate even—I have seen it done—"inadvertently" with "automatically": as though to say I trod on your toe inadvertently means to say I trod on it automatically. Or we collapse succumbing to temptation into losing control of ourselves,—a bad patch, this, for telescoping.[13]

All this is not so much a *lesson* from the study of excuses as the very object of it.

(9) *The exact phrase and its place in the sentence.*—It is not enough, either, to attend simply to the "key" word: notice must also be taken of the full and exact form of the expression used. In considering mistakes, we have to consider seriatim "by mistake", "owing to a mistake", "mistakenly", "it was a mistake to", "to make a mistake in or over or about", "to be mistaken about", and so on: in considering purpose, we have to consider "on", "with the", "for the", etc., besides "purposeful", "purposeless" and the like. These varying expressions may function quite differently—and usually do, or why should we burden ourselves with more than one of them?

Care must be taken too to observe the precise position of

[13] Plato, I suppose, and after him Aristotle, fastened this confusion upon us, as bad in its day and way as the later, grotesque, confusion of moral weakness with weakness of will. I am very partial to ice cream, and a bombe is served divided into segments corresponding one to one with the persons at High Table: I am tempted to help myself to two segments and do so, thus succumbing to temptation and even conceivably (but why necessarily?) going against my principles. But do I lose control of myself? Do I raven, do I snatch the morsels from the dish and wolf them down, impervious to the consternation of my colleagues? Not a bit of it. We often succumb to temptation with calm and even with finesse.

an adverbial expression in the sentence. This should of course indicate what verb it is being used to modify: but more than that, the position can also affect the *sense* of the expression, *i.e.*, the way in which it modifies that verb. Compare, for example:—

a_1	He clumsily trod on the snail.
a_2	Clumsily he trod on the snail.
b_1	He trod clumsily on the snail.
b_2	He trod on the snail clumsily.

Here, in a_1 and a_2 we describe his treading on the creature at all as a piece of clumsiness, incidental, we imply, to his performance of some other action: but with b_1 and b_2 to tread on it is, very likely, his aim or policy, what we criticise is his execution of the feat.[14] Many adverbs, though far from all (not, *e.g.*, "purposely") are used in these two typically different ways.

(10) *The style of performance.*—With some adverbs the distinction between the two senses referred to in the last paragraph is carried a stage further. "He ate his soup deliberately" may mean, like "He deliberately ate his soup," that his eating his soup was a deliberate act, one perhaps that he thought would annoy somebody, as it would more commonly if he deliberately ate *my* soup, and which he decided to do: but it will often mean that he went through the performance of eating his soup in a noteworthy manner or *style*—pause after each mouthful, careful choice of point of entry for the spoon, sucking of moustaches, and so on. That is, it will mean that he ate *with* deliberation rather than *after* deliberation. The style of the performance, slow and unhurried, is understandably called "deliberate" because each movement *has the typical look* of a deliberate act: but it is scarcely being said that the making of each motion *is* a deliberate act or that he is "literally" deliberating. This case, then, is more

[14] As a matter of fact, most of these examples *can* be understood the other way, especially if we allow ourselves inflexions of the voice, or commas, or contexts. a_2 might be a poetic inversion for b_2: b_1, perhaps with commas round the "clumsily," might be used for a_1: and so on. Still, the two senses are clearly enough distinguishable.

extreme than that of "clumsily", which does in both uses describe literally a manner of performing.

It is worth watching out for this secondary use when scrutinising any particular adverbial expression: when it definitely does not exist, the reason is worth enquiring into. Sometimes it is very hard to be sure whether it does exist or does not: it does, one would think, with "carelessly", it does not with "inadvertently", but does it or does it not with "absent-mindedly" or "aimlessly"? In some cases a word akin to but distinct from the primary adverb is used for this special role of describing a style of performance: we use "purposefully" in this way, but never "purposely".

(11) *What modifies what?* The Judge in *Regina* v. *Finney* does not make clear what event is being excused in what way. "If you think that indicates gross carelessness, then. . . . But if you think it inadvertence not amounting to culpability–*i.e.*, what is properly called an accident–then. . . ." Apparently he means that Finney may have *turned on the hot tap* inadvertently[15]: does he mean also that the tap may have been turned accidentally, or rather that *Watkins may have been scalded* and killed accidentally? And was the carelessness in turning the tap or in thinking Watkins had got out? Many disputes as to what excuse we should properly use arise because we will not trouble to state explicitly *what* is being excused.

To do so is all the more vital because it is in principle always open to us, along various lines, to describe or refer to "what I did" in so many different ways. This is altogether too large a theme to elaborate here. Apart from the more general

[15] What Finney says is different: he says he "made a mistake in the tap". This is the basic use of "mistake", where we simply, and not necessarily accountably, take the wrong one. Finney here attempts to account for his mistake, by saying that his attention was distracted. But suppose the order is "Right turn" and I turn left: no doubt the sergeant will insinuate that my attention was distracted, or that I cannot distinguish my right from my left–but it wasn't and I can, this was a simple, pure mistake. As often happens. Neither I nor the sergeant will suggest that there was any accident, or any inadvertence either. If Finney had turned the hot tap inadvertently, then it would have been knocked, say, in reaching for the cold tap: a different story.

and obvious problems of the use of "tendentious" descriptive terms, there are many special problems in the particular case of "actions". Should we say, are we saying, that he took her money, or that he robbed her? That he knocked a ball into a hole, or that he sank a putt? That he said "Done", or that he accepted an offer? How far, that is, are motives, intentions and conventions to be part of the description of actions? And more especially here, what is *an* or *one* or *the* action? For we can generally split up what might be named as one action in several distinct ways, into different *stretches* or *phases* or *stages*. Stages have already been mentioned: we can dismantle the machinery of the act, and describe (and excuse) separately the intelligence, the appreciation, the planning, the decision, the execution and so forth. Phases are rather different: we can say that he painted a picture or fought a campaign, or else we can say that first he laid on this stroke of paint and then that, first he fought this action and then that. Stretches are different again: a single term descriptive of what he did may be made to cover either a smaller or a larger stretch of events, those excluded by the narrower description being then called "consequences" or "results" or "effects" or the like of his act. So here we can describe Finney's act *either* as turning on the hot tap, which he did by mistake, with the result that Watkins was scalded, *or* as scalding Watkins, which he did *not* do by mistake.

It is very evident that the problems of excuses and those of the different descriptions of actions are throughout bound up with each other.

(12) *Trailing clouds of etymology.*—It is these considerations that bring us up so forcibly against some of the most difficult words in the whole story of Excuses, such words as "result", "effect" and "consequence", or again as "intention", "purpose" and "motive". I will mention two points of method which are, experience has convinced me, indispensable aids at these levels.

One is that a word never—well, hardly ever—shakes off its etymology and its formation. In spite of all changes in and extensions of and additions to its meanings, and indeed rather pervading and governing these, there will still persist the old idea. In an *accident* something befalls: by *mistake* you take the wrong one: in *error* you stray: when you act *deliberately* you act after weighing it up (*not* after thinking out ways and means). It is worth asking ourselves whether we know the etymology of "result" or of "spontaneously", and worth remembering that "unwillingly" and "involuntarily" come from very different sources.

And the second point is connected with this. Going back into the history of a word, very often into Latin, we come back pretty commonly to pictures or *models* of how things happen or are done. These models may be fairly sophisticated and recent, as is perhaps the case with "motive" or "impulse", but one of the commonest and most primitive types of model is one which is apt to baffle us through its very naturalness and simplicity. We take *some very simple action,* like shoving a stone, usually as done by and viewed by oneself, and use *this,* with the features distinguishable in it, as our model in terms of which to talk about other actions and events: and we continue to do so, scarcely realising it, even when these other actions are pretty remote and perhaps much more interesting to us in their own right than the acts originally used in constructing the model ever were, and even when the model is really distorting the facts rather than helping us to observe them. In primitive cases we may get to see clearly the differences between, say, "results", "effects" and "consequences", and yet discover that these differences are no longer clear, and the terms themselves no longer of real service to us, in the more complicated cases where we had been bandying them about most freely. A model must be recognised for what it is. "Causing", I suppose, was a notion taken from a man's own experience of doing simple actions, and by primitive man every event was construed in terms of this model: every event has a cause, that is, every event is an action done by somebody–if not by a man, then by a quasi-man, a spirit. When, later, events which are *not* actions are realised to be such, we still say that they must be "caused," and the word snares us: we are struggling to ascribe to it a new, unanthropomorphic meaning, yet constantly, in searching for its analysis, we unearth and incorporate the lineaments of the ancient model. As happened even to Hume, and consequently to Kant. Examining such a word historically, we may well find that it has been extended to cases that have by now too tenuous a relation to the model case, that it is a source of confusion and superstition.

There is too another danger in words that invoke models, half-forgotten or not. It must be remembered that there is no necessity whatsoever that the various models used in creating our vocabulary, primitive or recent, should all fit together neatly as parts into one single, total model or scheme of, for instance, the doing of actions. It is possible, and indeed highly likely, that our assortment of models will include some, or many, that are overlapping, conflicting, or more generally simply *disparate*.[16]

(13) In spite of the wide and acute observation of the phenomena of action embodied in ordinary speech, modern scientists have been able, it seems to me, to reveal its inadequacy at numerous points, if only because they have had access to more comprehensive data and have studied them with more catholic and dispassionate interest than the ordinary man, or even the lawyer, has had occasion to do. I will conclude with two examples.

Observation of animal behaviour shows that regularly, when an animal is embarked on some recognisable pattern of behaviour but meets in the course of it with an insuperable obstacle, it will betake itself to energetic, but quite unrelated, activity of some wild kind, such as standing on its head. This phenomenon is called "displacement behaviour" and is well identifiable. If now, in the light of this, we look

[16] This is by way of a general warning in philosophy. It seems to be too readily assumed that if we can only discover the true meanings of each of a cluster of key terms, usually historic terms, that we use in some particular field (as, for example, "right", "good" and the rest in morals), then it must without question transpire that each will fit into place in some single, interlocking, consistent, conceptual scheme. Not only is there no reason to assume this, but all historical probability is against it, especially in the case of a language derived from such various civilisations as ours is. We may cheerfully use, and with weight, terms which are not so much head-on incompatible as simply disparate, which just don't fit in or even on. Just as we cheerfully subscribe to, or have the grace to be torn between, simply disparate ideals—why *must* there be a conceivable amalgam, the Good Life for Man?

back at ordinary human life, we see that displacement behaviour bulks quite large in it: yet we have apparently no word, or at least no clear and simple word, for it. If, when thwarted, we stand on our heads or wiggle our toes, then we aren't exactly *just* standing on our heads, don't you know, in the ordinary way, yet is there any convenient abverbial expression we can insert to do the trick? "In desperation"?

Take, again, "compulsive" behaviour, however exactly psychologists define it, compulsive washing for example. There are of course hints in ordinary speech that we do things in this way—"just feel I have to", "shouldn't feel comfortable unless I did", and the like: but there is no adverbial expression satisfactorily pre-empted for it, as "compulsively" is. This is understandable enough, since compulsive behaviour, like displacement behaviour, is not in general going to be of great practical importance.

Here I leave and commend the subject to you.

INTENTION

G. E. M. Anscombe

What distinguishes actions which are intentional from those which are not? The answer that suggests itself is that they are the actions to which a certain sense of the question 'Why?' is given application; the sense is defined as that in which the answer, *if positive*, gives a reason for acting. But this hardly gets us any further, because the questions 'What is the relevant sense of the question "Why?"' and 'What is meant by "reason for acting"?' are one and the same.

To see the difficulties here, consider the question 'Why did you knock the cup off the table?' answered by 'I thought I saw a face at the window and it made me jump.' Now we cannot say that since the answer mentions something previous to the action, this will be a cause as opposed to a reason; for if you ask 'Why did you kill him?' the answer 'he killed my father' is surely a reason rather than a cause, but what it mentions is previous to the action. It is true that we don't ordinarily think of a case like giving a sudden start when we speak of a *reason for acting*. 'Giving a sudden start', someone might say, 'is not *acting* in the sense suggested by the expression "reason for acting".' Hence, though indeed we readily say *e.g.* 'What was the reason for your starting so violently?' this is totally unlike 'What is your reason for excluding so-and-so from your will?' or 'What is your reason for sending for a taxi?' But what *is* the difference? Why is giving a start or gasp not an 'action', while sending for a taxi or crossing the

Miss G. E. M. Anscombe is Lecturer in Philosophy and Rockefeller Research Fellow at Somerville College, Oxford. Her books include *Intention* (Oxford, 1958) and, with P. T. Geach, *Three Philosophers* (Ithaca, N.Y., 1961). She is also the author of numerous articles and the translator of Wittgenstein's *Philosophical Investigations*.

road is one? The answer cannot be 'Because an answer to the question "why?" may give a reason in the latter cases', for the answer may 'give a reason' in the former cases too; and we cannot say 'Ah, but not a *reason for acting;*' we should be going round in circles. We need to find the difference between the two kinds of 'reason' without talking about 'acting'; and if we do, perhaps we shall discover what is meant by 'acting' when it is said with this special emphasis.

It will hardly be enlightening to say 'in the case of the sudden start the "reason" is a *cause*'; the topic of causality is in a state of too great confusion; all we know is that this is one of the places where we do use the word 'cause'. But we also know that this is rather a strange case of causality; the subject is able to give a cause of a thought or feeling or bodily movement in the same kind of way as he is able to state the place of his pain or the position of his limbs. Such statements are not based on observation.

Nor can we say: 'Well, the "reason" for a movement is a cause, and not a reason in the sense of "reason for acting", when the movement is involuntary; it is a reason as opposed to a cause, when the movement is voluntary and intentional.' This is partly because in any case the object of the whole enquiry is really to delineate such concepts as the voluntary and the intentional, and partly because one can also give a 'reason' which is only a 'cause' for what is voluntary and intentional. *E.g.* 'Why are you walking up and down like that?'—'It's that military band; it excites me.' Or 'What made you sign the document at last?'—'The thought: "It is my duty" kept hammering away in my mind until I said to myself "I can do no other", and so signed.'

Now we can see that the cases where this difficulty arises are just those where the cause itself, *qua* cause, (or perhaps one should rather say the causation itself) is in the class of things known without observation.

I will call the type of cause in question a '*mental cause*'. Mental causes are possible, not only for actions ('The martial music excites me, that is why I walk up and down') but also for feelings and even thoughts. In considering actions, it is important to distinguish between mental causes and motives; in considering feelings, such as fear or anger, it is important to distinguish between mental causes and objects of feeling. To see this, consider the following cases:

A child saw a bit of red stuff on a turn in a stairway and asked what it was. He thought his nurse told him it was a bit of Satan and felt dreadful fear of it. (No doubt she said it was a bit of satin.) What he was frightened of was the bit of stuff; the cause of his fright was his nurse's remark. The object of fear may be the cause of fear, but, as Wittgenstein[1] remarks, is not *as such* the cause of fear. (A hideous face appearing at the window would of course be both cause and object, and hence the two are easily confused.) Or again, you may be angry *at* someone's action, when what makes you angry is some reminder of it, or someone's telling you of it.

This sort of cause of a feeling or reaction may be reported by the person himself, as well as recognised by someone else, even when it is not the same as the object. Note that this sort of causality or sense of 'causality' is so far from accommodating itself to Hume's explanations that people who believe that Hume pretty well dealt with the topic of causality would entirely leave it out of their calculations; if their attention were drawn to it they might insist that the word 'cause' was inappropriate or was quite equivocal. Or conceivably they might try to give a Humeian account of the matter as far as concerned the outside observer's recognition of the cause; but hardly for the patient's.

Now one might think that when the question 'Why?' is answered by giving the intention with which a person acts—a case of which I will here simply characterise by saying that it mentions something future—this is also a case of a mental cause. For couldn't it be recast in the form: 'Because I wanted . . .' or 'Out of a desire that . . .'? If a feeling of desire for an apple affects me and I get up and go to a cupboard where I think there are some, I might answer the question what led to this action by mentioning the desire as having made me . . . *etc.* But it is not in all cases that 'I did so and so in order to . . .' can be backed up by 'I *felt* a desire that . . .' I may *e.g.* simply hear a knock on the door and go downstairs to open it without experiencing any such

[1] *Philosophical Investigations* (Oxford, 1958) ¶ 476.

desire. Or suppose I feel an upsurge of spite against someone and destroy a message he has received so that he shall miss an appointment. If I describe this by saying 'I wanted to make him miss that appointment', this does not necessarily mean that I had the thought 'If I do this, he will . . .' and that it affected me with a desire of bringing that about which led up to my action. This may have happened, but need not. It could be that all that happened was this: I read the message, had the thought 'That unspeakable man!' with feelings of hatred, tore the message up, and laughed. Then if the question 'Why did you do that?' is put by someone who makes it clear that he wants me to mention the mental causes—*i.e.*, what went on in my mind and issued in the action—I should perhaps give this account; but normally the reply would be no such thing. That particular enquiry is not very often made. Nor do I wish to say that it always has an answer in cases where it can be made. One might shrug or say 'I don't know that there was any definite history of the kind you mean', or 'It merely occurred to me . . .'

A 'mental cause', of course, need not be a mental event, *i.e.*, a thought or feeling or image; it might be a knock on the door. But if it is not a mental event, it must be something perceived by the person affected—*e.g.* the knock on the door must be heard—so if in this sense anyone wishes to say it is always a mental event, I have no objection. A mental cause is what someone would describe if he were asked the specific question: what produced this action or thought or feeling in you? *i.e.*, what did you see or hear or feel, or what ideas or images cropped up in your mind, and led up to it? I have isolated this notion of a mental cause because there *is* such a thing as this question with this sort of answer, and because I want to distinguish it from the ordinary senses of 'motive' and 'intention', rather than because it is in itself of very great importance; for I believe that it is of very little. But it is important to have a clear idea of it, partly because *a* very natural conception of 'motive' is that it is what *moves* (the very word suggests that)—glossed as 'what *causes*' a man's actions *etc.* And 'what causes' them is perhaps then thought of as an event that brings the effect about—though *how*—*i.e.* whether it should be thought of as a kind of pushing in another medium, or in some other way–is of course completely obscure.

In philosophy a distinction has sometimes been drawn between 'motives' and 'intentions in acting' as referring to quite different things. A man's intention is *what* he aims at or chooses; his motive is what determines the aim or choice; and I suppose that 'determines' must here be another word for 'causes'.

Popularly, 'motive' and 'intention' are not treated as so distinct in meaning. *E.g.* we hear of 'the motive of gain'; some philosophers have wanted to say that such an expression must be elliptical; gain must be the *intention,* and *desire of gain* the motive. Asked for a motive, a man might say 'I wanted to . . .' which would please such philosophers; or 'I did it in order to . . .' which would not; and yet the meaning of the two phrases is here identical. When a man's motives are called good, this may be in no way distinct from calling his intentions good–*e.g.* 'he only wanted to make peace among his relations'.

Nevertheless there is even popularly a distinction between the meaning of 'motive' and the meaning of 'intention'. *E.g.* if a man kills someone, he may be said to have done it out of love and pity, or to have done it out of hatred; these might indeed be cast in the forms 'to release him from this awful suffering', or 'to get rid of the swine'; but though these are forms of expression suggesting objectives, they are perhaps expressive of the spirit in which the man killed rather than descriptive of the end to which the killing was a means–a future state of affairs to be produced by the killing. And this shows us part of the distinction that there is between the popular senses of motive and intention. We should say: popularly, 'motive for an action' has a rather wider and more diverse application than 'intention with which the action was done'.

When a man says what his motive was, speaking popularly, and in a sense in which 'motive' is not interchangeable with 'intention', he is not giving a 'mental cause' in the sense that I have given to that phrase. The fact that the mental causes were such-and-such may indeed help to make his claim intelligible. And further, though he may say that his motive was this or that one straight off and without lying–*i.e.* without saying what he knows or even half knows to be untrue—yet a consideration of various things, which may include the mental causes, might possibly lead both him and other people to judge that his declaration of his own motive was false. But it appears to me that the mental causes are seldom more than a very trivial item among the things that it would be reasonable to consider. As for the importance of considering the motives of an action, as opposed to considering the intention, I am very glad not to be writing either ethics or literary criticism, to which this question belongs.

Motives may explain actions to us; but that is not to say that they 'determine', in the sense of causing, actions. We do say: 'His love of truth caused him to . . .' and similar things, and no doubt such expressions help us to think that a motive must be what produces or brings about a choice. But this means rather 'He did this in that he loved the truth'; it interprets his action.

Someone who sees the confusions involved in radically distinguishing between motives and intentions and in defining motives, so distinct, as the determinants of choice, may easily be inclined to deny both that there is any such thing as mental causality, and that 'motive' means anything but intention. But both of these inclinations are mistaken. We shall create confusion if we do not notice (*a*) that phenomena deserving the name of mental causality exist, for we can make the question 'Why?' into a request for the sort of answer that I considered under that head; (*b*) that mental causality is not restricted to choices or voluntary or intentional actions but is of wider application; it is restricted to the wider field of things the agent knows about *not* as an observer, so that it includes some involuntary actions; (*c*) that motives are not mental causes; and (*d*) that there is application for 'motive' other than the applications of 'the intention with which a man acts'.

Revenge and gratitude are motives; if I kill a man as an act of revenge I may say I do it in order to be revenged, or that revenge is my object; but revenge is not some further thing obtained by killing him, it is rather that killing him is revenge. Asked why I killed him, I reply 'Because he killed my brother.' We might compare this answer, which describes a concrete past event, to the answer describing a concrete future state of affairs which we sometimes get in statements of objectives. It is the same with gratitude, and remorse, and pity for something specific. These motives differ from, say, love or curiosity or despair in just this way: something that *has happened* (or is at present happening) is given as the ground of an action or abstention that is good or bad for the person (it may be oneself, as with remorse) at whom it is aimed. And if we wanted to explain *e.g.* revenge, we should say it was harming someone because he had done one some harm; we should not need to add some description of the feelings prompting the action or of the thoughts that had gone with it. Whereas saying that someone does something out of, say, friendship cannot be explained in any such way. I will call revenge and gratitude and remorse and pity backward-looking motives, and contrast them with motive-in-general.

Motive-in-general is a very difficult topic which I do not want to discuss at any length. Consider the statement that one motive for my signing a petition was admiration for its promoter, X. Asked 'Why did you sign it?' I might well say 'Well, for one thing, X, who is promoting it, did . . .' and describe what he did in an admiring way. I might add 'Of course, I know that is not a ground for signing it, but I am sure it was one of the things that most influenced me'— which need *not* mean: 'I thought explicitly of this before signing.' I say 'Consider this' really with a view to saying 'let us not consider it here.' It is too complicated. The account of motive popularised by Professor Ryle does not appear satisfactory. He recommends construing 'he boasted from vanity' as saying 'he boasted . . . and his doing so satisfies the law-like proposition that whenever he finds a chance of securing the admiration and envy of others, he does whatever he thinks will produce this admiration and envy.'[2] This passage is rather curious and roundabout in its way of putting what it seems to say, but I can't understand it unless it implies that a man could not be said to have boasted from vanity unless he always behaved vainly, or at least very often did so. But this does not seem to be true.

[2] *The Concept of Mind* (London, 1949), p. 89.

To give a motive (of the sort I have labelled 'motive-in-general', as opposed to backward-looking motives and intentions) is to say something like 'See the action in this light.' To explain one's own actions by an account indicating a motive is to put them in a certain light. This sort of explanation is often elicited by the question 'Why?' The question whether the light in which one so puts one's action is a true light is a notoriously difficult one.

The motives admiration, curiosity, spite, friendship, fear, love of truth, despair and a host of others are either of this extremely complicated kind, or are forward-looking or mixed. I call a motive forward-looking if it is an intention. For example, to say that someone did something for fear of . . . often comes to the same as saying he did so lest . . . or in order that . . . should not happen.

Leaving then, the topic of motive-in-general or 'interpretative' motive, let us return to backward-looking motives. Why is it that in revenge and gratitude, pity and remorse, the past event (or present situation) is a reason for acting, not just a mental cause?

Now the most striking thing about these four is the way in which good and evil are involved in them. *E.g.* if I am grateful to someone, it is because he has done me some good, or at least I think he has, and I cannot show gratitude by something that I intend to harm him. In remorse, I hate some good things for myself; I could not express remorse *by* getting myself plenty of enjoyments, or *for* something that I did not find bad. If I do something out of revenge which is in fact advantageous rather than harmful to my enemy, my action, in its description of being advantageous to him, is involuntary.

These facts are the clue to our present problem. If an action has to be thought of by the agent as doing good or harm of some sort, and the thing in the past as good or bad, in order for the thing in the past to be the reason for the action, then this reason shows not a mental cause but a motive. This will come out in the agent's elaborations on his answer to the question 'Why?'

It might seem that this is not the most important point, but that the important point is that a *proposed* action can be questioned and the answer be a mention of something past. 'I am going to kill him.'–'Why?'–'He killed my father.' But do we yet know what a proposal to act is; other than a prediction which the predictor justifies, if he does justify it, by mentioning a reason for acting? and the meaning of the expression 'reason for acting' is precisely what we are at present trying to elucidate. Might one not predict mental causes and their effects? Or even their effects after the causes have occurred? *E.g.* 'This is going to make me angry.' Here it may be worth while to remark that it is a mistake to think one cannot choose whether to act from a motive. Plato saying to a slave 'I should beat you if I were not angry' would be a case. Or a man might have a policy of never making remarks about a certain person because he could not speak about that man unenviously or unadmiringly.

We have now distinguished between a backward-looking motive and a mental cause, and found that here at any rate what the agent reports in answer to the question 'Why?' is a reason-for-acting if, in treating it as a reason, he conceives it as something good or bad, and his own action as doing good or harm. If you could *e.g.* show that either the action for which he has revenged himself, or that in which he has revenged himself, was quite harmless or beneficial, he ceases to offer a reason, except prefaced by 'I thought'. If it is a proposed revenge he either gives it up or changes his reasons. No such discovery would affect an assertion of mental causality. Whether in general good and harm play an essential part in the concept of intention is something it still remains to find out. So far good and harm have only been introduced as making a clear difference between a backward-looking motive and a mental cause. When the question 'Why?' about a present action is answered by description of a future state of affairs, this is already distinguished from a mental cause just by being future. Here there does not so far seem to be any need to characterise intention as being essentially of good or of harm.

Now, however, let us consider this case:

Why did you do it?
Because he told me to.

Is this a cause or a reason? It appears to depend very much on what the action was or what the circumstances were. And we should often refuse to make any distinction at all between something's being a reason and its being a cause of the kind in question; for that was explained as what one is after if one asks the agent what led up to and issued in an action, but being given a reason and accepting it might be such a thing. And how would one distinguish between cause and reason in such a case as having hung one's hat on a peg because one's host said 'Hang up your hat on that peg'? Nor, I think, would it be correct to say that this is a reason and not a mental cause because of the understanding of the words that went into obeying the suggestion. Here one would be attempting a contrast between this case and, say, turning round at hearing someone say Boo! But this case would not in fact be decisively on one side or the other; forced to say whether the noise was a reason or a cause, one would probably decide by how sudden one's reaction was. Further, there is no question of understanding a sentence in the following case: 'Why did you waggle your two fore-fingers by your temples?'–'Because *he* was doing it;' but this is not particularly different from hanging one's hat up because one's host said 'Hang your hat up.' Roughly speaking, if one were forced to go on with the distinction, the more the action is described as a mere response, the more inclined one would be to the word 'cause'; while the more it is described as a response to something as having a *significance* that is dwelt on by the agent, or as a response surrounded with thoughts and questions, the more inclined one would be to use the word 'reason'. But in very many cases the distinction would have no point.

This, however, does not mean that it never has a point. The cases on which we first grounded the distinction might be called 'full-blown': that is to say, the case of *e.g.* revenge on the one hand, and of the thing that made me jump and knock a cup off a table on the other. Roughly speaking, it establishes something as a reason to object to it, not as when one says 'Noises should not make you jump like that: hadn't you better see a doctor?' but in such a way as to link it up with motives and intentions. 'You did it because he told you to? But why do what he says?' Answers like 'he has done a lot for me'; 'he is my father'; 'it would have been the worse for me if I hadn't' give the original answer a place among reasons. Thus the full-blown cases are the right ones to consider in order to see the distinction between reason and cause. But it is worth noticing that what is so commonly said, that reason and cause are everywhere sharply distinct notions, is not true.

VOLITION

G. N. A. Vesey

I

'Let us not forget this: when "I raise my arm", my arm goes up. And the problem arises: what is left over if I subtract the fact that my arm goes up from that fact that I raise my arm?'[1]

This is a question which would arise very naturally in trying to describe some of the effects of anaesthesia. William James[2] reports that if a patient who has lost sensation in one arm is asked to put the affected hand on top of his head while his eyes are closed, and is at the same time prevented from doing so, he will be very surprised on opening his eyes to find that the movement has not taken place. This, James says, is the rule rather than the exception in anaesthetic cases. Confirmation of this is to be found in case-histories reported in the medical journals.[3]

If one were to consider only such cases as these one might say that what is left over, if I subtract the fact that my arm goes up from the fact that I raise my arm, is

(a) 'It seems to me that I have raised my arm'.

But this is inadequate, since it invites the question, 'Why does it seem to you that you raised your arm? It was not from anything you saw or felt. What gave you the idea that you had

G. N. A. Vesey is Lecturer in Philosophy at King's College, University of London. He is the editor of *Body and Mind: Readings in Philosophy* (London, 1964) and the author of numerous articles.

[1] Wittgenstein, *Philosophical Investigations*, I, 621.

[2] *Principles of Psychology*, Vol. II, p. 105.

[3] For instance, J. D. Spillane, *Lancet*, 1942, i, p. 42, and J. Purdon Martin, *Lancet*, 1949, i, p. 51.

raised it?' One feels this to be a meaningful question, even if one cannot find words to answer it.

Furthermore, it may be simply false that it seems to the person that he has raised his arm. He may be well aware that it has not moved. He may even know himself to have lost the arm in question. It is in this connection that physiologists talk of 'phantom limbs'. A 'phantom limb' is not, of course, what we ordinarily mean by 'a phantom'; it is not an apparition, or a spectre. When medical people talk of a 'phantom limb' they are using the word 'phantom' in a technical sense, to refer to 'the seeming persistence of a part that was known to be gone, and the continued possession of many of its original attributes of form, position, and even voluntary movement'.[4] The point of using the word 'phantom' is that the limb seems to persist only to the person whose limb it was, and that it does not seem to persist even to him so far as what are usually referred to as 'the five senses' are concerned. Phantom limbs may be either painless or painful. Attempts to move painful phantom limbs usually result in an increase of the pain, but voluntary movement of painless phantom limbs 'is usually possible and often considerable'.[5]

Should we say that what is left over, if I subtract the fact that my arm goes up from the fact that I raise my arm, is

(b) 'I raised my phantom arm'?

The term 'phantom' in this phrase having been tailored to fit precisely the sort of cases we have been considering, there can be no question as to its being true that what is left over is a movement of a phantom arm. And there seems no reason (other than the practical one, that the present usage serves to distinguish cases in which there is no actual movement from normal cases) why we should not extend our use of this phrase so that in normal cases also there can be said to be the movement of a phantom arm. In normal cases the movement of the phantom arm will be materialised, so to speak, in the movement of a real arm. In abnormal cases this materialisation will be lacking.

But what would we achieve in answering the question thus? Have we, with talk of the movement of phantom arms,

[4] George Riddoch, *Brain*, 1941, Vol. 64, p. 197.
[5] Riddoch, *ibid.*, p. 218.

reached a point at which we can say 'Now I understand'? Or do we not, rather, feel the need to inquire further, 'But what is it to move a phantom arm?' For my own part I do not find talk of the movement of phantom arms a satisfactory way of answering the question, if only because the word 'phantom' has associations which are obviously out of place in this context.

One might well say of the patient mentioned by James, who had been prevented from moving his hand, that he had at least *tried* to move it. And hence that what is left over is

(c) 'I tried to move my arm'.

But this is unsatisfactory in that the patient may be unaware of any difficulty in moving his hand. Because of his anaesthesia it is not as if he could feel his hand being held down. From the patient's point of view it is not as if he had to try to move his hand, but as if he could actually, and easily, move it—or, at least, it is like this to him until he opens his eyes.

In short, 'He tried to move his hand' describes not so much what the patient did as what he did not do: he failed to qualify for the description 'He moved his hand'.

Suppose James' patient, when he found that his hand had not in fact moved, were to say,

(d) 'I did whatever would ordinarily have produced the movement'.

What he would mean by this is not immediately obvious. To make a piece of chalk fall to the floor I have to do something else, namely open my fingers, but (one feels like saying) to open my fingers there is not something else I have to do first. After all, they are my fingers, part of me. As Wittgenstein remarks,[6] 'When I raise my arm "voluntarily" I do not use any instrument to bring the movement about'.

It might be said that whether the movement takes place or not there occurs an outgoing of energy from the brain along one or other of the efferent nerves, and that this is what the patient really does.[7] This is 'what would ordinarily have pro-

[6] *Philosophical Investigations*, I, 614.

[7] Thus John Ladd, in 'Freewill and Voluntary Action', *Philosophy and Phenomenological Research*, 1951/52, writes: 'A person who has had a limb amputated may unsuccessfully will to move the absent

duced the movement'. The objection to this is not that there are no such outgoings of energy (for there are), nor that the agent is not conscious of them (certain psychologists[8] have held that the agent *is* conscious of them, as so-called 'feelings of innervation') but that any such outgoings of energy are not something the agent *does*. If, when asked what he was doing, a person were to reply, 'I am busy discharging energy into my efferent nerves', he would be making what Professor Ryle might call 'a category mistake joke'.

Let us now consider what might be called the 'traditional' answer to our question. It is, at the same time, another meaning which might be given to 'I did whatever would ordinarily have produced the movement'. It is

(e) 'I willed the movement to occur'.

Let us distinguish, first, two fairly common senses of the word 'will' in which it does not seem to be true to say that a person who moves his arm voluntarily, always 'wills' it to move.

The word 'will' is sometimes used in such expressions as 'He willed the waitress to look in his direction', and 'He willed the dice to fall with sixes uppermost'. A characteristic of this use of the word 'will' is that it makes no sense to talk of the person who does the willing, himself doing whatever it is he wills to happen. There is no 'doing' which fulfils 'He willed the waitress to look in his direction': he is not the waitress. In this sense of 'will' one only wills what one cannot do. So one does not, in this sense of 'will', will one's arm to move; one simply moves it.[9]

---

limb. Still he has *done* something, if it only be having had the appropriate imagery and discharging nervous energy into the formerly appropriate nerves.'

[8] See William James, *Principles of Psychology*, Vol. II, p. 493.

[9] If this sort of willing were to have effect it would constitute a case of what paranormal psychologists call 'psycho-kinesis'. It has been maintained by Professor J. C. Eccles, in *Nature*, 1951, pp. 53–57, and *The Neurophysiological Basis of Mind*, pp. 284–285, that such psycho-kinesis may well be the explanation of the effect of mind on brain in voluntary action. For a discussion of the idea that voluntary action is like willing other people to do things, see B. O'Shaughnessy, 'The Limits of the Will', *Philosophical Review*, 1956.

The word 'will' is also used when a person finds doing something very hard. We talk of a person willing himself to keep hold of a cliff edge, although the pain in his fingers is almost unbearable. And we talk of a person willing himself to appear cool and collected at an important interview. His 'willing himself' is largely a matter of encouraging himself not to give in, not to release his grasp or give way to worrying about the impression he is making. When there is no difficulty the person does not have to will himself.

It is not, or not only, a consideration of these two fairly common uses of the word 'will' which has led to its being said that what a person *really* does in moving some part of his body is to will that part of his body to move. The attraction of the 'I willed the movement to occur' answer does not lie in its being in accord with common usage. The point of giving this answer, and its meaning, is rather to be found in a certain philosophical argument purporting to show that voluntary movement is not at all what we ordinarily take it to be. To this argument, which might be called the 'causal' argument, we must now turn our attention.

II

To facilitate discussion of it, the causal argument[10] may be divided into three steps.

(1) It is a fact that when a person, as we say, 'moves his arm', the actual movement is caused by certain muscles contracting or expanding, which contractions or expansions are caused by impulses in the efferent nerves, which impulses are caused by certain physiological changes in the brain. Therefore what the agent *really* does is not to move his arm. But nor can it be held that what he *really* does is to make those physiological changes in his brain which are the starting point

[10] My formulation of the argument is based mainly on David Hume, *Enquiries*, Sections 51–53, and *Treatise*, Appendix (Selby-Bigge edition, p. 632); William James, *Principles of Psychology*, II, pp. 524–526; F. H. Bradley, *Collected Essays*, I, pp. 272–283, and *Mind*, N.S. xi, 1902, p. 441, and *Mind*, N.S. xiii, 1904, p. 1; and G. Dawes Hicks, *Proc. Arist. Soc.*, 1912–13, 'The nature of willing' (containing a translation of a passage from Hermann Lotze, *Medicinische Psychologie*, p. 288).

of the physical causal chain, since he is not even conscious of the nature of these changes. Therefore what he *really* does cannot be anything physical at all, but must be something of an altogether different kind, namely mental.

(2) Why it is that a certain mental state should produce, as it seems to, a certain physiological change in the brain, is wholly beyond our comprehension. (For the Cartesian philosopher, Arnold Geulincx, the idea of mind and body interacting was so unintelligible that he found it necessary to invoke God to supply the means of connection, by himself willing the appropriate bodily changes on the occasion of the mental states. On this theory the mental states are only the occasional causes of the bodily changes, and the theory is accordingly known as 'occasionalism'. Bradley substituted in place of God a variety of special dispositions to provide the connection. With reference to Bradley's use of the word 'disposition' Dawes Hicks remarked, 'I suspect that too often the notion of disposition does but serve the familiar device of providing a *tertium quid* between two modes of being that seem otherwise to resist the attempt to think of them as intelligibly connected'. Hume contented himself with remarking, 'So far from perceiving the connection between an act of volition, and a movement of the body, it is allowed that no effect is more inexplicable from the powers and essence of thought and matter'.) That is, we have no insight into why a certain mental state should be associated with a certain physiological change in the brain. For all we know, the mental states could have been what they are now and the bodily changes quite different. Consequently 'however manifest it may appear to us that in none of our bodily activities are we consciously so thoroughly at home as in regard to our own movements, however readily we may believe that we are self-acting, even down to the smallest details of such movements, yet in all this we are the victims of illusion'.[11]

(3) Why did we ever suppose ourselves to be 'at home' in our movements? Why are we 'the victims of the illusion that

[11] Lotze, *Medicinische Psychologie*, p. 288, as translated by Dawes Hicks. The Humean equivalent to the illusion that we are 'self-acting' would be the illusion that the immediate object of power in voluntary movement is the limb which is moved.

we are self-acting'? Why is it not immediately obvious to everyone that we do something of quite a different kind from a movement, namely something mental, which, by the grace of God (Geulincx), or of special dispositions (Bradley), results in a movement? The answer is that what characterises the mental state which results in, say, a movement of one's arm, is precisely that it is an uninhibited thought *of the arm moving*. It is this happy coincidence that accounts for the idea we have that we really do move our arms. If, in order to induce those physiological changes in the brain which are appropriate for the arms to move, we had to have an idea, not of the desired arm-movements, but of the necessary brain-changes, then we would never have supposed ourselves to be 'at home' in the movements of our arms: the arm-movements would always have seemed at a remove from us. Confirmation that the mental state of willing consists in having an idea of the movement desired, which somehow triggers off the causal chain ending in the movement (the so-called 'ideo-motor' theory) is to be found in such facts as that 'if an individual merely thinks intently of falling forward, swaying forward begins'. Voluntarily controlled actions are thus 'responses to auto-suggestions, either in the form of words or imagined actions or ideas of other kinds. In any determined voluntary action we stimulate ourselves verbally with commands to do or not to do an act.'[12]

III

Before attempting a reply to the first two steps of this argument it may be helpful to comment on, and expose some of the implications of, the final step.

Perhaps the most startling consequence of accepting the final step of the argument is that one is thereby involved in denying the validity of the customary distinction between voluntary and involuntary movements. This comes out most clearly in Bradley's treatment of the topic. Accepting, as he does, the ideo-motor theory, he writes:[13] 'An idea of a state

[12] J. P. Guilford, *General Psychology*, pp. 265–69.
[13] *Collected Essays*, I, pp. 275–6.

of my salivary glands or sexual organs will produce its existence in fact. We hear of those who can blush, shiver, sweat, or shed tears if their mind is set on it. And if we think of various sensations in parts of our bodies, we can produce them at will, and can induce at our pleasure other bodily alterations through emotional excitement. Now on the one hand, I believe, the view could not be sustained that our striped or voluntary muscles are here the necessary agents; and on the other hand to deny that these changes are volitional would be to confess oneself refuted. With the nature of the process, considered physiologically, I am not concerned; but, as will, it is merely a case of our law. Where we have had a bodily state A^1 with a psychical state B^1, then, when B^2 comes in, A^2 tends to appear; and, if an idea of A is what produces the result, that result is volition. . . . This is the essence of volition.'

In the light of this consequence of the ideo-motor theory it is hardly surprising that there have been attempts to disprove it, either by argument or by experiment. It may suffice to mention two such attempts, and an experiment of my own.

William McDougall writes:[14]

> The doctrine of 'ideo-motor action' is an exaggeration and distortion of the truth that every cycle of mental activity tends naturally and primitively to express itself in bodily movement. The 'ideo-motor theory' has been widely accepted and may be found dogmatically stated in many recent books. It asserts that every 'idea' is not only a state or act of knowing but also a tendency to movement; and this is made the basis of a widely accepted general theory of action, the 'ideo-motor theory'. The ideo-motor theory is most plausible in the case of 'ideas' of bodily movement. It has frequently been alleged that, if we think of a movement, that movement inevitably occurs, unless we somehow inhibit it. And one theory of volition asserts that volition is essentially the inhibition of 'ideas' which inhibit the 'idea' of movement. I cannot discover any substantial foundation for such assertions. It is clearly possible to think of such a movement as raising the hand, either as

[14] *Outline of Psychology*, pp. 290–1.

> a movement to be made or as a movement not to be made. And I can find no truth in the assertion that, when I think of such a movement, my limb fairly tingles with the tendency to move, and that it is necessary to exert some inhibitory power in order to prevent its movement. To merely think of a movement and to intend or to will a movement are entirely distinct. . . . The relation of our impulses, intentions and volitions to the action movements of our limbs remains entirely obscure, a part of the larger mystery of the relation between experience and bodily processes. The ideo-motor theory is a mistaken attempt to resolve this mystery.

McDougall does not say what he would regard as the proper way of going about resolving the 'mystery of the relation between experience and bodily processes'. But his use of the word 'mystery' suggests that he may think that it is not the sort of problem for scientists *qua* scientists to solve.

Professor C. T. Morgan approaches the problem from the point of view of a physiological psychologist. He writes:[15]

> What do we have to do in order to gain voluntary control of a response? It was at one time supposed that, if we could call to mind how the muscles would feel when moved in a certain way—in other words, if we had a clear memory of the proprioceptive sensations produced by the movement—we could then move those muscles appropriately. It was even sometimes supposed that such a memory of a movement must necessarily precede the movement which we desire to make.[16]
>
> Not only, however, is this anticipatory proprioception

[15] 'Voluntary Control of Movement', in Boring, Langfeld, and Weld, *Foundations of Psychology*, p. 50.

[16] For a revival of this theory see Professor C. A. Campbell, 'Self-activity and its modes', in *Contemporary British Philosophy, Third Series*, p. 93. Campbell holds that if a person has somehow forgotten what are the specific sensations associated with moving his leg, he cannot will to move it. His ground for this belief is his conviction, based on introspection, 'that the *immediate* object of our willing is not the movement of our leg but certain kinaesthetic and other sensations upon which, we have learned from experience, the movement of our leg normally supervenes'.

not necessary, but research has also shown that proprioception alone–or even when combined with a visual image of what the movement should be–is not a sufficient preliminary process to produce 'at will' a movement never before voluntarily initiated.

In certain experiments, persons who could not move their ears voluntarily had their ear muscles stimulated electrically so as to produce the movement. These persons felt the movement and saw it in a mirror. Still they could not move their ears voluntarily. In attempting to move them, they had the same sense of helplessness which they had experienced before the electrical stimulation. In their attempts, however, they moved the voluntarily controlled muscles of the brow, jaw, and cheek, in such a way that the muscles of the ear were accidentally moved with them. Thus the ear muscles were brought into the reaction pattern, with the result that there occurred both efferent impulses to the muscles and proprioception from their contraction. It was only then that the proprioception, by becoming a link in a reflex circle, helped to develop full voluntary control of the ears.

These facts give us a picture of the origin and development of voluntary movement. It is clear from them that the *first movement* of our muscle groups are unconscious and *involuntary*, and that they come under conscious voluntary control only later, after the muscles have been 'accidentally' innervated.

An experiment of which I have not found any mention in the psychology books, which illustrates Morgan's thesis, is the following. The subject is asked to bare his right arm, and to hold it, fully extended, palm downwards, horizontally in front of him. He is then asked to move his elbow anti-clockwise about 45 degrees *without moving his hand*. In all probability he will report the 'sense of helplessness' to which Morgan refers. He knows what is required, in the sense that he can imagine the movement occurring. He may even be able to imagine how it would feel. But he *cannot* obey the insturction.

Next he is asked to rest his hand flat on a table in front of him. He will find that he can now obey the instruction to move his elbow without moving his hand. He is no longer helpless. But once he takes his hand off the table he is likely to be as helpless as before. And remembering what it felt like to move his elbow without moving his hand is of no assistance.

If, however, he very gradually reduces the pressure of his hand on the table at the same time as he moves his elbow, he will be able to acquire the capacity to move his elbow, without moving his hand, when his hand is *not* resting on the table.

Someone might describe the situation by saying that the subject has learnt *how* to move his elbow without moving his hand. But if we ask the subject how he does it, what the secret is, there is nothing he can say. He can tell us how he acquired the capacity, and he can, while exercising it, say, 'This is how I do it'. Of course, if he is a neurologist, he may be able to explain how it is that he acquired the capacity by doing what he did. *But there is nothing he can say, about what is going on in his mind at the time he does it, which will enable someone else to make this sort of movement.* There is no 'secret' of voluntary action. If a person cannot raise one eyebrow without raising the other, then he cannot. But if he can, then there is nothing to it: he simply does it.

IV

Let us return now to the first two steps in the causal argument, the steps which lead to the conclusion, in Lotze's words, that the appearance of our being 'at home' in our own movements is an illusion.

What are we to make of the very first assertion in the argument, the assertion that arm movements are caused by muscles contracting and expanding, these in turn by nervous impulses, and so on? In the argument this is taken to imply that we are not 'at home' in our bodily movements, that the relation between the mental and the bodily sides of a voluntary movement is no more intimate than that between, say, thinking of something very frightening and sweating.

One way of responding to this would be to dismiss the causal account as irrelevant, and to refuse to countenance talk of what a person *really* does.

But if we dismiss the causal account as irrelevant it seems that we may also be involved in dismissing the question with which we began as meaningless. The patient who was asked to put his hand on top of his head did not do so—his hand did not move. But it was not as if he had simply ignored the request. On the contrary, he was surprised on opening his eyes to find that the movement had not taken place. Are we simply to say that he did not do anything, and leave it at that?

But this reconsideration of the question with which we began itself suggests an alternative to dismissing the causal account as irrelevant. We can say: its relevance has been over-played, as not only providing the reason for talking of what a person *really* does, but also as indicating what the content of such talk must be. We have taken the dose twice, so to speak. We have taken it once in accepting the necessity of introducing a terminology which is such that the truth or falsity of the statements in it is not dependent on the truth or falsity of statements about the body and how it is functioning. (That is, we recognise that we would never have occasion to say of anybody 'He is moving his arm' were it not for the fact that nervous impulses *do* cause muscles to contract, etc.; and we look for a way of describing what a person does—what he *really* does—which is truth-functionally independent of such facts.)

And we have taken the dose a second time in supposing that we are dictated in our choice of a terminology to describe what a person *really* does not only by the requirements (1) that it can truthfully be said of him that he does it no matter what happens in his body, what movements do or do not take place, etc., and (2) that it is something he is aware of doing, but also by the requirement (3) that it shall be whatever has been found to be the first link in the causal chain.

One might think that once the incompatibility of the second requirement and this additional one was seen—for a person is not aware of making physiological changes in his brain —it would be realised that one must have misunderstood the relevance of the causal account in adding this requirement. But such is the strength of the impulse (an impulse which finds expression in a most explicit manner in the works of J. C. Eccles, to which reference has already been made) to assimilate all explanation to explanation in terms of space and energy, that this objection is overcome by thinking of the mind (the events in which we are aware of, by definition) as a sort of energy-system, which is located either in the head itself, or in a higher dimensional space than the physical world,[17] and saying that what we *really* do are events in this energy-system, which 'influence' the brain.

The situation may be made somewhat clearer by comparing it with a parallel situation in the case of perception.

It may be pointed out that what colour a carpet looks to someone depends on the state of his nervous system. If he took certain drugs it might look quite different to him. His awareness of the carpet is thus subject to certain conditions —there being light, his having eyes, an optic nerve, etc. Here, just as in the case of voluntary action, a causal account can be given of a person's perception of a carpet as being, say, blue. And in the light of this causal account we may be invited to talk of what the person is *immediately* aware of.

Here again the relevance of the causal account can be overplayed. We can regard it as not only providing the reason for talking of what a person is *immediately* aware of, but also as indicating what the content of such talk must be. It provides us with a reason for introducing, if there is not one already, a terminology which is such that the statements in it are *not* subject to verification or falsification by reference to conditions under which we are observing something. And it is taken as indicating what the content of such talk must be, by those who say that what we are immediately aware of is a 'picture' which is somehow aroused in our minds as a result of certain physiological changes in our brains.[18] (If it were not too silly for words it would be said that what one was *immediately* aware of was the state of one's brain.)

Now in the case of perception we already have a terminology which is such that statements in it are not subject to verification or falsification by reference to conditions under

[17] J. R. Smythies, 'The Extension of Mind', *J. Soc. Psych. Res.*, 1951, pp. 477–502.

[18] J. A. V. Butler, 'Pictures in the Mind', *Science News 22.*

which we are observing something. We can say, 'What he is *immediately* aware of is *how the carpet looks to him*'. In using this phrase, 'how it looks to him', the conditions under which he observes the carpet are made truth-functionally irrelevant. He can always be mistaken about what he is aware of—the conditions under which he is observing may not be what he takes them to be—but he cannot be mistaken about how whatever he is aware of looks to him.

In saying 'He is *immediately* aware of how the carpet looks to him' we are not debarred from saying, concurrently, that he is *aware* of the carpet. We are not debarred from saying this because 'how it looks to him' is not another *thing*. And so it does not 'come between' the observer and the carpet. He is *aware* of the carpet *and* he is *immediately aware* of how it looks to him.

What we want, it seems, is an account of what a person *really* does, which is like the 'how the thing looks to him' account of what a person is *immediately* aware of. We want an account of what we *really* do which does not put something else in the place of what we *do*, which does not come between us and our bodily movements. (This, I take it, is the point of the remark Wittgenstein quotes, in *Philosophical Investigations*, I, 615, 'Willing, if it is not to be a sort of wishing, must be the action itself. It cannot be allowed to stop anywhere short of the action.')

The account we are led to give by treating the causal account as indicating what the content of such an account must be, is one which does put something else in the place of what we do. According to it the connection of mental state and bodily movement is purely contingent. 'For all we know the mental states could have been what they are now and the bodily changes quite different'. From this, the assimilation of voluntary movements to those involuntary ones which are the effect of, say, emotional excitement, follows quite naturally. I may be able to think of something so frightening that I start to sweat. I cannot tell, without experience of the connection, that thinking of something very frightening will ordinarily lead to sweating. That is, I can give a full description of what it is to think of something very frightening without it being evident that it leads to sweating. Similarly, according to this account, a full description of what a person *really* does in moving his arms could be given without it being evident that it ordinarily leads to his arms moving. It is as a consequence of *this* that we are said to be not at home in our movements, not self-acting in them. What one *really* does, on this account, would presumably be something one could do without ever having moved one's arms.

It is as if, in the case of perception, something could look to a person like a carpet without his knowing what it would be like to see a carpet.

V

The two requirements for a description of what a person *really* does in voluntary movement, if the causal account is taken only as providing a reason for such talk, are (1) that it can truthfully be said of him that he does it regardless of what happens in his body, what movements do or do not take place, etc., and (2) that it is something he is aware of doing.

In our language as it stands there simply is no short description which satisfies these requirements. There is no description of what a person *really* does which is as much a part of our everyday language as is the description, 'He moved his arm', of what he *does*. But there is no reason why we should not introduce some new expression, such as 'So far as he, but not necessarily his arm, was concerned, he moved his arm', or 'So far as the mental side of him as an agent is concerned, he moved his arm', at the same time stipulating that it is to work like 'He moved his arm', *except that it can be true even when 'His arm moved' is false.*

And thus is the question with which we began answered.

VI

I have tried to characterise the sort of thinking which often lies behind the use of the word 'will'. Any brief characterisation of this sort of thinking is bound to be open to misinterpretation. But if I had to put it briefly I would say that what lies behind the use of the word 'will' is the thought that the mind is only accidentally embodied. Its embodiment is an extrinsic, not an intrinsic, feature of it. Perhaps the clearest expression of this thought is to be found in the article by Dawes Hicks:[19] 'Seeing that for the realisation of a resolve or a purpose the conscious subject is at the mercy of an extraordinarily intricate conjunction of factors lying beyond the range of his inner life, seeing that the mechanism by means of which volition finds expression in the external world is completely hidden from him, the conclusion seems forced upon us that what specifically characterises volition as a fact of mind must be, to a large extent, at least, independent of the execution which is normally its consequent. The scope of willing, the content of the inner state which we call an act of will, would doubtless be enormously affected if execution habitually happened in a way other than that in which, as a matter of fact, it does happen, but the peculiar characteristic of willing as a state of mind might still be the same as it is now.'

What lies behind the preference for such an account of what a person *really* does in voluntary movement, as 'So far as he, but not necessarily his arm, was concerned, he moved his arm', is the thought that 'the scope of willing' and 'the peculiar characteristic of willing as a state of mind', so far from being independent of the movements a person actually makes, are conceptually parasitic on them. The mind, in its origins at least, is *necessarily* an embodied one.

It has been suggested[20] that an examination of the nature of voluntary activity may throw light on the freewill problem. Whether or not this is so depends on what one takes this problem to be.

One thing that can be said is this. Whereas any account on the lines of the ideo-motor theory readily lends itself to an interpretation of the action of mind on body in voluntary movement as causal (even if the cause is only an 'occasional' one), an account such as I have given does not readily lend itself to this interpretation. For if one knows that a person has moved his arm so far as the mental side of him as an agent is concerned, and one knows that his body is functioning properly, then one knows what part of his body will have

[19] *Ibid.*, p. 40.
[20] Campbell, *ibid.*, pp. 85–6.

moved. Hence (if one accepts the Humean thesis that if C is the cause of E then one cannot say, prior to experience of their conjunction, anything about E from a consideration of C alone) the action of mind on body in voluntary movement is not causal action.

Now the freewill problem may be taken to be the problem of explaining how a bodily movement can be accounted for in two different ways—in the 'physical' and the 'personal' ways—with each way seeming to give a complete accounting. This is how the freewill problem has been understood by, for example, those who see a solution in the 'physical' accounting not being as complete as had been thought.[21]

If this is taken to be the freewill problem then what has been said about volition *is* relevant. For if the 'personal' accounting is *not* a causal accounting then it does not conflict with the 'physical' accounting, which *is* causal. The problem is solved, not by denying either determinism or freewill but by showing there not to be a conflict between them.

[21] For example, J. C. Eccles, *The Neurophysiological Basis of Mind*, p. 272: 'The principal grounds for the theoretical belief that voluntary control of actions is an illusion are derived from the assumptions that science gives a deterministic explanation of all natural phenomena and that we are entirely within this deterministic scheme. In this context reference may be made to the recent discussion by Popper (*Brit. Journ. Phil. Sci.*, 1950, pp. 117–33, 173–95), in which he concludes that not only quantum physics but even "classical mechanics is not deterministic, but must admit the existence of unpredictable events". There are thus no sound scientific grounds for denying the freedom of the will, which virtually must be assumed if we are to act as scientific investigators.'

ACTION

A. I. Melden

We speak not only of the actions of infants, wild beasts, and lunatics but also of the actions of normal human beings in walking, talking, working, and playing. Yet we recognize an important difference between these two groups of cases. Infants, wild beasts, and lunatics may behave in ways that are fortunate or unfortunate to themselves and to others, but nothing done by such individuals is subject to moral criticism of any sort. Moral terms like "right" and "wrong" are appropriately applied only to the actions of normal and relatively mature human beings. In this paper I shall reserve the term "action" for the cases in which what an individual does can be in principle and in the appropriate circumstances the subject of moral review. This restricted usage of the term will enable us to avoid circumlocutions in addressing ourselves to the topic to be discussed: the relation between bodily movements and actions in the present restricted sense. When I perform an action, there is some bodily movement that occurs, but not every bodily movement counts as an action—not even those of normal adult human beings—since there are reflex movements, the activities of those who walk in their sleep, and the behavior of those under hypnosis. Hence it appears as though an action were a bodily movement of a special sort and that we need only specify the distinctive features of bodily movements that count as actions in order to elucidate the concept of an action. We are inclined, accordingly, to look for certain psychological factors in order to

A. I. Melden is Professor of Philosophy at the University of Washington, Seattle. He has contributed to various philosophical journals and is the author of *Rights and Right Conduct* (Oxford, 1959) and *Free Action* (London, 1961).

mark off bodily movements that count as actions from all those that do not. I shall argue that the familiar programs of analysis suggested by this approach rest upon fundamental misconceptions concerning the logical features of the concept of an action, and I shall then go on to indicate in outline at least the manner in which the concept of an action is related to that of a bodily movement.

I

It is difficult to resist the temptation to offer a simple summary formula in explanation of the concept of action, and, frequently, one of the first moves made in this direction is the suggestion that an action is a voluntary bodily movement. This, however, is to forget Aristotle's important reminder that the term "voluntary" does not help, since it is applied to a wide variety of bodily movements and serves only as a blanket term covering far too many different sorts of things.[1] Indeed, Aristotle regards the term "voluntary" as much too wide, since voluntary behavior is encountered in animals and small children who are exempt from moral criticism. And surely Aristotle is correct in rejecting the view that an action is a bodily movement that is chosen or deliberated, for "choice" and "deliberation" do not apply to spur-of-the-moment actions which we call "voluntary" and for which an agent is held responsible. When, for example, the traffic light turns red as I approach in my automobile, I do not in general deliberate and then choose to release the accelerator and apply the brakes. Indeed, most of the actions we perform are done without deliberation or choice. In most cases habits, desires, and impulses prevail—we act as we do as a matter of course, straight off, without reflection or pondering of any kind. But Aristotle's own elucidation of the term "voluntary" is wholly unilluminating; and the view which he seems to hold of the nature of action is less than satisfactory. Behavior is voluntary, he tells us, if "the moving principle is in a man himself."[2] What he means by a moving principle he does not

[1] *Nicomachean Ethics,* bk. III.
[2] 1110a. The translation is by Sir David Ross.

say, and so far the formula adds nothing to the various examples he cites and would mean nothing apart from them. But since Aristotle recognizes that infants and animals who are not responsible for what they do engage in voluntary behavior, even an adequate account of the concept "voluntary" will need to be supplemented by a further condition. As I understand his doctrine, this condition is that there be rational choice; but since not all actions are deliberated and chosen, e.g., spur-of-the-moment or impulsive acts, rational choice is introduced in connection with the formation of the states of character from which such impulsive actions are alleged to spring. We are responsible for impulsive actions since we are responsible for the states of character from which they spring; and we are responsible for such states even though we are not now masters of them, because rational choice was exercised in the actions which led to their formation. Hence an action would seem to be a case of behavior which is voluntary and in which, either in cause or in actual occurrence, there is rational choice.

But not even this will do, if we reflect upon the simple case in which, on the spur of the moment, one stops one's automobile when the traffic light turns red. The attempt to read deliberation and choice into the many cases of which this is only one instance by reference to some earlier choice to obey the relevant law whenever any occasion arises to which it applies is as fanciful as the attempt to discover some original covenant into which each of us has entered before engaging in our normal political dealings or some omnibus choice in favor of morality prior to the acquisition of the moral habits we exhibit in our normal moral affairs. When we do decide to learn to drive an automobile, we do not in general decide, in addition, to obey the traffic laws. For most of us, at any rate, there is no option in favor of such obedience—to learn to drive an automobile is to learn to operate the conveyance as we see it operated in the normal sort of way by stopping at the red light, starting at the green light, and so on. Until such practices have been acquired, there is a failure to operate the automobile with the requisite skill. We can of course imagine cases in which people do learn to drive cars in happy isolation from all traffic regulations, and we can imagine people whose first desire is to operate the controls of a car and who, on learning that there are laws governing its operation in traffic, then decide that they will observe the law; but for most of us, at any rate, it would be far more correct to say that the decision to obey the laws occurs only after we have learned how to obey by repeated practice, and only in those occasional situations in which it is burdensome to obey and on considering briefly whether we should, we then decide after all to do so. There are, therefore, actions in which either in cause or in actual performance no rational choice is involved.

It is the enormous variety of cases that defeats any attempt to provide a summary account of the nature of action in terms of bodily and psychological factors. Some of my actions are deliberate. I weigh alternatives and choose. Some of my actions are done with a motive but without deliberation and choice. When I slam the brakes on as the car ahead of mine suddenly stops, I do so with a motive—in order to avoid a collision—but without the choice I exercise when I consider quickly whether or not to run through the light that has just changed to red and thus risk a traffic fine. Some things I do without any motive. I pass the salt to my dinner companion not in order to please him or with any other motive or purpose in mind, but because I am polite. I act out of politeness rather than for the sake of politeness. Some things I do simply because I want to, or on the spur of the moment, and for no reason at all. If we consider the mental processes attending the relevant bodily movements, we find an enormous variation in what transpires. The cases range from those in which nothing that seems at all relevant happens except the occurrence of the bodily movement—one responds to the situation in which one finds oneself almost automatically, guided as it were by habit and the whole accumulation of past experience—to the cases in which force of mind, great effort, or internal struggles are involved as habit is resisted or passions and temptations conquered (the sorts of cases by reference to which meaning can be given to Plato's expression "the spirited element" and Prichard's term "setting oneself"). The characteristic philosophic vice of generalizing from special cases is involved in the familiar summary explanation of the concept of action in terms of various psychological factors or processes.

Perhaps the most frequent instance is the explanation given in terms of motives,[3] in which the preoccupation with the textbook examples of actions performed with ends in view leads the philosopher to ignore the very many sorts of actions in which no end in view is present at all.

There are still other formulae that need to be considered. Shall we say that bodily behavior is a case of action if it is free from compulsion? But animals and infants may move their limbs without compulsion. Indeed, there are internal compulsions that disqualify bodily movements as actions. Further, "compulsion" is as unilluminating as "voluntary." One is compelled by one's conscience (e.g., Luther's "Here I stand and can do no other"), but shall we say that there can be no conscientious action? One is compelled by hunger, but in different ways: the starving man reaches desperately for food, the hungry man steals a loaf of bread, and the man without any livelihood and faced with the prospect of hunger steals in order to avoid it—in all such cases one is compelled, but not in the same sense of the term. We need not multiply cases—what in one sense is compulsion is freedom from compulsion in another. The present formula is as unhelpful as Aristotle's "internal moving principle"; what is common to the great variety of cases that count as action is the verbal formula, and this, apart from a specification of the wide spectrum of cases falling under it, is wholly unilluminating.

When difficulties appear in the attempt to provide an analysis of an apparently categorical statement, the suggestion is often made that contrary-to-fact conditionals will do the trick. So in the present case it may be suggested that an item of bodily behavior is an instance of an action if the agent could have done otherwise, or if the agent could have done otherwise if he had chosen, or even if the agent could have done otherwise if he had chosen and he could have chosen. Here, again, the crucial phrase "could have done" provides us with only the semblance of an explanation. Consider the many different kinds of cases of which it would be true to say that a person could not have done otherwise. The man was insane, subject to compulsive desire, strong temptation, social

[3] See the latest instance in P. H. Nowell-Smith, *Ethics* (London, 1954), p. 114.

pressure; or he was misinformed, responding through habit, unthinking, or even bound by conscience. What in one sense a person could have done, in another he could not. So too with "could have chosen." A person could not have chosen to ignore his conscience, but it is correct to say even of those in whom conscience prevails that in some sense they could have chosen to do other than what conscience demanded.

Finally I shall consider another and even more desperate measure. It might be thought that the problem of dealing with the great variety of cases falling under the term "action" could be disposed of in the following way: Instead of taking a simple statement about a physical movement and conjoining with it some psychological statement about a motive, choice, or so on, we might construct a disjunction, each disjunct of which is itself a conjunction of two statements, one reporting bodily movement, the other some psychological factor. Such a proposal would indeed meet the requirement that our account of an action must fit the wide variety of cases; it would fail nonetheless. Suppose one of the disjuncts to contain a statement about the presence of a motive, then any physical movement in respect of which the agent has a motive will count as a moral action. Are we, however, to deny that animals, children, and even those occasional men who are not responsible for their conduct and who are, therefore, not blamed but hospitalized or otherwise confined have motives for their conduct? Consider, too, the fact that an action may be one done impulsively, on the spur of the moment, without reflection, choice, or motive. As far as the psychological phenomena are concerned, there need be nothing to distinguish such actions from those for which no responsibility is incurred by the agent. It is for this reason that the proposed disjunction is unsatisfactory—it will fit the wide variety of cases called "action" only by failing to distinguish such cases from those clearly excluded by the term. This is not to say that it would be impossible in principle to discover a disjunctive formula that would fit all those cases we call "action" and no others. It is perhaps possible that some elaborate disjunctive statement in terms of gross physical movements, the actions of synapses, or even the presence of peculiar feelings could be contrived which would fit action and only action. But such an elaboration, even if it were successful, would be perfectly futile; for it would provide us with a true statement of the conditions present at the time any action occurred, not with an elucidation of the concept.

These are the results with which we are faced: (1) Any formula that fits the wide variety of actions turns out on inspection to be useless because the key term must be employed in a variety of ways. For the bodily movements that count as actions constitute a very complex range or family of cases, not a single group with its characteristic borderline fringe. (2) The attempt to distinguish bodily movements that do, from those that do not, count as actions in terms of occurrent psychological processes is doomed to failure. What passes through my mind as I now act may be anything or nothing; it may be that all that happens is that without anything relevant passing through my mind, I just act.

II

If one considered the question "What is a chess move?" it is easy to see that each of the kinds of answers considered and rejected in the preceding section will not do at all. It may be, when I move my chess piece during a game, that all that happens is that my fingers push a piece from one square to another. As long as we confine our attention to bodily and psychological processes, there may be nothing to distinguish a chess move from the mere change of position of chess men resulting from an infant's random movements. And, clearly, the appeals to absence of compulsion (but consider the many sorts of moves called "forced"), to "could have beens," "would have beens," and even to the use of elaborate disjunctive functions, such as we considered in the preceding section, would be greeted with amusement. Nevertheless, to make a move in a game of chess is after all to engage in a bodily movement of some sort, so whatever else one is doing in saying that a move was made, is one not saying that a certain bodily movement took place? And, similarly, in the case of other actions, is it not a part of what one is saying, in saying that an action has taken place, that certain relevant movements of fingers, arms or legs, and so on, have occurred? Plausible as this may be, it is in my opinion mistaken.

1. If there were such a so-called descriptive component, then in order that I might know what I was doing in any given case, I would need to know what bodily movements took place, and this I could know only by observing my own movements. But if someone asks me, "Do you know what you have done?" the affirmative answer I give is in no way predicated upon any observation I may have made of my bodily movements. If my answer is in error (I gave the clerk a five, instead of a one, dollar bill), the error is not one of observation. When I do something and know what I am doing, it is not that I observe myself in action, and if I were to watch my arms, legs, and so on as I performed many of the familiar actions in which I engage, I would very likely fumble. But even when I take care in what I do, it is not that I observe my bodily movements and guide them as I would my child's movements as she learns to write, ride a bicycle, or skate. If someone were to say to me reproachfully, "You did not watch what you were doing" as I drove my car, he would not be reproaching me for failing to observe my bodily movements, nor would he be urging me to watch them if he were to say, "Watch what you are doing!"

2. Consider third-person statements. Unless A had engaged in a bodily movement of some sort, he could not have done what he did, and unless I had used my eyes in observing what had gone on, I could not have described his action as I did. But from this it does not follow that in describing A's action I am describing his bodily movements. For there are descriptions and descriptions, the physiologist's descriptions of muscle movements, my descriptions of the movements of arms and legs, and our familiar descriptions of actions—passing the salt hastily, paying one's bill distastefully, and so forth. To say that John paid his bill distastefully is not to say two things, one of which is that his body moved in a certain way, any more than to say the latter is to assert in part at least that such-and-such muscles were brought into operation. And because the latter must be true if his arms and legs moved as they did, it simply does not follow that in offering my description of the bodily movement, I am, among other

things, offering a physiological description of what took place. But there is just as much reason for saying this as for saying that a third-person action statement is a blend of diverse things, one of which is a descriptive component about the occurrence of a bodily movement.

The truth is that in saying as we do that A paid his bill, performed the castling maneuver, or passed the salt to his companion, we are in no way interested in the minutiae of bodily movements that may have taken place, just as one interested in the movements of arms, legs, and fingers, e.g., a dancer, may be sublimely ignorant of the physiological and biochemical changes that take place. Consider the example of the chess move. One who knows no chess may see only the movements of arms and fingers as odd-shaped objects are moved about on a checkered surface; one who knows the game may see a given offensive or defensive move taking place. The former simply does not know what takes place during the game, and the latter, far from offering a description that overlaps the former's curious description of what takes place, is saying something radically different in character.

3. But suppose a statement describing an action were a blend of diverse items, one being a description of a bodily movement. How must this "descriptive component" be supplemented in order that we may be provided with the force of a statement about an action? It will be apparent that the attempt to provide a supplement by means of another "descriptive" statement, to the effect that the movement is voluntary, chosen, and so forth, must lead to one of two consequences. Either the crucial term (e.g., "voluntary," "chosen," "motivated") is much too restrictive or it is too broad, or if no change in the application of the term "action" is to ensue, a shift must be made in the use of the crucial term (e.g., voluntary) and all of the puzzles about action reappear once more in connection with this new usage. If, however, the supplementation is to be made by means of disguised contrary-to-fact conditionals, the same dilemma faces us in a new guise. It will not do to say, for example, that an action which took place is a certain kind of bodily movement that could have been other than what it was in the sense in which any physical occurrence could have been other than what it was, or in the

sense appropriate to the familiar remark that a conscientious agent could not have acted otherwise. The sense of "could have been" required for the present purpose is just that sense involved in saying that the bodily movement counts as an action; but this does not help us.

It should not surprise us in view of these results to encounter even more drastic proposals. It has been agreed that the concept of an action is "fundamentally nondescriptive,"[4] and among those to whom this proposal seems only to generate new paradoxes, it would not be unreasonable to expect to find representatives of the indefinability thesis. It would be dangerous to generalize, but the appearance of this familiar triad of theories is due to a familiar mistake—the failure to attend to the relevant context in which expressions have a use. The pattern of thought is as follows: "Actions are happenings. Statements describing actions are true or false. What happens is always some bodily movement and need be nothing more than this. Hence, whatever else a statement about an action may do, it describes such a movement." The underlying mistake is that what occurs when an action is performed can be understood independently of its context and hence need only be a bodily movement. How this is so I want to illustrate by reference to the analogous problem of the nature of a chess move.

III

Consider the relatively artificial situation in which a chess move is made. Here there is an obvious change of context from the ordinary situation in which conduct occurs. There is little temptation to define a chess move in terms of bodily and psychological phenomena or to argue that the concept is "nondescriptive" or "indefinable." The concept is obviously social in character, logically connected with the concept of rules. How does this connection with the notion of rules

[4] Cf. H. L. A. Hart, "The Ascription of Responsibility and Rights," in *Proceedings of the Aristotelian Society* (1948–1949). Although Hart does not discuss the relation between action and bodily movement, he seems to regard the term "descriptive" as properly applicable to bodily movements.

enable us to distinguish between the random movements of an infant pushing chess pieces about on a checkered board and the chess moves of players? I want to argue that this distinction is intelligible only by reference to the notion of *following* or *observing* the given rules.

Central to the concept of a rule is the idea of obeying or following it. The notion of disobeying is dependent upon the more fundamental idea of obeying. Infants who push chess pieces about on a chessboard do not disobey or violate the rules of chess—they do not play chess at all. A chess player may violate the rule only after he has learned to obey. Without obedience there can be no disobedience, just as without the telling of the truth there can be no lying. Further, a rule is no mere statement which we can understand independently of the practice that is the obeying or the following of the rule. To understand the rule is to understand the kind of thing that would be obeying it, and it is only because we have followed or obeyed rules that any statement of a new rule, one we have not so far learned to follow, is intelligible. Again, to follow or obey a rule is not to repeat to oneself what the rule requires, reflect upon the situation in which one finds oneself in order to determine that it is one to which the rule applies, and then decide to obey it. Such an account, if it were true, would only serve to create a doubt that the person in question had learned the rule, for at best it could only describe the learner's fumbling, hesitating procedure.[5] Once we have learned the rules, we do not interpret the rule to apply to the given situation and follow this with a decision to obey—we simply obey.[6] And if in any given situation we choose to disobey, such choice is only parasitic upon the general practice in which no choice is exercised at all. Finally, obeying a rule is not something that can occur only once.[7] I do not mean that there may not be such a thing as a new rule

[5] Compare this account of obeying a rule with Prichard's account in "Duty and Ignorance of Fact," of coming to "know" that one has a duty. It is small wonder that in Prichard's account every claim that one has obeyed the rule is only problematical.

[6] See Wittgenstein's profoundly illuminating remarks in *Philosophical Investigations* on obeying rules, especially in § 219, "When I obey a rule, I do not choose, I obey *blindly*."

[7] Cf. Wittgenstein, *op. cit.*, § 199.

which is such that only one occasion arises to which it applies and such that after it has been obeyed only once it is then set aside. If such a case should ever arise, it would happen only because one had already learned what rules were in other situations and in learning these rules had engaged in the practice of obeying them. The point is that to obey a rule is to acquire a custom, habit, practice, and if only one instance suffices, this is owing to the derivative function of habits established with respect to other rules. Again, this is not to say that every instance of acting from habit or custom is a case of obeying a rule. "This is our practice," "this is what we do," need only express the things we do *as a rule,* in general, and through social habit, not the things we do in *following a rule.* Nevertheless, the familiar cases of obeying a rule are the cases in which the agent has acquired a habit, practice, custom—that way of thinking and doing that characterizes the man who knows his way about in situations by following the relevant rules. We need, therefore, to distinguish between the case in which what someone does *accords* with the rule and the case in which someone *follows* the rule. A child may push a piece called "the knight" from one square on a chessboard to another in such a way that what it does accords with the rule governing the piece, but in reporting this fact we need only observe the single item of behavior of the child. In saying of a child that it followed the rule, much more is at stake, namely, the question whether the child has learned the rules of the game (including the one concerning the knight) and in doing so has acquired the specific way of thinking and doing which is the playing of chess.

To attempt to understand a move in a game of chess in terms of bodily and psychological processes occurring at the time the agent makes his move is to leave out what is essential to the move—the fact that what transpires in the way of such occurrent processes is a case of following the rules. Similarly, to attempt to understand the concept of a chess player in terms of occurrent psychological processes, the order of percepts, or some presumed psychical substance is once more to ignore that feature of the agent that consists in the fact that he has learned by repeated doings and hence has acquired the practice of acting as he does. In both cases the circumstances in which the bodily and psychological processes occur are crucial; for what makes the bodily movement a case of a move is the fact that movement of the piece on the board is a case of following a rule, and what makes the agent a chess player is that he has acquired that custom or practice—that way of thinking and doing—that characterizes those who follow the rules of chess. Chess player and chess move are thus correlative notions, and neither can be understood in terms of processes, bodily or psychological, viewed in isolation from the rules that have been learned and the characteristic ways of thinking and doing thereby achieved. Hence it is not that a piece has been pushed from one square to another that constitutes a chess move but that the bodily movement is that of an agent who, during the course of a game, exhibits the characteristic practice in thinking and doing that he has acquired. For someone who does not know what it is to make a move in a game, no report of what transpires at the times the moves were made would make any sense at all, and, observe as he would, such a being would have *no* idea of what was going on. For someone who knew no chess but did know what it was to follow the rules of *some* game, the reports of such activities would be understood only in the most fragmentary way; he might know that a game was being played but would not know what was going on. It is only because we ourselves have acquired that practice of following the rules of chess—the characteristic custom of doing things on a chessboard in a way that we understand because we share it with others who play chess—that the reports of a game are understood by us and recognizes as true or false. The significance of the utterances we employ in reporting the activities on a chessboard is thus dependent upon the fact that we share with those involved in these activities the practices, in Wittgenstein's felicitous phrase, the form of life, of those who follow certain rules in the social transaction that is the playing of a game of chess.

Without this practice of obeying the rules, what we see is merely bodily movement. With it, we see this movement as a chess move, for we treat the physical movement made as a move in the play that takes place, and in our doing so, the physical movement that occurs takes on a wholly new aspect.

It is because we supply this practical context of acquired skill that we can understand the descriptive accounts of those who report to us the progress of a game; without it such accounts are unintelligible.

All this may be granted; but it will be objected that a chess move is only one very special kind of action. We act in all sorts of ways, even in sweeping the chessmen off the board, thus bringing the play to an abrupt end. With this I should certainly agree, but the case of the chess move is nonetheless important, for the very artificiality of the example may serve to remind us of what is too easily forgotten in the case of other types of action, namely, the crucial importance of the practical context of common or shared practices involved in following rules, applying criteria, observing principles, acting on policies, and so on. Actions do constitute a whole family of cases, but in various respects this practical context is essential to an understanding of the distinction between a bodily movement and an action.

IV

Consider some of the things we commonly do: we purchase food, drive automobiles, play, work, help and hinder our fellows. In all such activities, we have learned by imitating or following the instructions of others in obeying rules, employing criteria, following policies in the practices in which we engage. Thus in purchasing food our selection is guided by criteria for excellence, ripeness, and so on, and in paying for the items selected, our behavior is guided by various criteria and rules governing the use of currency. We act in such instances without reflection precisely because we have acquired the requisite skills. Or consider the enormously complex set of practices acquired by those driving their automobiles through traffic, responding to a variety of cues—the condition of the road surface, the sound of the motor, the presence of pedestrians and vehicles blocking the way, the signals of other motorists, the road signs, the traffic lights, and the instructions of the traffic police. In this complex set of practices we may recognize the observance of rules, the application of criteria, the response to instructions, the following of policies of safe, economical, or efficient driving, and so on. These practices are supplemented by other complicating and even supervening practices. One may drive an automobile in order to make up one's mind whether to purchase it or in order to test it, and throughout one will be guided in general in one's thinking and doing by the observance of moral rules and principles. It is not that there are practices and practices, each independent of the other, so that at one time one is driving an automobile, at another making a purchase, at another responding to the moral requirements of the situation. It is rather that we have a blending of the practices we have acquired, in the activities in which we engage, where various practices are themselves affected by the general practice of observing moral rules and principles. It is this ability to carry out a complex and organized set of practices in which throughout the agent is guided without reflection by moral rules that marks the achievement of responsibility. Even in the relatively artificial case of a chess move, what takes place when the move is made has to be understood in terms of the practice of observing not only the rules of chess but also those of good conduct and good manners, for these are involved in the agent's way of thinking and doing.

It is equally important to bear in mind the enormous difference between the permissive rules of chess and the prescriptive and justifying rules of morality, between the justification of the rules of traffic and the justification of the rules of morality, between the inevitable conflicts of rules (and the resulting exceptions) in the field of morality and the occasional predicament that may arise when the ill-formed rules of a game are discovered to be in conflict. Understanding a moral rule does involve understanding the kind of cases which may be excepted, but there cannot be any exception to the rules governing the movement of the knight in chess. These differences are so important that it is misleading to speak of the term "rule" as univocal.

One more comment on important differences: If I do not play chess, I shall not understand what a chess player does as his fingers push a piece from one square to another, but if I do not drive a car, it does not follow that I am incapable of knowing what someone at the wheel is doing when I see his arm pulling at the handbrake. Here we need to recall the reference made earlier to the derivative effects of the mastery of rules in order to see that this difference, important as it is, is no objection to the general contention. For the practices we share with others need not coincide precisely, indeed they cannot if there is to be diversity in the activities of individuals, but there must be enough similarity between the practices involved in different activities in order to allow for an understanding of one kind of activity which derives from the practice involved in another. Where there is no such similarity, as in the case of one who has never seen or heard of any game or as in the case of a bushman who has never seen or heard of machines of any sort, there is no understanding of what is being done, no matter how carefully attention is paid by such individuals to the bodily movements of agents when they engage, respectively, in games of chess or in the driving of automobiles.[8]

It is impossible within the limits of this paper to guard against all of the misunderstandings to which the analogy I wish to draw between chess moves and other actions may give rise. Briefly, I am maintaining that just as in the case of the concept of a chess move, so in the case of the concept of any action the context of practices in which rules are obeyed, criteria employed, policies are observed—a way of thinking and doing—is essential to the understanding of the difference between such bodily movements and actions. Just as this way of thinking and doing marks in the one case the chess player, so it marks in the other the responsible agent, one who has acquired a complex of practices, among others the practice of observing moral rules and principles. The concepts "action" and "moral agent" or "person" are thus correlative.[9] Because

[8] It is for this reason that anthropologists often need to enter into the practices of primitive tribes in order to understand their activities, their language—in short, their culture.

[9] Locke wisely rejects any attempt to define "person" in terms of ideas and an underlying immaterial substance. The concept, he tells us, is forensic and applies "only to intelligent agents capable of a law" and hence "concerned and accountable" (*Essay*, bk. II, ch. xxvii, sec. 26). It is this same correlativity of voluntary bodily behavior (i.e., action) and moral agent that leads Aristotle to remark about the individual whose unfortunate action was done by reason

we share so largely in our ways of thinking and doing, because in particular we are guided by moral rules and principles, we treat each other's bodily movements as actions, items of behavior for which the agent is responsible. Just as we supply a background of skills in understanding the bodily behavior of those engaged in playing chess, so we supply a complex background of skills in which rules are obeyed, criteria are employed, policies are observed, and so on, in understanding each other's behavior as action. This practical context—our common form of life—is crucial to our understanding. Without it we notice only bodily movements, and with it we see actions as we observe each other's behavior. Without it we employ the cool language of those who like coroners and physiologists are concerned to describe and explain bodily movements and effects, and with it we are enabled to participate in the use of discourse by which we impute responsibility to individuals when we treat them as persons or moral agents and their bodily movements as actions.

But this, it will be objected, is in effect to succumb to the philosophic vice of generalizing from very special cases—those actions performed in the social arena for which agents may be praised or blamed, such as cheating or dealing honestly in making purchases and driving with care or with unconcern for the safety of others. The very language employed for such conduct implies that the individuals referred to or treated are responsible moral agents and subject to praise or blame for what they do. But there are other cases of action, surely, with respect to which a specifically moral way of thinking and doing, the practice of observing moral rules, seems altogether out of bounds, so that the alleged correlativity of the terms "moral agent" and "person" is only evidence of unrestrained generalization from very special cases. My concluding remarks are directed at this objection.

In order to understand the concept of an action, we need to see how sentences in which typical action verbs are employed are used. Admittedly there is no single use. Some sen-

---

of ignorance that the terms "voluntary" and "involuntary" should not be applied to him in the event he does not repent, since such a being is a different sort of man and "should have a name of his own" (*Nicomachean Ethics*, 1110b).

tences are employed in praising or blaming (e.g., "*He* did it" uttered accusingly or "He *did* it" uttered exultingly by one watching a heroic rescue). Some sentences are employed with a view to determining whether blame is appropriate but where no blaming may actually occur (as in the hearings held in courts or during legislative fact-finding inquiries). Again, we may speak of actions where no verdict is anticipated, moral or legal. If my wife relates to me the various things she saw my neighbor doing, she might do so with a view to supporting the low opinion in which she holds him, but, equally, she may do so in order to make conversation or because she knows me to have a friendly interest in my neighbor's activities. And in giving me this information or in describing to me how he behaved, is she not speaking of just the sort of thing for which in appropriate circumstances any neighbor *can* be praised or blamed, action in the present sense of the term? For consider the remarks appropriate to such employments by my wife of sentences about the activities of my neighbor: "What on earth is he up to?" "I hope he will not leave the hole there; children may fall into it and hurt themselves," and so on. In reporting or describing as she does the actions of my neighbor, my wife does *not* employ the neutral language of those concerned to relate or describe bodily movements. It is rather to treat the bodily movements that did occur as behavior of a responsible agent, to impute to him not only the practices of those who have learned by imitation, following instructions, and so forth the ways in which tools are employed and activities of various sorts conducted but also the general practice of attending to the interests and well-being of others. If we consider the remarks appropriate to such employments of action sentences and contrast them with those appropriate to the behavior of lunatics, infants, and wild animals, it becomes clear that such normal uses of action sentences risk defeat on two quite distinct grounds: First, on learning that the individual engaged in the observed bodily movements is not responsible or morally competent and second, on learning that the alleged bodily movements did not occur (e.g., it was really someone else). For in such normal uses of action sentences, we ascribe responsibility to the individuals in question by treating the bodily behavior as action, and this we do by viewing it against the background of a set of practices, among others the practice of observing moral rules and principles. In short, we impute to the individual our common moral form of life.

There are cases, of course, in which sentences are employed in describing the behavior of our fellows and in which there is no ascription of responsibility. I have already mentioned the language of coroners and physiologists, in which a position of neutrality is taken with respect to the responsibility of the individual. But in what sorts of cases of an admittedly responsible agent would the question of common practices including that of observing moral rules be irrelevant? Would it be a case in which the individual raises his arm? But in that case we must not describe what the individual does as signaling, saluting, leading others in physical exercise drill, and so on. For these descriptions at once bring us within the social arena in which common forms of life have been achieved and by reference to which action statements can be understood and bodily movements treated as actions. No, we shall even have to deny that in raising his arm the individual was even pretending to engage in these activities, exercising, following the instructions of his physician, and so on. We shall have to rest content with the statement that he was simply raising his arm and never mind any further queries. But in that case, when the individual raises his arm what happens is that a bodily movement, not an action, occurs.

EMOTIONS

Errol Bedford

I

The concept of emotion gives rise to a number of philosophical problems. The most important of these, I think, concern the function of statements about emotions and the criteria for their validity. A solution to these problems is offered by what I shall call the traditional theory of the emotions, and I should like to begin by discussing some aspects of this. According to this view[1] an emotion is a feeling, or at least an experience of a special type which involves a feeling. Logically, this amounts to regarding emotion words as the names of feelings. It is assumed that to each word there corresponds a qualitatively distinct experience which may, although it need not, find "expression" in outward behavior. If it does, this

Errol Bedford is Senior Lecturer in Moral Philosophy at the University of Edinburgh. He is a contributor to the *Concise Encyclopaedia of Western Philosophy and Philosophers,* J. O. Urmson, ed., and has written a number of articles.

[1] The details vary. For example, it is very commonly held that every emotion must have an object, and therefore that it is an experience involving a "cognitive" element, not a pure state of feeling. "We must hold," writes McTaggart, "that the cogitation of that to which the emotion is directed, and the emotion towards it, are the same mental state, which has both the quality of being a cogitation of it, and the quality of being an emotion directed towards it" (*The Nature of Existence* [Cambridge, 1921 and 1927], II, 146). (I think it is important to ask what "directed towards" could mean here.) Russell claims that emotions also involve bodily movements. In *The Analysis of Mind* (London, 1921) he says that "an emotion —rage, for example—(is) a certain kind of process . . . The ingredients of an emotion are only sensations and images and bodily movements succeeding each other according to a certain pattern" (p. 284). To discuss the details of these theories would complicate, without affecting, my argument, which is meant to show that an emotion is not any sort of experience or process.

behavior entitles us to infer the existence of the inner feeling, and therefore to assert, with some degree of probability, statements of the form "He is angry." Looked at in this way, emotions naturally come to be thought of as inner forces that move us, in combination with, or in opposition to other forces, to act as we do. Briefly, anger is a specific feeling which leads the angry man to show the signs of anger (e.g., striking someone) unless he is willing to, and able to, suppress them. It follows, I take it, that to explain behavior by saying that a man acted as he did because he was angry, is to give a causal explanation, although, admittedly, a causal explanation of a special sort.

This is the accepted view of the older psychological textbooks. Stout distinguishes, indeed, between "emotional dispositions" (e.g., liking and disliking, hate and love) and "emotions," but he affirms that the emotion itself in which an emotional disposition is actualized is "always an actual state of consciousness" that, besides sensations and conative tendencies, "also involves specific kinds of feeling which cannot be explained away as resultants or complications of more simple elements."[2] Even James thinks that an emotion is a feeling, although he identifies the feeling with somatic sensations. In the famous passage in his *Principles of Psychology* he tells us that his theory is "that the bodily changes follow directly the perception of the exciting fact, and that our feeling of the same changes as they occur IS the emotion."[3]

I am going to argue that this involves a fundamental mistake: the logical mistake of treating emotion words as names, which leads in turn to a misconception of their function. There might, all the same, be more to be said for this view if it were less inadequate at the psychological level, if it did not presuppose a richness and clarity in the "inner life" of feeling that it does not possess. What evidence is there for the existence of a multitude of feelings corresponding to the extensive and subtle linguistic differentiation of our vocabulary for discussing emotions? This assumption gains no sup-

[2] G. F. Stout, A *Manual of Psychology*, 5th ed. (London, 1938), pp. 371 and 375.

[3] William James, *The Principles of Psychology* (New York, 1890), II, 449. James prints the passage in italics.

port from experience. Indignation and annoyance are two different emotions; but, to judge from my own case, the feelings that accompany indignation appear to differ little, if at all, from those that accompany annoyance. I certainly find no feeling, or class of feelings, that marks off indignation from annoyance, and enables me to distinguish them from one another. The distinction is of a different *sort* from this. (Perhaps I do not remember very clearly—but then is not this part of the difficulty, that the words "indignation" and "annoyance" do *not* call up recollections of two distinct feelings?) I might add that at the present time this is psychological orthodoxy. The author of the chapter on "Feeling and Emotion" in a standard textbook (Boring, Langfeld, and Weld's *Foundations of Psychology* [New York: Wiley, 1948]) remarks that "there is little evidence that a peculiar, unique type of consciousness accompanies and identifies the different emotions" (p. 100).

In any case, does the truth of such a statement as "He is afraid" logically require the existence of a specific feeling? I imagine that it would nowadays be generally conceded that emotion words are commonly used without any implication that the person they refer to is having a particular experience at any given time. But it may be said, granting this, that such expressions as "is afraid," "is angry," nevertheless gain their whole meaning from an indirect reference that they make to experiences, and can only be defined in terms of feelings. A man can feel angry as well as be angry; the expression "is angry" may not name an experience, but "feels angry" surely does, and all that can be meant by saying that someone is angry is that he is liable to, and sometimes does, feel angry. I do not think, however, that this argument can prove what it sets out to prove, i.e., that anger necessarily involves a specific feeling. In the first place, "feels angry" is often able to serve instead of "is angry." We can say, "I felt angry about it for days afterwards." A more important point is that one cannot understand what it is to feel angry without first understanding what it is to be angry. If we can assume the meaning of "is angry," or teach it (ostensively or by a descriptive account), we can go on to explain "feels angry" by saying that it is to feel as people often feel who are angry.

But how could we explain the expression "feels angry" without presupposing that the person we are explaining it to understands "is angry"? The only possible method open to us would seem to be this: to make him angry, e.g., by insulting him, and then to say to him, "Well, feeling angry is feeling as you feel now." The difficulty is that, if the view I am criticizing is correct, we cannot ensure in this way that we have taught him the meaning of the expression. We have to be certain that he has experienced a specific feeling. Yet it is logically possible that the insult (or other stimulus, and it is a crucial point that there is no *specific* stimulus) has failed in its object–it may have produced no feeling, or the wrong feeling, or so confused a mixture of feelings that he cannot discriminate the essential from the inessential (the matter is, if anything, even more difficult from his point of view). We cannot exclude this by arguing "He is angry, therefore he feels angry," for how are we to know that he is angry? *Ex hypothesi* his behavior is no proof of this. And having as yet no guarantee that he has grasped what the question means, we obviously cannot ask him whether he feels angry. Nor can we discover that he has understood the meaning of the expression by observing that he uses it in the same way as we do, for, *ex hypothesi* again, this will not prove that he means the same by it. The conclusion to be drawn, if I am right, is that being angry is logically prior to feeling angry, and therefore that being angry does not entail feeling angry, and a fortiori does not entail having any other feeling.

Now it may seem that this does not accord with the confidence we have in our beliefs about our own and other people's emotions respectively. But is this really so? We do not first ascertain that a man feels angry, and then conclude that he is angry. On the contrary, we realize that he is angry, and assume (perhaps wrongly) that he feels angry. Behavioral evidence for a statement about emotions is evidence in its own right, so to speak, and not because it entitles us to infer to private experiences. For if we have good grounds for the assertion that a person is jealous, we do not withdraw this assertion on learning that he does not feel jealous, although we may accept this as true. It is, after all, notorious that we can be mistaken about our own emotions, and that in this matter a man is not the final court of appeal in his own case; those who are jealous are often the last, instead of the first, to recognize that they are. This is scarcely consistent with the view that the criterion for identifying an emotion is the recognition of the special qualities of an experience; it is intelligible if the criteria are different from, and more complex than this. I am going to discuss these criteria shortly. For the moment, I only want to suggest that the traditional answer to the question "How do we identify our own emotions?" namely, "By introspection," cannot be correct. It seems to me that there is every reason to believe that we learn about our own emotions essentially in the same way as other people learn about them. Admittedly, it is sometimes the case that we know our own emotions better than anyone else does, but there is no need to explain this as being due to the introspection of feelings. One reason for this is that it is hardly possible for a man to be completely ignorant, as others may be, of the context of his own behavior. Again, thoughts may cross his mind that he does not make public. But the fact that he prefers to keep them to himself is incidental; and if they were known they would only be corroborative evidence, not indispensable evidence of a radically different sort from that which is available to other people. It is only in some respects, then, that each of us is in a better position to understand himself than anyone else is. Against this must be set the possibility of self-deception and a reluctance to admit that we are, for instance, vain or envious.

I must now meet what is, I think, the most serious objection that is likely to be made to this–the alleged impossibility of distinguishing, from an external observer's point of view, between real anger, say, and the pretence of it. It is sometimes claimed that although someone might behave as if he were angry, and give every appearance that he would persist in this behavior, there would still be a sense in which he might be shamming. What then is the difference between being angry and merely pretending to be? It may be held that it can only lie in the fact that the man who is pretending is not in the appropriate state of inner feeling. Now this objection plainly rests on the attempt to assimilate being angry to other cases of "being so-and-so" in which the only decisive evidence for whether someone is pretending or not is what he feels. One line of reply to it, therefore, would be to deny that there are any such cases. But it is doubtful whether this could be sustained. Pain is a specific sensation (or class of similar sensations) and it seems clear that being in pain does entail having that sensation, since "I am in pain but I don't feel anything" is self-contradictory. If so, it is possible for someone consistently to pretend to be in pain, and yet to be deceiving us. We might, of course, be unwilling to believe anyone who after showing all the signs of pain confessed that he felt no pain; but the point is, that *if* what he says is true, it entails the falsity of "He was in pain." Can we say that being angry is similar to being in pain in this respect? Let us contrast the cases of a man who is angry and another, behaving in a similar way, who is only pretending to be. Now it may well be true that the former feels angry, whereas the latter does not, but in any case it is not this that constitutes the difference between the fact that the one is angry and the fact that the other is only pretending to be. The objection rests on a misconception of what pretence is. There is necessarily involved in pretence, or shamming, the notion of a limit which must not be overstepped; pretence is always insulated, as it were, from reality. Admittedly, this limit may be vague, but it must exist. It is a not unimportant point that it is usually *obvious* when someone is pretending. If a man who is behaving as if he were angry goes so far as to smash the furniture or commit an assault, he has passed the limit; he is not *pretending*, and it is useless for him to protest afterwards that he did not feel angry. Far from his statement being *proof* that he was not angry, it would be discounted even if it were accepted as true. "He was angry, but he did not feel angry" is not self-contradictory, although it is no doubt normally false. If in a particular case it is difficult–as it may be–to settle the question, "Pretended or real?" that can only be because the relevant public evidence is inadequate to settle it. What we want is more evidence of the same kind, not a special piece of evidence of a different kind. Our difficulty in resolving the question "Is he really in pain?" on the other hand, arises from the fact that the only decisive evidence is evidence that he alone is in a position to give. (I think that even in the case of pretending to be in pain there is a limit, only it is exceptional in depending on a subjective condition. It is decisively passed if a person truly says "I feel pain." There may, of course, be inductive evidence for accepting or rejecting his statement.)

This is confirmed by the difference between the two questions "Do I really feel pain?" and "Do I really feel angry?" Since there is little room for doubt about the answer, the former is not a query that anyone is very likely to put to himself; it may even be said that it is a meaningless question. But I am inclined to think that it could be asked as a classificatory question, as roughly equivalent to "Is this pain or rather discomfort?" It is to be answered, if at all, by comparing the present feeling with other feelings definitely counted as pains, and considering whether it is sufficiently similar to be classed with them. One cannot resolve it by answering the question "Am I really in pain?" since the answer to that question must depend on the answer given to the first. By contrast, "Do I really feel angry?" is one of a class of similar questions that are common in everyday life. This question does not concern the comparison of feelings; in answering it one is trying to decide whether one is angry or not, and the answer "Yes" can be mistaken in a way that a similar answer to the question "Do I really feel pain?" cannot be.

II

Having, I hope, cleared the ground a little by putting some preliminary arguments against the traditional theory, I now want to consider whether an adequate alternative to it is provided by a dispositional theory of emotions, and to discuss the criteria for the use of emotion words. Can the concept of an emotion be fully elucidated without using non-behavioral, indeed non-psychological, concepts? I will try to justify the negative answer that I think should be given to this question.

To begin with, statements about emotions cannot be said to describe behavior; they interpret it.[4] The situation seems

[4] This is not to say that we do not also use the word "description" in such a way that (3) (immediately below) might form part

to be that emotional behavior, so to speak, is far from being homogeneous. The behavioral evidence for "He was angry" varies with the person and the occasion; in different cases it is not the same, and possibly it may not even be partially the same. Conversely, the same, or similar, behavior, can be differently, yet correctly, interpreted in different circumstances, for example as anger, indignation, annoyance, exasperation, or resentment. Accordingly, categorical descriptive statements, e.g., (1) "He raised his voice and began to thump the table," and hypothetical descriptive statements, e.g., (2) "If I had gone on teasing him he would have thrown something at me," are evidence for such statements as (3) "He was very angry," but they are not part of what these statements mean. Clearly, on hearing (3), it would be proper to ask for details, and such details could be given in (1) and (2). (1) and (2) would therefore give additional information to that already given in (3). To put the matter another way, (1), (2), and (3) are independent of one another in respect of truth and falsity. (1) may be true when (3) is false (a man can thump the table and raise his voice–to emphasize a point–without being angry), and (3) may be true although (1) is false (for not all angry men thump tables). The same holds of the relationships of (2) and (3). The truth of (2) is perfectly compatible with joining in the fun; anger, on the other hand, is consistent with not being prepared to throw things. I think that this would still hold if other statements were substituted for (1) and (2). It does not seem to be possible, therefore, to analyze (3) into a set, however complex, of categorical and hypothetical statements that describe individual behavior. (3) does not sum up, but goes beyond, the behavioral evidence for it, and it would always be logically possible to accept the evidence and deny the conclusion. Although when we say (3) we are in a sense talking about the behavior on which its truth rests, anger is not merely a disposition, and cannot be reduced to a pattern of behavior, actual or poten-

---

of a description of some incident. When I say that (3) does not describe I am making what could be looked on as a technical distinction between description and interpretation, which is meant to indicate a difference of order between (3) and (1) or (2). Higher order statements explain and interpret what lower order statements describe.

tial.[5] All that can be said about the logical relationships between (3) and such statements as (1) and (2) is that it is a necessary, but not a sufficient, condition for the truth of (3) that some statements such as (1) and (2) should be true, without it being possible to specify which.

This last assertion may be challenged in at least two ways. It might be said, first, that the phrase "necessary, but not a sufficient, condition" ought to be changed to "neither a necessary nor a sufficient condition." But since the only ground on which this could be maintained appears to be the traditional view, I shall not discuss it any further. I will only add that I do not believe that we either do, or should, take any notice of anyone's protestations that, for instance, he loves his wife, if his conduct offers no evidence whatever that he does. At the other extreme, those who want to be thoroughly behavioristic about emotions will argue that the phrase "necessary but not sufficient" should be amended to "both necessary and sufficient." What I am suggesting is that people who share the same information and the same expectations about another person's behavior may possibly place different emotional interpretations on that behavior, if their knowledge is confined to descriptive statements about it. It may be urged that this difference of opinion can be eliminated as further evidence of the same type comes to light, and that it can only be eliminated in this way. The assumption underlying this—that the criteria for assertions about emotions are purely behavioral—is not, however, borne out by an examination of the way in which we actually use emotion words. These words, when used without qualification, carry implications, not merely about behavior, but also about its social context. Consider the distinction between two emotions that have a close similarity, shame and embarrassment. The behavior of an embarrassed man is often not noticeably different from that of one who is ashamed; but there is an important difference between the respective situations they are in. In a newspaper article last year, Mr. Peter Davies, the publisher, was said to be "to his mild embarrassment" the original of Peter

[5] Let me give an analogy. "Jones is responsible for this muddle" is a statement about the behavior its truth is dependent on, although it is not shorthand for a set of statements describing that behavior.

Pan. The embarrassment is understandable, and the epithet appropriate, whether its application is correct or not. Yet we can say at once that if the writer of the article had alleged that Mr. Davies was "to his shame" the original of Peter Pan, this would have been incorrect; it is scarcely conceivable that it could be true. The reason for this is obvious, and it is logical, not psychological, since it has nothing to do with Mr. Davies' behavior, still less with his feelings. It is simply that the fact that Barrie modeled Peter Pan on him is not his *fault*—it was not due to an act of his, and there is nothing reprehensible about it anyway. In general, it is only true to say of someone "He is ashamed of so-and-so" if what is referred to is something that he can be criticized for (the criticism is commonly, though not perhaps necessarily, moral). It is, in other words, a necessary condition for the truth of the statement that he should be at fault. The word "embarrassed" is not connected in the same way with blame and responsibility; the claim that it makes is the vaguer and weaker one that the situation is awkward or inconvenient or something of that kind. "He was embarrassed" may impute a fault to someone else, but not to the person of whom it is said. (I do not mean that we may not also impute a fault to someone of whom we say this. Sometimes one puts oneself into an embarrassing situation, sometimes one finds oneself in it. I mean that we do not impute it *in* saying "He was embarrassed," in the way we do if we say "He was ashamed.") It may be pointed out that we can, after all, be ashamed of the faults of others. But I do not believe that this is true unless we accept the fault as our own; when, for instance, our children, or even our friends, commit antisocial acts in houses that we introduce them to. It is most unusual to be ashamed of the deeds of total strangers, although it is possible provided that responsibility is accepted through identification with the stranger in virtue of a common characteristic—"I was ashamed to see an Englishman lying dead drunk on the pavement." A Frenchman would be unlikely to say this, although rising to a still higher level of generality he might change "Englishman" to "European." (It is beside the point that such acceptance of responsibility may be irrational.) The connection between shame and responsibility is not, of course, ignored in the traditional theory of emotions. It appears as the doctrine that every emotion must have an appropriate object; that it is impossible (psychologically) to experience the feeling specific to shame unless you recognize that you are open to criticism. But there are no limits to what men may feel; we can only set limits to what they can say. This is merely the misrepresentation of a logical point as a piece of implausible a priori psychology.

The point of the example is to show that although knowledge of facts that is quite independent of knowledge of behavior cannot by itself establish a given interpretation of that behavior, it can be sufficient definitely to exclude it. I suggest, then, that it is possible to rebut the contention that, e.g., A is jealous of B's relationship with C, by showing that the claim that such an assertion makes about the situation which A is in, viz., that he is in a certain marital, professional, or other relationship (depending on the context) with B, is not satisfied. Certainly the contention that A is jealous is as a rule rebutted by evidence about his behavior which is inconsistent with its truth. The reason why the claim that A is in a certain relationship with B is usually unquestioned, is that it is very rarely false; the assertion that A is jealous is not usually made unless it is already known that the claim is satisfied, although it is frequently made on inadequate behavioral evidence. In general, then, this criterion is relevant to the *assertion* of statements, rather than the justification or rebuttal of statements that have *already* been asserted—it leads us to pick one word rather than another. For example, the decision whether to say that the driver of a car which has broken down for lack of water is indignant, or merely annoyed or angry, depends on whether the radiator is empty through (let us say) the carelessness of a garage mechanic who undertook to fill it for him, or through his own carelessness ("annoyed with myself" but not "indignant with myself"). Indignation, but not annoyance, seems to imply unfairness, particularly unfair accusation, or breach of an agreement. Thus, if the garage mechanic is later taxed with his carelessness, it could not be said that he was indignant, unless he was in a position to reply "But you said you would do it yourself, sir" or something similar.

Statements about emotions may also involve another, and somewhat different, type of commitment, which has an even closer bearing on the elucidation of their function. It can be illustrated in the contrast between hope and expectation, and I think this throws some light on the question why one is, and the other is not, usually counted as an emotion. The most apparent difference between them is that hoping for and expecting an event express different degrees of confidence that the event will happen. To expect something is to believe that it is more likely than not to happen. In the case of hope it is only necessary that it should not be an impossibility. This is, however, not the only, nor the most crucial, difference. Phrases which express a low degree of confidence, e.g., "I think it may . . . ," "Perhaps it will . . ." cannot be substituted without loss for "I hope that. . . ." The expression "I hope that . . ." implies, in addition to a very vague estimate of probability, an *assessment* of whatever is referred to in the clause that follows. I think it is clear that one cannot hope for something, although one can expect something, without judging it favorably in some respect, or from some point of view. Compare (1) "I don't favor a higher purchase tax but I expect it will be raised," with (2) "I don't favor a higher purchase tax, but I hope it will be raised." (1) Creates no surprise; (2) demands further explanation. Does he think it bad for the country, but profitable to him personally because he has a large stock of goods on which he has already paid tax? Does he regard it as unsound fiscal policy in general, but advisable temporarily in an inflationary economy? Failing an answer to questions such as these (2) is surely a puzzling remark, and (3) "I don't favor a higher purchase tax in any respect, but I hope it will be raised" seems to me to be self-contradictory. (Since—to mention one reason—one can only favor events under human control, and hope is not restricted in this way. "I favor . . ." does not precisely represent the implication of "I hope that . . . ," but it will do for the purpose of the present example. I need hardly say that it is not my intention in this paper to give an exhaustive—or, indeed, a more than roughly accurate—account of the particular concepts that I use as examples.) It is a psychological truism that men do not, with some exceptions, hope that their opponents will win; it is a truth of logic that they cannot hope that their opponents will win without approving of this in *some* respect. Thus "I hope that . . ." is commonly used to declare, or to commit oneself to, an allegiance, and although disagreement *about* hopes is disagreement about the interpretation of facts, disagreement *in* hopes is not—it is one of the forms that disagreement about value may take (e.g., "I hope the Socialists will get in." "Well, I don't. I think it would be a disaster for the country.") This is a further reason why it would be absurd to say that questions of the form "Do I feel regret for . . . ?" "Do I really hope that . . . ?" could be settled by introspection. "Do I really hope that the Tories will get in?" is plainly a question a wavering Tory supporter might put to himself. This may amount to asking himself whether, granted that he thinks a Tory government better than a Labour one, he is concerned enough about the election result, or whether he is not too indifferent to say, if he is honest, that he *hopes* for a Tory victory. If so, he will not answer it by searching his feelings, for they have nothing to do with the matter, but by reflecting, for example, that when the party's policy was attacked, he did not bother to defend it, or by remembering that after all he has agreed to do some canvassing. But it is just as likely, if not more likely, that the answer to the question will be a *decision* about his allegiance, reached by reconsidering the merits of the two parties. (Contrast "Do I really feel pain?" discussed above.)

To generalize from this example: emotion words form part of the vocabulary of appraisal and criticism, and a number of them belong to the more specific language of moral criticism. Normally, the verbs in their first-person use imply the speaker's assessment of something, and in their third-person use they carry an implication about an assessment by the person they refer to.[6] It is perhaps worth mentioning that there are certain cases in which a third-person statement gives the speaker's verdict on that person; a factor which certainly complicates discussions of character. Such terms as "vain," "en-

[6] But the words "right," "unreasonable," etc., when used to qualify third person statements sometimes serve as endorsements of, or refusals to endorse, this assessment on the speaker's part. I discuss this point below.

vious," and "resentful" are terms of censure.[7] There is an overlap between the lists of emotions, and the lists of virtues and vices that are given by philosophers. The overlap is not complete; some virtues (e.g., veracity) are not connected with emotions, and some emotions (e.g., regret) cannot be treated as elements of character and are not merits or defects.

So far I have discussed the conditions which appear to govern the truth and falsity of statements about emotions. While emotion concepts do not form an altogether homogeneous group, I believe that this is correct as a broad outline. But there is one respect in which it needs to be supplemented. This concerns the sense in which emotions (as opposed to statements about emotions) can be justified or unjustified, reasonable or unreasonable. It is fairly obvious, to begin with, that the behavioral criteria for the use of emotion words are not connected with the application of these predicates. The way in which a man behaves will determine whether he is or is not angry. But *if* he is angry, the behavioral evidence for this is not in itself relevant to the question whether his anger is justified or unjustified. On the other hand, if the claim that an emotion word makes about a situation is not satisfied, this is often indicated by saying that the emotion is unjustified or unreasonable. The attribution of the emotion, that is to say, is not withdrawn, but qualified. An example will make this clearer. Suppose that B does something that is to A's advantage, although A thinks that it is to his disadvantage (e.g., B, a solicitor administering A's affairs, sells some shares that A believes [wrongly] will appreciate in value). Now it would be misleading to say simply, except to a fully informed audience, "A resents what B did"—this surely carries the incorrect implication that B has injured A. To guard against this it is necessary to add "but his resentment is quite unjustified," or some equivalent expression. A's belief that B has done something that affects him adversely is, however, a necessary condition if the word "resentment" is to be used at all. The distinction between what the situation is, and what it is believed to be, is normally unimportant, and for this reason emotion words make an objective

[7] A point noted in respect of envy by Aristotle at *Eth. Nic.* 1107*a*.

claim unless special precautions are taken to exclude or cancel it (e.g., "He was afraid but no one else was" [there was no real danger], "Your surprise is quite unjustified" [the event was only to be expected]).

But this is not the whole story and the question whether an emotion is justified or not does not always turn on an issue of fact. There is a second group of emotions (not, I think, necessarily exclusive of the first) in respect of which the qualifications "unjustified," "unreasonable" refer to a different implication, and have quite a different force. Contempt, disgust, and pride are typical of this group. If I were to say that a music critic's contempt for Bartók was unjustified, I should not be asserting a fact; I should be challenging his assessment of Bartók. It is impossible to give any simple paraphrase of this remark, but it could be taken, in part, as more or less equivalent to saying that Bartók is a better composer than the critic allows. While the critic's assessment of Bartók determines, among other considerations, whether I shall assert or deny that he is contemptuous of Bartók, it does not determine whether I shall say that his contempt is justified or not; *that* depends on my opinion about his assessment.

How far can these distinctions be accounted for by theories in which emotion concepts are treated as psychological concepts? I am inclined to think that if an emotion were a feeling no sense could be made of them at all. It may be said that an emotion is unjustified when a feeling is inappropriate or unfitting to a situation. But I find this unintelligible. Feelings do not have a character that makes this relationship possible. In any case, the interpretation suggested is not what is meant by saying that, e.g., a critic's contempt is unjustified. In general, I do not think it can be maintained that logical predicates apply either to feelings or to sensations. What reasons could be given for or against a feeling, or for or against its "inappropriateness" to a situation? If someone were to say "I felt a pang this afternoon," it would be meaningless to ask whether it was a reasonable or unreasonable pang. The matter is different if he says "pang of regret," but the phrase "of regret" does not *name* the feeling, as I have already argued, and the pang of regret is justified, if it is, not as a feeling, but because his regret is justified. Nor do these predicates apply to bodily sensations, such as feeling giddy or having a pain in one's leg. This, I think, explains the fact that while we often say "You ought (or ought not) to be (or feel) ashamed (etc.)," we cannot say this of feelings[8]; a point that has created difficulties for moral philosophers who adhere to the traditional theory about emotions. Sir David Ross, for instance, recognizes that "ought" does not apply to feelings, and he assumes that from this it follows that it has no application to emotions, except in an "improper use." According to him "we cannot seriously say" e.g., "You ought to feel ashamed."[9] He is therefore constrained to interpret this remark as meaning that a certain feeling is "right or fitting" in the circumstances, which, as I shall argue shortly, misconstrues its point. If, however, we do not presuppose that the primary function of "I feel ashamed" is to report a feeling, there is no objection to allowing–what is surely the case –that "You ought to feel ashamed" employs "ought" in a perfectly "proper" sense, indeed in the same sense as in "You ought to apologize."

A dispositional theory of emotions may be thought to be on stronger ground, since it can be argued that behavior may be unreasonable or unjustified. To use a previous example again, to say that someone has an unjustified contempt for Bartók is to say, I take it, on this view, that certain categorical and hypothetical statements are true of him, and that these statements describe behavior that is unjustified. In other words, the assertion that contempt for Bartók is unjustified means that a certain pattern of preferential behavior is unjustified. But what is this pattern of behavior? Presumably it will consist in doing (or being prepared to do) things of this sort: switching off when Bartók's music is announced on the Third Programme, wasting free tickets for a concert of his

[8] In the same, i.e., moral, sense. A doctor might maintain that his patient ought not to feel any pain, when the physical condition is not as a rule painful or when he has given a dose of morphine that would alleviate the pain of most patients. "Ought not to" here means (roughly) "would not normally." He might equally be prepared to give a reason why a patient feels giddy, i.e., a causal explanation. This is not a reason *for* feeling giddy, which is an impossibility.

[9] Sir David Ross, *Foundations of Ethics* (London, 1939), pp. 45 and 55.

music, never buying records of Bartók, going for a walk when a neighbor plays his music on the violin, and so on; in short, choosing against this composer whenever a choice presents itself. Now let us suppose that contempt for Bartók is unjustified, as it undoubtedly is. Even so, this behavior may be perfectly reasonable or justified, and therefore cannot constitute an unjustified contempt for Bartók. It is open to a different interpretation, that the person who behaves in this way is simply uninterested in this composer's music, or in modern music generally. Consistently to choose against something is not necessarily to condemn it, or to be contemptuous of it, because this choice is susceptible of rational explanation in other ways.

III

I must now amplify what I have said in passing about the functions performed by statements that refer to emotions. It is generally assumed that these functions are to report feelings, or to report, predict or explain behavior. Now although some statements containing emotion words are used in these ways, and particularly as explanations, the force of the qualifications "unjustified" and "unreasonable" in itself suggests that this is much less common than might be thought, and my contention is that it would be a mistake to imagine that the primary function of these statements is to communicate psychological facts. Their principal functions are judicial, not informative, and when they are informative, it is often not merely psychological information that they give. Consider the following remarks, as they might be used in suitable contexts in everyday life:

(1) "They are very jealous of one another"
(2) "I envy Schnabel's technique"
(3) "I feel ashamed about it now"
(4) "I never feel the slightest pang of regret for what I did"
(5) "I am quite disgusted with the literary men" (Keats)
(6) "Well, I hope you are ashamed of yourself"
(7) "His pride in the Company's record is unjustified"
(8) "He is very disappointed in you."

I think these are all typical examples, and they have been chosen at random, except that I have taken care to ensure that in each case it is clear that the operative word is the emotion word, i.e., I have avoided such instances as "He is very disappointed by your failure to get there in time." Of these examples, the first is different from the rest, its point, I assume, being to inform the hearer that a certain relationship exists between the persons referred to, e.g., in a suitable context, that they are rivals in their profession. The other remarks have what I have termed, for want of a better word, a judicial function. (2) Praises Schnabel; it resembles, say, "Schnabel has a brilliant technique," although it is more tentative and personal, and implies more than this—it would only be said by another pianist. (3) is an admission of responsibility, or perhaps a plea in mitigation, and (4) is the justification of a choice. (5) and (6) imply highly unfavorable assessments. In (5) Keats condemns literary men, and he goes on (Letter of 8th October, 1817) to give part of his reasons for feeling disgusted by telling an anecdote about Leigh Hunt. The force of (6) seems to lie in its mixture of blame with imputation of responsibility—there are two general lines of reply to it, either (*a*) "No, I think I was quite right" or (*b*) "No, it wasn't my fault." (7) is either a way of saying that the person referred to is taking more credit than he deserves, or of saying that the Company's record is not as good as he believes. The normal conversational point of (8), I think, would be to convey blame.

In general then, the affinities of (1) to (8) are not with descriptive statements about what people feel and do, but with a different type of statement altogether. (4), for instance, is very close to "My choice was quite correct (sound, justified)" and (8) to "You have not done as well as he expected." These are not put forward as exact paraphrases; I only wish to suggest that they do not miss the point in the way that any psychological interpretation does. We do not counter such statements as (1) to (8), if we disagree, by challenging an alleged fact. If this is accepted, it can only be consistent with a psychological analysis of emotion concepts if either (*a*) a naturalistic theory of value is presupposed, or (*b*) these usages are treated as non-literal.

(a) It may be said that a judgment of value is a report or expression of an individual's feelings, and that it would not be surprising, therefore, if emotion words (reporting or expressing feelings) had a function somewhat similar to that of value words. I can only make one or two remarks about this here. Earlier on I discussed a moral emotion, shame, and tried to show that the concept of shame is logically dependent on the moral notion of wrong action. I believe, then, that there are specifically moral emotions in this sense only: that the use of some emotion words ("remorse," "shame," etc.) presupposes moral concepts. There are not specifically moral (or for that matter, aesthetic) experiences, and consequently no judgment of value can be a report, or an expression, of an experience. In the case of example (3), no statement that merely reported a feeling could be equivalent to it, since such a statement would not be an admission of responsibility. To accept responsibility for a past action (in the ordinary sense in which it is the opposite of taking credit for something), one has to admit that one did the action and to concede that it was wrong. But there is no experience which, taken in itself, is inconsistent with refusing to admit the one or concede the other. Even if there were a specific experience which always accompanied the admission of responsibility, this would be something logically accidental.

(b) It could be argued that although such words as "regret" and "pride" name emotions in their primary sense, they are used in a different sense in the examples. This will no doubt be turned by some into the objection that a consideration of such usages can throw no light on the nature of the emotions. What does this amount to? There exist uses of emotion words that are unquestionably figurative or metaphorical, e.g., "angry masses of cloud," "the raging waves of the sea foaming out their own shame." Statements (1) to (8) are precisely the literal uses that would be contrasted with these, and no one is likely to maintain, therefore, that they are figurative in the strict sense. It may more plausibly be argued that they are extended or derivative senses of emotion words. But what, then, are the senses from which they are extended or derived? No use of, e.g., "envy," "ashamed," or "pang of regret" appears to exist which is more basic, primary, or literal than that of the examples. There is perhaps a temptation to suppose, because we associate emotion with violent feelings and behavior, that the word "disgusted" is somehow being used more literally when it is used by or of a man who is actually feeling nausea, than it is by Keats in the sentence I have quoted. But all that this proves, it seems to me, is that the experiences of those who are disgusted are different on different occasions. No doubt, to be disgusted with the literary men is not the same as being disgusted with the state of the kitchen sink; the one criticism is moral, and the other is not; but there is a very close and intelligible connection between them which should not be obscured by treating one sense as more primary than the other.

IV

What kind of an explanation of behavior are we giving when we account for it in terms of emotions? I should like, in conclusion, to sketch the general lines on which I think this question ought to be answered. As this is no more than a corollary of the preceding discussion I can put it very briefly.

The traditional theory gives the answer that emotion words explain behavior by specifying its cause, i.e., a certain feeling or inner experience. But surely, when we ask what caused someone to do something, we usually neither expect nor receive an answer in terms of feelings. The answer takes the form of a reference to some external circumstance, if that is relevant, or to some thought, memory, observation, etc., that accounts for the action. If we refer to feelings at all, this appears to be a type of explanation that we fall back on as a last resort, because it is unilluminating and only one step removed from saying that the action is unaccountable. What seems to me to be wrong, then, on this score, with the traditional view is that it does not do justice to the explanatory power of emotion words. For the fact is that to know the feeling that may have preceded an action is not to understand it, or to understand it only very imperfectly. One can remember an action that one did many years ago, an action that one no longer understands, and the question "Why did I do it?" can remain in the face of the clearest recollection of what it felt like to do it. If emotion words merely named some inner experience that preceded or accompanied behavior, to explain behavior by using them would not give the insight that it does.

A quite different answer to this question is proposed by Professor Ryle in *The Concept of Mind.* Referring to what he calls "inclinations" or "motives," Professor Ryle writes, "The imputation of a motive for a particular action is not a causal inference to an unwitnessed event but the subsumption of an episode proposition under a law-like proposition" (p. 90). Again, "To explain an action as done from a certain motive is not to correlate it with an occult cause, but to subsume it under a propensity or behavior-trend" (p. 110). And as I understand him, explanation in terms of mood-words is of a generally similar character. Mood and motive explanations, despite their differences, have this in common, that they are explanations by reference to types of disposition (p. 97). Now although I have been simply following Professor Ryle in what he here denies, I find the positive side of this less adequate. It does not seem to me that emotion words explain merely in the relatively superficial way that dispositional words explain, if "the glass broke because it was brittle" is to be taken as a model, however rough, of this kind of explanation. To refer to a man's laziness or fondness for gardening is to account for what he does on a particular occasion by removing the need for a *special* explanation of it; by showing that his conduct is not in any way surprising or unusual, but part of the regular pattern of things that he does or is likely to do. To assimilate emotion words closely to dispositional words is to give an incomplete account of their explanatory function; they explain behavior more fully than could be done by saying, in effect, that it was only to be expected. ("To say that he did something from that motive is to say that this action, done in its particular circumstances, was just the sort of thing that that was an inclination to do. It is to say 'he *would* do that.'" *Ibid.* pp. 92–93.) I would suggest that emotion words go beyond this sort of explanation in two ways. First, they set the action to be explained, not merely in the context of the rest of an individual's behavior, but in a social context. "He was rude to you because he was jealous" resembles "I helped him because he was a friend" in accounting for his behavior by the reference it makes to his relationship with other people. Secondly, emotion words explain by giving one sort of reason for an action, i.e., by giving a justification, or partial justification, for it. "He refused an interview because of his contempt for journalists" explains the refusal by connecting it with an assessment made by the person whose behavior is referred to. In this respect it has some analogy with, for instance, "He reads Gibbon because he thinks highly of his style." Emotion concepts, I have argued, are not purely psychological: they presuppose concepts of social relationships and institutions, and concepts belonging to systems of judgment, moral, aesthetic, and legal. In using emotion words we are able, therefore, to relate behavior to the complex background in which it is enacted, and so to make human actions intelligible.

PRETENDING

J. L. Austin

In a recent paper[1] Mr. Errol Bedford argues that 'anger', like other words which would be said to be words for emotions, is not the name of a feeling, despite the existence of such espressions as 'feeling angry'. 'Anger', he argues, is not a name, nor is anger a feeling: there is no specific feeling that angry men as such feel, nor do we, to be angry, have to feel any feeling at all. With this thesis I am not concerned, but only with some remarks that he makes, quite incidentally, about pretending (and I realize it is hard on him to pick these out for intensive criticism). For he thinks that his view may be countered by referring to the case of someone *pretending* to be angry: is this not parallel to the case of someone *pretending* to be in pain, who precisely does not feel a certain feeling (pain) that the man who *is* in pain *does* feel—a feeling of which 'pain' surely is the name?

> Can we say that being angry is similar to being in pain in this respect? Let us contrast the cases of a man who is angry and another, behaving in a similar way, who is only pretending to be. Now it may well be true that the former feels angry, whereas the latter does not, but in any case it is not this that constitutes the difference between the fact that the one is angry and the fact that the other is only pretending to be. The objection rests on a misconception of what pretence is. There is necessarily involved in pretence, or shamming, the notion of a limit which must not be overstepped: pretence is always insulated, as it were, from reality. Admittedly this limit may be vague, but it must exist. It is a not unimportant point that it is usually

[1] *Proceedings of the Aristotelian Society*, 1956–7 [pp. 77–98].

obvious when someone is pretending. If a man who is behaving as if he were angry goes so far as to smash the furniture or commit an assault, he has passed the limit; he is not *pretending*, and it is useless for him to protest afterwards that he did not feel angry. Far from this statement being *proof* that he was not angry, it would be discounted even if it were accepted as true. "He was angry, but he did not feel angry" is not self-contradictory, although it is no doubt normally false. If in a particular case it is difficult —as it may be—to settle the question "Pretended or real?" that can only be because the relevant public evidence is inadequate to settle it. What we want is more evidence of the same kind, not a special piece of evidence of a different kind. Our difficulty in resolving the question "Is he really in pain?" on the other hand, arises from the fact that the only decisive evidence is evidence that he alone is in a position to give.

Since pain gets a perhaps undue share of attention in philosophy, and since Mr. Bedford is not shocking us about pretending to be in pain, let us here leave pain out of it, only remarking that if pretending to be in pain and pretending to be angry are actually as different as Mr. Bedford supposes then surely his statements about pretending, designed as they are to fit the case of anger, should be put in less general terms.

Our man, then, is 'behaving as if he were angry'. He scowls, let us say, and stamps his foot on the carpet. So far we may (or perhaps must?) still say 'He is not (really) angry: he is (only) pretending to be angry'. But now he goes further, let us say he bites the carpet: and we will picture the scene with sympathy—the carpet innocent, the bite untentative and vicious, the damage grave. Now he has gone too far, overstepped the limit between pretence and reality, and we cannot any longer say 'He is pretending to be angry' but must say 'He is really angry'. Mr. Bedford's language seems to me on the whole to mean positively that we must say this *because and in the sense that* behaviour of this extreme sort *constitutes* being really angry,[2] or is just what we mean by

[2] At least the bite 'constitutes the difference' between being really angry and pretending to be angry, the common element being pre-

'being really angry'. If, however, he only means, what he also says, that the extreme behaviour is decisive *evidence* that the man is really angry, that is not only a very different and slightly (if only slightly) more plausible thesis, but also one too weak to serve for his argument: for now we are still not told what really being angry, for which this is only the *evidence, is*, nor therefore shown that it does not involve, or even reside in, the feeling of a feeling–the evidence *might* be evidence that he is feeling a certain feeling.

We have primarily to consider whether Mr. Bedford is right in what he says we should *say*, rather than his claims about what is shown by our so speaking, if we do. If the man takes the bite, he *cannot* 'be pretending'–here surely Mr. Bedford carries the philosopher's professional addiction to furniture to a new pitch of positive concern for it. And if he does really mean that the difference in behaviour 'constitutes the difference between the fact that the one is angry and the fact that the other is only pretending to be', then he must be claiming, not only that once he has taken the bite we *cannot* (truly) say 'He is only pretending to be angry', which seems false, but also that if he merely stamps and goes no further we *cannot* (truly) say 'He is really angry', which seems patently false. I think it must on reflection be agreed that in whichever of the ways the man behaves it is open to us to say *either* 'He is angry' *or* 'He is only pretending to be angry', and that either statement can be in fact true, depending on the (other) circumstances of the case at least in addition to these features of his behaviour. It is common enough for someone who is really angry to behave in no way violently or even conspicuously: and if someone is pretending to be angry in some emergency where the success of the pretence matters seriously, more anyway than the integrity of any adjacent furniture (which may not even be his own and may in any case be insured), then surely he may hit upon biting the carpet as the very thing to clinch the deception.

Something has gone very wrong. Yet still there are in fact,

---

sumably such behaviour as scowling. Some may recall the textbook example, where it is only the hair on a gooseberry that stops it from being a grape: by a 'gooseberry', then, we mean simply a hirsute grape–*and* by a 'grape' likewise simply a glabrous gooseberry.

as we should expect, ways in which limits and the overstepping of limits are relevant to the concept of pretending, as to so many others. On a festive occasion you are ordered, for a forfeit, to pretend to be a hyena: going down on all fours, you make a few essays at hideous laughter and finally bite my calf, taking, with a touch of realism possibly exceeding your hopes, a fair-sized piece right out of it. Beyond question you have gone too far.[3] Try to plead that you were only pretending, and I shall advert forcibly to the state of my calf—not much pretence about that, is there? There are limits, old sport. This sort of thing in these circumstances will not pass as '(only) pretending to be a hyena'. True—but then neither will it pass as *really being* a hyena. The limit overstepped, a limitation upon violence as in the carpet-biting case, is not a boundary between pretending to be a hyena and really being a hyena, but between pretending to be a hyena and behaving like an uncivilized tough, or perhaps between *merely* pretending to be a hyena and pretending to be a hyena *with a difference* of some kind, with knobs on or with ulterior motives. So too if you begin to assault the bric-a-brac when told to pretend to be angry for a forfeit, we need not say that you must be really angry, but only that such antics are too bad and quite uncalled-for when pretending in such circumstances, or perhaps that you are taking advantage of the opportunity to further private aesthetic aims (in which case you may not really be pretending, but only pretending to pretend), or perhaps something else again quite different but still in its way satisfyingly censorious.

The moral is, clearly, that to be not pretending to be, and still more to be not only-pretending to be, is not by any means necessarily, still less *eo ipso*, to be really being. This is so even when the way in which we fail to be (only-) pretending is by indulging in excessively 'realistic' behaviour: but of course there are also numerous other kinds of cases, some to be mentioned later, in which we might be taken to be pretending and so may be said to be not pretending, where the reasons for which we are said not to be (only-) pretending are totally

[3] In these circumstances. But if Nero ordered you, in the arena, to pretend to be a hyena, it might be unwisely perfunctory *not* to take a piece right out.

different from this, and such that the notion that not-pretending ⊃ really being could scarcely insinuate itself. We must not allow ourselves to be too much obsessed by the opposition, in which of course there is *something*, between pretending and really being: not one of the following formulae is actually correct:

(1) not really being ⊃ pretending
(2) pretending ⊃ not really being
(3) not pretending ⊃ really being
(4) really being ⊃ not pretending.[4]

So set out these formulae lose, I realize, some of their attractiveness: but arguments like Mr. Bedford's show that they can attract; he has actually, if I am not mistaken, fallen principally for (3), which is not by any means the most tempting, though some of his arguments seem to favour (2), a quite independent matter.

'Pretend' is a verb used in various constructions, of which I have so far only mentioned 'pretend to be' followed by an adjective or adjectival phrase or by a substantive with the article: in such cases excessive behaviour will, as we have seen, commonly not produce the result that the performer 'really is', for example, angry. (I hesitate to say it, but surely the obvious reason is that 'being angry' does not consist merely in behaving publicly in some manner: to say this need not commit us to saying that being angry is the same as feeling angry—it is not, any more than being tired is the same as feeling tired—still less that 'anger' is the name of a feeling.) However, we have to consider also the construction in which 'pretend' is followed by 'to A' or 'to be A-ing', especially in cases where the verb 'A' is one which describes the doing of some *deed* (for example, 'bite' as opposed to, for example, 'believe'), and more particularly when that deed is of a pretty 'physical' kind (for example, biting as opposed to, for example, giving). If we now consider such a case as this: and if we remember one of the conditions that must be satisfied whenever I am pretending, viz. that there must be something,

[4] Actually, 'really' is, like 'actually', really a broken reed in philosophy. See how they twist and turn in example (3) below—the window-cleaner.

and something public, that I am actually doing, some action I actually am performing, in pretending and in order to pretend: then we may hope to have found *one* type of case in which what Mr. Bedford claims to hold of pretending in general does in fact hold.

Let us take the case where someone is to 'pretend to take a bite out of your calf'. Here it would be agreed that one thing he must *not* do,[5] however lifelike the pretence, is anything that could be correctly described as '(actually) taking a bite out of your calf': yet plainly too the action he has, in pretending, actually to perform is one which will be up to a point genuinely like the action he is pretending to perform (for what he is pretending is *here* to perform a public physical action), and might, but for precautions, pass over into it.[6] If he goes far enough he *will* have *really* done the thing he was only to pretend to do: and if he does not go so far, he *cannot* have really done *that* thing. Here, then, we seem to have a case on Mr. Bedford's pattern.

It is owing to the special features of cases of this kind that an impasse can arise over pretending to do something, say hole a putt, in circumstances, say in the presence of a surrounding crowd, where there seems to be nothing one can do at all like holing the putt which will not result in the putt's being actually holed.[7] It is easy to pretend to be sitting on a certain chair when it is half concealed behind a desk, less easy if it is in full view. (This is different from the less subtle type of case where one cannot pretend to do something because one can do neither it nor, often by the same token, anything even passably like it. Thus you cannot pretend to curl your trunk—though again, of course, if you help yourself to that curious object 'a pretend trunk', i.e. something of which we

[5] At least intentionally: I neglect complications about the unintentional.

[6] Of course there is too the rarish and quite different case in which a man pretending to be angry actually *becomes* angry—makes himself angry. I do not think this is of comparable interest.

[7] Doubtful, though not inexplicable, cases arise here, because of doubts as to how much is connoted by a putative description of a 'physical' action. Can I pretend to cough? Shall I, if I produce a coughing noise, have actually coughed? Or is 'to cough' different from 'to deliberately cough'?

pretend that it is your trunk, you can very likely curl that, and hence also very likely pretend to curl it.)

Is it however the case that at least when we are pretending to do or to be doing a physical action we are *universally* debarred from actually doing that action itself? We will consider three examples:

1. Two miscreants are surprised in the act and hastily agree, the wherewithal being handy, to pretend to be sawing a tree: in a trice the blade is humming to and fro a bare inch away from the bark. How good a pretence is that? And wouldn't they any longer be pretending to be sawing the tree if they allowed the teeth to bite in? Surely if they want the pretence to be convincing they should set about actually sawing the tree?

2. Yet surely again magicians pretend to saw girls, we've all seen one pretending very successfully to saw a girl in half. Would it really be still a pretence, and a more convincing one, if the teeth were biting in? Or wouldn't it rather have been transformed into grim reality?

3. That chap over there, he's all right I suppose, he's cleaning the windows, eh?

Ah, *him*, he's *pretending* to be cleaning the windows right enough, cleaning 'em a treat too: but I seen him taking note of the valuables through 'em all the time.[8]

To unravel these examples, we shall need a few more lemmas: we shall need to bring out more of the full features of the situation when we are pretending, which is moderately complicated. And first for that goddess fair and free (fairly fair, frailly free), divinest Etymology. *Prae-tendere* in Latin never strays far from the literal meaning of holding or stretching one thing in front of another in order to protect or conceal or disguise it: even in such a figurative use as that in Ovid's 'praetendens culpae splendida verba tuae', the words are still a façade to hide the crime. In English, we do not any longer explicitly refer, in the construction used with 'pretend',

[8] Here is another, trick, example, for exercise purposes only:—a man at a party decides, in an attempt to amuse, to pretend to behave vulgarly: the party, however, is of a type at which even to pretend to behave vulgarly is, alas, to behave vulgarly.

to that which the pretender is hiding or dissembling, which in Latin does appear in the dative case.[9] Nevertheless it seems clear that it still is an important feature of pretending, in classic cases if not in all, that the pretender is concealing or suppressing something.

In a case of pretending, then, there will typically be:

(PB) The pretence-behaviour, the actual public performance gone through in pretending, indulged in, as of course it is, for the sake of dissembling.

(Rd) The reality-dissembled, about which the audience is to be hoodwinked. This *may* on occasion include in part, or be wholly identical with

(RBd) Some real-behaviour-dissembled, as for instance when I am really engaged in biting the carpet but disguise this fact by pretending to be kissing it.

Thus when we speak of someone's angry behaviour being only a pretence, *one* thing with which this pretended anger is commonly being contrasted at least in our minds is (Rd) his real emotion, feeling, attitude, or what you will, which, whatever it is, is precisely not 'real anger'. In daily life, indeed, this contrast may be of more interest than the quite different contrast, which has been more stressed by philosophers, between

(PBm) The mere-pretence-behaviour, the actual public performance gone through in pretending, disregarding its motivation,

and

(GBs) The genuine-behaviour-simulated, which PBm is intended to resemble. This may be related to a further

(Gs) 'Genuinity'[10]-simulated, as genuinely behaving angrily is related, for example, to genuinely being angry.

[9] Indeed in English even the accusative case after 'pretend', as in, for example, 'He pretended sickness', though a venerable construction is by now archaistic. In the special construction 'pretending not to be' there is however a reference to what is being concealed.

[10] I am driven to this horrible word because I wish to use throughout the second contrast a different term from 'real', which I have kept for the first contrast.

When some simple contrast between 'pretence' and 'reality' comes up in discussion, it is all too often uncertain which of the things here listed is being contrasted with which.

To return now to our three examples. (2)—the girl-sawing—simply supports the rule suggested by the preceding discussion, that in pretending to do A you must not actually do A, or that PBm must not coincide with GBs. Defending this rule, we are tempted to try some special dodge to get out of (1)—the tree-sawing. The miscreants are 'pretending to be sawing the tree' and also 'they are sawing it' in fact, *but* perhaps they are pretending to 'be sawing' it in a sense that covers times earlier and later than the time during which they 'are sawing' it in fact: so that PBm does differ from GBs, it extends over a shorter stretch of time. Or perhaps we should not allow that they 'are (seriously) sawing' it, for example, in the sense that they are not embarked on an operation designed to terminate in the fall of the tree: but it is not clear what this means—suppose the police are suspicious and continue to hang around indefinitely? The case will then become like that of the man who pretends to be playing golf by playing a few strokes: can he prolong the pretence all round the course and yet not be actually playing golf? It is likely that by introducing 'seriously' (and of course it is true that their heart is not in sawing the tree, they are only doing it at all to cover up something) we are really already on the way to the treatment which we *must* use for example (3)—the window-cleaner.

Here surely no dodge will help us; we must allow that he is indeed actually cleaning the windows, from start to finish and throughout the whole time he is pretending to be cleaning them. But it is still a pretence, because what he is *really* doing all the time is something different, namely noting the valuables: he is only cleaning the windows to disguise and promote this other activity—RBd goes on during the course of

---

The Gs may stand to the GBs as, say, its 'motivation': then such an expression as 'pretending to be angry' will commonly run the two together. But where the GBs is something more purely 'physical', such as 'sawing a girl in half', the Gs, if any, is at a discount.

PB, which facilitates it and distracts attention from it. (In other cases RBd may actually be incorporated into PB as a camouflaged part of it.) It looks, then, as though it does not matter if PB does coincide with GBs, so long as the contrast between PB and RBd is preserved.[11]

It is worth noting once more that it will seldom be possible to decide with certainty that PBm does coincide exactly with GBs, because in so many cases GBs is apt to be described, and may only be describable, in terms which already import the Gs which underlines it: thus when someone is 'pretending to be angry', the GBs will be 'angry behaviour' or 'the behaviour of an angry man', a description which may be held already to mean that the actions are done 'in anger'. Only when the GBs is describable in pretty purely 'physical' terms which disregard 'motivation' and the like, for example, as 'sawing a girl', shall we be confident of the coincidence.

In the light of example (3), it can now be seen that the supposed rule that in certain cases, such as example (2), PBm must not coincide with GBs, is really only a marginal case of a more general rule. The essence of the situation in pretending is (not so much that my public behaviour must be non-genuine behaviour, as rather) that my public behaviour is meant to disguise some reality, often some real behaviour. From this it obviously follows, not only that PB must not coincide with RBd, in which case there would be no disguise, but also that PB must not coincide with *not*-RBd, in which case there would be nothing to be being disguised. Now in a case like that of the magician, the RBd precisely is, or includes, *not* actually sawing the girl in half, so that the GBs, sawing the girl in half, is equivalent to not-RBd: hence in such a case it follows directly from the more general rule that PB must stop short of being identical with GBs, as = not-RBd. This type of case, where Gs precisely equals or involves not-Rd, or GBs not-RBd, is of course quite a common one: 'pretending not to be' is a special variety of it.

At least in many cases there seems to be a clear difference

[11] Here is one of the similarities between 'pretence' and 'pretext'. A pretext may be not a genuine reason or not your real reason: a pretence may be something you are not genuinely doing or not what you are really doing.

in meaning between the expressions 'pretending to A' and 'pretending to be A-ing'. The former seems often to be preferred where it is being pointed out that PBm does not coincide with GBs, while the latter stresses that PB does not coincide with RBd. 'He is only pretending to clean the windows', i.e. what he is doing does not amount to genuinely cleaning the windows: but 'He is only pretending to be cleaning the windows', i.e. what he is really up to is something other than cleaning the windows. Take, again, Potter's gambit, where he makes three random moves and then resigns. If we say 'He's only pretending to play (chess)', we mean that that is not playing chess:[12] but if we say 'He's only pretending to be playing (chess)', we allow that in a way and for all we care he is playing chess, but we mean that he is really up to some deeper game. Children who are ignorant may typically be 'pretending to play chess': children, ignorant or not, who are up to mischief may typically be 'pretending to be playing chess'. The magician who is pretending to saw the girl, i.e. we reassure ourselves, not actually sawing her, may also be said to be 'pretending to be sawing her' if, whether he is or not (and naturally we presume not), he is surreptitiously engaged in something else rather crucial for the success of the illusion.

I should not, however, like to claim that this is the whole story about 'pretending to A' and 'pretending to be A-ing'. For consider two further cases:

4. Someone in the next room out of sight keeps up a string of remarks such as 'Check', 'Your move', &c., and occasionally taps pieces of wood together. We should say 'He is (only) pretending (for the benefit of us in the next room) to be playing chess', but scarcely 'He is (only) pretending to play chess'. Why is this?

5. A boy in an arm-chair is making tugging and twisting movements with his arms, accompanied by gear-change and other raucous noises. He is 'pretending to be driving a racing-car', but scarcely 'pretending to drive a racing-car'. Why? A *possible* answer is this. In neither case is the behaviour of the

[12] For some reason. For example, to be genuinely playing chess you must be making your moves with the object of winning, or at least of not losing.

pretending party sufficiently like the genuine article (GBs) for it to be in point to mark the distinction between the two. To pretend to drive a racing-car, he would need a racing-car: as it is, there is no serious prospect of deception. And in case (4) the deception is worked indirectly, mainly by words: if his actual actions were observed, there would again be no serious chance of deception. It might be urged, too, that both these cases of 'pretending to' have some affinity with 'pretending that', of which more later, which generally requires the continuous present tense after it. On the other hand, the difference between, say, 'pretending to sit' and 'pretending to be sitting' is at least sometimes clearly just the familiar difference between 'he sits' and 'he is sitting', so that it will not do to claim that the two forms of expression are used to mark any one single distinction.

So far we have not strayed very far from our starting-point, a consideration of the limits which must not be overstepped in the pretence-behaviour. Only in special cases is the limit between 'pretending to do A' and 'really doing A' of much interest, and even then it is of minor importance in clarifying the whole notion of pretending. When something claimed to be pretending is ruled out by reason of 'going too far', this will commonly mean something such as 'going beyond what was socially permissible on that occasion' rather than 'slipping into doing the actual thing'. But now further, there are other conditions of a quite general kind to which behaviour must conform if it is to qualify as pretence-behaviour: the following examples may serve to bring out some of them:

6. Trapped on a branch against the moon, we decide to pretend to be owls: you give a colourable hoot while I pull up my legs and hunch my shoulders up to my ears.

7. As I am engaged in filching one of your goats, you return inopportunely through the dusk: with a baffled snarl I bound off into the adjacent bush. Was this 'pretending to be a panther'? Or what if instead I slink about the kraal with menacing grunts?

8. Told to pretend to be a hyena at a party, you recline and appear to sleep.

9. In similar circumstances, you proceed to jump around

powerfully on your hind legs, boxing with your fists and fondling something in your pocket.

These are all somewhat facetious cases of 'pretending to be an' animal. It may be worth pointing out that 'pretending to be a hyena' in the let's-pretend, make-believe, party-forfeit way, is a very recent usage, perhaps no older than Lewis Carroll, and the same indeed seems to apply to at least most usages in which we pretend to be something other than ourselves. One of the most conspicuous facts in the history of the word 'pretend' is that of late it has come to be more popular and to be applied more widely than formerly.

In (6) I do better than you. We both *imitate* the owl, you perhaps rather better in voice than I in silhouette: but you stop short of pretending to be an owl, because you fail to attempt to disguise the fact that you are not one—mere imitation does not imply dissembling anything. In (7), while it seems clear that I am pretending if I slink around, this becomes much more doubtful if I bound away, *right* away and *promptly*: for it to be a clear case of pretending I, my human person, must *remain on the scene* to be hidden under the pretence, but as things are it is plainly preferring to be hidden under the bush. If, to startle me, you quack in a passable way from the undergrowth, you are scarcely pretending to be a duck (for you are not on the scene nor in need of disguise), as you would, however, be, very probably, if I trod on you in the dark and you quacked. Of course in all these cases you might be trying to *make me believe* that you were a panther or a duck: but not all such deceptions are achieved by pretending—I can make you believe I am angry by many methods without ever pretending to be angry.

In case (8), at the party, there is of course no question of my trying to convince you *seriously* that I am something other than myself; but still, on the party level, my performance must be convincing, I must dissemble my humanity under a simulated hyenity. I contrive to fail on both counts at once, because my behaviour is as much human as hyenine —how then could it distract attention from my humanity, to which so many other things point, or prompt anyone even to think specially of hyenas? A pretence must be not merely like but *distinctively* like the genuine article simulated: you will hardly pretend to be angry by simulating the behaviour of an angry man in perfect control of himself (though of course it might help if you were to *say* 'I am angry' too).

In (9), you evidently have a wrong idea of what a hyena is. The puzzle, such as it is, is exactly parallel to that about the man who, trying to draw a map of France, draws an outline which is that of Italy: its solution throws no special light on pretending, but rather on doing and intending to do in general—for pretending to be doing something is of course as good a case as another of doing something. You are meaning or trying to pretend to be a hyena, but actually behaving like a kangaroo: this is the correct and the shortest accurate way of describing the situation. There is *no* short answer to the question 'Is he pretending to be a hyena or isn't he?' nor to 'Is he pretending to be a hyena or a kangaroo?' since such simple expressions are not adequate to cope with such a complicated case.

It is quite misleading to handle pretending in the way it is so often handled, as identical with being (or being doing) except that some special feature is left out—and Mr. Bedford is no worse in this respect than those he is attacking, who say, for example, that pretending to be in pain is just the same as being in pain except that you do not feel pain, or that pretending to be angry is behaving like a really angry man only without feeling like one. Even if there were, what there is not, a general bar against PBm being the same as GBs, and even if it were possible, which even then it would not be, to give a *general* account of the precise way in which PBm must *always* fall short of GBs, still such an account would not explain pretending: for there are many situations in which I behave like an angry man without being really angry, which are nevertheless not cases of pretending. For example, I may be a rough diamond, or have odd manners, or be strangely insensitive, or not be attending to what I am doing: or I may be acting or rehearsing, or merely imitating or mimicking. And yet these are only some of the simplest things from which pretending has to be distinguished, much less near to it than, say affecting or shamming or feigning or posing as. To be pretending, in the basic case,[13] I must be trying to make others believe, or to give them the impression, by means of a current personal performance in their presence, that I am (really, only, &c.) *abc*, in order to disguise the fact that I am really *xyz*. To neglect to notice all this is to put in the bathwater without the baby.

Even so, we are far from having a full account of the nuances of pretending. For example, in a pretence there is for preference an element of the extempore, and in the situation that prompts it an element of emergency—there is at least something that has to be hidden. True, there are 'elaborate' pretences: but if there is too much of this, with making-up and dressing-up like an actor rather than a mimic or a diseuse, we begin to prefer to speak of, say, impersonation or imposture or disguise. To pretend to be a bear is one thing, to roam the mountain valleys inside a bearskin rather another. True, there are prolonged pretences—'How long', the cry goes up from the eternal drawing-room, 'must we two go on pretending to one another?'—but still we prefer to say that Col. Barker posed for twenty years as a man rather than that she pretended for twenty years. Again, if there is no sort of urgency to hide what we elect to hide, we may prefer to speak of a leg-pull or of affectation or a pose. Yet these are nuances, for it is probably legitimate enough, in these days, to extend 'pretending' to cover most of these cases if we do not care for precision, just as we can use 'pretended he was going to' to cover those cases where, more specifically, 'he made a feint', i.e. where he made a small movement in one direction to distract his opponent's defence, masking his true *intention*.

There remains, however, more to be said about one essential feature of pretending, namely that the pretender must be present and active in person to effect the deception by dint of his current behaviour. In the example of the panther above,

[13] I neglect here such parasitic cases as let's-pretending and pretending-to-oneself, besides, for the present, pretending-that. Still less have I space to take on 'pretensions', 'the Old Pretender' and the like: but it is not too difficult in fact to fit all these into their appropriate niches in the concept, and sometimes they shed light, as, for example, the contrast between 'affected' and 'pretentious' may help to point the contrast between affecting and pretending.

the awkwardness is not merely that what is to be disguised is not 'on the scene' to be disguised, but also that the pretender is not on the scene to do the disguising, features both essential to pretending though of course not essential to many other forms of deception. I may camouflage a factory as a housing estate, in order to deceive the enemy in an emergency, but this is not to pretend that it is a housing estate (still less does it pretend to be a housing estate). I may pretend to have been furious by emerging from the conference room breathing hard and making derogatory remarks about the proceedings: but not by leaving traces in the conference room—bitten carpets, maybe—designed to make you think I was furious at the time. In pretending, *contemporary behaviour* misleads as to *contemporary fact*, here the contemporary fact that I am not one recovering from or still suffering from the after-effects of fury, or mulling over fresh memories of fury.

This brings me to the last point I shall consider, the construction 'pretending that'. It may be the availability of this handy and flexible construction that has led to the ever increasing popularity of 'pretend', since such neighbouring verbs in the family as 'affect', 'feign', 'dissemble', and the like have never acquired a 'that' construction. It may even seem that, equipped with a that-clause, pretending achieves emancipation from some of the limitations inherent in pretending-to: when pretending-to I can deceive only as to *my own* states or activities, and contemporary ones at that, but surely when I 'pretend that it was in the garage yesterday' I deceive as to something other than my own states or activities, and something non-contemporary at that.

However, it is not easy to be certain that there is in fact any systematic difference between pretending-to and pretending-that, let alone that just suggested.[14] What is the difference between pretending to be on your way to Antarctica and pretending that you are on your way to Antarctica? Or between pretending not to remember her face and

[14] It might be relevant, but would take too long, to consider the other verbs ('hope', &c.) which can take both constructions: they are not particularly numerous.

pretending that you do not remember it? One feels inclined to say: with pretending-that the stress is on the suppression or concealment of knowledge or memory or thought or belief or awareness, in short of some 'cognitive state', and what is simulated is likewise some cognitive state.[15] Thus to pretend that you are in love with her is to dissemble your awareness that you are not, to pretend to be in love with her is to dissemble your indifference or aversion to her. Hence the fact, it might be argued, that in pretending-that the pretence-behaviour is particularly liable to take the form of verbal behaviour, since that is particularly apt for creating impressions about our cognitive states. Moreover the apparent emancipation of pretending-that can be on these lines both accounted for and discounted: when I pretend that it was in the garage yesterday I am still only dissembling *my own current* awareness (memory, knowledge, belief) that it was not: but of course awareness can be *awareness* of things other than my own states or activities, and of non-contemporary things.

Moreover it seems possible in this way to account for pretending-to-oneself or let's-pretending, the former of which strongly, if not exclusively, prefers the 'that' construction. Here we have a sort of 'make-believe'—we suppress our actual beliefs and simulate others.

Yet still in all cases of pretending-that, though it may be only a cognitive state that is simulated and though verbal devices may be often employed, it remains true that there is an immediate connexion with non-verbal behaviour. Pretending that I am on top of a mountain may seem a less active affair at first than pretending to be on top of a mountain, yet still it differs very considerably from merely imagining that I am on top of a mountain: pretending-that is a preliminary to or even accompanied by behaviour such as inhaling deeply or pointing downwards ('Let's pretend we're giraffes and eat the leaves'), while imagining-that is a preliminary perhaps only to asking myself certain questions—How should I feel?, &c., while my public behaviour will scarcely go beyond a faraway look, which is certainly no part of the imagining. For

[15] Yet it seems scarcely right to say: 'pretend that' = 'pretend to believe (or the like) that'.

this reason I can 'always' imagine, for example, that my prison walls are not there, but it may be 'no good' pretending they are not there, they are solid enough to stop me doing the things that follow on the pretending.

But how far can all this be pressed? Is pretending to be playing chess always so very different from pretending that you are playing chess, or again (perhaps still more) from pretending you are playing chess? Perhaps all that should be said is that the more it is a case of going through the motions the more likely we are to prefer 'to be playing' or 'to play': while the less this is necessary and the more we can put the deception across by verbal means or by simulating a belief the more we shall prefer the 'that' construction.

What, finally, is the importance of all this about pretending? I will answer this shortly, although I am not sure importance is important:[16] truth is. In the first place, it does seem that philosophers, who are fond of invoking pretending, have exaggerated its scope and distorted its meaning. In the second place, in the long-term project of classifying and clarifying all possible ways and varieties of *not exactly doing things*, which has to be carried through if we are ever to understand properly what doing things is, the clarification of pretending, and the assignment to it of its proper place within the family of related concepts, must find some place, if only a humble one.

[16] I dreamt a line that would make a motto for a sober philosophy: *Neither a be-all nor an end-all be.*

IMAGINATION

Gilbert Ryle

(1) *Foreword.*

I have mentioned the terminological fact that 'mental' is occasionally used as a synonym of 'imaginary'. A hypochondriac's symptoms are sometimes discounted as 'purely mental'. But much more important than this linguistic oddity is the fact that there exists a quite general tendency among theorists and laymen alike to ascribe some sort of an other-worldly reality to the imaginary and then to treat minds as the clandestine habitats of such fleshless beings. Operations of imagining are, of course, exercises of mental powers. But I attempt in this chapter to show that to try to answer the question, 'Where do the things and happenings exist which people imagine existing?' is to try to answer a spurious question. They do not exist anywhere, though they are imagined as existing, say, in this room, or in Juan Fernandez.

The crucial problem is that of describing what is 'seen in the mind's eye' and what is 'heard in one's head'. What are spoken of as 'visual images', 'mental pictures', 'auditory images' and, in one use, 'ideas' are commonly taken to be entities which are genuinely found existing and found existing elsewhere than in the external world. So minds are nominated for their theatres. But, as I shall try to show, the familiar truth that people are constantly seeing things in their minds' eyes and hearing things in their heads is no proof that there exist things which they see and hear, or that the people are seeing or hearing. Much as stage-murders do not have victims

Gilbert Ryle is Waynflete Professor of Metaphysical Philosophy at Oxford University and is the editor of *Mind*. His books include *The Concept of Mind* (London, 1949) and *Dilemmas* (Cambridge, 1956).

and are not murders, so seeing things in one's mind's eye does not involve either the existence of things seen or the occurrence of acts of seeing them. So no asylum is required for them to exist or occur in. . . .

(2) *Picturing and Seeing.*

To see is one thing; to picture or visualise is another. A person can see things, only when his eyes are open, and when his surroundings are illuminated; but he can have pictures in his mind's eye, when his eyes are shut and when the world is dark. Similarly, he can hear music only in situations in which other people could also hear it; but a tune can run in his head, when his neighbour can hear no music at all. Moreover, he can see only what is there to be seen and hear only what is there to be heard, and often he cannot help seeing and hearing what is there to be seen and heard; but on some occasions he can choose what pictures shall be before his mind's eye and what verses or tunes he shall go over in his head.

One way in which people tend to express this difference is by writing that, whereas they see trees and hear music, they only 'see', in inverted commas, and 'hear' the objects of recollection and imagination. The victim of *delirium tremens* is described by others, not as seeing snakes, but as 'seeing' snakes. This difference of idiom is reinforced by another. A person who says that he 'sees' the home of his childhood is often prepared to describe his vision as 'vivid', 'faithful' or 'lifelike', adjectives which he would never apply to his sight of what is in front of his nose. For while a doll can be called 'lifelike,' a child cannot; or while a portrait of a face may be faithful, the face cannot be any such thing. In other words, when a person says that he 'sees' something which he is not seeing, he knows that what he is doing is something which is totally different in kind from seeing, just because the verb is inside inverted commas and the vision can be described as more or less faithful, or vivid. He may say 'I might be there now', but the word 'might' is suitable just because it declares that he is not there now. The fact that in certain conditions he fails to realise that he is not seeing, but only 'seeing', as in dreams, delirium, extreme thirst, hypnosis and conjuring-shows, does not in any degree tend to obliterate the distinction between the concept of seeing and that of 'seeing', any more than the fact that it is often difficult to tell an authentic from a forged signature tends to obliterate the distinction between the concept of a person signing his own name and that of someone else forging it. The forgery can be described as a good or bad imitation of the real thing; an authentic signature could not be characterised as an imitation at all, since it is the real thing without which the forger would have nothing to imitate.

As visual observation has pre-eminence over observation by the other senses, so with most people visual imagination is stronger than auditory, tactual, kinaesthetic, olfactory and gustatory imagination, and consequently the language in which we discuss these matters is largely drawn from the language of seeing. People speak, for example, of 'picturing' or 'visualising' things, but they have no corresponding generic verbs for imagery of the other sorts.

An unfortunate result ensues. Among the common objects of visual observation there exist both visible things and visible simulacra of them, both faces and portraits, both signatures and forged signatures, both mountains and snapshots of mountains, both babies and dolls; and this makes it natural to construe the language in which we describe imaginations in an analogous way.

If a person says that he is picturing his nursery, we are tempted to construe his remark to mean that he is somehow contemplating, not his nursery, but another visible object, namely a picture of his nursery, only not a photograph or an oil-painting, but some counterpart to a photograph, one made of a different sort of stuff. Moreover, this paperless picture, which we suppose him to be contemplating, is not one of which we too can have a view, for it is not in a frame on the wall in front of all of our noses, but somewhere else, in a gallery which only he can visit. And then we are inclined to say that the picture of his nursery which he contemplates must be in his mind; and that the 'eyes' with which he contemplates it are not his bodily eyes, which perhaps we see to be shut, but his mind's eyes. So we inadvertently subscribe to the theory that 'seeing' is seeing after all, and what is 'seen' by him is as genuine a likeness and as genuinely seen as is the oil-painting which is seen by everyone. True, it is a short-lived picture, but so are cinematograph-pictures. True, too, it is reserved for the one spectator to whom it and its gallery belong; but monopolies are not uncommon.

I want to show that the concept of picturing, visualising or 'seeing' is a proper and useful concept, but that its use does not entail the existence of pictures which we contemplate or the existence of a gallery in which such pictures are ephemerally suspended. Roughly, imaging occurs, but images are not seen. I do have tunes running in my head, but no tunes are being heard, when I have them running there. True, a person picturing his nursery is, in a certain way, like that person seeing his nursery, but the similarity does not consist in his really looking at a real likeness of his nursery, but in his really seeming to see his nursery itself, when he is not really seeing it. He is not being a spectator of a resemblance of his nursery, but he is resembling a spectator of his nursery.

(3) *The Theory of Special Status Pictures.*

Let us first consider some implications of the other doctrine, that in visualising I am, in a nearly ordinary sense of the verb, seeing a picture with a special status. It is part of this doctrine that the picture that I see is not, as snapshots are, in front of my face; on the contrary, it has to be not in physical space, but in a space of another kind. The child, then, who imagines her wax-doll smiling is seeing a picture of a smile. But the picture of the smile is not where the doll's lips are, since they are in front of the child's face. So the imagined smile is not on the doll's lips at all. Yet this is absurd. No one can imagine an unattached smile, and no doll-owner would be satisfied with an unsmiling doll plus a separate and impossible simulacrum of a smile suspended somewhere else. In fact she does not really see a Cheshire smile elsewhere than on the doll's lips; she fancies she sees a smile on the doll's lips in front of her face, though she does not see one there and would be greatly frightened if she did. Similarly the conjuror makes us 'see' (not see) rabbits coming out of the hat in his hand on the stage in front of our noses; he does not induce us to see (not 'see') shadow-rabbits coming out of a second spectral hat, which is not in his hand, but in a space of another kind.

The pictured smile is not, then, a physical phenomenon, i.e. a real contortion of the doll's face; nor yet is it a non-physical phenomenon observed by the child taking place in a field quite detached from her perambulator and her nursery. There is not a smile at all, and there is not an effigy of a smile either. There is only a child fancying that she sees her doll smiling. So, though she is really picturing her doll smiling, she is not looking at a picture of a smile; and though I am fancying that I see rabbits coming out of the hat, I am not seeing real phantasms of rabbits coming out of real phantasms of hats. There is not a real life outside, shadowily mimicked by some bloodless likenesses inside; there are just things and events, people witnessing some of these things and events, and people fancying themselves witnessing things and events that they are not witnessing.

Take another case. I start to write down a long and unfamiliar word and after a syllable or two, I find that I am not sure how the word should go on. I then, perhaps, imagine myself consulting a dictionary and in some cases I can then 'see' how the last three syllables are printed. In this sort of case it is tempting to say that I am really seeing a picture of a printed word, only the picture is 'in my head', or 'in my mind', since reading off the letters of the word that I 'see' feels rather like reading off the letters from a dictionary-item, or a photograph of such an item, which I really do see. But in another case, I start writing the word and I 'see' the next syllable or two on the page on which I am writing and in the place where I am to write them. I feel rather as if I were merely inking in a word-shadow lying across the page. Yet here it is impossible to say that I am having a peep at a picture or ghost of a word in a queer space other than physical space, for what I 'see' is on my page just to the right of my nib. Again we must say that though I picture the word in a certain place, printed in a certain type, or written in a certain handwriting, and though I can read off the spelling of the word from the way I picture it as printed or written, yet there exists no picture, shadow or ghost of the word and I see no picture, shadow or ghost of it. I seem to see the word on the page itself, and the more vividly and sustainedly I seem to see it, the more easily can I transcribe what I seem to see on to my paper with my pen.

Hume notoriously thought that there exist both 'impressions' and 'ideas', that is, both sensations and images; and he looked in vain for a clear boundary between the two sorts of 'perceptions'. Ideas, he thought, tend to be fainter than impressions, and in their genesis they are later than impressions, since they are traces, copies or reproductions of impressions. Yet he recognised that impressions can be of any degree of faintness, and that though every idea is a copy, it does not arrive marked 'copy' or 'likeness', any more than impressions arrive marked 'original' or 'sitter'. So, on Hume's showing, simple inspection cannot decide whether a perception is an impression or an idea. Yet the crucial difference remains between what is heard in conversation and what is 'heard' in day-dreams, between the snakes in the Zoo and the snakes 'seen' by the dipsomaniac, between the study that I am in and the nursery in which 'I might be now'. His mistake was to suppose that 'seeing' is a species of seeing, or that 'perception' is the name of a genus of which there are two species, namely impressions and ghosts or echoes of impressions. There are no such ghosts, and if there were, they would merely be extra impressions; and they would belong to seeing, not to 'seeing'.

Hume's attempt to distinguish between ideas and impressions by saying that the latter tend to be more lively than the former was one of two bad mistakes. Suppose, first, that 'lively' means 'vivid'. A person may picture vividly, but he cannot see vividly. One 'idea' may be more vivid than another 'idea', but impressions cannot be described as vivid at all, just as one doll can be more lifelike than another, but a baby cannot be lifelike or unlifelike. To say that the difference between babies and dolls is that babies are more lifelike than dolls is an obvious absurdity. One actor may be more convincing than another actor; but a person who is not acting is neither convincing nor unconvincing, and cannot therefore be described as more convincing than an actor.

Alternatively, if Hume was using 'vivid' to mean not 'life-like' but 'intense', 'acute' or 'strong', then he was mistaken in the other direction; since, while sensations can be compared with other sensations as relatively intense, acute or strong, they cannot be so compared with images. When I fancy I am hearing a very loud noise, I am not really hearing either a loud or a faint noise; I am not having a mild auditory sensation, as I am not having an auditory sensation at all, though I am fancying that I am having an intense one. An imagined shriek is not ear-splitting, nor yet is it a soothing murmur, and an imagined shriek is neither louder nor fainter than a heard murmur. It neither drowns it nor is drowned by it.

Similarly, there are not two species of murderers, those who murder people, and those who act the parts of murderers on the stage; for these last are not murderers at all. They do not commit murders which have the elusive attribute of being shams; they pretend to commit ordinary murders, and pretending to murder entails, not murdering, but seeming to murder. As mock-murders are not murders, so imagined sights and sounds are not sights or sounds. They are not, therefore, dim sights, or faint sounds. And they are not private sights or sounds either. There is no answer to the spurious question, 'Where have you deposited the victim of your mock-murder?' since there was no victim. There is no answer to the spurious question, 'Where do the objects reside that we fancy we see?' since there are no such objects.

It will be asked, 'How can a person seem to hear a tune running in his head, unless there is a tune to hear?' Part of the answer is easy, namely that he would not be seeming to hear, or fancying that he heard, a tune, if he were really hearing one, any more than the actor would be simulating murder, if he were really murdering someone. But there is more to be said than this. The question, 'How can a person seem to hear a tune, when there is no tune to be heard?' has the form of a 'wires and pulleys' question. It suggests that there exists a mechanical or para-mechanical problem (like those that are properly asked about conjuring-tricks and automatic telephones), and that we need to have described to us the hidden workings that constitute what a person does, when he fancies himself listening to a tune. But to understand what is meant by saying that someone is fancying that he hears a tune does not require information about any ulterior processes which may be going on when he does so. We already know, and have known since childhood, in what situations to describe people as imagining that they see or hear or do things. The problem, so far as it is one, is to construe these descriptions without falling back into the idioms in which we talk of seeing horse-races, hearing concerts and committing murders. It is into these idioms that we fall back the moment we say that to fancy one sees a dragon is to see a real dragon-phantasm, or that to pretend to commit a murder is to commit a real mock-murder, or that to seem to hear a tune is to hear a real mental tune. To adopt such linguistic practices is to try to convert into species-concepts concepts which are designed, anyhow partly, to act as factual disclaimers. To say that an action is a mock-murder is to say, not that a certain sort of mild or faint murder has been committed, but that no sort of murder has been committed; and to say that someone pictures a dragon is to say, not that he dimly sees a dragon of a peculiar kind, or something else very like a dragon, but that he does not see a dragon, or anything dragon-like at all. Similarly a person who 'sees Helvellyn in his mind's eye' is not seeing either the mountain, or a likeness of the mountain; there is neither a mountain in front of the eyes in his face, nor a mock-mountain in front of any other non-facial eyes. But it is still true that he 'might be seeing Helvellyn now' and even that he may fail to realise that he is not doing so.

Let us consider another sort of imaging. Sometimes, when someone mentions a blacksmith's forge, I find myself instantaneously back in my childhood, visiting a local smithy. I can vividly 'see' the glowing red horseshoe on the anvil, fairly vividly 'hear' the hammer ringing on the shoe and less vividly 'smell' the singed hoof. How should we describe this 'smelling in the mind's nose'? Ordinary language provides us with no means of saying that I am smelling a 'likeness' of a singed hoof. As has been said already, in the ordinary daylit world there are visible faces and mountains, as well as other visible objects, which are pictures of faces and mountains; there are visible people and visible effigies of people. Both trees and reflections of trees can be photographed or reflected in mirrors. The visual comparison of seen things with the seen likenesses of those things is familiar and easy. With sounds we are not quite so well placed, but there are heard noises and heard echoes of noises, songs sung and recordings of songs played, voices and mimicries of them. So it is easy and tempting to describe visual imaging as if it were a case of looking at a likeness instead of looking at its original, and it may pass muster to describe auditory imaging as if it were a case of hearing a sort of echo or recording, instead of hearing the voice itself. But we have no such analogies for smelling, tasting or feeling. So when I say that I 'smell' the singed hoof, I have no way of paraphrasing my statement into a form of words which says instead 'I smell a copy of a singed hoof'. The language of originals and copies does not apply to smells.

None the less, I may certainly say that I vividly 'smell' the singed hoof, or that its smell comes back to me vividly, and the use of this adverb shows by itself that I know that I am not smelling, but only 'smelling'. Smells are not vivid, faithful or lifelike; they are only more or less strong. Only 'smells' can be vivid, and correspondingly they cannot be more or less strong, though I can seem to be getting a more or less strong smell. However vividly I may be 'smelling' the smithy, the smell of the lavender in my room, however faint, is in no degree drowned. There is no competition between a smell and a 'smell', as there can be a competition between the smell of onions and the smell of lavender.

If a person who has recently been in a burning house reports that he can still 'smell' the smoke, he does not think that the house in which he reports it is itself on fire. However vividly he 'smells' the smoke, he knows that he smells none; at least, he realises this, if he is in his right mind, and if he does not realise it, he will say not that the 'smell' is vivid, but, erroneously, that the smell is strong. But if the theory were true that to 'smell' smoke were really to smell a likeness of smoke, he could have no way of distinguishing between 'smelling' and smelling, corresponding to the familiar ways in which we distinguish between looking at faces and looking at likenesses of them, or between hearing voices and hearing recordings of voices.

There are usually ocular ways of distinguishing between things and snapshots or effigies of them; a picture is flat, has edges and perhaps a frame; it can be turned round and turned upside down, crumpled and torn. Even an echo, or a recording, of a voice can be distinguished, if not audibly, at least by certain mechanical criteria from the voice itself. But no such discriminations can be made between a smell and a copy of a smell, a taste and a likeness of a taste, a tickle and a dummy-tickle; indeed, it makes no sense to apply words like 'copy', 'likeness' and 'dummy' to smells, tastes and feelings. Consequently we have no temptation to say that a person who 'smells' the smithy is really smelling a facsimile or likeness of anything. He seems to smell, or he fancies he smells, something, but there is no way of talking as if there existed an internal smell replica, or smell facsimile, or smell echo. In this case, therefore, it is clear that to 'smell' entails not smelling and therefore that imaging is not perceiving a likeness, since it is not perceiving at all.

Why, then, is it tempting and natural to misdescribe 'seeing things' as the seeing of pictures of things? It is not because 'pictures' denotes a genus of which snapshots are one species and mental pictures are another, since 'mental pictures' no more denotes pictures than 'mock-murders' denotes murders. On the contrary, we speak of 'seeing' as if it were a seeing of pictures, because the familiar experience of seeing snapshots of things and persons so often induces the 'seeing' of those things and persons. This is what snapshots are for. When a visible likeness of a person is in front of my nose, I often seem to be seeing the person himself in front of my nose, though he is not there and may be long since dead. I should not keep the portrait if it did not perform this function. Or when I hear a recording of a friend's voice, I fancy I hear him singing or speaking in the room, though he is miles away. The genus is seeming to perceive, and of this genus one very familiar species is that of seeming to see something, when looking at an ordinary snapshot of it. Seeming to see, when no physical likeness is before the nose, is another species. Imaging is not having shadowy pictures before some shadow-organ called 'the mind's eye'; but having paper pictures before the eyes in one's face is a familiar stimulus to imaging.

An oil painting of a friend is described as lifelike, if it makes me seem to see the friend in great clarity and detail, when I am not actually seeing him. A mere cartoon may be lifelike without being at all similar to a lifelike oil painting of the same person. For a picture to be lifelike it is not necessary or sufficient that it should be an accurate replica of the contours or colouring of the subject's face. So when I vividly 'see' a face, this does not entail my seeing an accurate replica, since I might see an accurate replica without being helped to 'see' the face vividly and *vice versa*. But finding a picture of a person lifelike or 'speaking' entails being helped to seem to see the person, since that is what 'lifelike' and 'speaking' mean.

People have tended to describe 'seeing' as a seeing of genuine but ghostly likenesses, because they wanted to explain vividness or lifelikeness in terms of similarity, as if, for me vividly to 'see' Helvellyn, I must be actually seeing something else very similar to Helvellyn. But this is erroneous. Seeing replicas, however accurate, need not result in 'seeing' vividly, and the speakingness of a physical likeness has to be described, not in terms of similarity, but in terms of the vividness of the 'seeing' which it induces.

In short, there are no such objects as mental pictures, and if there were such objects, seeing them would still not be the same thing as seeming to see faces or mountains. We do picture or visualise faces and mountains, just as we do, more rarely, 'smell' singed hoofs, but picturing a face or a mountain is not having before us a picture of the face or mountain, it is something that having a physical likeness in front of one's nose commonly helps us to do, though we can and often do do it without any such promptings. Dreaming, again, is not being present at a private cinematograph show; on the contrary, witnessing a public cinematograph show is one way of inducing a certain sort of dreaming. The spectator there is seeing a variously illuminated sheet of linen, but he is 'seeing' rolling prairies. So it would invert the true state of affairs to say that the dreamer is regarding a variously illuminated sheet of 'mental' linen; for there is no mental linen, and if there were, seeing it variously illuminated would not be dreaming that one was galloping over the prairies.

The tendency to describe visualising as seeing genuine, but internal, likenesses, reinforces and is reinforced by the Sense Datum Theory. Many holders of this theory, supposing, erroneously, that in 'seeing' I am seeing a peculiar paper-less snapshot, though one which, oddly, cannot be turned upside down, think that *a fortiori* in seeing proper I am seeing a peculiar non-physical colour expanse. And supposing, erroneously, that having a visual sensation is descrying a flat patchwork of colours spread out in 'a private space', they find it all the easier to say that in imaging we are scanning a more ghostly patchwork of colours hung up in the same gallery with that original patchwork of colours. As in my study there may be both a person and a shadow or a portrait of that person, so in my private sight-gallery there might be both sense data and reproductions of sense data. My objections to the interpretation of picturing as picture-seeing do not in themselves demolish the Sense Datum Theory of sensations; but they do demolish, I hope, the ancillary theory that picturing is looking at reproductions of sense data. And if I am right in saying that having a visual sensation is wrongly described as some sort of observing of a patchwork of colours, since the concept of sensation is different from the concept of observing, it will follow, as can be established on other grounds, that imaging is not only not any sort of observing of anything; it is also not having a sensation of a special sort. Seeming to hear a very loud noise is not being in any degree deafened, nor is seeming to see a very bright light being in any degree dazzled. So far are ideas from being impressions of a special sort, that to describe something as an idea, in this sense, is to deny that an impression is being had.

(4) *Imagining.*

It will probably be asked, 'What then is it for a person to fancy that he sees or smells something? How can he seem to hear a tune that he does not really hear? And, in particular, how can a person fail to be aware that he is only seeming to hear or see, as the dipsomaniac certainly fails? In what precise respects is 'seeing' so like seeing that the victim often cannot, with the best will and the best wits, tell which he is doing?' Now if we divest these questions of associations with any 'wires and pulleys' questions, we can see that they are simply questions about the concept of imagining or make-believe, a concept of which I have so far said nothing positive. I have said nothing about it so far, because it seemed necessary to begin by vaccinating ourselves against the theory, often tacitly assumed, that imagining is to be described as the seeing of pictures with a special status.

But I hope I have now shown that what people commonly describe as 'having a mental picture of Helvellyn' or 'having Helvellyn before the mind's eye' is actually a special case of imagining, namely imagining that we see Helvellyn in front of our noses, and that having a tune running in one's head is imagining that one has the tune being played in one's hearing, maybe in a concert-hall. If successful, then I have also shown that the notion that a mind is a 'place', where mental pictures are seen and reproductions of voices and tunes are heard, is also wrong.

There are hosts of widely divergent sorts of behaviour in the conduct of which we should ordinarily and correctly be described as imaginative. The mendacious witness in the witness-box, the inventor thinking out a new machine, the constructor of a romance, the child playing bears, and Henry Irving are all exercising their imaginations; but so, too, are the judge listening to the lies of the witness, the colleague giving his opinion on the new invention, the novel reader, the nurse who refrains from admonishing the 'bears' for their subhuman noises, the dramatic critic and the theatre-goers. Nor do we say that they are all exercising their imaginations because we think that, embedded in a variety of often widely different operations, there is one common nuclear operation which all alike are performing, any more than we think that what makes two men both farmers is some nuclear operation which both do in exactly the same way. Just as ploughing is one farming job and tree-spraying is another farming job, so inventing a new machine is one way of being imaginative and playing bears is another. No one thinks that there exists a nuclear farming operation by the execution of which alone a man is entitled to be called 'a farmer'; but the concepts wielded in theories of knowledge are apt to be less generously treated. It is often assumed that there does exist one nuclear operation in which imagination proper consists; it is assumed, that is, that the judge following the witness's mendacities, and the child playing bears, are both exercising their imaginations only if they are both executing some specifically identical ingredient operation. This supposed nuclear operation is often supposed to be that of seeing things in the mind's eye, hearing things in one's head and so on, i.e. some piece of fancied perceiving. Of course, it is not denied that the child is doing lots of other things as well; he roars, he pads around the floor, he gnashes his teeth and he pretends to sleep in what he pretends is a cave. But, according to this view, only if he sees pictures in his mind's eye of his furry paws, his snow-bound den and so on, is he imagining anything. His noises and antics may be a help to his picturing, or they may be special effects of it, but it is not in making these noises, or performing these antics, that he is exercising his imagination, but only in his 'seeing', 'hearing', 'smelling', 'tasting' and 'feeling' things which are not there to be perceived. And the corresponding things will be true of the attentive, if sceptical, judge.

Put as bluntly as this, the doctrine is patently absurd. Most of the things for which we ordinarily describe children as imaginative are ruled out in favour of a limited number of operations the occurrence and qualities of which it is difficult to ascertain, especially from relatively inarticulate children. We see and hear them play, but we do not see or hear them 'seeing' or 'hearing' things. We read what Conan Doyle wrote, but we do not get a view of what he saw in his mind's eye. So, on this theory, we cannot easily tell whether children, actors or novelists are imaginative or not, though the word 'imagination' came to be wielded in theories of knowledge just because we all know how to wield it in our everyday descriptions of children, actors and novelists.

There is no special Faculty of Imagination, occupying itself single-mindedly in fancied viewings and hearings. On the contrary, 'seeing' things is one exercise of imagination, growling somewhat like a bear is another; smelling things in the mind's nose is an uncommon act of fancy, malingering is a very common one, and so forth. Perhaps the chief motive from which many theorists have limited the exercises of imagination to the special class of fancied perceptions is that they have supposed that, since the mind is officially tri-partitioned into the Three Estates of Cognition, Volition and Emotion, and since imagination was born into the first, it must therefore be excluded from the others. Cognitive malpractices are notoriously due to the pranks of undisciplined Imagination, and some cognitive successes are in debt to its primmer activities. So, being an (erratic) Squire of Reason, it cannot serve the other masters. But we need not pause to discuss this feudal allegory. Indeed, if we are asked whether imagining is a cognitive or a non-cognitive activity, our proper policy is to ignore the question. 'Cognitive' belongs to the vocabulary of examination papers.

(5) *Pretending.*

Let us begin by considering the notion of pretending, a notion which is partly constitutive of such notions as those of cheating, acting a part, playing bears, shamming sick and hypochondria. It will be noticed that in some varieties of make-believe, the pretender is deliberately simulating or dissimulating, in some varieties he may not be quite sure to what extent, if any, he is simulating or dissimulating, and in other varieties he is completely taken in by his own acting. On a small scale this can be illustrated by the child playing bears, who knows, while in the well-lit drawing-room, that he is only playing an amusing game, but feels faint anxieties when out on the solitary landing, and cannot be persuaded of his safety when in the darkness of a passage. Make-believe is compatible with all degrees of scepticism and credulity, a fact which is relevant to the supposed problem, 'How can a person fancy that he sees something, without realising that he is not seeing it?' But if we pose the parallel questions, 'How can a child play bears, without being all the time quite sure that it is only a game? How can the malingerer fancy that he has symptoms, without being perfectly confident that they are only his fancies?' we see that these questions, and many others like them, are not genuine how-questions at all. The fact that people can fancy that they see things, are pursued by bears, or have a grumbling appendix, without realising that it is nothing but fancy, is simply a part of the unsurprising general fact that not all people are, all the time, at all ages and in all conditions, as judicious or critical as could be wished.

To describe someone as pretending is to say that he is playing a part, and to play a part is to play the part, normally, of someone who is not playing a part, but doing or being something ingenuously or naturally. A corpse is motionless, and so is a person pretending to be a corpse. But a person pretending to be a corpse is, unlike the corpse, trying to be motionless, and, again unlike the corpse, he is motionless from the wish to resemble a corpse. He is, perhaps, deliberately, skilfully and convincingly motionless, whereas the corpse is just motionless. Corpses have to be dead, but mock-corpses have to be alive. Indeed, they have to be not only alive, but also awake, non-absent-minded and applying their minds to the part they are playing.

Talking about a person pretending to be a bear or a corpse involves talking obliquely about how bears and corpses behave, or are supposed to behave. He plays these parts by growling as bears growl and lying still as corpses lie still. One cannot know how to play a part without knowing what it is like to be or do ingenuously that which one is staging; nor can one find a mock-performance convincing or unconvincing, or dub it skilful or inefficient, without knowing how the ingenuous performance itself is conducted. Pretending to growl like a bear, or lie still like a corpse, is a sophisticated performance, where the bear's growling and the corpse's immobility are naive.

The difference is parallel to that between quoting an assertion and making it. If I quote what you asserted, then what I say is just what you said; I may even say it in just your tone of voice. Yet the full description of my action is not at all like that of yours. Yours was, perhaps, an exercise of the skill of a preacher; mine is that of a reporter or mimic; you were being original; I am being an echo: you said what you believed; I say what I do not believe. In short, the words I utter are uttered, so to speak, as they would be written, inside inverted commas. The words you uttered were not. You spoke in *oratio recta*; I may intend what I say to be taken as if in *oratio obliqua*. In the same sort of way, while the bear just growls, the child's growling is, so to speak, inside inverted commas. His direct action is, unlike the bear's, one of representation, and this obliquely embodies growling. Yet the child is not doing two things at once, any more than I, in quoting you, am saying two things at once. A mock-performance differs from the ingenuous performance which it represents, not in being a complex of performances, but in being a performance with a certain sort of complex description. A mention of the ingenuous performance is an ingredient in the description of the mock-performance. The noises issuing from the child may be as similar as you please to those issuing from the bear, just as the noises issuing from my lips may be as similar as you please to the noises you made in your homily, but the concept of such mock-performances is logically very different from that of the ingenuous performances. In describing their authors, we use quite different batteries of predicates.

Is a forged signature the same sort of thing as a genuine signature, or is it a different sort of thing? If the forgery is perfect, then the one cheque really is indistinguishable from the other and so, in this sense, they are exactly the same sort of thing. But forging a signature is quite unlike signing; the one requires what the other does not, the wish and the ability to produce marks indistinguishable from a signature. In this sense they are completely different sorts of things. The whole ingenuity of the forger is exerted in trying to make his cheque a perfect facsimile of the authentic cheque, the signing of which had taken no ingenuity. What he is after has to be described in terms of the similarity between writings, just as what the child was after has to be described in terms of the similarity between his noises and the bear's noises. Deliberate verisimilitude is a part of the concept of copying. The very likenesses between copies and their originals are what make activities of copying different in type from the activities copied.

There are lots of different sorts of pretending, different motives from which people pretend and different criteria by which pretences are assessed as skilful or unskilful. The child pretends for fun, the hypocrite for profit, the hypochondriac from morbid egotism, the spy, sometimes, from patriotism, the actor, sometimes, for art's sake, and the cooking instructress for demonstration purposes. Let us consider the case of the boxer sparring with his instructor. They go through the motions of serious fighting, though they are not fighting seriously; they pretend to attack, retreat, punish and retaliate, though no victory is aimed at, or defeat feared. The pupil is learning manoeuvres by playing at them, the instructor is teaching them by playing at them. Yet though they are only mock-fighting, they need not be carrying on two collateral activities. They need not be both punching and also pulling their punches; both laying traps and also betraying the traps they lay; or both plying their fists and also plying propositions. They may be going through only one set of movements, yet they are making these movements in a hypothetical and not in a categorical manner. The notion of hurt enters only obliquely into the description of what they are trying to do. They are not trying either to hurt or to avoid hurt, but only to practise ways in which they would hurt and would avoid hurt, if engaged in serious fights. The cardinal thing in sparring is abstaining from giving punishing blows, when one could, i.e. in situations in which one would give such blows if the fight were serious. Sham-fighting is, to put it crudely, a series of calculated omissions to fight.

The central point illustrated by these cases is that a mock-performance may be unitary as an action though there is an intrinsic duality in its description. Only one thing is done, yet to say what is done requires a sentence containing, at the least, both a main clause and a subordinate clause. To recognise this is to see why there is no more than a verbal appearance of a contradiction in saying of an actor, playing the part of an idiot, that he is grimacing in an idiotic manner in a highly intelligent manner; or of a clown that he is deftly clumsy and brilliantly inane. The scathing adjective attaches to the conduct mentioned in the subordinate clause of the description and the flattering adjective or adverb to the activity mentioned in the main clause, yet only one set of motions is executed. Similarly, if I quote a statement, you might correctly characterise what I say both as 'accurate' and as 'inaccurate', for it might be a highly inaccurate statement of the size of the National Debt quite accurately quoted, or *vice versa*. Yet I have uttered only one statement.

Acts of pretending are not the only ones the descriptions of which incorporate this dualism between the direct and the oblique. If I obey an order, I do the thing I am told to do and I comply with the command; but as I comply with the command by doing the thing, I execute only one action. Yet the description of what I do is complex in such a way that it would often be correct to characterise my conduct by two seemingly conflicting predicates. I do what I am told from force of habit, though what I am ordered to do is something which I am not in the habit of doing; or I obey like a good soldier, though what I am ordered to do is something which it is a mark of a bad soldier to do. Similarly, I may do wisely in following advice to do something unwise, and I may with difficulty carry out a resolve to do something easy. In Chapter VI, Section (6) we found it convenient to distinguish verbally between higher order tasks and lower order tasks, and between higher order performances and lower order performances, meaning by a 'higher order task', one the description of which incorporates the mention of another task of a less complex description. It will be realised that the fact that the movements made in the execution of one task are entirely similar to those made in the execution of another is compatible with the descriptions of the tasks being not only different but different in type in the way indicated.

To return to pretending. The frame of mind of a person pretending to be cross is different from that of a person who is cross, and different from it not just in the fact that the former is not cross. He is not cross, though he acts as if he were; and this simulation involves, in some way, the thought of crossness. He must not only possess, but in some way be using, the knowledge of what it is for someone to be cross. He intentionally models his actions upon those of a cross man. But when we say that putting on the behaviour of a cross man involves having the thought of crossness, we run a certain risk, namely the risk of suggesting that pretending to be cross is a tandem process consisting of one operation of meditating about crossness, shepherding a second operation of performing the quasi-cross actions. Such a suggestion would be wrong. Whether or not pieces of make-believe happen to be preceded by, or interlarded with, pieces of describing or planning, it is not in this way that make-believe involves the thought of what is simulated. The business of trying to behave in ways in which a cross man would behave is itself, in part, the thought of how he would behave; the more or less faithful muscular representation of his poutings and stampings is the active utilisation of the knowledge of how he would comport himself. We concede that a person knows what the publican's temper is like if, though he is unable to give to himself, or to us, even a lame verbal description of it, he can yet play the part to the life; and if he does so, he cannot then say that he is unable to think how the publican behaves when annoyed. Mimicking him *is* thinking how he behaves. If we ask the person how he thinks the publican acted, we shall not reject a response given by impersonation and demand instead of response given in prose. Indeed, so far from the concept of pretending to be cross requiring for its elucidation a causal story about operations of planning shepherding operations of acting quasi-crossly, the converse is the case. To explain the sense in which planning a line of conduct leads to the pursuance of that line of conduct, it is necessary to show that executing a planned task, is doing, not two things, but one thing. But the thing done is an act of a higher order, since its description has a logical complexity, like that which characterises the descriptions of pretending and obeying. To do what one has planned to do and to growl like a bear are both relatively sophisticated occupations. To describe them, we have obliquely to mention doings, whose description embodies no corresponding oblique mentions. Of the same type are acts of repenting of what one has done, keeping a resolution, jeering at another's performance and complying with the rules. In all these cases, as well as in many others, the doing of the higher order acts involves the thought of the lower order acts; yet the phrase 'involves the thought of' does not connote the collateral occurrence of another, cogitative act.

One variety of pretending is worthy of mention at this point. A person engaged in a planning or theorising task may find it useful or amusing to go through the motions of thinking thoughts which are not, or are not yet, what he is disposed ingenuously to think. Assuming, supposing, entertaining, toying with ideas and considering suggestions are all ways of pretending to adopt schemes or theories. The sentences in which the propositions entertained are expressed are not being ingenuously used; they are being mock-used. There are, metaphorically speaking, inverted commas round them. Their employer is wielding them with his intellectual tongue in his cheek; he utters them in a hypothetical, not in a categorical frame of mind. Very likely he advertises the fact that he is wielding his sentences in a sophisticated and not in a naive way by using such special signals as the words 'if', 'suppose', 'granting', 'say' and so on. Or, he may talk aloud, or to himself, in a sparring, instead of a fighting tone of voice. But he may still be misunderstood and accused of seriously meaning what he says, and then he has to explain that he had not been committing himself to what he had been asserting, but only considering just what he would have been committing himself to, had he done so. He had been trying out the thought, perhaps to give himself practice in it. That is to say, supposing is a more sophisticated operation than ingenuous thinking. We have to learn to give verdicts before we can learn to operate with suspended judgments.

This point is worth making, partly for its intimate connection with the concept of imagining and partly because logicians and epistemologists sometimes assume, what I for a long time assumed, that entertaining a proposition is a more elementary or naive performance than affirming that something is the case, and, what follows, that learning, for example, how to use 'therefore' requires first having learned to use 'if'. This is a mistake. The concept of make-believe is of a higher order than that of belief.

(6) *Pretending, Fancying and Imaging.*

There is not much difference between a child playing at being a pirate, and one fancying that he is a pirate. So far as there is a difference, it seems to come to this, that we use words like 'play', 'pretend' and 'act the part', when we think of spectators finding the performance more or less convincing, whereas we use words like 'fancy' and 'imagine' when we are thinking of the actor himself being half-convinced; and we use words like 'play' and 'pretend' for deliberate, concerted and rehearsed performances, whereas we are more ready to use words like 'fancy' and 'imagine' for those activities of make-believe into which people casually and even involuntarily drift. Underlying these two differences there is, perhaps, this more radical difference, that we apply the words 'pretend' and 'act the part', where an overt and muscular representation is given of whatever deed or condition is being put on, while we tend, with plenty of exceptions, to reserve 'imagine' and 'fancy' for some things that people do inaudibly and invisibly because 'in their heads', i.e. for their fancied perceptions and not for their mock-actions.

It is with this special brand of make-believe that we are here chiefly concerned, namely what we call 'imaging', 'visualising', 'seeing in the mind's eye' and 'going through in one's head'. Even people who might allow that sparring consists in going through some of the motions of fighting in a hypothetical manner will not readily allow that the same sort of account holds good of seeing Helvellyn in one's mind's eye. What motions are there here to go through in a hypothetical manner? Even though in describing how the dipsomaniac 'sees' snakes we use inverted commas, as we do in describing how the child 'scalps' his nurse, or how the boxer 'punishes' his sparring partner, it will be urged that the force of these commas is not the same in the two sorts of cases. Picturing is not sham-seeing in the way that sparring is sham-fighting.

We have, I hope, got rid of the idea that picturing Helvellyn is seeing a picture of Helvellyn, or that having 'Lillibullero' running in one's head is listening to a private reproduction, or internal echo, of that tune. It is necessary now to get rid of a more subtle superstition. Epistemologists have long encouraged us to suppose that a mental picture, or a visual image, stands to a visual sensation in something like the relation of an echo to a noise, a bruise to a blow or a reflection in a mirror to the face reflected. To make this point more specific, it has been supposed that what is taking place, when I 'see', or 'hear', or 'smell', corresponds to that element in perceiving which is purely sensuous; and not to that element which constitutes recognising or making out; i.e. that imaging is a piece of near-sentience and not of a function of intelligence, since it consists in having, not indeed a proper sensation, but a shadow-sensation.

But this opinion is completely false. Whereas an unknown tune may be played in a person's hearing, so that he hears the tune without knowing how it goes, we cannot say of a person in whose head a tune is running that he does not know how it goes. Having a tune running in one's head is one familiar way in which knowledge of how that tune goes is utilised. So having a tune running in one's head is not to be likened to the mere having of auditory sensations; it is to be likened rather to the process of following a familiar tune, and following a heard tune is not a function of sentience.

Similarly, if I peer through a hole in a hedge on a misty day, I may not be able to identify what I see as a watercourse flowing in spate down a mountainside. But it would be absurd for someone to say 'I vividly see something in my mind's eye, but I cannot make out even what sort of a thing it is'. True, I can see a face in my mind's eye and fail to put a name to its owner, just as I can have a tune in my head, the name of which I have forgotten. But I know how the tune goes and I know what sort of a face I am picturing. Seeing the face in my mind's eye is one of the things which my knowledge of the face enables me to do; describing it in words is another and a rarer ability; recognising it at sight in the flesh is the commonest of all.

We saw in the previous chapter that perceiving entails both having sensations and something else which can be called, in a strained sense, 'thinking'. We can now say that to picture, image or fancy one sees or hears also entails thinking, in this strained sense. Indeed, this should be obvious, if we consider that our picturing of something must be characterisable as more or less vivid, clear, faithful and accurate, adjectives which connote not merely the possession but the use of the knowledge of how the object pictured does or would really look. It would be absurd for me to say that the smell of burning peat comes vividly back to me, but that I should not recognise the smell, if the peat were smoking in my presence. Imaging, therefore, is not a function of pure sentience; and a creature which had sensations, but could not learn, could not 'see', or picture, things any more than it could spell.

A person with a tune running in his head is using his knowledge of how the tune goes; he is in a certain way realising what he would be hearing, if he were listening to the tune being played. Somewhat as the boxer, when sparring, is hitting and parrying in a hypothetical manner, so the person with a tune running in his head may be described as following the tune in a hypothetical manner. Further, just as the actor is not really murdering anyone, so the person picturing Helvellyn is not really seeing Helvellyn. Indeed, as we know, he may have his eyes shut, while he pictures the mountain. Picturing Helvellyn, so far from having, or being akin to having, visual sensations, is compatible with having no such sensations and nothing akin to them. There *is* nothing akin to sensations. Realising, in this way, how Helvellyn would look is doing something which stands in the same relation to seeing Helvellyn as sophisticated performances stand to those more naive performances, whose mention is obliquely contained in the description of the higher order performances.

But there remains, or appears to remain, a crucial difference, which may be brought out thus. A sailor, asked to demonstrate how a certain knot is tied, finds that he has no cord with which to demonstrate. However, he does nearly as well by merely going through the motions of knotting a cord empty-handed. His spectators see how he would tie the knot by seeing how he manoeuvres his hands and fingers without any cord in them. Now although he is, so to speak, hypothetically knotting cord, still he is really moving his hands and fingers. But a person picturing Helvellyn with his eyes shut, while he is certainly enjoying, so to speak, only a hypothetical view of the mountain, does not seem to be really doing anything. Perhaps his non-existent visual sensations correspond to the sailor's non-existent piece of string, but what corresponds to the movements of his hands and fingers? The sailor does show the spectators how the knot would be tied; but the person visualising Helvellyn does not thereby show to his companion its contours or its colouring. Does he even show them to himself?

This difference between the two varieties of make-believe is, however, nothing but a consequence of the difference between perceiving something and bringing something about. This difference is not a difference between bringing something about privily and bringing something about overtly, for perceiving is not bringing anything about. It is getting something or, sometimes, keeping something; but it is not effecting anything. Seeing and hearing are neither witnessed nor unwitnessed doings, for they are not doings. It makes no sense to say 'I saw you seeing the sunset', or 'I failed to watch myself hearing the music'. And if it makes no sense to speak of my witnessing, or failing to witness, a piece of hearing or seeing, *a fortiori* it makes no sense to speak of my witnessing, or failing to witness, a piece of fancied hearing or fancied seeing. No hearing or seeing is taking place.

In the concert-hall a man's neighbour can, perhaps, see him beating time to the music and even overhear him half-whistling or half-humming to himself the tune the band is playing. But not only do we not say that his neighbour sees, or overhears, him hearing the music, as he sees or overhears him accompanying it, but we do not say, either, that his neighbour fails to witness him hearing the music. 'Secretly' and 'openly' do not attach to 'hearing', as they can attach to 'cursing' and 'plotting'. A *fortiori*, while his neighbour in the train may detect him beating time to a tune that is running in his head, he does not claim either to detect, or to fail to detect, his 'hearing' of the imagined tune.

Next, as we saw in the last chapter, following a known tune involves not only hearing the notes, but also much more than that. It involves, so to speak, having the proper niche ready for each note as it comes. Each note comes as and when it was expected to come; what is heard is what was listened for.

This listening for the due notes entails having learned and not forgotten the tune and is therefore a product of training and is not a mere function of aural sensitiveness. A deafish man may follow a tune better than one who hears it better.

A person listening to a moderately familiar tune may on some occasions describe himself as having got the tune wrong, meaning by this that, though he was not himself playing or humming the tune, but only listening to it, yet here and there he listened for notes other than those which were really due to come; and he was taken by surprise to hear a particular movement beginning when it did, though he also recognised that it was his mistake to be surprised. It must be noticed that his error about the course of the tune need not have been, and ordinarily would not have been, formulated in a false sentence, private or public; all he 'did' was to be listening for what was not due to come, in place of what was due to come, and this listening for notes is not a deed done, or a series of deeds done.

This very point brings us to the case of a person following an imagined tune. To expect a tune to take one course, when it is actually taking another, is already to suppose, fancy or imagine. When what is heard is not what was listened for, what was listened for can be described only as notes which might have been heard, and the frame of mind in which they were listened for was therefore one of erroneous expectancy. The listener is disappointed, or abashed, by what he actually hears. A person going through a tune entirely in his head is in a partially similar case. He, too, listens for something which he does not get, though he is well aware all the time that he is not going to get it. He too can get the tune wrong, and either realise, or fail to realise, that he does so, a fact which by itself shows that imaging is not merely the having of sensations or sensation-echoes, since this could not be characterised as the acceptance of either a wrong or a correct version of a tune.

Going through a tune in one's head is like following a heard tune and is, indeed, a sort of rehearsal of it. But what makes the imaginative operation similar to the other is not, as is often supposed, that it incorporates the hearing of ghosts of notes similar in all but loudness to the heard notes of the real tune, but the fact that both are utilisations of knowledge of how the tune goes. This knowledge is exercised in recognising and following the tune, when actually heard; it is exercised in humming or playing it; in noticing the errors in its misperformance; it is also exercised in fancying oneself humming or playing it and in fancying oneself merely listening to it. Knowing a tune just is being able to do some such things as recognise and follow it, produce it, detect errors in the playing of it and go through it in one's head. We should not allow that a person had been unable to think how the tune went, who had whistled it correctly or gone through it in his head. Doing such things *is* thinking how the tune goes.

But the purely imaginative exercise is more sophisticated than that of following the tune, when heard, or than that of humming it; since it involves the thought of following or producing the tune, in the way in which sparring involves the thought of fighting in earnest, or in the way in which uttering something at second hand involves the thought of its first hand utterance. Fancying one is listening to a known tune involves 'listening for' the notes which would be due to be heard, were the tune being really performed. It is to listen for those notes in a hypothetical manner. Similarly, fancying one is humming a known tune involves 'making ready' for the notes which would be due to be hummed, were the tune actually being hummed. It is to make ready for those notes in a hypothetical manner. It is not humming very, very quietly, but rather it is deliberately not doing those pieces of humming which would be due, if one were not trying to keep the peace. We might say that imagining oneself talking or humming is a series of abstentions from producing the noises which would be the due words or notes to produce, if one were talking or humming aloud. That is why such operations are impenetrably secret; not that the words or notes are being produced in a hermetic cell, but that the operations consist of abstentions from producing them. That, too, is why learning to fancy one is talking or humming comes later than learning to talk or hum. Silent soliloquy is a flow of pregnant non-sayings. Refraining from saying things, of course, entails knowing both what one would have said and how one would have said it.

Doubtless some people on some occasions of imagining tunes fancy themselves not merely passively hearkening but also actively producing the notes, just as most imagined discourse contains not only imagined hearing but also imagined speaking. Very likely, too, people who imagine themselves producing noises tend to activate slightly those muscles which they would be activating fully, if they were singing or talking aloud, since complete abstention is harder than partial abstention. But these are questions of fact with which we are not concerned. Our concern is to find out what it means to say, e.g. that someone 'hears' something that he is not hearing.

The application of this account to visual and other imagery is not difficult. Seeing Helvellyn in one's mind's eye does not entail, what seeing Helvellyn and seeing snapshots of Helvellyn entail, the having of visual sensations. It does involve the thought of having a view of Helvellyn and it is therefore a more sophisticated operation than that of having a view of Helvellyn. It is one utilisation among others of the knowledge of how Helvellyn should look, or, in one sense of the verb, it is thinking how it should look. The expectations which are fulfilled in the recognition at sight of Helvellyn are not indeed fulfilled in picturing it, but the picturing of it is something like a rehearsal of getting them fulfilled. So far from picturing involving the having of faint sensations, or wraiths of sensations, it involves missing just what one would be due to get, if one were seeing the mountain.

Certainly not all imaging is the picturing of real faces and mountains, or the 'hearing' of familiar tunes and known voices. We can fancy ourselves looking at fabulous mountains. Composers, presumably, can fancy themselves listening to tunes that have never yet been played. It may be supposed, accordingly, that in such cases there is no question of the imaginary scene being pictured right, or of the tune still under composition being 'heard' to go otherwise than as it really goes; any more than Hans Andersen could be either accused of misreporting the careers of his characters, or praised for the factual fidelity of his narratives.

Consider the parallels of pretending and quoting. An actor on one day plays the part of a Frenchman; on the next day he has to play the part of a visitor from Mars. We know how the former representation might be convincing or unconvincing; but how could the latter? Or I might start by quoting what you have said and go on by giving utterance to what you would or could have said. We know what it is for a quotation to be accurate, but a pretence quotation cannot be either accurate or inaccurate; it can only be, in some remoter sense, in character or out of character, by being, or failing to be, the sort of thing that you would or could have said. None the less, the actor is pretending to give a convincing representation of the man from Mars, and I am pretending that I am quoting your very words. It is just a piece of double representation. A boy mimicking a boxer sparring is in a similar case, for he is not fighting and he is not rehearsing fighting; he is staging some of the moves of a person rehearsing fighting. He is mock-mock-fighting. As the predicates by which we comment on fighting do not attach to sparring, so the predicates by which we comment on sparring do not attach to mimicries of sparring. Correspondingly, not only do the predicates by which we comment on our view of Helvellyn not attach to the manner in which we picture Helvellyn, but also the predicates by which we comment on our visualisations of Helvellyn do not attach to our visualisations of Atlantis or Jack's Beanstalk. None the less, we pretend that this is how Atlantis and the Beanstalk would have looked. We are doing a piece of double imagining.

We are now in a position to locate and correct an error made by Hume. Supposing, wrongly, that to 'see' or 'hear' is to have a shadow-sensation (which involves the further error of supposing that there could be shadow-sensations), he put forward the causal theory that one could not have a particular 'idea' without having previously had a corresponding sensation, somewhat as having an angular bruise involves having been previously struck by an angular object. The colours that I see in my mind's eye are, he seems to have thought, traces somehow left by the colours previously seen by me with my eyes open. The only thing that is true in this account is that what I see in my mind's eye and what I hear 'in my head' is tied in certain ways to what I have previously seen and heard. But the nature of this tie is not at all what Hume supposed.

We saw that mock-actions presuppose ingenuous actions, in the sense that performing the former involves, in a special sense, the thought of the latter. A person who had not learned how bears growl, or how murderers commit murders, could not play bears, or act murders. Nor could he criticise the acting. In the same way, a person who had not learned how blue things look, or how the postman's knock sounds, could not see blue things in his mind's eye, or 'hear' the postman's knock; nor could he recognise blue things, or postman's knocks. Now we learn how things look and sound chiefly and originally by seeing and hearing them. Imaging, being one among many ways of utilising knowledge, requires that the relevant knowledge has been got and not lost. We no more need a para-mechanical theory of traces to account for our limited ability to see things in our mind's eyes than we need it to account for our limited ability to translate French into English. All that is required is to see that learning perceptual lessons entails some perceiving, that applying those lessons entails having learned them, and that imaging is one way of applying those lessons. Addicts of the trace theory should try to fit their theory to the case of a tune running in someone's head. Is this a revived trace of an auditory sensation; or a series of revived traces of a series of auditory sensations?

(7) *Memory.*

It is convenient to append to this discussion of imagination a brief excursus on remembering. We must begin by noticing two widely different ways in which the verb 'to remember' is commonly used.

(a) By far the most important and the least discussed use of the verb is that use in which remembering something means having learned something and not forgotten it. This is the sense in which we speak of remembering the Greek alphabet, or the way from the gravel-pit to the bathing-place, or the proof of a theorem, or how to bicycle, or that the next meeting of the Board will be in the last week of July. To say that a person has not forgotten something is not to say that he is now doing or undergoing anything, or even that he regularly or occasionally does or undergoes anything. It is to say that he *can* do certain things, such as go through the Greek alphabet, direct a stranger back from the bathing-place to the gravel-pit and correct someone who says that the next meeting of the Board is in the second week in July.

What, in this use, is said to be remembered is any learned lesson, and what is learned and not forgotten need have nothing to do with the past, though the learning of it of course precedes the condition of not having forgotten it. 'Remember' in this use is often, though not always, an allowable paraphrase of the verb 'to know'.

(b) Quite different from this is the use of the verb 'to remember' in which a person is said to have remembered, or been recollecting, something at a particular moment, or is said to be now recalling, reviewing or dwelling on some episode of his own past. In this use, remembering is an occurrence; it is something which a person may try successfully, or in vain, to do; it occupies his attention for a time and he may do it with pleasure or distress and with ease or effort. The barrister presses the witness to recall things, where the teacher trains his pupils not to forget things.

Recalling has certain features in common with imagining. I recall only what I myself have seen, heard, done and felt, just as what I imagine is myself seeing, hearing, doing and noticing things; and I recall as I imagine, relatively vividly, relatively easily and relatively connectedly. Moreover, much as I imagine things sometimes deliberately and sometimes involuntarily, so I recall things sometimes deliberately and sometimes involuntarily.

There is an important connection between the notion of not-forgetting and the notion of recollecting. To say that a person either actually is recalling something, or can recall, or be reminded of it, implies that he has not forgotten it; whereas to say that he has not forgotten something does not entail that he ever does or could recall it. There would be a contradiction in saying that I can or do recollect the incidents that I witnessed taking place at a picnic, though I no longer know what occurred there. There is no contradiction in saying that I know when I was born, or that I had my appendix removed, though I cannot recall the episodes. There would be an absurdity in saying that I do or can recall Napoleon losing the Battle of Waterloo, or how to translate English into Greek, though I have not forgotten these things; since these are not the sorts of things that can be recalled, in the sense of the verb in which what I recall must be things that I have myself witnessed, done or experienced.

Theorists speak sometimes of memory-knowledge, memory-belief and the evidence of memory, and, when discussing the 'sources' of knowledge and the ways by which we come to know things, they sometimes talk as if memory were one such 'source' and as if remembering were one such way of coming to know things. Memory is, accordingly, sometimes ranged alongside of perception and inference as a cognitive faculty or power; or remembering is ranged alongside of perceiving and inferring as a cognitive act or process.

This is a mistake. If a witness is asked how he knows that something took place, he may reply that he witnessed it, or that he was told of it, or that he inferred to it from what he witnessed or was told. He could not reply that he found out what took place either by not forgetting what he had found out, or by recalling finding it out. Reminiscence and not-forgetting are neither 'sources' of knowledge, nor, if this is anything different, ways of getting to know. The former entails having learned and not forgotten; the latter is having learned and not forgotten. Neither of them is a sort of learning, discovering or establishing. Still less is recalling what took place using a piece of evidence from which certain or probable inferences are made to what took place, save in the sense that the jury may infer from what the witness narrates. The witness himself does not argue 'I recall the collision occurring just after the thunder-clap, so probably the collision occurred just after the thunder-clap'. There is no such inference; and even if there were, the good witness is one who is good at recollecting, not one who is good at inferring.

Certainly the witness may be forced to admit, even to his surprise, that he must have been drawing on his imagination, since, for one reason or another, he could not have been recalling what he professed to be recalling; in other circumstances he may volunteer that he himself has doubts whether he is recalling, or making things up. But it does not follow from the fact that alleged reminiscences may be fabrications that veracious reminiscences are discoveries or successful investigations. A person who is asked to tell what is known of the Milky Way, or to draw a map of the rivers and railways of Berkshire, may say and draw things which he does not know to represent the facts, and he may be surprised to find that he has been doing this, or be uncertain whether he is doing it. But no one thinks that telling and drawing are 'sources' of knowledge, ways of finding things out, or bits of evidence from which discoveries can be made by inference. Telling and drawing things are, at best, ways of conveying lessons already learned. So is recalling a conning of something already learned. It is going over something, not getting to something; it is like recounting, not like researching. A person may recall a particular episode twenty times in a day. No one would say that he twenty times discovered what happened. If the last nineteen reviewings were not discoveries, nor was the first.

The stock accounts given of reminiscence give the impression that when a person recalls an episode belonging to his own past history, the details of the episode must come back to him in imagery. He must 'see' the details 'in his mind's eye', or 'hear' them 'in his head'. But there is no 'must' about it. If a concert-goer wishes to recollect just how the violinist misplayed a certain piece, he may whistle the bungled tune, or play it on his own fiddle just as the artist had done it; and, if he repeats the mistake faithfully, he is certainly recollecting the artist's error. This might be his only way of recalling how the artist had gone wrong, since he may be poor at going over tunes in his head. Similarly a good mimic might recapture the preacher's gestures and grimaces only by reproducing them with his own hands and on his own face, since he may be poor at seeing things in his mind's eye. Or a good draughtsman may fail to recollect the lines and the rigging of a yacht, until he is given a pencil with which to delineate them on paper. If their mimicries and delineations are good and if, when they go wrong, their authors duly correct them without being prompted, their companions will be satisfied that they have recollected what they had seen, without desiring any additional information about the vividness, copiousness or connectedness of their visual imagery or even about its existence.

No one would say that the concert-goer, the mimic or the draughtsman had got to know anything by reproducing the misplayed tune, the preacher's gestures, or the lines of the yacht, but only that they had shown how the tune had been heard to be misplayed, how the preacher had been seen to gesticulate and how the yacht had been seen to be shaped and rigged. Reminiscence in imagery does not differ in principle, though it tends to be superior in speed, if otherwise greatly inferior in efficiency; and it is, of course, of no direct public utility.

People are apt grossly to exaggerate the photographic fidelity of their visual imagery. The main reason for this exaggeration seems to be that they find that very often, particularly when suitably prompted and questioned, they can give very comprehensive, detailed and well-ordered verbal descriptions of episodes at which they have been present. They are then tempted to suppose that, since they can describe such bygone episodes nearly as well now as they could have done during their occurrence, they must be checking their narratives against some present replicas or souvenirs of the vanished scene. If a description of a face is about as good in the absence as in the presence of the face, this must be due to the presence of something like a photograph of the face. But this is a gratuitous causal hypothesis. The question, 'How can I faithfully describe what I once witnessed?' is no more of a puzzle than the question, 'How can I faithfully visualise what I once witnessed?' Ability to describe things learned by personal experience is one of the knacks we expect of linguistically competent people; ability to visualise parts of it is another thing that we expect in some degree of most people and in high degree of children, dress-designers, policemen and cartoonists.

Reminiscing, then, can take the form of faithful verbal narration. When it does so, it differs from reminiscence by mimicry and reminiscence by sketching inasmuch as what took place is told and not portrayed (though the telling often embodies some dramatic portrayal as well). Clearly, here, too, no one would wish to speak as if narration were either a 'source' of knowledge, or a way of acquiring knowledge. It belongs not to the stages of manufacture and assembly, but to the stage of export. It is akin not to learning lessons, but to reciting them.

People are, however, strongly tempted to think that vivid visual recall must be a sort of seeing and therefore a sort of finding. One motive of this mistake may be brought out as follows. If a person learns that a naval engagement has taken place, without himself having been a witness of it, he may deliberately or involuntarily picture the scene in visual imagery. Very likely he soon settles down to picturing it in a fairly uniform way whenever he thinks of the battle, much as he is likely to settle down to describing the episode in a fairly uniformly worded narrative, whenever he is called on to tell the story. But though he cannot, perhaps, easily help picturing the scene in his now routine manner, still he recognises a difference between his habitual way of picturing scenes of which he was not a witness and the way in which unforgotten episodes of which he was a witness 'come back' to him in visual imagery. These, too, he cannot help picturing in a uniform way, but their uniformity seems to him compulsory and not merely settled by repetition. He cannot now 'see' the episode as he pleases, any more than he could originally have seen it as he pleased. He could not originally have seen the thimble elsewhere than on the corner of the mantelpiece, since that is where it was. Nor, however hard he tries, can he now recall seeing it elsewhere, for all that he can, if he likes, imagine seeing it lying in the scuttle. Indeed he may well imagine seeing it in the scuttle, while repudiating someone else's allegation that that is where it was.

The reader of a report of a race can, subject to certain restrictions imposed by the text of the report, first picture the race in one way and then deliberately or involuntarily picture it in a different and perhaps conflicting way; but a witness of the race feels that, while he can call back further views of the race, yet alternative views are rigidly ruled out. This is what makes it tempting to say that reminiscence by imaging has in it something analogous to scanning a photograph, or to listening to a gramophone record. The 'cannot' in 'I cannot "see" the episode save in one way' is tacitly assimilated to the mechanical 'cannot' in 'the camera cannot lie', or in 'the record cannot vary the tune'. But in fact the 'cannot', in 'I cannot "see" the episode save in one way' is like that in 'I cannot spell "Edinburgh" as I like'. I cannot write down the correct letters in the correct order and at the same time be writing down any other arrangement of letters; I cannot be spelling out 'Edinburgh' as I know it should be spelled out and also be spelling it out in any other way. Nothing forces my hand to spell it in one way rather than another; but simple logic excludes the possibility of my both producing what I know to be the required spelling and producing an arbitrary spelling in one and the same operation. Similarly, nothing forces me to do any picturing at all, or to do my picturing in this way rather than that; but if I am recalling how the scene looked when I witnessed it, then my picturing is not arbitrary. Nor in making my way from the gravel-pit to the bathing-place am I forced to take this rather than any other footpath. But if I know that this is the right path, then I cannot, in logic, both take the path known to be the correct one and also take any other path.

Consider again the case of the concert-goer who reproduces the violinist's mistake by whistling the bars as the violinist had misplayed them. The only sense in which he 'has' to whistle as he does, is that he will not be reproducing the violinist's mistake if he whistles anything else. He whistles what he whistles because he has not forgotten what he heard the violinist do. But this is not a cause-effect 'because'. His whistling is not causally controlled or governed either by the violinist's misperformance, or by his own original hearing of it. Rather, to say that he has not forgotten what he heard is to say that he can do some such things as faithfully reproduce the mistake by whistling it. As long as he continues to bear in mind the violinist's mistake, he continues to be able and ready to do some such things as to show what the mistake was by faithfully re-performing it. This is what is meant by 'bear in mind'.

If a child is set to recite a poem, but gets it wrong, or partly wrong, we do not say that he has recited the poem. Nor is a misquotation a sort of quotation. If we are told that someone has spelled or construed something, we do not ask,

'But did he get it right?', since it would not be spelling or construing if it were misspelling or misconstruing. But of course there do exist uses of these verbs in which they have the same force as the phrases 'try to spell', or 'try to construe'. In these uses they can be significantly qualified by 'unsuccessfully'.

'Recall', save when it means 'try to recall', is in the same way a 'got it' verb. 'Recall unsuccessfully' and 'recall incorrectly' are illegitimate phrases. But this does not mean that we have a privileged faculty which, given its head, carries us to our destination without our having to be careful. It means only that if, for example, we picture incidents otherwise than as we know they looked, then we are not recalling, any more than we are quoting, if we ascribe other words to a speaker than those which we know he uttered. Recalling is something which we sometimes have to try hard and which we often fail to bring off; and very often we do not know whether we have brought it off or not. So we may claim to have recalled something and later be persuaded to withdraw the claim. But though 'recall' is a 'got it' verb, it is not a verb of finding, solving or proving. Rather, like 'reciting', 'quoting', 'depicting' and 'mimicking', it is a verb of showing, or is at least affiliated to such verbs. Being good at recalling is not being good at investigating, but being good at presenting. It is a narrative skill, if 'narrative' be allowed to cover non-prosaic as well as prosaic representations. That is why we describe recollections as relatively faithful, vivid and accurate and not as original, brilliant or acute. Nor do we call people 'clever' or 'observant' merely because things come back to them well. An anecdotalist is not a sort of detective.

IMAGINATION

J. M. Shorter

In his chapter on Imagination,[1] Professor Ryle seeks to show that 'seeing things in the mind's eye does not involve the existence of things seen or the occurrence of acts of seeing them', and that 'The question "Where do the things and happenings exist which people imagine existing?" is a spurious one'. His argument appears to run as follows. When we say someone 'sees' something we mean something quite different by the word "'see'" from what we mean when we say he sees something. The inverted commas are important. 'Whereas they (people) see trees and hear music, they only 'see' and 'hear' the objects of recollection and imagination.' Again 'A person who says that he 'sees' the home of his childhood is often prepared to describe his vision as 'vivid', 'faithful', 'life-like', adjectives which he would never apply to his sight of what is in front of his nose.' This shows how entirely different 'seeing' is from seeing. What then is the difference between the two? To 'see' something is to imagine that one sees something. 'Having a mental picture of Helvellyn is imagining that we see Helvellyn in front of our noses, and having a tune running in one's head is imagining that one has the tune being played in one's hearing'. The point of such phrases is that they are factual disclaimers. They deny that we saw Helvellyn and do not assert that we saw something else, namely a sort of copy of Helvellyn, or a mental image. Mental images therefore do not exist. We do not see them, and it is a spurious question to ask about their locations.

J. M. Shorter is a professor at Canterbury University College, Christchurch, New Zealand. His articles have appeared in *Mind*, *Analysis*, and the *Australasian Journal of Philosophy*.

[1] *Concept of Mind.* Ch. viii [pp. 117–153].

Now it may be admitted that 'seeing' something is not to be described as seeing a special sort of copy of something. Though it is not very far out in some cases of 'seeing'. For example, we may say " 'See' an oasis" or "See a mirage". Apart from this, however, most of what Ryle says is not correct.

In the first place he seems a little arbitrary in deciding what are and what are not spurious questions. 'Do mental images exist?' is a genuine question to which the answer is that they do not. On the other hand 'Where do they exist?' is spurious. This way of talking suggests a parallel between 'Do unicorns exist?' and 'Where are they to be found?' The latter may be regarded as spurious because there are not any unicorns. But 'spurious' is surely the wrong word here. In a philosophical context 'spurious question' implies 'meaningless question'. But in this case the question makes perfect sense, but, the world being what it is, it just does not arise. Anyone who asks it is misinformed about the empirical facts. In the case of images this is not the case. What Ryle really seems to have in mind is that both questions make no sense. Both arise from thinking that any question that may be asked about such things as tables, chairs, or unicorns, can also be asked about mental images. However, this point need not be pressed. It is not uncommon to express the fact that it is nonsense to talk of something existing by saying that it does not exist. It is a more or less recognised alternative to saying that the question about its existence is a spurious one. But it is dangerously misleading to combine both ways of talking.

There are, however, other errors. Ryle fails to make any distinction between the various senses of the word 'see' when it is used in inverted commas. It is this failure which makes his account of visualising seem plausible. Indeed he does not just blur or ignore such distinctions, but positively denies their existence. Visualising, or having Helvellyn before the mind's eye, is 'a special case of imagining'.[2] A man suffering from delirium tremens may imagine that he sees snakes. A perfectly healthy person, casting his mind back to his holiday in the Lakes, may imagine that he sees Helvellyn. Presumably

[2] *Op. cit.*, p. 256 [p. 129].

the only reason that we do not use the word 'visualise' in the first case is that the man is in a peculiar state. This is clearly incorrect. If a man imagines that he sees snakes, he is mistaken, he thinks he sees snakes but does not. If he visualises snakes, he may do this quite deliberately and does not think there are really any snakes about. The concept of imagining is to be illuminated by distinguishing visualising or picturing from the sort of imagining that a drunkard does, not by identifying the two. One can see that it is wrong to identify the two from the fact that, as Ryle points out, we can use with the verb 'to picture' adverbs like 'faithfully'. But can the drunkard's 'vision' be described as faithful any more than our 'sight' of something in front of us?

It is illuminating to make explicit the reason why we can use words like 'vivid', 'faithful' and 'lifelike' in connexion with picturing or visualising. The reason is that the logic of words like 'picture', 'visualise', and 'see in the mind's eye' is to some extent parallel to that of 'depict', and 'draw a picture of'. We can depict something vividly, faithfully or in a lifelike manner, or we can picture something in these ways. Thus when it is said that 'seeing in the mind's eye is one thing and seeing is another', there are two points to be added. First 'see in the mind's eye' is a misleading expression in a way that 'picture' is not. The analogue of 'seeing' and picturing is not seeing, but depicting. Second, seeing in the mind's eye or picturing, what might best be called "'depicting'", is not the same thing as depicting. It is depicting only in a metaphorical sense and is not even metaphorical seeing.

This analogy (partial logical parallelism) between depicting and visualising throws light on a number of points. It shows what is wrong with saying that visualising Helvellyn is the same thing as seeing an image of that mountain. It is wrong for the same reason that it is wrong to say that drawing a picture of Helvellyn is drawing a picture of a picture of Helvellyn. When I depict Helvellyn it is Helvellyn itself I depict, not the picture I make while depicting Helvellyn. The things I can visualise are just the things I can depict, real physical objects like lions, or else imaginary ones like unicorns, not pictures in the one case or visual images in the other. Again Ryle says that visualising is not a matter of 'pure sentience'. But this is not because visualising belongs to that aspect of perceiving that might be described 'in a strained sense' as thinking. It is because visualising does not correspond to perceiving at all. Visualising is not mock-seeing. Visualising is *doing* something in a way that seeing is not doing something, and more in a way that depicting *is* doing something. One can be ordered to depict or to visualise something, one cannot be ordered to see it.

We have now shown that visualising something is not seeing a mental image of something. We have not shown that we do not see mental images. This, however, would have to be something different from visualising, just as seeing a picture is different from depicting something. We have stated that the logic of 'visualising' is parallel to that of 'depicting'. We do see pictures. So, if the parallel was complete, we would see mental pictures also. That is to say the expression 'see a mental picture' would have a use. But it has not got a use. It is not normally used. Moreover, when it is introduced by philosophers it is supposed to be synonymous with 'visualise something', and to elucidate what we mean by this phrase. In this case it is not parallel to 'see a (real) picture', which is not synonymous with 'depict something'. The parallel is just not complete, and this is a fact about the English language. It is not, however, *just* a fact about language. For it is a fact about the non-linguistic world that it is not of such a nature that it would be convenient to give a use to the expression 'see a mental image'. One might express this, not improperly, by saying that the parallel between depicting and visualising extends only a certain way. The same applies to other questions such as 'Do mental images exist?', 'Are they in a space of their own?' and so on. We have no use for such expressions as 'Such and such a mental image is no longer in existence'. Such expressions have no use because we do not do anything that it is natural to describe in these terms. Let us make this point clearer by indicating what it would be like to 'visualise' in a way that might tempt us to give a use to these expressions. To do this it is necessary to use familiar words in an extended sense, as is usually the case when we are describing phenomena different from any we have met before. This procedure is justified, though it must be used with care, and is in accordance with ordinary practice. We are not debarred from extending the use of a word where convenient, and others usually contrive to understand what we are getting at provided that they are co-operative. Suppose that when we visualised anything the image stayed put until we visualised it being rubbed out. If we had visualised a house and then wanted to visualise a triangle, we should have to visualise a house and a triangle side by side unless we first 'rubbed out' the house. Perhaps we might visualise a triangle superimposed on a house, but that would be confusing. Again suppose there is a limit to the number of things we can visualise, if we go on visualising new things without 'rubbing out' the images of the old ones. That is to say we just cannot produce another image to the right of our right hand image, and so on. Moreover, if we visualise things very small we can get more on to our 'mental screen'. Now, if things were like this, it might be convenient to ask questions that it is in fact not proper to ask. One might ask 'Is that mental picture you produced yesterday still in existence, or have you rubbed it out?' Or, 'Where is it?'; to which the reply might be 'At the bottom left hand corner of my mental screen.' If this were so, it would be as correct to say 'mental images exist' as it is to say 'physical objects exist'. Both these statements would be logical statements to the effect that statements like 'that chair no longer exists' or 'the image of the chair I had yesterday no longer exists', have a use in English. That mental images do not exist is therefore best described as both a logical and an empirical fact. Alternatively one might say that it can be taken in two ways. (1) Such expressions as 'That image no longer exists' have no use. (2) The world is such that it is not convenient to give a use to such expressions. The former expresses a linguistic, the latter a non-linguistic fact.

We may now examine more closely the various senses of "'see'". It was by confusing these different senses that Ryle was led to equate seeing in the mind's eye with imagining that one sees. We say someone 'sees' something in a variety of different situations. At the cinema we may 'see' a car driving along the road. Now in this sense the theory of 'seeing' that Ryle attacks comes into its own. We do really see a picture of a car. Only this sort of 'seeing' has nothing to do with imagination. A case which has something to do with imagining, and is fairly like this is that of 'seeing' an oasis. We can say either "'see' an oasis" or 'see a mirage', but not "'see' a mirage". Similarly at the cinema it is wrong to say "'see' a picture of a car". A mirage, however, is not a picture of anything. What is the difference between the expressions "'see' an oasis" and 'imagine that you see an oasis'? It is that the latter tends to be reserved for cases where one is taken in or is in some danger of being taken in. An old hand at desert travelling might be said to have 'seen' several oases in the course of a journey, but he would indignantly deny having imagined that he saw any. 'He imagined he saw' is closer to 'He thought he saw'; Though perhaps the former implies that he definitely did not see, whereas the latter suggests only that he may not have done. The former is in fact a factual disclaimer, whereas the latter expresses doubt about the facts. These two same expressions cover a wide range of phenomena. The man who has an hallucination thinks he sees and imagines he sees. In a normal state of mind I might quite gratuitously think I see something when there is nothing there. Now to describe all these cases we may use the word "'see'" (*i.e.* 'see' in a special tone of voice). But none of them are at all like seeing in the mind's eye. If I have an hallucination, I do not see anything in my mind's eye. I do not visualise anything. I make a mistake about whether I see or whether I do not see something. I think I see something, but I do not. But when I visualise Helvellyn, I do not make any sort of mistake at all. Nor am I even tempted to do so, as in the case with the sufferer from delirium tremens who knows what is wrong with him but still cannot help being frightened by the snakes he 'sees'. I cannot deliberately 'see' snakes, but I can quite deliberately visualise Helvellyn, and to do this is not to indulge in a bit of self-deception. One can imagine that one sees Helvellyn, and one can visualise Helvellyn. They are two quite different things. One exception to this may be worth noticing. If I say to someone 'Imagine that you see Helvellyn', this means the same as 'Visualise Helvellyn'. The usage in the imperative does not correspond to that in the indicative. It is easy to see why this is so. One cannot order someone to be mistaken, so one clearly cannot use 'imagine' in the imperative in a sense that implies error. This is presumably why 'imagine that' in the imperative comes to mean the same as 'visualise'.

Another description given by Ryle of visualising is that it is sham-seeing.[3] We have seen that this is wrong in that if visualising is sham-anything it is sham-depicting. Is it then sham-depicting? In a way it is, and this has been one of our main points so far. But it is not sham-depicting in the way that sparring is sham-fighting. Sham-depicting in this sense would be drawing something in the air with your finger, going through the motions of depicting without actually producing a picture. Just as in sparring one goes through the motions of fighting without actually punching hard. Sham-seeing would presumably consist in pretending to see something when one did not. Visualising is not sham-anything. It does not involve any sort of pretence, or the going through of any motions. It may, however, be involved in pretence and make-believe, and often in fact is. If I trace a triangle with my finger on a sheet of paper, I usually visualise a triangle on the paper at the same time. I visualise the lines I do not actually draw. If I pretend to see a boat I probably visualise one. Moreover, if I really enter into the spirit of the thing, I may almost take myself in. An actor may find it hard to return from the world of fancy to that of reality. Visualising is an ingredient in make-believe, and make-believe may shade off into delusion. Perhaps there is no hard and fast line between cold-blooded visualising and one sort of imagining that I see. Nevertheless there is some visualising that has no element of pretence or deception about it. Suppose that someone sets me a fairly simple problem in geometry. He says, 'There is a rectangle with its longest side horizontal. The bottom left hand angle is bisected. What side of the rectangle will be cut if the bisecting line is produced?' Now if I am very familiar with this sort of thing, I may be able to produce the answer pat without any thought. If I am very unfamiliar with geometry, I may have to draw a diagram. It may, however, be enough to mock-draw the diagram with my finger. Or, better than this, I may just visualise the rectangle instead and get the answer that way. This brings out how

[3] *Op. cit.*, 264 ff. [138 ff.].

wrong it is to describe visualising as a sort of abstaining.[4] Rather visualising is a substitute for doing something else. Similarly it is wrong to describe reading to oneself as merely abstaining from reading out loud. One way of doing this is not to read at all. But reading to oneself is a way of spending the afternoon. One cannot spend the afternoon in abstaining from going for a walk. Of course visualising may involve refraining from drawing. I may want very much to draw a diagram. In complicated cases it is so much easier than solving the problem in one's head. I may refrain in order to exercise my powers of visualising. Usually, however, I do not have any such urge to draw, and so cannot be said to refrain. One cannot refrain from doing what one does not want to do. One just does not do it. Often one combines visualising and drawing. One draws so much, and this enables one to visualise the rest.

So far we have dealt mainly with visual imagery. Auditory imagery cannot be dealt with in quite the same way. There is nothing in the realm of sound that corresponds to depicting. One can reproduce a sound, but one cannot make a model of it. Without going into all the differences between 'seeing' and 'hearing', which are mainly the result of the differences in the logics of the words 'hear' and 'see', many of the conclusions we have reached about visualising apply here also. 'Hearing' a tune in one's head is not the same as imagining that one hears a tune. It is not pretending to hear, it is not mock-hearing. It is no sort of abstaining.

We have seen that the verb 'imagine' is often used when there is no question of anyone doing any visualising, 'hearing', 'smelling' or 'tasting'. In other constructions, however, it is used to refer to just this sort of thing, as for example in sentences like 'He imagined himself doing so and so'. Sentences like this imply that the subject was engaged in various sorts of imagery. If I imagine myself playing tennis, I 'see' what I would see, 'feel' what I would feel, 'hear' what I would hear, if I were really playing tennis. If I imagine someone else playing tennis, I 'see' and 'hear' what I would see and hear if I were watching him play tennis. It is partly for this reason that imagining myself looking at something is not the same as

[4] *Op. cit.*, p. 270 [p. 143].

visualising that thing. Similarly 'hearing' a tune is not the same as imagining oneself humming it or imagining oneself listening to it. At least if I myself was asked to imagine myself humming a tune, part of what I should do would be to visualise myself from the 'outside', so to speak, in a humming attitude. However perhaps different people would do different things when asked to imagine themselves doing something. Perhaps, if one was asked to imagine oneself playing tennis, one might visualise what a spectator of oneself would see. This is an empirical matter to be decided only by asking people what they do.

I now want to consider another question about visualising to which no very satisfactory answer has yet been given. Why cannot a man blind from birth visualise anything? Is the impossibility logical or empirical? Ryle makes it a purely logical matter. It is like the impossibility of pretending to be a bear if one does not know what a bear is. To take a parallel example from depicting, one cannot depict the Taj Mahal if one has no idea of what it is like. Now this is correct as far as it goes. But the fact remains that a man who has never seen a bear may (logically) do just what someone might do who was in fact giving a skilful imitation of a bear. A blind man might take a pencil in his hand and produce on a sheet of paper a good likeness of Mr. Churchill. Now to say that it is logically impossible for a blind man to portray Churchill is misleading in that it suggests that he cannot (logically) produce the likeness. Similarly it may be misleading to say that a blind man cannot visualise anything. May it not be logically possible for him to do something we might describe as 'visualising without knowing it'? What would we say if a man came to see for the first time late in life and stated that he had always been able to visualise in a way, though he had not known that that was what he used to do? To state baldly that the impossibility of a blind man's visualising is logical is to commit oneself in advance to answering the above question. We would have to say that whatever he did it was not any sort of visualising. It is to say that no imaginable occurrence would lead us to say that a man who had never seen anything could visualise. This is not to find a logical impossibility but to extend language in such a way as to manufacture one. One would make a similar mistake if one said the impossibility was empirical. For to say this is to say that there are certain imaginable situations that would lead one to say a blind man could visualise, but that in fact they never arose. What then are we to say? It is tempting to say that the sentence 'This blind man can visualise' is meaningless because we do not know what would count as a blind man visualising. But this will not do either, because it is certainly meaningful and true to say that no blind man can visualise. If it is meaningful to say that a blind man cannot visualise, it cannot be meaningless to say that he can. However, the position is not really very puzzling. I can safely say something is not green even if I do not quite know what 'green' means, provided I know that the object in question is not green. Similarly I can say that a blind man cannot visualise, because I know that nothing he does would count as visualising, even though I am not clear what would count, and even though it is not clear whether anything would count. All I know is that some things would come nearer to counting than others, and that no decision has been made as to the correct terms in which to describe them because they have not occurred and no decision has been needed.

Let us now consider the use of such phrases as 'being imaginative', 'having a vivid imagination' and so on. In general Ryle seems to be right. There is no nuclear operation that consists in exercising the imagination. But I do not think that a man's excellence at visualising counts at all in favour of saying that he is imaginative. Nor does constant indulgence in make-believe make a child imaginative. The notion of imagination is close to that of originality. If the child's make-believe is dull, or if he always makes believe about the same thing in the same sort of way then he shows that he lacks imagination. If I can visualise complicated diagrams, solve problems in my head, or have a good visual memory, this does not mean I am imaginative. There is no specific connexion between visualising and make-believe on the one hand and imaginativeness on the other. I can, of course, show my imaginativeness in my make-believe just as I can in story telling, or producing a play, but I can also show my lack of imagination in these ways. The phrase 'he has no imagination' tends to be used particularly, though not exclusively, of our ability to put ourselves in someone else's place, and to understand how others feel about things. Many other expressions too tend to have their own special uses, but we need not go into that here.

Part of the answer to the very vague question "What is imagination?" has now been given. Visualising must be distinguished from other sorts of 'seeing', and not confounded with them. Roughly to visualise is to *do* something, whereas to 'see' snakes is not to do something. Again we are not talking of any sort of 'seeing' when we say that someone is imaginative. Of course, there are further distinctions that can be made. For example, we have not considered a number of expressions in which the word 'imagine' occurs. We have talked as if 'see in the mind's eye' is synonymous with 'visualise'. This is not quite true. Apart from this, however, it may still be felt that certain questions have been left unanswered which are not touched by the procedure we have so far followed. What, positively, is visualising? Granted that visualising is doing, what exactly is it that we do when we visualise? Now, if these questions are taken in one way, they are unanswerable. But the desire to ask them may be allayed by seeing why they cannot be answered. It may be that what is wanted is a description of visualising that would enable someone who could not visualise to know what visualising is.

But ultimately the only answer to the question about 'what visualising is' is something like, 'It is what you do when you solve a geometrical problem in your head, remember someone's face and so on'. Similarly if a man has never had a pain, you cannot make him understand just what it is like to have a pain. You can perhaps give him some idea by saying it is a very unpleasant bodily sensation. You can give a man who cannot visualise some idea of what it is like, by saying things like, 'It is the visual analogue of having a tune running in your head'. If this is not the sort of thing that is wanted, then there is nothing that is wanted. However, there do remain certain other questions about imagery to which some sort of answer can be given. These may be expressed in a vague form as follows: 'Are there mental images?' 'Are mental images things?' 'What sorts of things are they?'

The best way of approaching such questions is to ask whether mental images can be said to be vague, and by comparing together describing, visualising, and depicting. The relevance of this will become clearer as we proceed.

Some philosophers have held and some have denied that such images can be vague, indeterminate, non-specific and general. Consider for example the view expressed by Sartre in *The Psychology of Imagination*, Chapter I, §5:

> 'To be vaguely conscious of an image is to be conscious of a vague image. We are far from Berkeley and Hume who denied the possibility of general images *or* non-specific images—Berkeley's error lay in ascribing to the image conditions that apply only to perception. A hare vaguely perceived is nevertheless a specific hare. But a hare which is the object of a vague image is a vague hare.'

Now such a view as this may appear paradoxical or even nonsensical. So at least it would have seemed to Berkeley. One can bring out the nature of the paradox by putting the matter in a way that seems to involve a denial of the law of excluded middle. Suppose that I have an image of a head that is non-specific about baldness, is this not rather queer? For presumably this head must be neither bald nor not bald nor even a half-way house with just a few hairs. Again it will not do to say that what is visualised is a head without a top (*e.g.* a scalped head) so that the question of its baldness cannot arise. For to visualise such a head is quite different from visualising a head without considering the question of baldness at all.

Yet at the same time there does seem to be a point in saying that images are in some way non-specific. For if one tells someone to visualise something, and then asks about some detail of what he visualised, he is often unable to give an answer. I may say 'visualise a rabbit', and then ask 'What color did you visualise it as having?' Sometimes the reply will be something like this, 'It did not have any particular colour, the question of colour did not enter my head'. Or again he may say he visualised something as red, but not be able to say whether it was scarlet or crimson. Can one here avoid talking of an image that is red but no particular shade of red by saying that the image was perhaps scarlet but that the visualiser did not notice this? This would be an attempt to preserve the analogy between images and things, for one can notice that the wallpaper is red without noticing what particular shade of red it is. But this will not do. Not only have we got no established use for expressions like 'notice a feature of my mental image', but if we did decide to apply it in the situation we are now considering, we would still be unable to give criteria establishing what the overlooked feature was like, what the colour really was. But we do have such criteria in the case of the wallpaper, and this is just what gives the word 'notice' its point. In fact we do not preserve the analogy with seeing an object just by using the word 'notice' in this context, for the word is left without point.

There seems then to be something of a dilemma. It is both natural and paradoxical to describe mental images as vague or non-specific. Now there are a number of different things that incline one to say that images are vague, a number of senses in which they may be said to be vague. One of these senses may be clarified and isolated by comparing visualising with describing. The ways we use these words run parallel to a considerable extent. Visual images are always images *of* something, and so are descriptions. We may visualise men as bald and we may describe them as bald. We may visualise or describe something correctly or incorrectly, and if we want to check on our accuracy, we must do the same thing in either case, go and have a look at the object in question. Visualising and describing can be done in greater or less detail.

Let us consider what it is for a description to be vague, and see if there is anything at all analogous in the case of visual images. There is clearly nothing at all odd in speaking of a vague or non-specific description. If a description is non-specific about colour, this means only that the colour of the object was not mentioned, or that it was described only in vague or general terms, as being light or dark. A man may not be described as being neither fair-haired nor not fair-haired, but in an incomplete description he may well be neither described as fair nor described as not fair. His hair may not be mentioned. There is no paradox in this. Let us then try to manufacture one that is like the one that arose about imagery.

To do this one must say not, 'The man was described neither as bald nor as not bald', but instead 'The description was neither bald nor not bald'. The absurdity of this way of talking is of course obvious. Descriptions are not material objects and cannot sensibly be said to have or not to have the characteristics that belong to such objects. Now we may note that to construct the paradox about visualising we had in that case too to talk in an artificial way. We do not normally speak of red mental images, any more than we speak of red descriptions. We visualise red things and we visualise things as red. It does not sound odd to say, 'The man was visualised neither as fair nor as dark' instead of 'The image was neither fair nor dark', or 'The image was of a man who was neither fair nor not fair'. Shall we then say that to talk in this way about imagery is as absurd as to speak in a parallel way about descriptions? Is it impossible to ascribe to mental images the properties of material objects or at least analogous properties? Is the vagueness of visualising just like that of describing, and do all puzzles vanish once this is pointed out? We may say that part of the desire to say that images are vague springs from this likeness between visualising and describing. Descriptions and images have to be *of* something and this is why they can both be described as vague, indeterminate and so on. The things they are 'of' cannot sensibly be said to have this sort of vagueness.

Nevertheless we must not assume that our original difficulty about saying that images are vague has now been dispelled. No trouble arises about descriptions because they clearly cannot be said to have the properties that material objects do. But to ascribe such properties to images is not so obviously absurd. To put the matter in another way, we are tempted to think of images as things, though of a special sort. Like pictures, it seems that they can be regarded in two ways, as objects in their own right as well as representations of other things.

How far then are they like pictures? What is the need or justification for introducing a word like 'visual image' at all?

We can approach this question by asking why it is we need a word like 'picture' to which nothing corresponds in the case of describing, and then seeing if there is any similar need in the case of visualising. In some respects we can liken depicting to describing. The police can circulate both pictures and descriptions of criminals for roughly the same purpose. Reading a description of a murderer and looking at his picture both enable one to say 'So that's what he's like'. One may talk of descriptions metaphorically by using words that apply literally to pictures. One may call a description a caricature, a pen portrait or a verbal picture. Portraits and descriptions can be accurate or inaccurate representations, detailed or not detailed, lifelike or not lifelike. Portraits and descriptions have to be *of* something. More detailed parallels can be worked out. A bald description is rather like a conceptual or schematic drawing. An impressionistic picture in which much is suggested is like a vivid but oblique description. However, there is one big difference about the ways we can talk about the two. For pictures are things, just as much as the things they are pictures of. For this reason one can ascribe to pictures the properties that one can ascribe to other material objects. A statue can have no hand, and this does not mean that it is a statue of a man without a hand. In saying that a statue has no hand we are not thinking of it in its representational aspect, but, so to speak, as a thing in its own right. We cannot do this in the case of a description. The case of a picture is rather more complicated. We can speak of a picture as a thing, as when we say that it is brightly coloured, and do not mean it is a picture of something brightly coloured. Also we have phrases like 'the man in the picture' where the object is thought of as a man (a picture-man). We may say 'this (picture) hand is delicately drawn' or 'this (picture-) hand has blurred edges' and we do not mean that it is a picture of a hand with blurred edges. A statue may be regarded as a stone man as well as a statue of a man in stone. For all these reasons we need a word like 'picture' or 'statue' to which ordinary material object adjectives may be applied. Now quite clearly a mental image is not an object, but it may be in some way analogous to one in that it is useful to have a way of talking about visualising that does not refer to the representative aspect of visualising. It seems to me that in fact there *is* this much excuse for the introduction of the word 'image'. It is a fairly well known fact that it is often difficult to visualise the faces of people we know very well. We can get so far, we can perhaps put in the outline of the head, but the features elude us. Now when people describe this they tend to say things like this. 'I tried to visualise the face but all I got was a blur', or 'His face was a blur' or 'It was a blur'. Now we may ask 'What was a blur?' What does 'His face' refer to? It does not refer to the face we are trying to visualise, nor do we mean that we visualise his face as blurred. What we are referring to is something analogous to the 'face in the picture', the picture-face. The blur does not represent anything in the face visualised. It is, so to speak, a feature of the image in its own right. Similarly there is such a thing as visualising a scene in black and white, as opposed to visualising a black and white scene. If we do this and are asked what colour we visualised the sky as being, we may say 'I didn't visualise it as any particular colour, the whole thing was various shades of grey'. 'The whole thing' is not the scene but what is best called the image of it, or the mental picture of it. The word 'picture' is a good one here because of the analogy between painting in black and white and visualising in black and white. Of course, there is danger here. One may press the analogy too far, and talk of seeing mental images as though having produced them one could afterwards do something analogous to examining them. This is one of the ways in which mental images are not like pictures.

The answer to the question 'Are there mental images?' is contained in the above discussion. There is no straight answer because the purport of the question is not clear. If it is taken as meaning 'Do people visualise things?' then the answer is that they do. On the other hand a desire to deny that there are images may spring from a number of sources. We do not need a word like 'image' in the normal course of events, and it may be felt that its introduction is not justified. More particularly the denial that there are images may be at bottom a rejection of a philosophical account of imagination that is felt to be misleading, and to lead to the asking of absurd and therefore unanswerable questions. This appears to be part of the motive for Ryle's denial that there are images. The concept of visualising is not illuminated but obscured by saying that it consists in seeing a private picture located in the mind. In so far as it is some such theory as this that is denied, we may agree with Ryle. But it will not do to express this by saying there are not images. It is very natural to talk of visual images, and we can make ourselves understood when we do so. I have argued that it is sometimes more convenient to talk about images than to use more normal forms of expression. For these reasons the denial that there are images seems quite paradoxical to the educated non-philosopher. It is far better to say that there are mental pictures, and at the same time issue a warning against asking questions about them that can sensibly be asked only of real pictures. There remains the question 'What sorts of things are images?' The answer to this may be put briefly thus: 'They are the same sorts of things as pictures and descriptions. They are a sort of half-way house between pictures and descriptions.' This answer as it stands is of course very misleading, and its meaning is not obvious. It is intended merely as a short-hand reminder of our earlier comparison of the concepts of describing, visualising, and portraying. Moreover, this answer is not the whole story. Rather it illustrates a method of answering questions like "Are there mental images?". This method is to try to talk about visualising in the same sort of language as we talk about depicting and about pictures, and to see how far such a way of talking is possible and useful. We draw certain distinctions in our talk about pictures, how far can parallel distinctions be made in talking about mental pictures? In this article this method has been applied to one very important part of the field. We can talk about pictures without talking about what they are pictures of. How far is it convenient and possible to talk in a similar way about mental pictures?

REMEMBERING

B. S. Benjamin

Nothing is so uniquely personal to a man as his memories. Our inner lives revolve around their contemplation, and in guarding their privacy we seem almost to be protecting the very basis of our personalities. Most of our remembering is done in private and though we speak of sharing our memories with others there seems to be a sense in which we could no more share a memory than we could share a pain; the best that we can do is to try to describe it. Yet unlike pains and aches, feelings of anger or of amusement, there are no natural and public signs of memories. We do not have to learn how to keep our recollections private as we have to learn to suppress feelings of amusement, boredom and discomfort. To the prefatory expression "I remember" there seems to attach the aura of a voluntary disclosure about oneself. It would seem, then, natural and indeed essential to construe the concept of remembering upon the model of an avowal about one's state of mind, about one's inner and inaccessible experiences. It is indeed traditional to approach the concept of remembering as though it has this kind of logic; in this paper I shall argue that such an approach is radically at fault.

Although it is not my purpose either to examine particular theories of memory as they bear upon the problem, or to do justice to the literature in the field by subjecting it to detailed criticism, I shall attempt to mention what seem to me to be typical and mistaken moves made in analysing the concept. And I shall begin by considering Hume's analysis as it is presented in the *Treatise*, because not only does it present in its

B. S. Benjamin (1925–63) was Senior Lecturer in Philosophy at Australian National University. His articles appeared in *Mind* and *The Australasian Journal of Philosophy*.

purest form a thesis which I wish to attack, but it has exerted a powerful influence upon subsequent analyses of remembering.

According to Hume, to remember something is to have a special kind of mental experience in the form of a mental image different from any other kind of image or idea. In part, of course, he was led to talk of 'an idea of the memory' by his faculty psychology, but it is important to notice that although the days of faculty psychology are over we still feel compelled to think of the memory in a not very dissimilar way. Although psychologists and neurologists still know practically nothing about the "brain mechanism" which enables us to recall past experiences and previously acquired skills, it seems natural to think of the memory as a unitary function of some sort, and from this it is easy to conclude that our memories, being the products of a single process, must in some way be stamped with the sign of their manufacture. This is one feature of the problem which suggests that the task set to any philosophical theory of memory is to detect those characteristics of the mental experience of remembering that will serve to isolate and define it. There is another puzzle which leads one in the same direction. How do we know that certain of our images and thoughts are images of, and thoughts about, the past? How do we know, if we are trying to remember say the look of a town, that none of the images we can summon are right, that none of them are memory images, and then, suddenly, that this one is a memory image?

Hume's general concept of the mind as an entity which can perceive only its own thoughts, inevitably suggested an answer to these questions, which also did justice to the solution suggested by a faculty psychology. For if one holds that a second order perception is involved in all thinking, it is natural to apply to this second order perceiving an analysis that is obvious and seems perfectly adequate to account for certain features of first order perception. The commonplace that one defines words referring to physical objects by attempting to isolate those features of a physical object that are necessary and unique to it was applied by Hume to the "objects" of second order perception. The impressions of sense, the ideas of memory and the ideas of imagination differ from each other, he said, with respect to their strength and vivacity, hence perception (first order), remembering and imagining may be defined in terms of relative strength and vivacity.

Professor Ryle has mentioned the absurdities involved in the classical theory of second order perception, but it is worth pointing out here that the difficulties involved in talking of perceiving an impression of sense (or a sense datum) are not by any means so obviously involved in talking about perceiving one's mental image. Most students, when they first read Hume, are struck by the strangeness of his suggesting that the impressions of sense differ from the images of memory only in degree, in a way that they do not think it strange to suggest that the images of memory and those of imagination might so differ. This is not surprising, for although no one has quite been able to describe how one should set about obeying a request to attend to one's impression of sense or sense datum of an object, as distinct from looking at the object itself, everyone knows how to attend to a mental image of an object. In ordinary discourse we use the verbs of perception in this second order sense quite naturally, as when we speak of hearing the tune we heard last night or of seeing the accident as clearly as if it were occurring in front of one's eyes, and only a philosopher would feel obliged to supply inverted commas for the verbs in this use. Furthermore, not only can one describe the contents of an image but one can also discriminate between and report upon properties of the image as a whole; for example, upon its comparative vividness, intensity, blurriness, definition, and so on. I conclude, then, that when Hume suggested that the images of memory and those of imagination differ intrinsically in respect of their relative strength and vivacity, he was not making a suggestion that is difficult to understand and implausible in the way that his similar remarks about the impressions of sense are.

It is generally agreed, however, that the characteristics of strength and vivacity of an image fail to mark off unambiguously our rememberings from our imaginings. For quite often the images of our imaginings and fantasies are very much more vivacious and vivid than are many of our memory images. Usually this standard criticism of Hume's theory is made with the suggestion, explicit or implied, that if only we were sufficiently attentive and ingenious we could discern what combination of characteristics invariably attend our rememberings and are absent when we are imagining. A number have been suggested, *e.g.* that our rememberings are accompanied by a feeling of familiarity, that this feeling makes us apply the concept of pastness to the image, and so on, though I think it is rarely suggested that such characteristics provide the criteria of remembering as Hume maintained his did. The trouble with this criticism is that it fails to expose the real nature of Hume's failures and in fact it simply encourages speculations which must prove equally inadequate.

Hume's theory of remembering is the purest example of what I might call the mental datum theory: that to remember is to have a certain sort of mental datum or experience, and to tell others what one remembers is to inform them of the details of this datum (usually thought to be an image). So far in this paper I have been chiefly concerned to point out considerations which make this a natural theory to put forward. I wish now to show that it is an impossible thesis to maintain in any form.

No first person statement that asserts an inner experience like the possession of an image, a certain sort of feeling or sensation, can be corrected by a third person. It must be accepted as true or rejected as a lie; it cannot be shown to be mistaken. If I say that I have a vivid image of a tree before me, my hearers can, in principle, disbelieve me on the grounds that I am lying, though it is very difficult to imagine what such grounds might be. But it would make no sense to accuse me of being mistaken about the matter. The concept of mistake only applies to cases where it is both theoretically possible to obtain independent evidence on the matter and to explain how the mistake arose. There is no way at present known of obtaining evidence independent of a man's word as to whether or not he has a mental image of the sort he claims to have. It is sometimes suggested, indeed, that avowals of one's state of mind or body are in principle incorrigible and hence self-certifying. But I suggest this is an incorrect way of stating the point. We are under no logical obligation to accept the truth of an avowal and avowals of certain types of inner experience are regarded as corrigible by indirect evidence. To mention only one example, claims to be in pain are sometimes rejected on the evidence of medical authorities when there is a recognised correlation between the described pain and a physiologically morbid condition. But malingerers are lying, not mistaken. The important logical difference between statements about one's inner and private experiences and statements about the external and public world does not run along the cleavage line of corrigible and incorrigible assertions, but along the gap separating claims that may be true, mistaken or deceitful, and those that can only be true or deceitful.

Sometimes, like George IV, people have entirely delusive memory experiences; more frequently, they claim to remember something when there is independent evidence to show that they must be mistaken in so thinking. It is this fact that theories of memory like Hume's cannot account for. It is plain that on Hume's theory one must have either veridical memories or be lying, for no one can be mistaken as to whether or not he has an image of a certain strength and vivacity. This is the point at which the analogy between first and second order perception ceases to hold. We can explain how we made the mistake of taking an overcoat on the floor to be the body of a man: the light was bad, we had lost our spectacles, we were too far away to see properly. But one needs no light by which to see a mental image, no oculist can attend to the defects of the inner eye, and try as we may we can neither approach nor retreat from our images. We use no organs to detect our images, states of mind and sensations; they are separated from us by no medium; there is no mechanism to go wrong; there is no inference made into which error could creep.

The absurd necessity that Hume's theory would impose upon us of declaring to be a liar anyone who thought himself to be remembering when he was not, clearly follows equally from any revised version of the theory. There are no special images, accompanying feelings of familiarity, or intense convictions that one is truly remembering and so on, from the experiencing of which it follows conclusively that one is indeed remembering. This follows from the fact that any claim to remember, no matter how confidently it may be based upon the possession of clear and distinct images, feelings of familiarity and so on, may in principle be falsified by evidence of a non-subjective kind. For instance, I may be absolutely certain that I can remember meeting a friend in the street yesterday. Yet, if it were proved that the friend whom I thought I remembered meeting had been at that time a hundred miles away, I would have to accept the fact that I could not possibly remember meeting him and that I must have imagined the occurrence. It follows from this corrigibility of claims to remember, that no mental datum or combination of mental data can possibly function as sufficient criteria of remembering as the Humean type of theory suggests they do. Or, to put the point in the way I have been doing, one can only maintain the enterprise of taking mental data to be sufficient criteria at the expense of rendering it impossible to talk of people making honestly mistaken memory claims.

It is well worth noticing that mental data of the type I have been considering do not function as necessary criteria of remembering either. Hume's doctrine that one remembers *if* one has an *image* of a certain kind has only recently been abandoned in the face of a mass of psychological evidence to the contrary. Indeed, some would seem to have abandoned the memory-image theory with the poignant reluctance of the theorist confronted with impossibly indigestible facts. The facts are certainly indigestible, but the weak points in a conceptual analysis (which every philosophical theory of memory should be) may be detected independently of experimental evidence, and in this case one can certainly show without recourse to experimental evidence that the possession of mental imagery is not a necessary condition (or criterion) of remembering. For example, if a barrister conducting a cross-examination attempted to throw doubt on the reliability of a witness's memory by demonstrating, *per impossibile*, that the witness's account was unaccompanied by mental imagery, no one in the court would understand his point at all. We have tests to decide or to help us decide whether or not people remember and some of these are tests for the presence or absence of necessary conditions, but the possession or lack of possession of images is not one of these tests.

By substituting for 'mental image' any other mental datum

in the example above, one can see similarly that no specific mental datum need be present before one can be said to remember.

To avoid misunderstanding, it should be mentioned that of course these arguments do not apply to any non-introspectible concomitant of remembering, *e.g.* such as a certain pattern of neural discharge. It may well be discovered that phenomena of this kind are necessary to remembering, but non-introspectible or unconscious mental phenomena in the nature of the case do not, and could not, usefully function as *criteria* of remembering, which is the point in question.

Modern versions of the memory image theory avoid the notorious flaw in Hume's theory by attempting to account for the fact of honest but mistaken memory claims. The core of the modified version is the suggestion that a memory image is a representative image of a past perceptual experience, and when one makes an honest mistake of memory one is faithfully reporting or observing an image that fails to represent the past experience. This is unobjectionable so far as it goes, but if the argument above, showing that images have no necessary role in remembering, is correct, it follows that this theory fails to expose any part of the logical structure of the concept at all, and merely describes a phenomenon that may or may not take place.

It is, furthermore, obvious that anyone who assigns to the memory-image a central role in the analysis of remembering must explain the connexion or lack of connexion between our rememberings when memory-images naturally are likely to occur, as in our memories of places and faces, and those when they are not, as for instance when we remember how to tie a running bowline or the first four lines of *Paradise Lost*.

It is worth considering one such attempted explanation, made by Professor Broad in *The Mind and Its Place in Nature*. In a chapter entitled "Memory" in that work he says that the word "memory" is highly ambiguous in the sense of covering "a number of very different acts"; thus we use the verb "to remember" in different senses when we speak of remembering a set of nonsense-syllables, a poem, a proposition in Euclid, how to swim, and people and places, because in each case *what* we remember differs from the others. Given this technique of discriminating different senses of the verb "to remember", Broad is able to declare the sense in which we remember past perceptual experiences (when imaging is most likely normally to occur), to be different from other cases, most of which, he suggests, can be called instances of remembering only by courtesy.

Professor Broad's contention that 'remembering' is an ambiguous word which has many senses would be of the first importance if true. There are, however, several reasons for denying its truth, at least in the form in which he presents it. In the first place it is plainly incorrect to assert that, for example, in the claims 'I remember her face', 'I remember her name and telephone number', 'I remember how to rhumba', one could possibly mistake what was being claimed, through an ambiguity of 'remember', in the way that one might mistake or misunderstand the claim 'I have been to the bank'. Neither is it apparent that more subtle distinctions of sense are involved as in 'I feel a penny', 'I feel sick' and 'I feel happy'. The differences of sense involved in the latter cases can be indicated by the blatant inappropriateness of certain questions asked of one or more of the claims, which are quite appropriate if asked of others, *e.g.* what is the location of what you feel? what did you feel it with? and so on. But Broad does not elicit distinctions of sense in the verb 'to remember' in the same straight-forward way. Instead, he first states an implied analysis of the concept of remembering from which distinctions can be seen to follow, by declaring that remembering is an act, and then not unreasonably concludes that the very different activities involved in, *e.g.* remembering how to swim (bodily activity), the lines of a poem (rote activity), someone's face (the mental activity of having an image), and so on, must be reflected in different senses of the word we use to refer to these differing acts. But such distinctions rest upon the highly contentious assertion that remembering is the name of an act or set of different acts, and is in no way a straight-forward statement about usage as the previous examples were. Indeed, the implausible conclusion which follows from this theory, and which Professor Broad draws, that there is no connexion whatever between the senses of 'remember' elicited, might be taken as *prima facie* evidence of its falsity.

The only way to decide whether remembering and its cognates are radically multivocal, or substantially univocal as I wish to maintain, is to re-analyse the concept to see whether or not a uniform core of meaning is preserved in its use in different contexts. This I shall attempt to do, and in the course of my argument it will, I think, become quite clear that it is not possible to construe remembering as an act, except of course in the entirely empty sense in which one might say that every active verb must denote an act.

Before I proceed to this analysis something further is needed to do justice to at least one of the points which Broad wished to make. For anyone, irrespective of whether or not he takes remembering to be simply an activity, might well be greatly struck by the difference between remembering a past perceptual experience, and remembering a poem or how to swim. The difference seems to lie in the fact that whereas it in no way seems necessary for one's remembering the lines of a poem or how to swim to be accompanied by introspectible mental experiences, it is difficult to understand how one *could* remember a perceptual experience without an experience *analogous* to the original one taking place. For example, what would it be like to remember the very tones of a voice without in some sense hearing the voice again, or to recollect in detail the view up the High from Magdalen Bridge without seeing it in one's mind's eye? Then again, when one goes over the events of the day one usually does so not by telling oneself the story of what occurred but by seeing, hearing and feeling again in memory fragments of one's perceptual experiences, in short, by a sort of reliving of the day's events. What I shall call, for want of a better phrase, reliving, is undeniably typical of our remembering of perceptual experiences, and the memory-image theory is an attempt to do justice to this fact, as also is Broad's assertion that remembering has different senses.

Whether the phenomenon of reliving is marked by a distinction in sense of 'remember' is a question that may be decided the better when the remaining analysis has been made. It is fairly obvious, however, that the notion of reliving is capable far better than that of a memory image of accommodating the recall of non-visual perceptual experiences and, hence, that the memory-image theory has the trivial defect of over-narrowness. What is less obvious is whether the argument against the memory-image theory presented earlier has equal weight against the broader reliving theory.

It is certainly no more a standard *test* of remembering to enquire whether a person is in some way reliving what he claims to remember, than it is to enquire if he has an image of it. But one might now feel tempted to argue that it does not follow from the fact that this is not a standard test, that reliving is nevertheless not a necessary ingredient of remembering past experiences. We may investigate this possibility by setting up the hypothetical case of a man who was perfectly well able to describe his past perceptual experiences and yet denied that he underwent the experience of reliving in any way at all. Some people might wish to argue that he must be reliving the experiences he describes—otherwise how could he describe them? and that either he fails to understand what we mean by the phrases 'reliving', 'seeing or hearing vividly in recollection' and so on, or that he undergoes his reliving in a very curious way (as, for example, some hold that people with freakish ability to calculate in their heads *must* perform sums terribly fast and unbeknown to themselves).[1]

It would take us too far off the course this paper must follow to consider the really interesting points this argument involves. Two, however, may be noted. First, the ability to image sensory experiences does vary widely from person to person, so the disagreement may well have a factual basis.[2] Second, it is a genuine puzzle sometimes to know what is to count as an image. For instance, what the writer *presumes* is his memory image of the High from Magdalen Bridge is so fleeting, blurred and thin that, if, as it were, it could be cap-

[1] A phenomenon interesting in this connexion is reported in a recent note on "Loss of Visualisation" by Sir Russell Brain, *Proc. of the Royal Society of Medicine*, April 1954, Vol. 47, No. 4.

[2] An informative and brief account of such differences is given in "The Measurement of Mental Images" by P. L. Short, *Penguin Science News*, No. 24.

tured for the requisite time, it would undoubtedly prove impossible to draw it; yet he can describe the view to himself and others. Would this count as an image, a reliving? One tends to put an end to such a question, I think, by wearily agreeing that it *must* be an image.

The really important point at issue, though, may be decided, whether or not this preliminary question can be. If reliving is a necessary condition of remembering a past experience, then, were we to find someone who could describe to himself and to others his experiences without any reliving of them, it would have to follow that he was not *really* remembering. I do not think that this point could be sustained. Our subject would give a perfectly adequate memory-performance; he would pass all the standard tests of remembering; we could not even say that he is not good at remembering, in the usual sense of the phrase. All that we could say of him is that he does his remembering in a curious fashion, and, at the most, that remembering is for us a much richer experience than it is for him, that, perhaps, it means *more* to us than it does to him. But the phrase 'means more' in this context has somewhat the same force that it has in the observation that doing addition means more to me than it does to a bank teller; we both add, but whereas his answers come almost automatically, I reach mine by means of agonised and laborious little sums.

If only because we are *taught* to add, there is little temptation of us to confuse our personal methods of doing it with the notion of adding itself. It is perhaps largely because remembering is a natural phenomenon, something which we do not have to learn, that we feel ourselves to be authorities on the subject and that our personal methods and techniques will have some necessary connexion with the logical structure of the concept. But a concept used in public discourse could not be so dependent upon the vagaries of private experiences, the nature of which, as we have seen, it is not even easy to describe. For it to have a standard meaning its use must be standardised, and reference to the experiences of reliving undergone by individuals, plainly, could hardly be suitable for this. In fact, because of our preoccupation with our *experiences* of remembering, we tend to simply ignore the standard uses to which we put the concept in our discourse. It is to these that we must now turn.

I referred earlier to the fact that a claim to remember is in principle falsifiable or verifiable by observations which are in no way connected with the state of mind of the person making the claim. The following example illustrates still further points of difference between the logic of statements about one's state of mind and statements containing the verb 'to remember' or its cognates. But this is incidental to the present purpose of the example, which is to provide further material for the study of how the concept actually behaves when used in discourse. Suppose two men, each of whom is thoroughly acquainted with the painting of a certain artist. This artist has painted a view familiar to each, and one man has seen the painting and the other has neither seen it nor had it described. Now suppose we ask each man to try and picture the painting to himself and then to tell us what the painting is like. The man who has seen the painting before will probably claim to remember it, and we can test his claim by getting him to describe it to us. Should his statement be such that it would count as a description of the painting, it must be allowed that he remembers it. Should his statement not be a description of the painting,[3] or should he be unable even to begin a description, we would have to declare that he did not remember the painting; in the first case that either he was guessing or confusing the painting with another one; in the second, unless he suffered from a speech defect or the painting was such that a verbal description presented great difficulty, simply that he had failed to remember it. We could hardly expect the other man to be able to describe the painting, but it is just possible that, knowing the scene and being familiar with the artist's 'vision', palette and so on, he could tell us sufficiently well what the painting was like. But even were his answer to be in substance exactly the same as that of the man who remembered the painting, and even if both were to have similar mental pictures, the second man would not be remembering the painting but guessing what it was like, and even if he were honestly to believe himself to

[3] What would count or not count as a description in this type of context will be discussed later.

be remembering it, it could not follow that he was. Alternatively, if the first man had quite forgotten that he had seen the picture and had then told us what it was like, thinking he was guessing, we should be forced to declare that in fact he was remembering the picture although he was unaware that he was doing so.

The obvious point which this example illustrates is the independence between on the one hand, the state of mind, mental imagery and so on, of the person who claims to remember or not remember the painting and, on the other, the factors which, on appeal, *decide* whether the claim is to be accepted or rejected and reformulated as a guess or an imagining. As was mentioned earlier, that memory claims are verifiable in principle by recourse to publicly ascertainable facts[4] indicates a marked difference between the logic of these assertions and those reporting a mental experience. An even more striking distinction lies in the fact that if a claim to remember is rejected *in toto*, it is immediately reclassified, as for instance 'you couldn't remember such an occurrence because it never took place; you must have imagined it or guessed it or made it up'. Each of us has been subject to such corrections and unquestionably we were not being convicted of linguistic incompetence; neither, as we have seen, could it be for mistaking the nature of our (conscious) mental experience. What sort of mistake, then, were we committing?

An answer suggests itself most strongly when one notices the way in which rejected memory-claims are corrected: you didn't remember, you imagined, dreamt, guessed it, and so on. We use these forms of emendation when certain of the conditions which must be fulfilled before remembering can take place, have not been fulfilled; for example, when someone claims to remember seeing an occurrence which in fact never took place, or, if it did, which he could not have been in a position to witness. In such a case, the statement presented as a memory-claim or the unexpressed thought which is taken

[4] This is not always possible, of course, *e.g.* when we remember our dreams, feelings and so on. But we treat our memories of such things *as though* they are verifiable independently, in as much as everyone would admit that it is possible that his memory of, *e.g.* his dream, is mistaken or faulty.

to be a memory, cannot have come to mind as a result of the memory process, *i.e.* as the retention of past experience, for the experience never took place. To correct the claim with 'you must have imagined, dreamt, guessed it', and so on, answers the question which the denial that remembering took place poses, namely, How then did he come to think of it? by ascribing to him a mental process different to the one originally claimed.

I think that it would be true to say that the everyday view of remembering is simply that it is the final stage of a causal process and that the memory is some sort of causal device or mechanism. The fact that in our language remembering is opposed by other process words like imagining, guessing, inventing, making-up, dreaming, and so on, is itself evidence of this belief. The view that remembering should be thought of as part of a causal process is, of course, fundamental to psychology and to neurologists attempting to find the brain mechanism responsible for the phenomenon. The process view also underlies the extensions made to the concept of memory when, under the influence of the new evolutionary biology, the notion was applied to races and groups, or in our own day when we apply it to inanimate objects capable of certain involved causal processes, as when we speak of calculating machines having a memory.

The fact that it makes some sense (although also different senses) to talk of human memory, race memory, machine memory and so on, indicates how central to the concept of memory is the process-analysis. Add to this the point that if we are to explain the phenomenon of memory we undoubtedly have to assume that a process of some sort is responsible, and one is led to enquire whether the analysis of remembering into a process-concept may not solve the problems which the analyses so far mentioned have been unable to meet. For one thing, reference to an underlying mental process provides a common factor in our use of the memory words over a wide range of differing contexts, and would thus appear to explain our usage. For another, it would seem to avoid the difficulty raised by honest but mistaken memory-claims, as there is no reason why privileged access should extend to unconscious mental processes.

There is, however, something very curious entailed by this suggestion. On the one hand, even now very little is known about the processes involved in human memory.[5] On the other, it is frequently possible to establish with certainty that a person remembers something. The consequence of the process analysis would be, then, that we can establish with certainty that on occasions the working of an assumed and unknown process has taken place. It also involves the novel information that when we claim to remember, what we are really claiming is that we are undergoing a certain mental process. If this were so it is undoubtedly true that the vast majority of people when they claim to remember something, simply do not know what it is that they are claiming.

These conclusions are quite unacceptable. But the difficulties involved in construing the concept as a process concept do not necessitate the equally unpalatable course of maintaining that it is not a process concept. The assertion that a person remembers something does involve, or is taken to involve, the ascription to that person of a certain mental process undergone. But it also involves far more, and that of a character vastly more important to the purposes of everyday life in which the concept finds employment. In its constant everyday use it finds employment, I suggest, as one of a group of concepts which we use to classify statements according to their truth-value.

The group described earlier as process concepts opposed to remembering likewise serve the same purpose. But the properties which, in the previous context, it was natural to assume were properties belonging to the utterer of a statement—that *he* is guessing, imagining, inventing, dreaming, etc.—I wish now to point out are properties which, in the first place, belong to the statement itself.

A statement is classified as a guess when it is not backed by evidence which would yield it as a conclusion; an inference

[5] There are, of course, highly informed speculations about its nature. See, *e.g. The Neurophysiological Basis of Mind,* by J. C. Eccles, Oxford. For a discussion of certain special difficulties that accounts of the nature of the memory mechanism must face, see, "In Search of the Engram" by K. S. Lashley, *S.E.B. Symposia,* vol. IV, Academic Press, N.Y., 1950.

when it is so backed; an invention, story, dream or imagining when it bears no relation, descriptive or evidential, to the facts which it purports to be about, when the statement is presented as a claim to remember. (To *preface* a statement with, *e.g.* 'this story', 'my dream', etc., is to declare that it does not purport to be about any facts.) These rough summaries, which are not meant to be characterisations let alone definitions, serve to bring out two points. First, that to classify a statement under any one of these or similar heads is to label it with regard to its truth-value. Second, that it is, so to speak, to write upon the label the support or lack of it which the statement possesses. Thus the labelling of an assertion as a guess informs people that the support or grounds backing the assertion is of a certain kind, and that although the information asserted is unlikely to be true, it just may be so (it may be a shrewd guess). Though the remaining process verbs I mentioned, and the far larger set that I have not mentioned, would each need individual treatment (which I shall shortly give in the case of remembering) in order to demonstrate that they are used to classify assertions, the sample that I have given is sufficient to indicate the nature of this linguistic function. It may be observed that it is clearly necessary in the interests of efficient communication that we should apprise one another, where possible, of the logical status of the assertions we make. The enormous difficulties and frustrations reported by people who have experienced living in primitive societies where such distinctions are not made is sufficient witness of this. On the other hand, except in certain rare instances, it is not apparent that the constant exchange of autobiographical prefaces to our remarks would be particularly useful or interesting. The man who purveys information solely about himself is a bore.

Although the fact that it is grammatically correct to refer the actions denoted by active verbs to the actor (I guess, he guesses, etc.) clearly plays a large part in leading us to misconstrue sentences containing verbs of the group which concerns us simply as sentences giving information about the actor, this linguistic fact is not the whole of the matter. Even though the logical propriety of employing active verbs at all in these contexts might now seem dubious, it equally seems unavoidable. On the one hand, that the making of assertions or the thinking of thoughts of logically different kinds necessarily involves a doing or activity seems guaranteed by the "causal principle"; on the other, it is a matter of experience that frequently the production of different sorts of assertions (or thoughts) is preceded by typically different mental doings, experiences or processes. The fact of the matter is that these verb forms play a multiple role in discourse; they are used simultaneously to label the logical status of an assertion or thought, and to refer to the activities or processes which are causally responsible for the assertion. Neither role can be reduced to the other, but it is important to see that one is logically primary.

That the process role is secondary showed itself in the case of remembering, in that no types of mental experiences or thought processes were found to be either necessary or sufficient conditions of remembering. Equally, the primacy of the logical status marking role appears when it is realised that the conditions which are necessary and sufficient are those relating to the truth value and truth conditions of the statement of what is remembered, *e.g.* my claim to remember seeing Jones hit Smith is correct only if Jones did hit Smith and I witnessed the occurrence. Once the relationship existing between the two roles is clear it is not difficult to see why the experiences which typically enter into our remembering have no part in the logical structure of the concept. They could never provide conclusive tests of whether remembering has taken place or not because what the tests must be designed to determine is whether the putative memory is veridical (*e.g.* whether Jones did hit Smith, etc.). If the assertion 'I remember p' is true then it follows that one's memory processes worked correctly, but the truth of the assertion is not logically dependent on the workings of the memory process. This point can be seen more clearly in the following logically analogous case. The test of whether an electronic calculating machine is working correctly (and was designed correctly) lies in the correctness of its calculations. The tests of correctness are of course logically related to the rules of the calculus employed, not to an electronic process. The production of a calculation is causally dependent upon the functioning of some process, mechanical or mental, which employs certain mathematical procedures, just as the production of a memory is causally dependent upon some individual's memory processes. But logical dependence cannot be assimilated to causal dependence (or *vice versa*) as the theories of remembering examined earlier in fact attempt to do. For instance, even if a totally error-free calculating machine were developed, so that it became practicable to say that the correct answer to a complex calculation is the answer given by the machine, the machine's answer would still in principle be verifiable and the relations between logical and causal dependence remain unchanged. Human memories are not perfect, and whenever anything of importance hangs upon an individual's memory claim we endeavour to verify it. But although in practice we never accept as quite conclusive those experiences, whatever they may be, which lead a man to state with honest conviction 'I *know* I remember', we do accord them the status of strongly presumptive signs of remembering. If our memories were uniformly excellent then undoubtedly we would drop our practice of verifying claims to remember, except as a check for mendacity, and treat them *as if* they were self-certifying. But even in this remote contingency, the primacy of the status labelling role would remain unchanged.

What I have referred to as the 'logical status labelling' role played by the mental process verbs must be elucidated further in the case of remembering. To preface one's remarks with the phrase 'I remember . . .' (or a cognate) is to indicate to one's audience that you certify the truth and accuracy of the information you are about to give or which you claim to be able to give or to the correctness of the performance you will or could undertake. The nature of the status-label affixed to p in a statement of the form 'I remember p', might, in part, be paraphrased 'p is true (or this performance is an instance of p) and you have *my* word for it'. In this, the role of these expressions is notably parallel to that of 'I know', and this comes out in the fact that very frequently we can employ either verb with indifference both to the intended and understood sense of the utterance, *e.g.* 'do you know/remember his name?', 'do you know/remember Ohm's Law?' and so on. It similarly shows itself in the fact that if one remembers p it entails that one knows p. The reverse, of course, does not hold. One may use the verb 'to remember' only to certify statements or performances relating to the past, whereas we can, by the use of 'know' certify statements about the past, present or future. I propose to mark this common linguistic role by describing each concept as a certificatory concept. We may now understand the concept of knowledge to be our most general certificatory concept, and the concept of remembering to be specialised in the respect just mentioned.

It might at first seem that the certificatory role is at once too obvious and too unimportant to be worth the mention. For the norm of communication is essentially the exchange of information supplied in all sincerity. We expect perfectly ordinary statements like 'the car is outside', 'it was raining yesterday', 'I can see him coming' to be true, and hence there is a perfectly good sense in which one can say that the mere utterance of apparently informative statements commits the utterer to standing by the truth of his statements. But this very fact makes it obviously desirable to have expressions which underline our committal to the truth of our assertions, and which can be used to stress the fact that the information is certified. I shall turn shortly to consider the contexts in which we do and do not use 'remember'; here, it may be noticed that a phrase like 'body of knowledge' can be translated into 'body of certified information', and 'theory of knowledge' into 'theory of certification' with some gain in illumination. A further gain stems from the power to explain certain features of the logical grammar of the concepts which this way of looking at them allows.

If one proffers information accompanied by the formula 'I remember (that) p' or 'I know (that) p', then, should p turn out to be false, to be misinformation, one is forced not merely to admit the falsity of the information, but also that one did not remember, that one did not know. One is forced by the rules of language formally to eat one's own words. One may attempt to explain the existence of such a rule by pointing out that, at least in the case of the verb to remember and the verbs of perception, which are also subject to this rule, one is dealing with what Ryle has called achievement words.

This is both true and useful, for one can talk here of trying or of failing to achieve the desired result, *e.g.* of trying or failing to remember, to see, to hear and so on; and success may sometimes indeed be accompanied by a very real feeling of achievement. But one cannot make this point of the verb 'to know': it is not clear what could be meant by 'trying to know', or 'failing to know', except in the acquaintance sense of the word where the rule does not apply. The reason for this difference is undoubtedly that the verbs of 'achievement' are also process (or procedure) verbs whereas the verb 'to know' in its relevant sense is not. Processes may or may not work, they need suitable conditions ('the light is too bad to see', 'it happened too long ago for me to remember the details', 'my ears are full of water'); and sometimes they can be made to work ('turn on the light then you'll see', 'if you remember what you did before that it might come back', 'you'd better see a doctor'). If a process fails to work one must withdraw a claim which implies that it has worked. But the fact that this rule of formal withdrawal applies equally to the verb to know, which is not a process verb, suggests that there must be more behind the rule than reference to processes which may or may not have taken place. The remaining explanation emerges, I suggest, if one sees the rule also as a device, embodied in the language, to protect the integrity of certificatory expressions. Words may be abused, suffer debasement and lose their force, and if it were not for the presence in the language of a formal rule of this nature, certificatory expressions would soon lose the special emphasis which makes them so valuable.

It is important to notice that because we use the verb 'to remember' as a mark that the information we are giving is true and correct, it does not follow that memory can never play us false, that we cannot make a mistake in our remembering, that one either remembers or one doesn't. If a man were to make three mistakes in a recitation of the *Ode to a Nightingale* no one could sensibly accuse him of failing to remember the poem, unless it happened to be an occasion when perfection was required. On the other hand, if he were to get his telephone number wrong, we would say that he simply doesn't remember it rather than say merely that he made some mistakes. We have no hard and fast rules for what is to count as a correct description, an accurate summary, getting an account right, knowing a street or an argument or a poem. Hence, we cannot state hard and fast rules for what is to count as remembering, for we treat remembering as a function of the truth, correctness and accuracy of a statement (or performance). We evaluate the truth or accuracy of a statement by taking into account the demands of the context and situation in which it is made, and express this evaluation by choosing terms from, so to speak, a rough scale of expressions. For example: 'completely accurate', 'fairly accurate', 'inaccurate', 'quite true', 'partly true' and so on. Likewise we evaluate and express the truth or accuracy of what is remembered. For example, 'he remembered it perfectly', 'he half-remembered it', 'he didn't remember it at all' and so on. Similarly we may diminish the claim to correctness implied by the use of the verbs 'to remember', 'to recollect', 'to know' by prefacing them with, *e.g.* 'I seem to . . .', 'I think I . . .', 'I believe I . . .' and so on. The object of such qualifications is of course to warn the listener that there is, to a varying degree, some doubt about the correctness of the information which will follow and that, having given due warning, the speaker cannot be blamed if his listener puts too much weight upon his words.

A noteworthy consequence of the certificatory role of remembering may be seen in the fact that it is only rarely necessary to bring up the notion of remembering in our everyday discourse. Now one could generate a sense of the verb to remember such that from the *demonstration* that one has not forgotten p, *i.e.* that one has produced or performed p, it would follow that one remembers p. This sense would fully accord with the requirements of the process concept of memory, as the latter embodies precisely the rule just used to generate the new sense of remember. Hence, the skills and information that may be said to be memory-dependent, *i.e.* which we may forget (perhaps as a result of injury to the brain) may now be said to be remembered when they are actualised. Thus one could speak of Englishmen conversing or writing in English as 'remembering words in the English language', of accountants doing accounts as 'remembering how to add', and one might murmur as one signs one's name 'I've remembered my name again'.

The absurd inappropriateness of these examples if 'remember' is understood in its usual sense, illustrates the opposition between the two senses. It is not, of course, an opposition that permits the crude exposure of its existence by denying that in these examples one remembers one's name or one's language, for such a denial would for each sense entail that one had forgotten them. The inappropriateness would lie in bringing up the notion of remembering in its usual sense at all in such connexions.

Two very closely related factors determine when it is appropriate to bring up the notion of remembering in ordinary discourse. It would clearly be nearly as pointless to remark the functioning of one's memory processes each time they work as it would be to remark the fact that one breathes and is in full possession of one's faculties; that one has possession of one's faculties is usually sufficiently evident. The introduction of one's remarks with the phrase 'I remember' or the ascription to the remarks or performances of others as remembered has point just because we reserve the use of these expressions for occasions when there is some possibility that one may not remember whatever happens to be in question. Thus the absurd examples given above would be sensible remarks only if made in a context in which there was reason to believe that the person of whom they are made was suffering an impairment of his faculties, or was a child who was actually learning this information or these skills. As a result of this restriction of application, the very bringing up of the question of remembering actually implies the possibility of forgetting. Compare the rudeness of 'do you remember your name?' with 'what is your name?' or 'do you remember what you had for breakfast today?' with 'do you remember what you had for breakfast three weeks ago?' Part of the absurdity of the earlier examples lies in the ineptness of *implying* that, for instance, a sane and sober accountant might have forgotten how to add.

Similar considerations determine the occasions on which it would be sensible to use a certificatory expression. We never bring up the notion of remembering unless there are grounds for supposing that an assertion may need checking or that a performance might be faulty, and in such circumstances it is obviously fitting to employ a certifying expression. By the same token it would be otiose to employ an expression with this force when one's hearers stand in no need of personal assurances about the truth of what is uttered. For instance, no one would say either 'I remember' or 'I know that $2 + 2 = 4$' although he certainly does know it and, in the special first sense, he certainly does remember it.

The contrast which I have drawn between the special sense and the ordinary sense of the verb to remember lies, of course, more properly, between the concept of memory and the concept of remembering. The concept of memory is the concept of a storage system, but the concept of remembering is not its natural corollary, that of the wholesale removal from store of the goods and chattels of experience. Rather, as I have briefly attempted to show, it is devoted to the removal, not of special articles, but of any articles when conditions are such that the transaction deserves attention.

It is now possible to attempt an answer to the question which we deferred, namely, whether remembering has a unitary sense maintained in all contexts, or whether it is importantly multi-vocal.

If the arguments put forward in this paper are correct, it is plain that in their primary linguistic role as certificatory concepts the verb to remember and its cognates preserve a unitary sense in all contexts. Things as various as assertions, thoughts, images, feelings, bodily performances and so on, may be similar in respect of their logical status as having been remembered. It is the secondary process attributing role that misleads theorists on the topic and invites speculations about differing senses of the verb. Whether there is a single process responsible for the phenomenon of remembering is a question on which no lay opinion would merit consideration, and in the absence of an accepted view about the nature of the process it seems correct to suggest that generally the verb has an utterly vague secondary sense, rather than a cluster of differing ones. But it remains quite open to individuals to nominate specific process references should they wish to, and it is apparently the case that sometimes this does occur, as when people, impressed by the characteristic way in which their own memories come to them, take the verb to have reference to these private happenings. In such cases there seems no reason why one should not talk of differing secondary senses of the verb, so long as it is clearly understood that such senses are private ones, and do not provide the material upon which an analysis of the concept must be founded.

PLEASURE

Gilbert Ryle

What sort of a difference is the difference between taking a walk which one enjoys and taking a walk to which one is indifferent? (1) It might be suggested that it is, in genus if not in species, the sort of difference that there is between walking with a headache and walking without one; and that somewhat as one walker may recollect afterwards not only the ordinary acts and incidents of his walk, but also the steady or intermittent pains that he had had in his head while walking, so another walker who has enjoyed his walk might recall both the ordinary acts and incidents of his walk and also the steady pleasure or the intermittent pleasures that had been concomitant with the walk. It might even be suggested that as one walker may recollect that his headache had become specially acute just as he reached the canal, so another might recollect that his pleasure had become specially acute just as he reached the canal.

A person who made such a suggestion need not hold that to enjoy a walk is itself to have a special bodily sensation or series of bodily sensations concurrent with the walking. He might admit that while we can ask in which arm an agreeable or disagreeable tingle had been felt, we could not ask in which arm the agreeableness or disagreeableness of it had been felt. He might admit, too, that in the way in which pains yield to local or general anaesthetics, enjoyment and distaste are not the sorts of states or conditions for which anaesthetics are appropriate. But he might still suggest that pleasure is a non-bodily feeling, in supposedly the same generic sense of "feeling" as pain is a bodily feeling. If sophisticated enough, he might suggest that pleasure is a specific, introspectible Erlebnis, where a headache is a specific bodily Erlebnis. Now a sensation or Erlebnis, like a tingle, may be agreeable, disagreeable or neutral. If enjoying and disliking were correctly co-classified with such Erlebnisse or feelings, one would expect, by analogy, that one could similarly ask whether a person who had had the supposed pleasure-feeling or dislike-Erlebnis had liked or disliked having it. Enjoying or disliking a tingle would be, on this showing, having one bodily feeling plus one non-bodily feeling. Either, then, this non-bodily feeling is, in its turn, something that can be pleasant or unpleasant, which would require yet another, non-bodily feeling, . . . ; or the way or sense, if any, in which pleasure and distress are feelings is not in analogy with the way or sense in which tingles are feelings.

There are other places where the suggested analogy between pleasure and tingles collapses. If you report having a tingle in your arm, I can ask you to describe it. Is it rather like having an electric shock? Does it mount and subside like waves? Is it going on at this moment? But when you tell me how much you are enjoying the smell of peat smoke in my room, you cannot even construe the parallel questions about your enjoyment. Nor is your inability to answer due merely to the very important fact that in order to attend to my questions you have to stop attending to the smell, and so cannot still be enjoying it. You cannot answer my questions even in retrospect. There is no phenomenon to describe, except the smell of the peat smoke.

(2) The enjoyment of a walk might, however, be co-classified by some, not with feelings like tingles, but with feelings like wrath, amusement, alarm and disappointment—which is a very different use of "feeling." It could be urged that though the walker would not naturally say that he had felt pleased all the time or had kept on feeling pleased, still he could quite naturally say such things as that he had felt as if he were walking on air, or that he had felt that he could go on for ever. These dicta, which would certainly suggest that he had enjoyed his walk, should, on this second view, be construed as reporting a passion or emotion, in that sense of those words in which a person who is scared, thrilled, tickled or surprised is in the grip of a more or less violent passion or emotion.

This second assimilation too collapses. The walker may enjoy his walk very much, but he is not, thereby, assailed or overcome by anything. A man may be too angry or surprised to think straight, but he cannot enjoy his walk too much to think straight. He can be perfectly calm while enjoying himself very much.

Panic, fury and mirth can be transports, convulsions or fits, but the enjoyment of the smell of peat smoke is not a paroxysm like these—not because it is very mild, where they are violent, but because it is not the sort of thing that can be resisted, whether successfully or unsuccessfully. It cannot be given way to either. It is not a gale or a squall, but nor is it even a capful of wind. There is no conquering it or being conquered by it, though there is certainly such a thing as conquering or being conquered by the habit of indulging in something or the temptation to indulge in it.

(3) There is the third, though surely not the last use of "feeling" in which moods or frames of mind like depression, cheerfulness, irritability and *insouciance* are often called "feelings." Typically, though not universally, a mood lasts some hours or even a day or two, like the weather. But the mood of irritability is unlike the emotion or passion of anger, not only in its typical duration and not only in being more like squally weather than like a squall, but also in not having a particular object. A man is angry with his dog or his tie, but his irritability has no particular object, except, what comes to the same thing, The Scheme of Things in General. To be irritable is to be predisposed to lose one's temper with no matter which particular object. A person in a cheerful or energetic mood is predisposed to enjoy, *inter alia*, any walk that he may take; but what he enjoys is this particular walk. His enjoyment of it is not the fact that he is predisposed to enjoy any occupations or activities. Moreover he enjoys his walk only while taking it, but he had felt cheerful or energetic, perhaps, ever since he got out of bed. So enjoying something is not the same sort of thing as being or feeling cheerful. On the contrary, the notion of being cheerful has to be explained in terms of the notion of pleasure, since to be cheerful is to be easy to please.

Sensations, emotional states and moods can, in principle,

all be clocked. We can often say roughly how long a tingle or a headache lasted, very roughly how long a fit of rage or amusement lasted, and extremely roughly how long a mood of depression or cheerfulness lasted. But pleasure does not lend itself to such clockings. The walker can, indeed, say that he enjoyed his walk until it began to rain, two hours after he started out; or the diner can say that he enjoyed, though decreasingly, every bite of Stilton Cheese that he took until satiety set in with the penultimate bite, and that this series of bites took about six minutes. But he cannot clock the duration of his enjoyment *against* the duration of the thing he enjoyed. He can, at best, divide the duration of the walk or meal into the parts which he enjoyed and the parts which he did not enjoy. The enjoyment of a walk is not a concomitant, e.g. an introspectible effect of the walking, such that there might be two histories, one the history of the walk, the other the history of its agreeableness to the walker. In particular there would be a glaring absurdity in the suggestion that the enjoyment of a walk–might outlast the walk–unless all that was intended was that the walker enjoyed the walk and then enjoyed some after-effects or memories of the walk; or that the walk had made him cheerful for some time afterwards.

Psychologists nowadays often avoid idioms which suggest that enjoying a walk is having a special feeling while one walks, by speaking instead of the "hedonic tone" of the walker. This new idiom, apart from performing its one antiseptic function, does not by itself advance very much our conceptual enquiry. It does not make clear what sort of a thing pleasure is. Is the hedonic tone the sort of thing that could, conceivably, be induced by drugs or hypnosis–as Dutch courage and somnolence can be induced? Could a person be qualified by hedonic tone, without his doing or having anything in particular to enjoy doing or having? So let us try to make a more positive move of our own.

Sometimes I enjoy a smell, sometimes I dislike it, and very often I am quite indifferent to it. But I could not enjoy it, dislike it or be indifferent to it if I were totally oblivious or unaware of it. I cannot say, in retrospect, that I liked the smell but did not notice it. I could, of course, enjoy a complex of smells, views, cool air and running water without paying special heed to any one of them. But I could not have enjoyed just that complex, while being totally oblivious of any one of those components of it. This "could not" is not a causal "could not." To say that a person had enjoyed the music, though too preoccupied to listen to it even as a background noise, would be to say something silly, not to report a *lusus naturae*. Unnoticed things, like ozone in the air, may certainly cause us to feel vigorous or cheerful. There may well be such an unnoticed cause of our being predisposed to enjoy, *inter alia*, the food and the music. But then we do not enjoy the ozone, but the food and the music; and of these we cannot be both oblivious and appreciative.

Similarly, when a person temporarily forgets his headache or tickle, he must cease, for that period, to be distressed by it. Being distressed by it entails not being oblivious of it. But just what is this connection between enjoying and attending, or between being oblivious and being undistressed? What, to begin with, is there to be said about the notions of attention and oblivion themselves?

When we consider the notion of attending, a subject which we consider far too seldom, we are apt to fancy that we have to do with some nuclear, one-piece notion; as if, for example, all attending were comparable with just switching on and aiming a torch in order to see what is there whether we see it or not. But in real life we use a wide variety of idioms for attending, most of which will not quite or even nearly do duty for one another. Some of these idioms correspond not too badly with the model of the torch-beam; others do not correspond with it at all.

For example, if at the prompting of someone else I come to notice a previously unnoticed smell, the way I become alive to the smell has some kinship with the way the hedgehog comes to be seen when the torch-beam is directed upon it. But then the way in which a strong smell so forces itself on my attention that I cannot *not* notice it is much more like a piece of barbed wire catching me than like an object being picked out by my exploring torch-beam.

When we describe someone as writing or driving carefully, we are describing him as attending to his task. But he is not, save *per accidens*, taking note of the things he is doing, since he is playing not an observer's part, but an agent's part. He is taking pains to avoid, among other things, ambiguities or collisions, where noticing a strong smell does not involve taking pains at all.

Consider some other differences between the functions of such idioms as those of noticing, heed, being careful, being vigilant, concentrating, taking interest, being absorbed, giving one's mind to something, and thinking what one is doing. When excited or bored, I may not think what I am saying; but to say this is to say less than that I am talking recklessly. I may be interested in something when it would be too severe to say that I am concentrating on it; and I may concentrate on something which fails to capture my interest. Attention is sometimes attracted, sometimes lent, sometimes paid and sometimes exacted.

Philosophers and psychologists sometimes speak of "acts" of attention. This idiom too is partially appropriate to certain contexts and quite inappropriate to others. When a person is actually bidden by someone else or by himself to attend, there is something which with some effort or reluctance he *does*. Where his attention had been wandering, it now settles; where he had been half-asleep, he is now wide awake; and this change he may bring about with a wrench. But the spectator at an exciting football match does not have to try to fasten or canalise his attention. To the question "How many acts of attention did you perform?," his proper answer would be "None." For no wrenches had occurred. His attention was fixed on the game but he went through no operations of fixing it. The same man, listening to a lecture, might perform a hundred operations of fixing his attention and still fail to keep his mind on what was being said. Acts of attending occur when attending is difficult. But sometimes attending is easy; and sometimes it is difficult, sometimes impossible not to attend.

Even where it is appropriate to speak of acts of attention, the word "act" carries very little of its ordinary luggage. In ordinary contexts we apply very multifarious criteria in determining what constitutes one act. Perhaps making one move in chess is performing one act; perhaps doing enough to warrant prosecution is performing one act; and perhaps getting from the beginning to the end of a speech without being side-tracked is one act. But a person who has, say, hummed a tune from beginning to end, not absent-mindedly but on purpose and with some application, has not performed two acts or accomplished two tasks, one of humming plus one of giving his mind to reproducing the tune; or, at any rate, he has not performed two acts in that sense of "two acts" in which it would make sense to say that he might have done the second but omitted the first. Giving his mind to reproducing the tune is not doing something else, in the way in which a person sawing wood while humming is doing something else besides humming. We should say, rather, that a person who hums a tune with some concentration is humming in a different way from the way in which he hums automatically, for all that the difference might make no audible difference. It makes his humming a different sort of action, not a concomitance of separately performable actions.

I suggest that explicit talk about such things as heed, concentration, paying attention, care and so on occurs most commonly in instruction-situations and in accusation-situations, both of which are relatively small, though important sections of discourse. Elsewhere, even when talking about human beings, we tend to make relatively few explicit mentions of these things, not because it would be irrelevant, but because it would be redundant to do so. The notions are already built into the meanings of lots of the biographical and critical expressions which we use in talking to people and about them. In partly the same way we do not often need to make explicit mention of the special functions of particular utensils and instruments; not because they have not got functions, but because the names of these utensils and instruments themselves generally tell us their functions. The gunsmith does not advertise "Guns to shoot with."

When, in our philosophising, we do remember how notions of care, vigilance, interest and the like are built into the meanings of lots of our biographical and critical expressions, we may still be tempted to assimilate all of these notions to the two special notions that are cardinal for pedagogues and disciplinarians, of *studying* and *conforming*. We then find that our resultant account of the spectator's interest in an exciting game has a smell of unreality about it. For he is not taking pains to improve his wits, or dutifully abiding by any rules. He is attending, but not in either of these special modes of attention. Being excited or interested is not being sedulous; it is, more nearly, not-having-to-be-sedulous.

The general point that I am trying to make is that the notion of *attending* or *giving one's mind to* is a polymorphous notion. The special point that I am trying to make is that the notion of *enjoying* is one variety in this genus, or one member of this clan, i.e. that the reason why I cannot, in logic, enjoy what I am oblivious of is the same as the reason why I cannot, in logic, spray my currant-bushes without gardening.

Let us consider again the moderately specific notion of *interest*. To be, at a particular moment, interested in something is certainly to be giving one's mind to it, though one can give one's mind to a task, without being interested in it. The notions of *being fascinated, carried away, being wrapped up in, excited, absorbed, puzzled, intrigued,* and many congeners, clearly tie up closely, though in different ways, with the notion of interest. Now to say that someone has been enjoying a smell or a walk at least suggests and maybe even implies that he has been interested in the smell or in the exercise and the incidents of the walk—not that he gave his mind to them in e.g., the sedulous way, but rather that his mind was taken up by them in a spontaneous way. This is, of course, not enough. Alarming, disgusting and surprising things capture my attention without my having to fix my attention on them. So do pains and tickles.

I should like, at this stage to be able to answer these questions:—What is it, in general, to give one's mind to something? What, more specifically, is it to give one's mind to something in the mode of being interested in it? What, finally, is it to give one's mind to something in that special dimension of interest which constitutes enjoyment? I cannot do this, but will throw out a few unscholastic remarks.

It will not, I think, be suggested that interest is either a separable process or activity or a peculiar feeling. Even if there are acts of attention, there are not acts of interest, or pangs of it either. *En passant,* it is just worth mentioning that a person might be, for a spell, wholly taken up with something, like a smell or a taste, though he would not claim that the smell or taste had been interesting—or of course boring either. We tend to reserve the adjective "interesting" for what provokes hypotheses or even for what would provoke hypotheses in the best people. A connoisseur might find a wine interesting; the ordinary diner might describe it as piquant or attractive or just nice.

Think of the partly metaphorical force of the expressions "absorbed" and "occupied." When the blotting-paper absorbs the ink, we picture the ink as unresisting and the blotting-paper as having the power. It thirstily imbibes every drop of the docile ink and will not give it up again. Somewhat similarly, when a child is absorbed in his game, he—every drop of him—is sucked up into the business of manipulating his clockwork trains. All his thoughts, all his talk, all his controllable muscular actions are those of his engine-drivers, signalmen and station-masters. His game is, for the moment, his whole world. He does not coerce or marshal himself into playing, as, maybe, his conscripted father does. Else there would be some drop of him which was recalcitrant to the blotting-paper. Yet when we say that he is wholly absorbed in his game, we do not accept the entire parallel of the ink and the blotting-paper. For the blotting-paper had been one thing and the ink-blot another. But the game which absorbs the child is nothing but the child himself, playing trains. He, the player, has, for the moment, sucked up, without resistance, every drop of himself that might have been on other businesses, or on no business at all.

Or think of the notion of occupation. Victorious troops occupy a city; its police, administration, communications and commerce are managed according to the policy or the whims of the victors. The citizens' public and private doings are subject to the permission and perhaps to the direction of their new masters. Yet there are different kinds of occupation. The city may be managed tyrannically, stiffly, amicably, paternally or fraternally; and while the citizens may feel like slaves or helots or infants, they might feel like adolescents who are being shown how to be free; how to manage themselves. Somewhat so a person who is occupied in reading may feel oppressed; but he may feel merely shepherded, or advised, or partnered, or trusted, or left to his own devices. But here again, the parallel is only fragmentary, since here both the citizens and the occupying troops are the reader himself. He is under the control and he is the controller. It is his policy or his whim that directs and permits those doings of his own which, if he were unoccupied, would otherwise be without these directions and permissions—and therefore be quite different doings.

There is an important objection which could be made against both of these attempted illustrations. It could be said that I have in fact been sketching an elucidation of the notions of absorption and occupation which fails for the reasons for which a *circulus in definiendo* ruins an attempted definition. To say that the child who is totally absorbed in a game has all his thoughts, conversation and controllable muscular movements sucked up into the one activity of playing trains would be simply to say that being absorbed in A involves not being absorbed in B, C or D. To say that a person who is occupied in reading brings and keeps all his doings under a unified control is only a long-winded way of saying that while he is engaged in reading, he is not engaged in bicycling or conversing; and these are truisms. I hope that I mean something less nugatory than this. A man who is not employed by one employer may not be employed by any other. He may be employable, but unemployed. Or he may be unemployable. Somewhat similarly, a person who is not taking an interest in A, need not be taking an interest in anything else. He may be inert, i.e. asleep or half-asleep. But he may not be inert and yet not be taking an interest in anything at all. He may be the victim of *ennui*, in which case he actively yawns, fidgets, wriggles, scratches, paces up and down and whistles; yet he may do all of these things absent-mindedly or mechanically. He is restless but not employed; energetic but not occupied. He does plenty of things, but not on purpose, carefully with zeal or enjoyment. He is accomplishing nothing, for he is essaying nothing. He is merely responding to stimuli. The right thing to say would perhaps be that the child's game sucks up not all his thoughts, conversation and controllable muscular movements but rather all his energies.

These energies, when so sucked up, become the thinking, conversing and manipulating that constitute his playing. But this notion of energies seems a rather suspicious character.

What is the point of pressing analogies or even plays upon words like these? One point is this. Where, as here, unpicturesque discourse still eludes us, the harm done by subjugation to one picture is partly repaired by deliberately ringing the changes on two or three. If they are appropriate at all, they are likely to be appropriate in different ways and therefore to keep us reminded of features which otherwise we might forget. The analogy of the blotting-paper may remind us of what the analogy of the torch-beam would, by itself, shut out of our heads, namely the facts—the conceptual facts—that there can be attending where there is no switching on of attention, and that there can be attending where there is no question of exploring or discerning. The analogy of the military occupation of a city may keep us in mind of the conceptual facts, which the other analogies do not bring out, that giving one's mind to something may but not need involve mutinousness, reluctance or even dull acquiescence. One's mind may be given readily and it may be given with zest. Not all control is oppression. Sometimes it is release. Both the analogy of the blotting-paper and the analogy of the fraternal military occupation are meant to indicate, in a very unprofessional way, the conceptual region in which pleasure is located. But, at best, the real work remains to do.

THE CONCEPT OF HEED

U. T. Place

I. *Introduction*

Do the words and expressions which the subject uses when he makes his introspective report, refer to internal events going on inside him? If they do, it is difficult to see why we should not use the subject's statements in order to formulate and verify hypotheses about such processes. If they do not it is difficult to see what reason we should have for believing in the existence of the sort of events which are described in the text-books of introspective psychology. If, as is suggested in this paper, some of them do and some do not, it becomes extremely important for the psychologist to be able to discriminate between the two cases.

Now in so far as the language of the introspective report is the 'psychological' language of ordinary speech, this is the question which has recently been exercising the minds of the philosophers; and in at least one case (Ryle, 1949) the conclusion that has been reached is preponderantly negative. In his book *The Concept of Mind* Ryle has attempted to show that the traditional view which holds that mental states and processes are private internal occurrences within the individual is mistaken. He does not deny that some of the statements which we ordinarily make about people, refer to states and activities of the individual that are 'private' or 'covert' in the sense that only the individual himself can report their occurrence. He would maintain, however, that such statements constitute only a small minority of the statements we make about our own and other people's minds.

U. T. Place is a member of the department of psychology at Central Hospital, near Warwick, England, and a contributor to *The British Journal of Psychology*.

I shall argue in this paper that the number of mental concepts which do entail a reference to covert states and activities of the individual is much larger than Ryle is prepared to admit. In particular it will be contended that a reference of this kind is involved in our ordinary use of such expressions as 'being conscious of' or 'paying attention to something', 'observing', 'watching', 'looking', 'listening', 'seeing', 'hearing', 'smelling', 'tasting', 'feeling', 'noticing', 'perceiving' and 'recognizing'.

II. *The Concept of Heed*

The key notion in Ryle's account of what is traditionally referred to as our 'apprehension of the external world' is the concept of 'heed'. As he himself points out (p. 136), this notion of 'heed', or 'heeding' is closely related to the concept of 'consciousness' which is the basic concept in all the traditional theories of mind. While heed does not carry quite the same theoretical load as does the notion of consciousness in the traditional theories, it is employed by Ryle in his analysis of a wide range of mental concepts, and a large part of his case against the view that mental concepts entail a reference to covert states, processes and activities, would seem to depend on his ability to show that paying heed is not a covert activity.

Ryle defines the notion of 'heeding' or 'minding' as embracing such concepts as 'noticing, taking care, attending, applying one's mind, concentrating, putting one's heart into something, thinking what one is doing, alertness, intentness, studying and trying'. Concepts which 'entail, but are not entailed by, heeding' include 'enjoying, disliking, pondering, searching, testing, debating, planning, listening, relishing, calculating and scrutinizing' (p. 136), looking (p. 232), observing, watching, descrying (p. 207) and recognizing (p. 223). Remembering something, according to Ryle (pp. 91 and 137–9) involves having paid heed to it at the time, while being conscious of sensations in one's body or objects in one's environment is evidently synonymous with heeding or noticing them (pp. 157–8). It will be seen from this that Ryle's concept of heed corresponds more closely to the traditional concept of attention than to that of consciousness. On the traditional theories consciousness is the basic notion of which attention is a special active or conative form. For Ryle on the other hand, it is 'attending' or 'heeding' which is the basic concept, and no distinction is drawn between paying attention to something and being conscious of it.

III. *The Contemplative Theory of Heed*

The traditional or, as Ryle calls it, the 'contemplative' theory of heed or attention and consciousness in the form in which I wish to defend it, may be stated as follows. The expression 'paying attention' refers to an internal activity of the individual presumably of a non-muscular variety whereby he exercises a measure of control over the vividness or acuteness of his consciousness of (*a*) the sensations to which he is susceptible at that moment, or (*b*) such features of the environment as are impinging on his receptors, without necessarily adjusting his receptor organs or their position in any way. In paying attention to something the individual is regulating the vividness of his consciousness of the object or sensation in question and hence the number of its features of which he is conscious. The expression 'being conscious of something' refers to a peculiar internal state of the individual which normally accompanies any reasonably intense stimulation of his receptor organs, the particular form assumed by the individual's state of consciousness at a given moment being determined by the pattern of physical energies impinging on his receptor organs at the time.

Being conscious of something is by definition a necessary condition of the individual's being able to give a first hand report on that something either at the time or later. It is not, however, a sufficient condition of the individual's ability to make such a first hand report, since it is possible for someone to be conscious of things which he cannot put into words, without his actual capacity to verbalize being in any way disturbed. Likewise, though here the relationship is probably contingent rather than necessary, the successful performance of any skilled activity depends to a greater or lesser extent on the individual paying attention to, i.e. maintaining a vivid consciousness of, relevant features of the situation and his own activity with respect to it; but the mere fact that someone is paying attention to what he is doing does not entail that the performance will be adapted to the demands of the task.

IV. *Ryle's Objections to the Contemplative Theory*

Ryle's first objection to this type of theory (pp. 136–37) is that it leads to a *reductio ad absurdum* in those cases where we speak of watching carefully or attentively. He points out that it is always possible to ask of a spectator, whether he has been a careful or a careless one. In order to interpret this on the contemplative view, he suggests, we should have to postulate an additional process of watching his watching, which is present in the careful spectator and absent in the careless one. This interpretation leads to an infinite regress, since it would always be sensible to ask whether or not this watching of one's watching was done carefully or not. There is, however, no reason why the contemplative view should force us to adopt this particular interpretation. As Ryle himself points out (p. 136), minding can vary in degree. There is, therefore, no reason why we should not say that the difference between the careful and the careless spectator lies in the amount of heed that each pays to the scene before his eyes. The careless spectator is not one who fails to watch his watching, nor is he completely oblivious of what is going on, he merely pays insufficient heed to it. What distinguishes the careful spectator from the careless one are the detailed and accurate reports which he is able to furnish as a result of the richness and vividness of the impressions with which his more active heed-paying provides him.

Ryle's second objection to the traditional theory of attention is that it fails to account satisfactorily for those cases where we speak of applying our minds to some task, such as whistling or driving a car. In this case, he argues (p. 138), we are not doing two things, whistling and minding, driving the car and attending to our driving; we are performing a single activity in a certain way. He points out in support of this contention that we cannot stop driving the car and continue our heed-paying. This argument, however, is singularly unconvincing. The fact that we cannot stop driving and continue our heed-paying merely shows that we cannot continue to pay heed to something that is no longer there to pay heed to. We do not normally lapse into unconsciousness after applying the hand-brake; we turn our attention to other things. On the other hand the fact that one can, if one is sufficiently foolhardy, continue to drive and cease to pay heed to what one is doing would suggest *prima facie* that there are two distinct processes going on here. Ryle is doubtless right in pointing out that in driving with care one is not doing two things at once in quite the same sense as one is when one is walking along and humming at the same time. In humming and walking at the same time one is performing two distinct sets of muscular movements simultaneously. When heeding and driving occur together, on the other hand, there is only one set of muscular movements, those of manipulating the controls; and in that sense there is only one activity being performed. No one, however, supposes that heed-paying is a separate set of muscular movements occurring alongside the muscular movements involved in driving. Nor is heeding thought of as an unrelated activity going on at the same time as the driving. It is a peculiar sort of internal activity which controls the movements of the driver's limbs, by regulating his consciousness of the stimuli to which he responds.

V. *The Dispositional Theory of Mental Concepts*

Although Ryle has failed to produce any conclusive objections to the contemplative theory, it is clear that if he can give a plausible account of the logic of 'heed concepts' which dispenses with the assumption that they refer to peculiar private events within the individual, we should undoubtedly be led to prefer such a theory on the grounds of parsimony. We must therefore examine the account which Ryle has offered of the logic of these concepts in order to discover whether or not it constitutes a satisfactory alternative to the traditional view.

The peculiarity of mental concepts as a class is that in order to determine whether or not someone knows, believes, understands, recognizes, remembers, wants, feels, is enjoying, attending to or thinking about something, you either have to cross-examine him or else observe considerable stretches of his behaviour before you can settle the question with any degree of confidence. This logical peculiarity is traditionally explained on the assumption that these mental concepts refer to invisible states and processes within the individual, whose existence and nature can only be determined with certainty by the individual in whom they occur, although it is usually possible also for an external observer to make reliable inferences about them by observing the behaviour to which they give rise.

Ryle's explanation of this logical feature is quite different. He supposes that mental concepts, or at least most of them, refer to what may be called behavioural dispositions, i.e. capacities, tendencies or temporary dispositions to behave in a certain way. To assert that someone has a capacity or tendency to behave in a certain way on this view is not to say anything about what is going on here and now, it is to assert a hypothetical proposition about how the individual could or would behave if certain circumstances were to arise. Hypothetical propositions of this kind can only be verified by investigating the behaviour of the individual under the conditions supposed. The proposition 'X can swim', for example, can only be verified by observing X's behaviour when in the water. Similarly with the proposition 'X knows the date of the battle of Salamis': unless you happen at that moment to hear X say 'Salamis was fought in 480 B.C.', you would either have to wait for the chance of hearing his reactions when called upon to exhibit his knowledge of ancient history, or else adopt the more practical course of testing his knowledge by asking the appropriate question. The reason why it is often necessary to cross-examine the individual in order to discover what he knows, is not that knowing is a peculiar internal state or activity of the individual of which he alone is directly apprised; it is that an important part of what we mean when we say that X knows the date of the battle of Salamis is that he can give you the correct date when asked to do so.

With a few notable exceptions of which 'cogitating', 'visualizing' and 'having sensations' are the most important, Ryle attempts to apply this type of explanation to all the mental concepts treated in his book. In most cases moreover the attempt has proved remarkably successful. To my way of thinking there can be little doubt that the dispositional account which he gives of such concepts as 'knowing', 'believing', 'understanding', 'recognizing', 'remembering', 'intending' and 'wanting' is substantially correct. It is only with his attempt to apply it to such concepts as 'attending to', 'observing' and 'being conscious of something' that I wish to quarrel.

VI. *Ryle's Application of the Dispositional Theory to Heed Concepts*

Ryle contends (pp. 137–39) that to say that someone is paying attention to what he is doing entails that he has at least two important dispositions, (*a*) the disposition under favourable circumstances to remember and give a first hand report on what it is he has been paying heed to, and (*b*) the disposition to adapt his performance to the various demands of the task as they arise. Now it is quite true that if we are told that someone is paying close attention to what he is doing, we normally expect him to be able to answer questions about his activity and to have made at least a better showing at the activity than if he had not been applying his mind to the same extent. It is also true, as Ryle points out, that we frequently conclude from the fact that someone is unable to answer questions about something that has been said in his presence, or from his failure in certain skilled performances, that he has not been paying attention to what was said or to what he was doing. But it does not follow from this that to say that someone is paying attention entails that he has the disposition to do these things. A schoolmaster frequently concludes from the fact that a boy has got the wrong answer to a mathematical problem, that he has set about it in the wrong way. Yet this would not lead us to say that to set about a problem in the right way entails a disposition to get the right answer. We only conclude that the boy must have used the wrong method if we know that his capacities are such that he could not have avoided getting the right answer had he used the correct method. Similarly, we only attribute someone's failure in a skilled activity to lack of attention if we know that his capacities are such that no other explanation of his failure is possible. One would hardly expect someone who had never been near an aeroplane before to be able to meet the demands of the task of piloting one, however closely he attended to what he was doing.

On the view which I am urging, the individual who pays attention is more likely to succeed in so far as he becomes acutely conscious of those features of the situation which are relevant to the successful performance of the task. Close attention to his own activity will be of no avail to the unskilled person because he has not learnt to discriminate between the relevant and irrelevant features. On the other hand an acute consciousness of the details of his own activity in relation to the environment may actually detract from the efficiency of performance in the case of an individual who has learnt to make many of the adjustments involved automatically. Thus we frequently say of someone whose skill is already well developed that his performance suffered because he paid too close attention to what he was doing. It is difficult to see what meaning could possibly be attached to this statement on a dispositional theory of attention.

In claiming that 'attending' entails 'being able to say something about what is going on', Ryle is on stronger ground. It is certainly true that it would be extremely odd to say that someone was paying attention to something, but could tell you absolutely nothing about it. But it is arguable that this is merely because one cannot pay attention to something without at least noticing the thing to which one is paying attention. There is no doubt that to say one has noticed something entails that one has the capacity to mention it and point it out, but to say that one has noticed something and to say that one has paid attention to it, are not, as Ryle appears to think, to say the same thing. 'Noticing' is an achievement concept like 'recognizing', 'perceiving', not an activity concept like 'pondering' or 'attending'. 'Noticing', 'perceiving', or 'recognizing', are the achievements that result from the activities of looking, listening and attending. If one looks, listens or attends one normally notices or recognizes something or other, but one can also attend and fail to notice; one can look and fail to see, listen and fail to hear. When we say that we have failed to notice anything, what we really mean is that we have failed to notice anything remarkable or anything additional to what we have already noticed. You can hardly be said to have paid attention, if there was nothing at all which you could be said to have noticed as a result of your attending. But it does not follow from the fact that A notices more about the situation than *B* that A was paying closer attention. The man who pays closer attention usually notices more, but the relationship is contingent rather than necessary.

VII. *Ryle's Account of the Logic of Heed Concepts*

The expression 'paying attention to something' exhibits the distinctive logical characteristics which are normally associated with words and expressions which refer to activities. The fact that it is perfectly good sense to speak of someone being engaged in paying attention to something, while it is nonsensical, for example, to speak of someone being engaged in knowing or understanding something, clearly shows that 'paying attention' or 'heed' is an activity expression in contrast to dispositional verbs like 'expect', 'know', 'like', and 'believe' or achievement verbs like 'understand', 'remember', 'recognize', 'perceive' and 'infer' where such a combination would be nonsensical.

It might be objected that 'attending' differs from those verbs which unquestionably refer to activities in that it is not sensible to use it in conjunction with adverbs like 'quickly' or 'slowly'. We can say 'he slowly began to pay attention to his surroundings', but not 'he paid slow attention to his book for five minutes and then rapid attention to the black-board'. There are, however, a number of expressions which can properly be described as 'activity verbs' of which the same is true. For example we can say 'he slowly took hold of the hammer' but not 'he held the hammer slowly for five minutes'. The analogy between 'attending' and 'holding' seems generally very close.

In support of his contention that 'attending' is not an ordinary activity verb, Ryle draws attention to the curious fact that it is always possible to replace a 'heed verb' by a 'heed adverb'. We can speak, to use his examples, of 'reading attentively', 'driving carefully' and 'conning studiously' just as readily as we can of 'attending to the page in front of one', 'taking care in one's driving', and 'applying one's mind to the task of translation' (p. 138). Ryle contends that the adverbial form is the more accurate way of expressing what is meant when a 'heed concept' is used. To say that someone is doing something heedfully, he maintains is merely to say that he is doing it in a certain way or in a certain frame of mind, i.e. with a disposition to adapt his performance to the various demands of the task as they arise and to answer questions about it.

On this theory the fact that 'paying attention' behaves like an ordinary activity word is explained on the assumption that the phrase 'paying attention to something' is analysable into two parts, (*a*) a categorical statement that a certain activity is taking place, and (*b*) a hypothetical or dispositional statement about how the individual in question would behave if certain contingencies were to arise. Ryle calls it for this reason a 'mongrel categorical statement'. The categorical part of the statement from which it derives its logical characteristics, is however, extremely uninformative. It asserts merely that some unspecified activity is being performed. In order to discover the nature of this activity we must find out what it is that the individual in question is paying attention to. As Ryle points out (p. 143) to say that someone is paying attention is an incomplete statement, unless we are told or unless it is obvious from the context of the remark what it is that he is paying attention to. On this view the part of the supposed meaning of the phrase which refers to the performance of an activity is strictly speaking redundant, since it must always be supplemented by a specification of the activity which is being performed.

In his lengthy discussion of 'mongrel categorical expressions' (pp. 140–7) Ryle is at pains to try to explain how it is that the fact of attention or inattention can be used to explain the failure or success of the individual in the activity he is performing. He shows convincingly enough that we can explain the bird's flying south by saying that it is migrating, without implying that migration is an additional process superimposed on the activity of flying south. The statement that the bird is migrating explains the behaviour of the bird by bringing the particular behaviour in question under the general rule that birds of certain species change their habitats at certain times of the year. Unfortunately he does not explain how the analogy is to be applied in the case where we explain the failure of an individual to complete a task satisfactorily or to give an adequate report on what was happening, by saying that he was not paying sufficient attention. It is difficult in this case to see what the general rule involved could be, unless it is the rule that if you don't pay attention you won't be able to carry out the activity you are performing satisfactorily or give an adequate first hand report on what went on. On Ryle's analysis of attention this general proposition reduces to the tautology 'unless you are disposed to give a first hand report on what is going on and to carry out what you are doing satisfactorily, you won't be able to give a first hand report on what is going on or carry out the activity you are performing satisfactorily'.

VIII. *The Objection to Ryle's Account of the Logic of Heed Concepts*

Although Ryle fails to produce any conclusive reasons for adopting his theory of 'attending' in preference to the traditional account, it is difficult to produce any decisive arguments against it as long as we restrict the discussion to the special case where we speak of someone paying attention to what he is doing. His case breaks down, however, once we try to apply it to those cases where we are said to pay heed to an object in our environment or to some feeling we have, without being engaged in any other activity with respect to it. Ryle castigates the traditional theorists for 'misdescribing heed in the contemplative idiom' (p. 137), but he himself overlooks in developing his own theory the important cases where paying heed to something is purely a matter of watching, listening, observing or contemplating. Ryle explains the fact that 'attending' exhibits the usual characteristics of an activity verb, rather than those of a dispositional verb, on the assumption that verbs like 'attending' and 'heeding' assert the occurrence of the activities which are being performed attentively. There is no special activity called 'attending', there is only the attentive performance of an activity. The logical consequence of this theory is that the individual's own activities are the only sorts of things to which attention can be paid. If Ryle's theory were correct it should be nonsensical to talk of someone paying attention to anything other than an activity which he himself is performing. In fact, of course, we can speak with perfect propriety of the paying attention to any kind of object, phenomenon or sensation which is visible, audible, tangible, or otherwise perceptible. In such cases there is no activity which is being performed attentively or heedfully. To attend in such cases is merely a matter of contemplating or observing the object or phenomenon in question. We cannot say that when we pay heed to something we are watching it, listening to it, observing or contemplating it heedfully, since as Ryle himself points out (pp. 207 and 223), words such as 'watching', 'listening', 'observing' and 'descrying' already entail that heed is being paid. These expressions do not refer to activities like driving a car which can be performed with or without heed, they refer to special forms of the activity of heed-paying itself. It makes nonsense to say that someone was observing, watching, contemplating or listening to something without paying any attention to it, whereas it makes perfect sense to speak of someone driving without paying any attention to what he is doing.

The inadequacy of Ryle's account appears most clearly when we examine the account which he gives of expressions like 'being conscious of', 'observing', 'watching' and 'listening'. To be conscious of the sensations in a blistered heel according to Ryle (pp. 157–58) is to pay heed to them; but what is the activity which is being performed attentively or heedfully here? It would seem from his long discussion of 'observation' (ch. VII) that for Ryle to say that one is observing something is to say that one is paying heed to the sensations derived from it, and 'watching' and 'listening' by the same token, refer to the paying of heed to visual and auditory sensations respectively. But we cannot say that 'having sensations' is the activity which is being performed heedfully in these cases, since to have a sensation itself entails paying at least some heed to the sensation. We can speak of failing to notice the sensations which one would have had if one had paid attention to them; but to say that one had a tingling sensation in the left toe without noticing it is nonsense. Ryle accuses the traditional theory of being unable to provide a sensible account of the difference between a careful and a careless observer, but his own theory, while giving a plausible account of carefulness, fails to explain the activity of observing.

IX. *The Dispositional Theory Restated*

Although Ryle has failed to provide a satisfactory account of consciousness, attention and observation in terms of dispositional theory of mental concepts, it would be unwise to conclude that such an account cannot be given. Ryle's account fails mainly because he overlooks the fact that our own activity is not the only sort of thing to which we can pay attention. The possibility of providing a plausible dispositional theory which takes account of our consciousness of and attention to objects, phenomena and sensations is not ruled out. Indeed it is not difficult to suggest the form which such a theory might take.

We have seen that although paying attention to what one is doing does not entail being prepared to meet the demands of the task in hand, it cannot be denied that to pay attention to something entails noticing and hence being able to say something about it. It must also, I think, be conceded that it involves being ready to encounter something, although one need not be prepared to encounter the sort of thing that is actually there. This, however, cannot be all that we are saying when we say that someone is attending to something, since we can be ready to behave in a manner appropriate to the presence of some object or event in our immediate environment without actually being conscious of it. Our disposition to act in this way may be a result of something we have been told, some inference we have drawn or some observation made a few moments previously. In such cases we might be said to know, remember or suspect that it was there, but we would not be observing, attending to or conscious of it. In order for us to be conscious of something our disposition to react to its presence must result from its impingement on our sense organs at the time.

With the qualification that the disposition must result from sensory stimulation, it becomes quite plausible to maintain that to be conscious of something is to be ready to react both verbally and otherwise to the presence of some object or event in one's immediate environment. On this theory the contribution of attending to skilled performance would be explained by pointing out that unless the individual is disposed to react in a manner appropriate to the presence of the relevant features of his own activity and the environmental situation in which it takes place, he is not likely to be very successful.

On this view 'consciousness', 'attention' and 'observation' refer to a temporary state of readiness for something. You would therefore expect them to exhibit the logical features of expressions referring to temporary states of affairs. Expressions like 'being conscious' or 'aware of' do exhibit these logical characteristics. Words like 'attending', 'observing', 'watching', 'looking' and 'listening', on the other hand, exhibit the logical behaviour characteristic of expressions which refer to activities. This fact as we have seen, appears to provide a formidable obstacle to any dispositional theory of the meaning of these words. Nevertheless the difficulty can probably be overcome without appealing to any kind of internal process or activity, by examining the notion of 'activity' itself. It is at least arguable that when we speak of an individual's activities, of the things he does, we refer to those changes in him which can be induced by such things as commands, entreaties, instructions and deliberations. Any changes whether muscular or non-muscular which he can decide or be asked to bring about in himself are things which he does. Paying attention and observing are not muscular movements, nor are they movements of a mysterious transcendental musculature, they are, so the theory might run, changes in the individual's short term dispositions, readinesses or sets (to use a term which has a wide currency in the psychological literature) which can be induced by appropriate commands, requests or by decisions on the part of the individual himself.

In the light of these considerations we may restate the dispositional theory of attention, observation and consciousness as follows: to observe or pay attention to something is to bring about a change in oneself such that the impingement of the object or phenomenon in question on one's receptor organs prepares one to respond both verbally and otherwise in a manner appropriate to the presence of something; while to be conscious of something is to be so disposed.

X. *The Case for the Traditional View*

Stated in this way my quarrel with the dispositional theory is less substantial than my agreement with it. My contention is not so much that it is wrong as that it is incomplete. It is incomplete because it makes no reference to the internal state of the individual which enables him to describe and respond appropriately to the presence of objects in his vicinity. On the view which I wish to defend, when we use what Ryle calls a 'heed concept', we are not merely referring to the disposition to respond in a manner appropriate to the presence of the thing in question and specifying how that disposition is brought into being, we are also referring to an internal state of the individual which is a necessary and sufficient condition of the presence of such a disposition. I shall now try to present arguments in support of this contention.

One of the major weaknesses of Ryle's account of mental concepts is, as he himself recognizes, his retention of the traditional extended use of the term sensation (ch. VII). He is compelled to retain this use in order to provide something —having a sensation—which the observer of an object can be said to do heedfully. One of the advantages of the revised form of the dispositional theory which I have stated is that it dispenses with the necessity for this concession to the traditional misappropriation of mental concepts. But although it dispenses with the necessity of abusing the concept of sensation, it runs into serious difficulties when applied to those cases where we do speak of being conscious of or of attending to our sensations, i.e. in those cases where our state of consciousness results from interoceptive or proprioceptive stimulation or from the various twists and quirks of our sensory apparatus, rather than from the impingement on our sense organs of any specifiable state of affairs in our environment.

Suppose that having applied pressure to my eyeball, I am conscious of a sensation of light. According to the revised dispositional theory this means that I am disposed to react to the presence of something. But what is it that I am disposed to react to? It cannot be the pressure on my eyeball, since to be conscious of light sensations is not the same thing as being conscious of pressure applied to the eyeball. But it cannot be the presence of the sensation either. Sensations, as we have seen, do not exist independently of our consciousness of them. There are not two things, my sensation and my consciousness of it, in the way that there are two things, a penny and my consciousness of the penny. The occurrence of a sensation entails someone's consciousness of that sensation.

To be disposed to react to a sensation therefore would be to be disposed to react to one's consciousness of that sensation. In other words we now have an infinite regress of dispositions, instead of the infinite regress of ghostly operations which appears so frequently in Ryle's criticisms of the traditional theories. We might be tempted to meet this objection by supposing that to say that someone is conscious of a sensation of light is to say that he is temporarily disposed to react as he would normally do if there had been a flash of light. But to be disposed to react as if there were a flash of light, would be to believe or be tempted to believe that a flash had occurred; whereas it makes perfectly good sense to say that he was conscious of a vivid sensation of light, yet it never occurred to him for one moment to suppose that there had been any actual flash of light. In other words an individual's state of consciousness is something over and above any dispositions which it arouses in him.

An objection which applies to any attempt to give a dispositional account of consciousness and attention is the objection that it always makes sense to ask the individual to describe what it is like to watch, listen, observe or be conscious of something, whereas it does not make sense to ask him what it is like to have a certain capacity or tendency. We can only describe what something is like if it is an object, situation or occurrence. We can describe, characterize or define such things as relationships, capacities and tendencies, but we cannot describe what they are like. We can describe what a car is like, but we cannot describe what its horsepower is like; we can describe what it is like for one billiard ball to strike another and propel it forward, but we cannot describe what the causal relationship is like; we can describe what it is like to swim or what it is like to realize that one can swim, but not what it is like to be able to swim; we may be able to describe what it is like to be told or call to mind the fact that whales are mammals, but we cannot describe what it is like to know or believe that they are. If to be conscious of something were merely to be disposed to react in some way, it should be logically impossible for us to describe what it is like to be conscious of something. In fact there is no logical impossibility here. We are continually describing what it is like to watch, look at, listen to or feel things.

It might be objected with some justification here that what we describe is not our consciousness, but the things we are conscious of. As we have seen, part of what is meant by saying that someone is conscious of something is that he can say something about it. It is certainly true that when we describe some object in our environment of which we are conscious, our description is a description of the object itself, and not, as has sometimes been supposed, a description of our consciousness of that object. It is also true that we cannot describe the state of being conscious in abstraction from the things we are conscious of. But that does not mean that we do not on occasions describe our consciousness of things as distinct from describing the things themselves. When we say, to use a familiar example, that the penny looks elliptical when viewed at an angle, we are not describing the penny, nor are we describing the image which it projects on our retina; we are describing what it is like to look at a penny from that particular angle; we are saying that it is somehow like looking at an ellipse viewed full face. When we say this, moreover, we do not imply that we are disposed to act in a manner appropriate to its being an ellipse. The elliptical shape of the penny is not an optical or a psychological illusion (cf. Ryle's discussion of this problem pp. 216–18).

When we describe a state of consciousness, we usually do so by comparing being conscious of one thing with being conscious of another. Nevertheless there are one or two expressions like 'pleasant', 'unpleasant', 'vivid', 'dim', 'acute' and 'vague' which we apply to the states of consciousness themselves. These are somewhat unusual adjectives to apply to a state of readiness. Furthermore the difference between vividness and dimness, acuteness and vagueness is difficult to explain on a dispositional theory of consciousness. The only possible interpretation on such a theory is in terms of the appropriateness of the behaviour, for which one is prepared, to the presence of whatever it is one is conscious of. Acute consciousness, however, does not guarantee the appropriateness of the resulting behaviour. The statement 'his consciousness of his own ineptitude was so acute that he was unable to do anything about it', makes perfectly good sense. It also describes a situation with which some of us are only too painfully familiar. If we recognize that consciousness is some sort of internal state of the individual these discrepancies between the intensity of the individual's consciousness and the adequacy of the behaviour for which it prepares him, no longer constitute a problem.

Finally, there are considerations of a more general nature. If there were no decisive arguments either way, we should probably prefer the dispositional to the internal process theory of consciousness and attention on the grounds of parsimony. As against this must be set the fact that in every other case where verbs having 'activity' characteristics are involved, it has been found impossible to apply a purely dispositional analysis, and in at least one group of cases the reference to internal processes within the individual cannot seriously be denied. The cases I have in mind here are thinking (in the sense of thinking about or thinking to oneself), pondering, calculating, imagining, dreaming, visualizing and doing mental arithmetic. Ryle (p. 27) has made a strong case for the view, that when we talk about someone thinking (in the relevant sense), pondering, calculating, or imagining we are not asserting the occurrence of any internal process or activity. He contends that the activity referred to, although sometimes covert, as when it consists of visualizing or performing mental arithmetic, need not be so. It may equally well consist in some entirely overt performance such as drawing, talking out loud to oneself or playing a game of make-believe. To assert that someone is thinking or imagining does not discriminate between these two possibilities. This argument disposes or, at least appears to dispose of, the view that words like 'thinking' and 'imagining' necessarily assert the occurrence of covert activities, but there is no suggestion that these are dispositional concepts. Nor is there any attempt to deny that thinking sometimes consists in a purely covert process or that expressions like 'dreaming', 'visualizing' and 'mental arithmetic' refer to such processes. If this is conceded with respect to 'dreaming', 'visualizing' and 'mental arithmetic', it is difficult in view of the weight of traditional and common-sense opinion and the lack of any positive evidence against it, to see why a similar concession should not be made with respect to 'attending', 'observing', 'watching', 'looking' and 'listening'.

Concepts like 'observing', 'watching', 'listening' and 'being conscious of' are, in fact, closely related to concepts like visualizing and dreaming in a way, which is extremely difficult to explain, if the former are regarded as dispositional concepts. For if we want to explain what sort of thing this business of visualizing or dreaming is, the answer which immediately suggests itself is to say that visualizing something is like watching it except that there is nothing there really and you don't have to have your eyes open. Now if to watch something is merely to bring about a change in oneself such that the impingement of the thing in question on one's eyes prepares one to respond both verbally and otherwise in a manner appropriate to there being something there, this explanation becomes completely unintelligible. Apart from the fact that both visualizing and watching are things which the individual can be said to do, it is exceedingly difficult on this theory to find anything which the two cases have in common. We cannot say that to visualize is to be disposed to act and speak as if there were something impinging on one's eyes when in fact there is not. Any one who is so disposed would be suffering from a visual hallucination, and although having a visual hallucination may be said to involve visualizing, we can visualize things perfectly well without being hallucinated. The similarity between visualizing something and watching it lies in the internal state of the individual which is brought into being, not in the behavioural dispositions which that state induces.

XI. *Conclusions*

If the above arguments prove what I think they prove, are we back where we started at the beginning of Ryle's inquiry? Do these arguments merely put the Ghost back into the Machine? I do not think so. So far as I am aware, the criticisms I have made of the dispositional theory apply only to the dispositional analysis of consciousness and heed concepts generally. The dispositional analysis of intelligence, knowledge, belief, motives and memory remains unaffected, except in so far as these concepts involve dispositions to pay attention to or become conscious of certain features of one's environment. Indeed, since Ryle himself appears to accept the view that words like 'watching', 'listening' and 'observing' entail a reference to a covert process of having sensations, it is only in the case of the heedful performance of muscular activities that the view which has been urged in this paper differs from the account which Ryle has given as far as recognizing a reference to covert states and processes is concerned. On Ryle's view, however, these processes are relatively unimportant; we learn to talk silently to ourselves in order not to disturb others; we could plan our course of action on paper, but it is often more convenient to do it in our heads. If, on the other hand, our very ability to describe and adapt our behaviour to the objects and phenomena which impinge on our sense organs, is dependent on a special state of affairs within ourselves, which can itself be described by the person in whom it occurs, the reference which is made to such a process in our use of expressions like 'attending', 'observing' and 'being conscious' can hardly be brushed aside as a matter of no great significance. If such a view is accepted, we can hardly avoid raising the question which Ryle has dodged persistently throughout his book, namely the question: 'What are these curious occurrences within ourselves on which we can give a running commentary as they occur?' Lack of space unfortunately precludes any discussion of this fascinating problem here. It is my belief, however, that the logical objections to the statement 'consciousness is a process in the brain' are no greater than the logical objections which might be raised to the statement 'lightning is a motion of electric charges'.

THE LOGIC OF PLEASURE

Terence Penelhum

In *The Concept of Mind*[1] and elsewhere Professor Ryle has attempted to establish the thesis that most mental-conduct words are used to refer not to private episodes, but to dispositions which manifest themselves in predominantly public performances, and that the traditional dualism of Mind and Body, which requires its adherents to construe these words as names of private episodes, is therefore to be rejected as leading to, and deriving its strength from, a basic misdescription of their use. This thesis seems to me to be made out very successfully in the case of a large number of concepts, among them those of intelligence, knowledge, belief, and understanding; it is clearly false (and Ryle does not deny this) in the case of such concepts as those of pains, sensations, and bodily feelings. Between these there is a group of concepts which are particularly puzzling because there seems to be reason to suggest a dispositional interpretation, and reason to suggest a private-episode interpretation, and reason to feel misgivings about both. In this group are 'heeding,' 'attending,' 'trying,' 'being conscious of,' 'seeing,' 'noticing,' and 'expecting.' Each requires independent discussion; I propose in this paper to discuss another member of this class of concepts, namely that of pleasure or enjoyment.

The Episode-View of Pleasure

An obvious view to take of the noun 'pleasure' is that it is the name of a certain type of private episode, analogous

Terence Penelhum is a member of the department of philosophy at the University of Alberta, Canada. His articles have appeared in several American and British journals.

[1] Gilbert Ryle, *The Concept of Mind* (London, 1949).

perhaps to feelings or sensations. To say that someone took pleasure in something would therefore be to say that it caused him to experience this feeling. This feeling would, normally at least, occur at the same time as the activity or experience which is its cause; and it could vary in intensity–some (e.g., Bentham) have held that its intensity is calculable to a degree which could guide us in our choice of actions which lead to it.

This becomes less plausible when attention is directed away from the *noun* 'pleasure,' which, like most nouns, suggests there is some process or entity to which it refers, to other expressions which can be substituted for it in most contexts, but are not nouns, e.g., 'enjoy,' 'like,' 'be amused by,' etc. Ryle's attack on the view that pleasure is an episode rests largely on pointing out forcefully the affinities between 'pleasure' and these latter expressions, and the relative implausibility of adopting an episodic interpretation of them.

I wish now to examine his criticisms, and to show that they do not refute the episode-view, but merely necessitate some refinements in it. I shall then argue that, thus refined, it is true, and that Ryle's own dispositional view cannot in this case account for the facts.

Ryle's Criticisms of the Episode-View

The following points are collected from three places in which Ryle discusses the concept of pleasure: *The Concept of Mind* (to be referred to hereafter as CM), Lecture IV of *Dilemmas*[2] (to be referred to as D), and his contribution to the symposium with Professor W. B. Gallie called "*Pleasure*" in the Aristotelian Society Supplementary Volume for 1954[3] (to be referred to as PAS).

(1) (D page 58) The assumption that pleasure is a feeling or sensation has led to its being coupled with pain, so that the two are thought of as opposite ends of the same scale, like North and South. But this is very misleading. It is clearly reasonable to classify pain as a feeling, at least in many cases.

[2] Gilbert Ryle, *Dilemmas* (Cambridge, England, 1954).

[3] Aristotelian Society *Supplementary Volume* XXVIII *Belief and Will* (London, 1954) [pp. 195–205].

For this reason we can ask whether a pain is shooting or stabbing, and where it is ('Where does it hurt?'). We cannot, however ask whether the pleasure is shooting or stabbing, or where it is ('Where does it please?' is nonsense). This would indicate that 'pleasure' is not a feeling- or sensation-word in the way that 'pain' is.

(2) (D 58) We can say of any sensation that it is pleasant or unpleasant or neutral. The same sensation might be found pleasant at one time, unpleasant at another, and be neither enjoyed nor disliked on a third occasion. If enjoying something consisted in having a sensation at the same time, then it would presumably make sense to ask whether this sensation itself were pleasant or unpleasant or neutral. To answer that it was unpleasant or neutral would produce a contradiction, to answer that it was pleasant would lead to 'a redundancy or worse.'

(3) (PAS 135 [195]) The meaning of the sinister 'or worse' in the above is probably revealed by Ryle's argument that the episode-view leads to an infinite regress (a form of absurdity which he frequently, and often correctly, claims to follow from the episodic interpretation of mental concepts). If one asked of the pleasure-feeling (and if pleasure were a feeling the question would be quite proper) whether it was pleasant, and were to get the answer 'Yes,' then this, on the episode-view, would mean that it in its turn was accompanied by another pleasure-feeling; the same question could in turn be asked about *this* feeling, which would generate a third-order pleasure-feeling, and so on ad infinitum.

(4) *a.* (D 60–61, CM 132) It makes sense to say that any given sensation might occur without those processes which it is normally found to accompany. It makes sense, for instance, to say that a pain might occur in the foot without there being any evidence of the sort of injury which is normally found to give rise to such a pain (my example). Such statements may very well be false, but what they assert is conceivable. If pleasure is to be construed according to the episode-view, we should be able intelligibly to make the same suggestion about it, but this is not in fact possible. To say to someone who plays golf 'just for pleasure' that you have found a way of his getting the pleasure without having to bother with the golf

is to utter a manifest absurdity. To do something for pleasure is to do it for itself, not for something to which it is an unfortunately necessary means. You cannot just 'have pleasure'; you can only take pleasure *in* something. 'Enjoy' is a transitive verb: we must always enjoy *something*; there is no sense to the sentence 'I was just enjoying.' (To inject another case of my own: the apparent exception of the phrase 'enjoy oneself' is only apparent, because on any occasion when it is used it is assumed from the context that the person who is enjoying himself is finding *something* pleasant. The mother telling her children as they leave to enjoy themselves knows, or thinks she knows, what it is that they are going to enjoy themselves doing.) It is always sense to say of any episode that it could occur in isolation; this cannot be said of enjoyment; so enjoyment is not an episode.

(4) *b*. (D 59, PAS 138 [198]) Closely connected with the above: any process which accompanies another might continue after the other had stopped; but my enjoyment of a walk does not continue after the walk. (If I am enjoying anything after the walk, it is remembering the walk, or something else entirely.) The pleasure I take in an activity cannot be 'clocked' in the way in which the activity can:

> . . . when I enjoy or dislike a conversation, there is not, besides the easily clockable stretches of the conversation, something else, stretches of which might be separately clocked, some continuous or intermittent introspectible phenomenon which is the agreeableness or disagreeableness of the conversation to me. I might indeed enjoy the first five minutes and the last three minutes of the conversation, detest one intermediate stage of it, and not care one way or the other about another stage. But if asked to compare in retrospect the durations of my enjoyings and dislikings with the durations of the stretches of the conversation which I had enjoyed or disliked, I should not be able to think of two things whose durations were to be compared. (D 59)

(5) (CM 107–108) Although someone playing a game might experience certain feelings, intense or otherwise, during the course of it, he would certainly resist the suggestion

that the only parts of it he enjoyed were those at which those feelings occurred; he might very well claim to have enjoyed the *whole* game. So enjoyment cannot be identified with any concomitant feelings.

(6) (D 59) A sensation or feeling can often distract our attention from whatever we are doing. It is clearly absurd to suggest that our enjoyment of something might distract us from it, but this would be possible if enjoying it consisted in having a sensation at the same time as it.

(7) (D 58–9, PAS 136 [196]) In general, Ryle claims that enjoying something and having feelings or sensations stand in quite different relations to *heeding* or *paying attention.* The relation between the concepts of pleasure and heed forms the core of Ryle's positive theory; for the moment I will just state his use of it to attack the episode-view. I can be absorbed in a sensation yet pay no heed to what has caused it, or I can attend to what causes it and not to it; but I cannot attend to my enjoyment of something to the exclusion of that which I am enjoying, and I cannot therefore separate the enjoying of it from the attending to it with the intention of concentrating on the latter to the exclusion of the former.

(8) There is finally the general Rylean argument (not stated specifically in this connection, but used so basically in CM that its application here can be assumed) that if pleasure were a private process no one could ever know that anyone else was at a given time enjoying something, except as the result of a very shaky inference from his external behavior, and that since this is in obvious contradiction to the fact that we do often claim to know with certainty that people are enjoying what they are doing, it follows that such knowledge is not the result of inference from overt events to covert ones.

The above criticisms purport to establish that to call pleasure an episode is to make a category-mistake. This mistake reveals itself in the fact that if pleasure-words *did* belong to the category they would have to belong to on the episode-view, *viz.*, the same category as feeling- and sensation-words, certain questions could be asked and statements made using them which are actually absurd. They must, therefore, belong to a different category, and the episode-view is false. I shall now take each of these criticisms in turn and evaluate it.

Evaluation of Ryle's Criticisms.

(1) (See also (5), (6), (7) below.) Ryle's purpose here is to show that 'pleasure,' which is not the name of a localizable sensation, should not be likened to 'pain,' because this *is* a class-word for a certain set of localizable sensations. I shall argue that this view does not show pleasure to be non-episodic, but in itself it is, I think, basically correct. Unfortunately, however, the situation is not quite as simple as this, because:

(i) as W. B. Gallie points out (PAS pp. 147–50) 'pleasure' is sometimes used to refer to certain kinds of localizable sensation, as in the case of sexual pleasure or 'the pleasures of the stomach';

(ii) 'pain' is not only used to refer to certain sensations, but also in another, apparently non-localized sense, as in the phrase 'a painful experience.' Both senses are found in the sentence 'This hurts me more than it hurts you.' If the schoolmaster says this to the pupil while chastizing him, it would be not only rash but logically inappropriate for him to reply "Where does it hurt you?"[4]

This complicates, but does not vitiate, Ryle's main point, which might be re-presented as follows: Both the words 'pleasure' and 'pain' have a localized use (call it the α-use) and another (apparently unlocalized, but anyway distinct) use (call it the β-use). In sense α they name certain well-known sensations; in sense β they do not.[5] When I ask What Pleasure Is, or what is meant by saying someone is enjoying himself, I am asking about 'pleasure'-β. This must be the case, because

(i) It always makes sense to say that one of those sensa-

[4] I owe this very apt example, as well as the clarification of this ambiguity in 'pleasure' and 'pain,' to the very helpful comments of my colleague, Professor A. M. Mardiros.

[5] I would think it was in part the confusion between these two senses of 'pleasure' that caused the persistent interpretation of Ethical Hedonism, at least on the part of its less perceptive opponents, as a purely sensualist doctrine.

tions we refer to as 'pleasures' is occurring, but the person to whom it is occurring is not enjoying it; so the enjoyment which most people customarily feel in the presence of such a sensation cannot be identified with the sensation itself.

(ii) There are, we can pride ourselves, many things we enjoy besides localized sensations.

The same points can be made in the case of 'pain.'

(i) In sense β it could be replaced by 'displeasure' or 'dislike.' Any pain in sense α might be experienced without displeasure—even with pleasure (otherwise the masochist, who has problems enough, would find himself a logical absurdity).

(ii) Similarly, also, there are many things besides organic pains that we dislike.

[This is perhaps the place to suggest, in parenthesis, that the order of priority between the α and β senses seems different in the two cases. 'Pain' can be argued to be originally a class-word for a set of unwelcome sensations, and to have acquired a derived application to the state of mind which these sensations (though not only these sensations) produce in most people, whereas 'pleasure' might seem originally to be a name for a state of mind we are in when enjoying something and to have acquired a derived application to certain localized sensations which give rise to this state of mind in the majority of us (though not only to these sensations, as is clear when we recall the existence of such phrases as 'the pleasures of philosophy'). The reason for this suggestion is the considerable lack of correspondence between pleasure-idioms and pain-idioms, in spite of the similarities already mentioned: for one thing, the dissimilarities Ryle mentions (see (1) above) indicate that the α-use of 'pleasure' and its cognates is less common than the α-use of 'pain' and *its* cognates; for another, the β-use of 'pain' is rather more stilted and uncommon than the β-use of 'pleasure.'

This cannot be developed further here, and is only incidental. But if it is true it might explain why Ryle chose to emphasize the non-sensory character of enjoyment by his over-simple contrast between 'pleasure' and 'pain.' He is in fact contrasting 'pleasure' -β and 'pain' -α; but this is less misleading than it might appear, since he is in each case dealing with the more basic of the uses of the word.]

So I agree with Ryle that enjoyment is not to be identified with any of the commonly-enjoyed sensations we call 'pleasures.' I would add, further, that it cannot be a localized sensation *accompanying* these others, for we could then sensibly ask what portion of the anatomy it was located in–not only whether, but where, we were pleased.

But it does not follow from the fact that 'pleasure' is not a sensation-word that it is not an episode-word, perhaps even the name of some diffuse and unlocalizable feeling. Nothing so far rules out this possibility, even the fact that we do not talk of shooting or stabbing pleasures, since we are not given to referring to our unlocalizable feelings in such terms either. It remains to be seen whether any of Ryle's other objections is enough to refute the episode-view in such a form. In what follows I shall assume for the sake of brevity that the episode-view of pleasure represents it as some episode *other than* a localized feeling or sensation.

(2) I do not feel there is much substance in this criticism. It amounts to saying what I think is true, that we do not talk about enjoying our enjoyment of something. Granted this, it seems to me that the episode-view can explain it quite easily. It claims that the enjoyment of something consists in its being *accompanied* by the pleasure-episode. So the reason why we cannot talk of enjoying enjoyment is that the pleasure-episode cannot accompany itself (for nothing can do this). Pleasure would share with such undeniable episodes as headaches the logical inability to occur in pairs. Hence it is senseless to ask whether pleasure is itself pleasant or unpleasant (or, therefore, neutral); this fact, however, is quite compatible with the view that it is an episode.

(3) This answer would remove the danger of a regress, since it would prevent our giving the incriminating reply which Ryle claims leads to one.

(4) *a*. I do not feel *quite* sure that there are *no* situations in which we would speak of 'unattached' pleasure; and if there were such situations this would clearly count strongly in favor of the episode-view. But I am not unsure enough to press the point. So let it be conceded that we cannot conceive the enjoyment of something (e.g., golf) taking place without the occurrence of that which is enjoyed. We must

first be clear in what sense this is true and in what sense not. We might, after all, quite truthfully tell a golfer that he can get the pleasure without the golf if by this we meant simply that he might be enjoying some *other* activity, like drinking in the clubhouse. But in this sort of case we would still not talk of him as 'just enjoying.' Ryle is not, I take it, denying that instead of enjoying one thing we can be enjoying another; I rather take him to be denying that enjoyment can occur *alone*, i.e., in the absence of any event or episode which could be connected with it as its cause or object (be what we are enjoying). He is correct in his denial, but this does not show that enjoyment is not an episode. What it shows is that enjoyment is a *response:* the particular kind of episode we call 'enjoyment' is a response we make to stimuli—this is part of the meaning of the word 'enjoy,' and part of the explanation of its being a transitive verb. Now should the episode which, *when it occurs as the result of a stimulus,* we call 'enjoyment,' ever occur in the *absence* of anything we could regard as a stimulus, then even though this episode were, on this occasion, identical phenomenologically with the corresponding response-episode, we should just not *call* it 'enjoyment,' because of its isolation. Whether this logical fact about 'enjoyment' is actually the result of the fact that this episode never *does* occur in isolation (or even whether this is a fact at all) is irrelevant; I do not feel at all certain about this, though it does appear likely.

One might compare the episode when occurring as a response and when occurring (if it ever does) not as a response with the same statement occurring as an answer to a question and not as an answer to a question. One might also compare the inference from the fact that pleasure cannot (logically) occur alone to the conclusion that it is not an episode or occurrence at all, to an imaginary inference from the fact that an answer cannot (logically) occur alone to the conclusion that an answer is not an occurrence.

So the fact that enjoyment cannot in logic take place by itself does not prove that it is not an episode. The episode-view can accommodate this fact by saying enjoyment is an episode which is a response to a stimulus, and which would have to go under another name if it took place without a stimulus.

(4) *b.* This is still not answered, for it might after all be the case that a response should outlast its stimulus, and I do not think this can be held with regard to pleasure. If enjoyment did persist after a stimulus, it would have to be enjoyment 'of' something else, not of the original object at all. It is not possible to deal with this point before examining the connection of enjoyment with attention.

(5) Although I must admit to being rather unclear about the relationship between enjoyment and the feelings (e.g., tingles, thrills, transports, glows) that are associated with it, I do not feel they need present any problem for the episode-view. Ryle is correct in pointing out that the occurrence of such feelings during the course of a game which I enjoy is neither a necessary nor a sufficient condition of my enjoying it, and that I would certainly not, as a rule, claim to have enjoyed only those parts of the game at which they occurred. But although they are not to be *identified* with the enjoyment of the game, they may surely contribute to it: I suggest they contribute to the enjoyment of the game simply because they are occasioned *by* the game and are themselves pleasant–in other words, they are just part of the complex of events I am enjoying, and if the enjoyment of the whole complex is intensified by their occurrence, this is because they are particularly pleasant. If it should be said that on this account they would be likely to distract from the game, the retort is that they do–one may very well stop and savor feelings of this sort; this would only be of consequence to our theory if these feelings were mistakenly identified with the enjoyment of the game.

Having avoided the pitfall of identifying such incidental feelings with the pleasure of the game, we can see that the possibility of this latter's being an episode is as open as it was before. All that we have established with regard to it is that if it *is* an episode, it is distinct from *these* episodes.

(6) This point has considerable force, and to answer it requires a further clarification of the form in which the episode-view is to be held. I have already abandoned the sensation-form of it. So far, however, it might still be held

that pleasure is a *feeling* of some unlocalized kind, like a feeling of feverishness or malaise, perhaps. The objection now being considered makes this impossible. One can always say of a feeling in this sense that it might distract us from whatever we were doing or experiencing when it occurred. The only way of holding that pleasure is a feeling and not admitting that it can distract from whatever we are taking pleasure in is to say that it just happens that *this* feeling is one which does not distract from, but rather increases our degree of attention to, what it accompanies—in other words, to accept the criticism but deny it is enough to make the retention of the feeling-classification impossible. One could do this, but it would clearly involve a *decision* about the future use of the word 'feeling,' for Ryle is clearly right in holding that the logic of this word as it is *now* used is such that this would be an innovation. This is enough to prove his point, that 'pleasure' is logically different from the words we use to mention feelings. This linguistic decision would also have the disadvantage of leaving the mysterious fact that this feeling had this special feature quite unexplained.

But all this shows is that we should not classify pleasure as a *feeling*. It does not show that it is not a psychological *episode,* unless one holds that all psychological episodes are feelings, or that all psychological episodes can be distracting, and I can see no good reason for saying either. What is required is a re-statement of the episode-view in a form which does not construe pleasure as either a sensation or a feeling. This I shall shortly try to produce.

(7) The above involves an acceptance of *this* criticism of the episode-view in the forms in which I have abandoned it. I shall try to show in what follows that, in another form, it can take account of the important facts Ryle here points out.

(8) The answer to this general point in the case of pleasure is that our knowledge of whether *other people* are enjoying themselves *is* inferential; that it is quite often hard to be sure whether our guests are enjoying our company or not, though presumably *they* know without any effort. It is, of course, very easy at other times: the signs, we say, are unmistakable, obviously they are enjoying the party. But it seems to me that here we are still relying on inference, and are simply assert-

ing that the inference is easy to make with confidence. We may not like (or philosophers may not like) the fact that our knowledge of a lot of psychological facts about others is inferential, but it is. In this respect pleasure and pain are similar. Far from being a *reductio ad absurdum* of the episode-view, this is a source of its plausibility.

For, when all is said and done, there is something *obviously* right about the episode-view, which does not depend on adherence to dualist dogma but to the obvious facts of our experience. I shall try later to specify more precisely some of the facts which lend weight to it.

Ryle's Positive Account of Enjoyment

Most of what Ryle says about enjoyment is negative, designed to refute the episode-view. He does, however, point out as crucial the intimate relationship between enjoying and heeding, or paying attention (PAS 139ff, [199ff] CM 132, D 58–9). It is logically impossible to claim that I am enjoying something and yet paying it no attention. It is, of course, possible to pay attention to something without enjoying it. So enjoyment entails, but is not entailed by, heed. This is the position as stated in CM 136, where Ryle gives a specimen list of 'heed concepts' (which includes those of noticing, taking care, concentrating, and taking an interest); enjoying and disliking are not in the list, but are said to 'connote' heeding, to entail it without being entailed by it. The connection is put more strongly in PAS, where Ryle stresses that the notion of attending is not a 'nuclear, one-piece notion,' but that there are a large variety of different idioms which belong together loosely in a family, of which 'attending to' might serve as the generic name. (One might also suggest 'being aware of,' 'not being oblivious of'). Here he states that 'enjoying' is a member of this family:

> The general point I am trying to make is that the notion of *attending* or *giving one's mind to* is a polymorphous notion. The special point that I am trying to make is that the notion of *enjoying* is one variety in this genus, or one member of this clan, i.e. that the reason why I cannot, in

logic, enjoy what I am oblivious of is the same as the reason why I cannot, in logic, spray my currant-bushes without gardening. (PAS 142) [202]

I do not think these two accounts are intended to differ. Both amount to the following:

(i) Enjoying entails attending, i.e., it would be self-contradictory to say that someone was enjoying something and yet not paying any attention to it.

(ii) This is not the whole story about enjoying, since there are a large family of concepts of which (i) is true which do not entail enjoying.

This explains the fact (see the answer to (6) above) which is not explicable if enjoyment is construed as a feeling, that it does not distract us from what we are enjoying. It does not do this because enjoyment is a *kind* of attention: a person's attending to something is part of what we mean by *saying* he is enjoying it. (It also explains (4) *b.*–I cannot, in logic, attend to what is no longer present.) So attending and enjoying are not two separate episodes that always mysteriously go together: at most one is *part* of the other–assuming, what is still *sub iudice*, that either of them is an episode at all.

It is this latter that Ryle denies, for reasons which, in the case of enjoyment, I have already considered. He not only claims (very plausibly) that 'enjoyment' is a heed-concept, but also claims (less plausibly) that heed-concepts are not episodic but dispositional. My own view can be put roughly by saying that I accept the first and deny the second.

I have no space to criticize Ryle's general theory of heed-concepts; it has in any case been done with great clarity and perceptiveness by U. T. Place, in a recent paper[6] with which I find myself in full agreement. I shall instead construct a Rylean account of enjoyment (one, that is, which applies to this concept the sort of analysis Ryle suggests for all the members of this family) and examine it.

To claim that any concept is dispositional is to claim that someone making a statement applying it to a thing or person does not make a categorical assertion to the effect that any

[6] U. T. Place, "The Concept of Heed," *British Journal of Psychology* (November, 1954) [pp. 206–26].

episode, public or private, is occurring, but uses a linguistic device for making a definite or indefinite set of hypothetical statements about what that thing or person would do if certain circumstances obtained. This analysis is very suitable for such psychological concepts as those of intelligence or generosity. But the difficulty it faces with heed-concepts in general and enjoyment in particular is that statements applying these do seem to have an irreducibly categorical element. When we say someone is attending to, or enjoying, something, we do seem to be asserting that something is taking place; the very use of the continuous present tense indicates this. Ryle tries to accommodate this fact by saying that such statements are 'mongrel-categoricals,' that is, they are partly categorical and partly hypothetical. Insofar as they are categorical they assert the occurrence of the activity that is being heedfully or enjoyably done; the rest of their meaning is to be construed dispositionally.

To illustrate with the statement 'Jones is enjoying digging': this is categorical in that, and only in that, it asserts Jones is digging. It does not assert that anything else is *occurring*, e.g., an episode called enjoyment. Enjoying digging is not doing two things (CM 108); it is doing one thing in a certain manner or frame of mind. This latter can be represented by a series of hypotheticals such as: 'If he gets hot he will not notice,' 'If he is interrupted he will resent it,' 'If we offer to relieve him he will refuse,' 'If it begins to rain he will persevere,' and so on. There is of course no definite series of such hypotheticals, any more than there are only a certain set of hypotheticals into which we can 'unpack' the statement that Jones is intelligent. But it is this *type* of explanation that shows the difference between 'Jones is digging' and 'Jones is enjoying digging,' and which enables us to explain this difference without recourse to a 'ghostly' episode going on at the same time as the wielding of the spade.

This account is clearly more economical than the episode-view, and it would be more acceptable for this reason if it could account for all the facts. I wish to show that it cannot.

Evaluation of Ryle's Positive Account

The following positive points about the logic of pleasure seem to me to tell very strongly against the dispositional view and in favor of the private-episode view:

1. As mentioned above (reply to 8), there is no doubt that my knowledge of whether other people are at any time enjoying themselves is inferential. I have to infer this from what they say and do. This in itself is quite compatible with a dispositional account of pleasure, since the only way of deciding whether someone has a given disposition is to judge this from what they say and do, i.e., to see what happens when the protases of some of the hypotheticals into which the relevant disposition-statement can be broken down are fulfilled. For instance, if I claim Jones is generous, this can be unpacked into specimen hypotheticals like 'If asked for money in a worthy cause, he will give some'; the way to test the claim that he is generous is to see what he does when he *is* asked for money in a worthy cause. Similarly, it is true that in the case of others I have to infer from evidence of a like sort whether or not they are enjoying something. Now, as Ryle points out, in the case of dispositions like generosity I have to use exactly the same method of inference as other people to decide whether *I* have the disposition. I have no 'privileged access' to my own generosity or intelligence. My own knowledge of my character is inferential, and my inferences are, for well-known reasons, often less reliable than other people's. This seems to me a very strong argument in favor of a dispositional view of character-traits and abilities, and against the postulation of such things as private intelligence- and generosity-episodes.

But this works both ways. If enjoyment were a disposition, my knowledge that *I* was enjoying myself would be inferential, just like my knowledge that others are doing so. This is obviously not the case. In this respect enjoying oneself is logically like having a pain.

It will not do to claim that since dispositions may manifest themselves in private as well as public happenings I may have a greater *quantity* of evidence in favor of the proposition that I am enjoying myself than others have, and try to use this to explain the difference between my knowledge that I am enjoying myself and their knowledge that I am. It will not do because talk of *evidence* for such a proposition in my own case is out of place. Just as *I* do not *need* evidence for the claim that I have toothache, because I unfortunately *have* that for which others need evidence, so I and only I know *without* evidence whether I am enjoying something or not. I do not, though everyone else does, have to *ascertain* whether I am finding something pleasant. This fact is entirely to be expected if pleasure is a private episode, and very hard to explain if it is a disposition.

2. This is intimately connected with 1. There is no distinction between saying that something seems to me pleasant, and saying it actually *is* pleasant to me. There is no sense to the claim that I feel I am enjoying something but may be mistaken. When I am making statements about *my own* enjoyment the phrases 'seems pleasant' and 'is pleasant' are interchangeable. If X seems pleasant to me, then it is. I can sometimes perhaps be doubtful whether my present state of mind is one of enjoyment or not ('I am not sure whether or not I like this picture'), but *if I feel sure then I cannot be wrong*, provided of course I make no claims about what other people would enjoy, and no claims about what I am enjoying beyond the statement that I am enjoying it.

Plato made a mistake over this. He tried (see *Republic*, Book IX) to distinguish between genuine and illusory pleasures, the former being those that were not, and the latter being those that were, preceded by the discomfort of lack or craving. He claimed that the latter were illusory, since they seemed more pleasant than they really were by contrast with the discomfort preceding them. But this is a mistake, because it entails that when, I, e.g., enjoy eating after feeling hungry I am deluded, since I think I am enjoying something more than I really am. But I cannot think I am enjoying something more than I really am. If eating seems pleasant to me then it is, and if it seems more so to me when I do it after hunger than when I do it on a full stomach, then it is.

This situation, which is logically similar to that which obtains when we report our pains and feelings (for one has to construct very recondite imaginary occasions to fit remarks like 'I seem to have toothache but I may be wrong'), is quite intelligible on the private-episode view. But it is not easy to account for on the dispositional view, since for reasons discussed above it is quite possible for me to seem to myself to possess a dispositional characteristic like generosity or intelligence and yet lack it.

3. It is hard to see how a convincing explanation could be given on the dispositional view of *degrees* of enjoyment. We would have to say that the difference between Jones' enjoying his digging a little and his enjoying it a great deal lay in the possibilities of the situation only, e.g., in the degree of difficulty that would be encountered in interrupting him, the degree of perseverance he would show under stress, etc. This is possible, but surely less plausible than holding that these factors are merely *effects* of the different degrees of his enjoyment.

4. Ryle's account of enjoyment as a frame of mind in which we do things entails that the only things we can enjoy are activities of our own. (This point is an adaptation of one made by Place in attacking Ryle's general theory of heed-concepts.) It makes it impossible to enjoy what someone *else* is doing, or something which is not anyone's action at all. Yet we do in fact talk of enjoying the actor's performance, the clown's antics, the Prime Minister's discomfiture, or the view. 'Enjoy' is a transitive verb, which has no use unless it has an object as well as a subject, but there is nothing in its grammar to necessitate that the object is some activity of the subject. This fact is quite intelligible if enjoyment is an occurrence, a mental state of the attention-family, but not if it is just a manner in which the enjoyed activity is done, because in these cases the activity (if there is one at all) is done by someone else.

A possible way out is to insist that what we are enjoying *is* some activity of our own, *viz.*, that of watching or noticing the actor's performance. But this clearly entails the un-Rylean view that watching and noticing are activities, and therefore occurrences, and although I would not resist this, to hold it in the interest of a dispositional theory of enjoyment would be to construe one heed-concept as episodic and another as dispositional, which is hardly compatible with claiming that both are species of the same genus. What *is* compatible with this is claiming that *all* heed-concepts are episodic, and that some form of attention is part of the meaning of the word 'enjoyment.'

The implication of the above seems to me to be this: in order to avoid the obviously false view that we can never know whether other people are enjoying themselves or not, Ryle has misrepresented the very fact which *shows* this view to be false. This is the fact that, normally, when someone is enjoying himself this affects his behavior in certain ways, and that the behavior which results enables us to infer that he is enjoying himself. Ryle misrepresents this by *identifying* the tendency to behave in these revealing ways with the enjoyment which causes it and of which it is the sign[7].

Conclusion

I would like to end by summing up the positive points which have emerged in the foregoing, and adding one or two more. In doing this I shall be trying to present the rudiments, but no more, of a purified episode-theory of enjoyment.

There is no doubt that elucidating the mode of use of the class of concepts to which 'pleasure' and its cognates belong is difficult and often baffling, and that the episodes to which they relate are elusive and hard to describe. But this does not make these episodes mythical. It is hard to *describe* what it feels like to have a headache or a toothache, but these *occur*. How much can one say positively about enjoyment?

(i) It, too, *occurs*; it is, in other words, an episode and not a disposition.

(ii) But when it occurs it generally affects the actions of the person to whom it is occurring so that certain short-term dispositional statements can be made about him. Their truth could be explained by reference to its occurrence; and their independent confirmation furnishes *evidence* of its occurrence.

[7] This is symptomatic of a general tendency in CM—see F. N. Sibley, "A Theory of the Mind," *Review of Metaphysics* (December, 1950).

(iii) Although it can be classed as an episode, it cannot be classed as a sensation or as a localized or unlocalized feeling; though there are certain well-known sensations and feelings which we almost invariably like, others which we almost invariably dislike, and some to which we are indifferent.

(iv) Ryle's basic insight that enjoyment is a variety of heed seems to me to be sound. In maintaining this together with an episode-view of pleasure I am clearly maintaining that other varieties of heed are also episodes. I have not tried to argue this here, but would merely refer the reader to Place's paper, and mention that Ryle seems in PAS (see pp. 140–43 [195–7]) half-ready to admit this himself. I would hold that heed-concepts denote a special class of mental episodes distinct from sensations and feelings; it is because they occur that we are able to respond to and report on what happens around us. I have already mentioned, however, *some* ways in which enjoyment, as one of them, *is* analogous in its logic to sensations and feelings.

(v) One way in which enjoyment differs from such kinds of heed as paying attention, concentrating, or applying oneself, and resembles such kinds as being absorbed, attracted, or interested, is the fact that it is something we cannot do at will. Aristotle noticed (1172*b* 20) that one cannot ask to what end we are pleased, what the purpose of our pleasure is. Hand-in-hand with this goes the fact that one cannot be commanded to enjoy something in the way one can be commanded to concentrate on it. What one *can* do is begin by concentrating on it in the hope that this state of concentration, which requires effort, will give way to one of enjoyment, which does not. The only way a command to enjoy something can be understood is as an order to attend to something which there is reason to anticipate you will enjoy after a time. When this intended result does not follow, we get experiences like parties which 'never really begin.' (Compare the commands 'Try to forget,' and 'Distract yourself.') Enjoyment, then, can only be commanded indirectly; in itself it must (logically) be effortless. It is not an activity, which could be done well or badly, though one can, in these ways, go through certain activities with the intention of arousing it. Aristotle (1174*b* 15) came as near as anyone to characterizing this essential passiveness of pleasure in his famous statement that it is something which supervenes like the bloom of youth.

(vi) Enjoyment, then, is an effortless form of attention, a response which is drawn *by* something and not directed *to* it. (Any effort tends to be *away from* rather than toward the object of enjoyment.) It may be, though it does not have to be, continuous with some form of directed attention which gives place to it. When it occurs it tends to make us wish for the prolongation of whatever aroused it.

(vii) It can have degrees, indicated by adjectives like 'intense,' 'moderate,' 'profound,' and its effects will vary with its degree.

(viii) It occurs at a definite time, but never alone, since no form of attention can (logically) do so. We can and do report its occurrence. It can last a long or short period of time, and come sooner or later, but (see Aristotle 1173*a* 30, Ryle D 60) it cannot be characterized as fast or slow. (Nor can the having of a pain.)

(ix) It is because enjoyment is passive and not an activity, because it cannot occur in isolation or be fast or slow that it is tempting to agree with Ryle when he says that, e.g., enjoying digging is not doing two things. There may not be two activities, but there *are* two events, taking place.

The above does not pretend to be complete. More needs to be said, especially about the difference between enjoyment and other forms of effortless attention (mere absorption, horrified fascination), and about the differences in use between the various words in the enjoyment-family. But this is not possible here: I have no space, and (at least with regard to the former point) no inspiration.[8]*

[8] On the former point there is much of value in Gallie (PAS), on the latter there are some interesting suggestions in Chapter 10 of P. H. Nowell-Smith's recent Pelican, *Ethics*.

* After this paper was in proof, there appeared an interesting article by Mr. Gerald E. Myers (in the *Journal of Philosophy*, Vol. LIV, No. 7, March 28, 1957), in which the author uses some of the shortcomings of Ryle's views on pleasure to raise "general reservations" about "Ryle's kind of 'ordinary-language' philosophizing". While I would also object to those of Ryle's arguments which Mr. Myers picks out for criticism, I would disagree with this wider purpose. It is a not uncommon mistake to identify the use in the phi-

losophy of mind of methods akin to Ryle's with the adoption of Ryle's conclusions, and if my own arguments are right they show in one instance how wrong this is. If the user of a philosophical technique comes up with the wrong answers, it is not necessarily because he is using an unsound method; it could also be because he is, on this occasion, misusing a sound one.

SLEEPING AND WAKING

Margaret Macdonald

"There exist", lamented Descartes, "no certain marks by which the state of waking may be distinguished from sleep."[1] This is disastrous because in sleep occur "those painted representations . . . in the likeness of realities"[2] which men call dreams and mistake for their originals. They finally discredit the plain man's belief in the existence of an external world which can be known by perception. Mistaken waking perceptions begin its discredit and the process of liquidation is completed by dreaming. Waking illusions and hallucinations deceive, but in dreams everything deceives. One, therefore, who dreams that he is in New York when he is, in fact, asleep in bed in London ought never to trust his senses again. It is useless for him to protest that after dreaming he wakes, for he must prove that he does not dream that he wakes and that what he perceives after waking is not another dream. Since he cannot do this, and, indeed, neither Descartes nor any other philosopher has given the slightest, intelligible hint of what would constitute such a proof, he is condemned to incurable scepticism of the senses.

I wish to challenge two assumptions in this slide. (1) The assumption that waking illusions and hallucinations constitute with dreams a progressively degenerating perceptual series differing only in degree of deception. (2) The assump-

Margaret Macdonald (1903–56) was Reader in Philosophy at Bedford College, University of London. She was the editor of an anthology, *Philosophy and Analysis* (Oxford, 1954) and of the journal *Analysis*, as well as a contributor to many other books and journals.

[1] *First Meditation. A Discourse on Method etc.* Everyman edition, p. 81.

[2] *Ibid.*

tion that dreams are 'painted' or any other kind of representation of what is perceived or experienced when awake. I admit that, in some sense, these are both very natural assumptions. Indeed, the almost universal agreement of philosophical and other reflective literature on the question seems to show that there is a practically irresistible temptation to treat dreaming as a form of illusory perception and dreams, like illusions, as counterfeit physical realities. Both these assumptions are profoundly mistaken. They are excused by certain similarities in ordinary discourse about dream and waking experience. But these have been so stressed as to conceal far more important differences. I shall argue that neither the logic of discourse about waking realities and illusions nor that of their representations applies to dreams. Nor, in consequence, the distinction between 'appearance' and 'reality'; 'seems' or 'looks to be' and 'is' and the parallel distinction between 'good' and 'bad' imitation. In short, that none of the criteria appropriate to waking life apply to dreams. The failure to realise, or the ignoring of this by philosophers has caused much confusion of the Cartesian kind in the philosophy of perception. I shall, then, begin by discussing some important differences between waking illusions and dreams. I include among waking illusions both those perceptions of an object as it appears but is not and those completely hallucinatory. By 'dreams' I refer only to what occurs during sleep. I exclude day dreams and waking imagery.

One glaring difference between dreams and waking illusions is that the latter, except perhaps for the totally insane, occur in a context of real objects with which they can be compared. Normally, not all waking experience is equally delusive. (It is because it is so for the completely insane that they must be protected.) The distant mountain looks small and blue through the haze, though it is over 4,000 feet high and covered with vegetation. To the right is something which may be a rock or a goat, I am not sure which. But at my feet is green grass, above hot sun and just ahead a tree which offers shade. About the existence and qualities of these objects there is no doubt. The stick *looks* but is not *really* bent in the water, but the water *is* and does not merely *feel* wet to an immersed hand. But may not the colours of all objects be distorted by wearing, *e.g.* brown spectacles? True, but their shapes, tactual and other qualities are unaffected. Similarly, the rattle of the train may compete for attention with the hallucinatory voices of imaginary persecutors. A real companion will confirm the first but not the second. The visionary Banquo is compared by the guilty Macbeth with his astonished flesh and blood guests, their abandoned meal and the familiar furniture of the banqueting hall. Moreover, an illusion or hallucination very often (though not, perhaps, always) fits into its context. The objects seen through brown spectacles are not all brown, but they all have some colour and it could have been brown. Either a rock or a goat might equally well be in a field. There are bent sticks as well as straight sticks which look bent in water. Banquo might have entered alive, but battered, after fighting with his assailants. There could be a lake on the horizon though what is seen happens to be a mirage. From which it follows that the objects of illusory waking perception are, in some sense, located among the real objects which form their context. It is perfectly sensible to compare the apparent size of the distant mountain with the real size of the tree near at hand; to assert that the hallucinatory voices come from behind the victim or whisper in his right ear; that Banquo's ghost crossed the room and took his place at the table. True, there are differences. A camera will record the relative shapes and sizes of mountain and tree much as they are perceived; the bent appearance of the stick in water; the object which may be rock or goat, but it will not record Banquo's ghost. Nor will a microphone transmit the voices of imaginary persecutors. Nevertheless, whatever distinctions may be made between perceptual and physical space, or between different uses of the word 'place'; for the unsophisticated perceiver illusory objects certainly appear among and in spatial relations to other perceived objects.

None of this applies to dreams. The contents of dreams do not appear in a context of real objects, for there are none. It makes sense to say, "Banquo's ghost appeared at the banquet" but it would be nonsense to say "My dream of Westminster Abbey appeared between the window and the wardrobe". Correct expressions of such an experience would be,

"I dreamed that Westminster Abbey was between my window and wardrobe" or "In my dream Westminster Abbey appeared there". For the contents of my dreams are not contents of my room. In fact, dreams are rarely of the place in which the dreamer is dreaming. But even when they are, they are not that place and their contents are not the objects nor in any spatial or other relation to the objects of that or any other place. 'In a dream' is a tricky phrase which helps to create this confusion. My wardrobe is in my bedroom; the stick looked bent, in a stream; the hallucinatory mouse ran, across a carpet. All these descriptions inform one of the whereabouts of certain perceived objects. But to the question, "Where did you meet Bernard Shaw?" the answer, 'in a dream' would be silly. It locates no meeting place. A dream is not a queer kind of stream, carpet or banqueting hall in which one may meet either real or illusory objects. No dream is a place. But neither is it not a place. 'In a dream' is not equivalent to 'No-where'. Rather is it nonsensical to ascribe the contents of a dream to a dream as their place. It is highly significant that for the adverbial phrase 'in a dream' one can always substitute some part of the verb 'to dream'. "I saw Westminster Abbey in a dream" is equivalent to "I dreamed that I saw Westminster Abbey". This sort of equivalence does not hold of proper adverbs of place. "I met him in Africa" cannot be alternatively expressed by "I Africa-met him". There may appear to be idioms which refute this. "I put the apples in a box" may, *e.g.* be expressed by "I boxed the apples". But then one will find that the verb disguises a reference to place. "I boxed the apples" means "I put the apples in a box" because 'boxed' = 'put in a box'. But "I dreamed" does not mean "I placed something in a dream". It does mean "I experienced something in a dream" or (another alternative) 'while dreaming'. These translations show that 'in a dream' is utterly different from 'in a place'. Similar differences exist for time references. When I dream (in April, 1952) that I win a fortune on the Derby (in June, 1952) do I win a fortune in April, when I dream, or in June, when the race is run? The answer is that neither makes sense. All that is true is that I have a certain dream on a certain date but that neither clocks nor fails to clock, its incidents. It is absurd to ask when they occur. Some people may prefer to say that the notions of space and time are very different in dreams and in waking life. So be it. I wish only to stress how very different they are. So different that 'I dreamed', 'in a dream', 'when dreaming', seem much more properly classified as indications of state than of place and time.

Dreams and waking illusions also differ in respect of confirmation. Not only are waking illusions compared with their neighbouring real objects but there are recognised ways of testing their character and when and where they exist. One removes coloured spectacles and sees the real colours of objects; walks to the mountain and finds its proper size; investigates the doubtful object and discovers whether rock or goat; tries, without avail, to strike the visionary Banquo; watches the cat sit down in the place in which the hallucinatory mouse appears; notices that the imaginary voices began again, as usual, at 9 a.m. In short, there are procedures for determining whether any waking perception is veridical or illusory. One perception is checked or corrected by others. These procedures may not have been precisely formulated, but neither are they haphazard and without any order or rule and they are constantly and deliberately employed when a perception is doubted. "Is this a dagger that I see before me? Let me try to clutch it. I cannot, so it is not." He tries to touch in order to prove that the object is, or is not, real. *This is logically impossible in a dream.* It is not that it is much more difficult to determine whether what is perceived in dream is real or illusory; that one is too tired, vague and confused; but rather that it makes no sense to assert that one could employ any confirming technique in a dream. For one would but dream such employment. It would be absurd to say, "I dreamed that I saw King's College Chapel but on looking more closely I discovered that it was really Westminster Abbey". What can be meant by 'looking more closely' and 'discovering' that one was mistaken in a dream? Only, surely, that one dreamed that one looked and discovered and a dream cannot bear witness for or against itself. The answer to this has always seemed obvious. Admittedly, while dreaming, one cannot confirm that Westminster Abbey and not King's College Chapel was perceived but on waking up one finds that neither was present. What is perceived after waking proves the unreality of what is dreamed. "Thank goodness", we exclaim, on waking from nightmare, "it was only a dream". But I suggest that this obvious answer is wrong. For it assumes that 'waking up' is a method of proof, which is very queer. When was it learned and what are its rules? We learn from experience, example, tuition the procedures, already mentioned, for testing perceptual validity. These are refined upon in scientific theory and practice and chosen for their success as means to the end of obtaining empirical knowledge. But no one chose or was instructed by his teachers to wake up as the best method of making experiments. Waking up is not done by rule, in order to get information or for any other conscious purpose. "First make sure you are awake" does not occur on the first page of text books of methodology as a fundamental principle of scientific method. Waking, like sleeping, is a process of nature, not of logic. Indeed, how could 'waking up' be a procedure for testing perceptions? For such procedures are designed to show what exists and where, at the time of testing. Testing an illusory perception substitutes now the real for an apparent quality of an object; a real for an apparent object in the same context. The real colour, size, shape, etc. of an object *are*, now, roughly, where its apparent colour, size, shape, etc., *appear*; some other object *is* now where an illusory object *appears*; air, and not a dagger or ghost; sand, not water; carpet but no snakes. So it is perfectly sensible to say, "I thought the mountain could not be as low as it looked from a distance, so I went nearer and found that it was very high"[3] or "It looked like a

[3] I admit difficulties about some of these cases, especially about place and position. *E.g.* how can a high mountain be said to occupy the same place as that in which a low mountain appears? Does this not require a distinction between different kinds of space, *e.g.* physical and perceptual? I think, however, I may ignore these refinements for my present purpose. I will observe only that no one would ordinarily say that the mountain was in a different place from that in which it differently appears. One approaches the same place from which it appears small and is found to be large. Nor does it move or would be said literally to grow (and so come to occupy a larger place) during this journey. No difficulties are solved by multiplying spaces.

dagger so I tried to grasp it but met only empty air" but it would be absurd to say "I dreamed that I saw the Eiffel Tower so I awoke and found it was only the bedpost". For the bedpost was not being misperceived when I dreamed that I saw the Eiffel Tower, nor did the Eiffel Tower appear where the bedpost now *is*. The bedpost, as W. S. Gilbert might say, "has nothing to do with the case". The drunkard may console himself with "No, there isn't a real snake on the carpet, it is only one of my turns" but the dreamer cannot wake to exclaim, "Thank goodness, there isn't a real corpse on the floor". For the dream corpse never was on the floor to which he wakes and the murder may have been dreamed to occur ten years ago and not five minutes before he wakes on Friday, 18th April, 1952. So if there is no 'it' here and now of which one can say "It seemed to be something else" there is nothing which waking up can confirm. When a dreamer wakes his dream vanishes and its contents cannot, therefore, be checked for they no longer exist in any context for comparison. They may be remembered but not corrected. Dreams are thus incorrigible by waking experience. Since they are not corrigible by dream experience it seems to follow that they are totally incorrigible. But, again, what rather seems true is that dreams are neither corrigible nor incorrigible; the notion of corrigibility cannot significantly be applied to dreams. They neither conform nor fail to conform to criteria of physical reality. Consequently, they do not appear or seem to be what they are not and so do not qualify for the categories of either perceptual appearance or reality. In this dreams differ fundamentally from waking illusions which are opposed as appearances to physical realities. For one means by 'waking illusion' an object which is perceived to be or to be a quality of, a physical object and is found by subsequent experience to be a fraud.

This difference may be shown in reverse. A waking illusion is a perception which may lead to error. True, it need not always do so. One may become wary and refuse to be deceived. The experienced traveller and even the experienced drunkard cease to be taken in by mirages and pink rats. They are, so to say, disillusioned. But deception is always possible from the nature of what is perceived. It appears so like what it is not. Weaker, or less sophisticated, percipients succumb without resistance. Rash, foolish or prejudiced they fail to get the right answer they intend from experience. I did not want to take the wrong bus when too tired or lazy to distinguish '8' from '2'. I intended to get the right one and was shocked to find myself at Piccadilly Circus instead of Victoria. I should have known better and could have avoided my mistake and thus the inconvenience. Even when a mistake is not my fault, when an illusion is rare or unfamiliar to me, I wish I had been forewarned so that I could have guarded against error by being more alert, wary, dispassionate. To be deceived by a waking illusion is to be frustrated in a genuine attempt to know what exists. This cannot sensibly be said to occur in dreams. A dreamer is not trying, and failing, to be right about what he dreams. When he dreams that he sees, touches and even enters Westminster Abbey he is not failing, despite his best efforts, to achieve an intended visit to Westminster Abbey. He is not trying to do something right and getting it wrong. So he cannot be reproached for being so foolish as to imagine that he could visit Westminster Abbey in a dream. To dream what one dreams is neither wise nor foolish; successful nor unsuccessful. No precautions can be taken against it, except, perhaps, that of remaining permanently awake. According to Descartes a dreamer supposes that what he dreams are real objects and incidents and is thus deceived. But this is false. At most a dreamer may dream that he affirms the reality of what he dreams. But he is not deceived even in so doing since he cannot be undeceived. Nor can he be cautious and clever in guarding against error in his dreams nor lucky in being right without taking such precautions. Just as waking up is not a method of discovery, so falling asleep is not falling into error. "I dreamt that I dwelt in marble halls" does not imply "I then (or ever) did dwell in marble halls" but neither does it imply, still less mean the same as, "I mistakenly believed that I dwelt in marble halls". For, as in the converse situation of waking up, what rule has been broken, test omitted or misapplied which constitutes this mistake? When in waking life Macbeth believes that the visionary Banquo is real he believes that something which he sees could also be touched, fed, warmed, argued with and he is wrong. But no such tests can be applied in dreams and this is part of what is asserted by "I dreamt". This inability to apply tests is logical, not physical or psychological. But when it is logically impossible that tests which prevent or correct mistake should be applied then it is nonsensical to assert that mistake can occur. No one can be deceived where no distinction can be made between what is and is not deceptive. A dreamer is thus neither correct nor mistaken about what he dreams. While dreaming, a dreamer cannot significantly be said to know or truly or mistakenly believe any proposition about the contents of his dreams. But a person can, and very often does, assert false propositions about his illusory waking perceptions.

I have indicated probably only some of the differences between dreams and waking illusions which could be unveiled. There are also many differences within waking illusions, to consider which would take me too far from my main task. Undoubtedly, the philosophical dump labelled 'Illusions' contains a great variety of displaced perceptions. This brief discussion has, however, I hope, shown that much which can be significantly said of waking illusions cannot be said of dreams and conversely. Or, in other words, that the use of 'dream' differs in ways important for philosophers to note from that of words for waking illusions. Indeed, it may be thought too much has been proved, too great difference shown. For, according to me, it is senseless to affirm that what is dreamed is either illusory or real or that one can or cannot be mistaken about it. This sounds a strange conclusion. One thinks, if I dream of a snake my dream must contain, if not a snake then an illusory or pretence snake. For do I not perceive something snake-like and is not this fact the reason for Descartes' doubt? My answer is that whether or not something is real depends upon what is meant by 'real'. There is nothing which is real in general. 'Real' by itself has no meaning. But there are significant, particular uses of this word and what does not conform to the criteria for these uses is, in relation to them, unreal. 'Snake' is used for a certain kind of physical object. What might, but does not, conform to the criteria of physical reality is not a real physical object, *e.g.* a real snake. It is, therefore, correctly termed an illusory, *i.e.*

an unreal object of that kind. But none of the criteria of physical reality can sensibly be applied to dreams. In dreams anything may happen; nothing is ruled out. So the question whether what one dreams is a real or illusory physical object is quite unanswerable. The conditions for answering it do not exist. But, if so, how were philosophers, like Descartes, misled into classifying dreams with illusions? Why did it seem inevitable or even plausible, to conclude that though waking illusions discredit, dreams totally destroy the reliability of sense perception? How did anyone ever come to connect veridical perceptions, illusions, hallucinations and dreams? What could tempt philosophers to slide into total scepticism of the senses?

The main source of this temptation is contained in a previous question, "When I dream of a snake do I not perceive something snake-like?" It is due to the fact that many sentences which describe dreams resemble those which describe waking perceptions by sharing the common vocabulary of sensation-verbs; 'see', 'hear', 'touch', 'smell', etc. So that the following statements might all be true: "I saw a rabbit"; "I thought I saw a rabbit but found I was mistaken"; "I dreamed that I saw a rabbit". A subsidiary cause is the fact that, after waking, one can, and often does, remember dreams and compare these memories with waking perceptions. So, it is argued, if I sometimes perceive or seem to perceive a physical object and can remember and describe what I dream in perceptual terms then I must have been perceiving and perceiving some perceptible object when I dreamed. If not, why should I use the vocabulary of sensation? But if I was perceiving in dreams and find on waking that there was nothing to perceive how do I know that what I perceive when awake is not also a dream and so by what right do I ever trust my senses? Descartes' proof that the state of waking cannot be distinguished from sleep depends upon these facts (*a*) that dreams are remembered (*b*) that what is so remembered resembles an object or combination of objects perceived when awake.[4] Thus, noticing that it is in fact very difficult for him to doubt that he is sitting before a fire, clad in a dressing

[4] *Loc. cit.*

gown, writing the Meditations, he "cannot forget" that he has often believed in dreams that he was "in these same familiar circumstances" and woken to find himself deceived.[5] So, how can he be sure that he is not always deceived? The answer to part of this should now be plain. The criteria of 'real' and 'illusory' physical object which apply to the perceptions of waking life do not apply to the contents of dreams. So that when "we, in dreams, behold the Hebrides", it is neither true nor false that the Hebrides exist. Nor are we being deceived or not deceived about them. Words which are the complements of sensation verbs function differently when used of dreams and of any objects perceived in waking life. But so also do the sensation verbs. From the fact that I saw the Hebrides in a dream it does not follow that I *saw* any more than that which I saw was the Hebrides. Nor does it follow that I seemed to see or thought I saw but later found that I was mistaken, found that I was having an image or some other sensation. For, as with the objects of a dream, no such correction can be made during or after dreaming. So that it makes no sense to say either that one perceives or does not perceive in a dream. Some people again may prefer to say that this shows only that sensation verbs and their complements are used differently of dreams and the objects of waking perception. For example, some philosophers will say that what I perceive when I dream that I see the Hebrides is a sense datum of or related to the Hebrides. They also say that whenever I perceive what I directly perceive or am acquainted with is a sense datum and that the difference between dreaming and other forms of perception consists in the difference of relation between dream and other sense data and physical objects. This relation, however, has never been explained. Or, they distinguish two senses of 'perceive', *viz.* perceive_1 or "directly perceive" in which one perceives all sense data, including the contents of dreams, and perceive_2 in which one perceives physical objects and this will not apply to dreams.[6] But, again, apart from the fact that no one has yet clearly explained how perceive_1 applies to all perception,

[5] *Ibid.*

[6] *Cf.*, for example, Moore, G. E. "The Status of Sense Data" and "Some Judgments of Perception", *Phil. Studies*, pp. 168, 220 ff.

including that of physical objects, to suppose that it does so apply blurs too much the distinction between dreaming of and perceiving objects. It is very true that sensation verbs and their complements are used differently of dreams and in other contexts. But also the same words are used. The question is whether these uses can be more than exemplified, whether any attempt to characterise them further results, in effect, in their assimilation to each other or to those of another type. Again, when Descartes asks how he can be sure he is not always dreaming he seems to ask for a crucial experiment to determine an infallible mark of separation between the states of waking and sleeping. But in what state is such an experiment to be performed? If in either that of waking or sleeping this presupposes that its result is already known. Descartes gives no hint of a possible third state. He is obviously operating with the model of an experiment in waking life to determine between two theories which appear to explain the same facts. But the analogy fails. For it is logically impossible to perform such an experiment in respect of the state in which and only in which all experiments whatever can be performed. He may also be interpreted as trying to identify the use of the sensory vocabulary for dreams with (*a*) its use for physical objects and waking illusions, (*b*) with idioms appropriate to pictures, stories, plays and similar forms of representation. For, he suggests, if what are perceived in dreams are not physical objects they must–like illusions–be shams, forgeries or fictions–'painted representations' of realities. I have tried to show that the first identification leads to nonsense. I will now discuss the second.

According to this, then, which is a very common interpretation and not confined to Descartes, if I did not behold the Hebrides in a dream and must have seen *something*, this could only have been a picture or likeness of the Hebrides. But, a fact which Descartes and others have tended to overlook, one is not always a passive spectator in dreams. One dreams of travelling, eating meals, holding conversations with others, engaging in many and often violent activities. Perhaps the relative immobility of philosophers when writing about perception has led them to treat dreams as sheer spectacles of which the only valid questions to ask are, "Is it a real scene?" or "Is it a fair copy?". But dreams are often more like dramas in which the dreamer plays a leading role then presentations which he contemplates. However, its defenders could accept this extension without substantially modifying their view that dreams are substitute or imitation realities. Dreams are a copy or enactment of the objects and incidents of waking life. Professor Ryle has pointed out that the 'copy' metaphor is inapplicable to waking imagery.[7] The grammar of 'picture', 'representation', 'fake', 'imitation', is quite different from that of 'image'. A picture, copy or any other kind of duplicate, however cleverly and carefully executed, can always be distinguished from its original or it would not be a copy but the original. Copies have their own peculiar characteristics. They are executed in a certain material, with paints on canvas, in plastic instead of leather, recorded on a wax disc, worm-holed by a gimlet and not by termites. None of these is a characteristic of images. To try to stretch the analogy by inventing an etherial, mental material from which copies are produced by a ghostly artist is just to show that the analogy has evaporated and so to talk nonsense. This is also true of dreams. If "we are such stuff as dreams are made on" the poet does not disclose the nature of this material. The same lack of analogy also exists between dreams and the enactment of actual or imagined incidents from real life. Despite their feeling of activity dreams are no more dramas than pictures. Dream scenes are not pasteboard stage 'sets'; no lanthorn "doth the hornéd moon present". Dreams do not take place on a stage, in a theatre, nor are their participants, including the dreamer, performing players. These may be thought trivial objections. 'Drama' and 'dramatic performance' are vague terms applied to a widely varying family of histrionic forms. Surely one may compare dreams to dramas without requiring that they conform to all the paraphernalia of full-scale theatrical performance? I do not deny this, but my point is different and more general. The analogy attempted by all these comparisons is between dreams and, roughly, the arts and crafts. Pictures, plays, novels, even fakes and forgeries have to be made and some of them produced and performed. I have said that dreams do not conform to

[7] *Cf. The Concept of Mind*, Chapter VIII [pp. 117–53].

the standards of reality. But the arts also have their standards and canons. Even the expert forger prides himself on a decent job. But dreams are not produced by a dreamer trying to achieve artistic merit. They are not artefacts. Nor would it be appropriate to praise or condemn them by the canons of art criticism or craftsmanship. Most dreams, I suspect, would hardly qualify as pictures for the walls of a village schoolroom or as theatre for the repertoire of the feeblest company of barn-stormers. But even if they were as perfect as a Cézanne canvas or as a play of Racine performed by the stars of the Comédie Française they still would not fulfil nor fail to fulfil the conditions of art any more than those of reality. For they have neither function. One no more falls asleep in order to become an artist or craftsman than to become a scientist or ignoramus. Works of art, like Kubla Khan, may be suggested by dreams but they are not dream compositions. For to compose or create a work of art is to produce a certain result from deliberate intent with appropriate materials and in accordance with artistic criteria. Dreams may have subconscious causes; they do not have conscious aims. 'Bad dreams' are not bad because they are bad imitations or inferior works of art. Dreams have no standards. Or, rather, it is senseless to apply the notion of standards to dreams.

Another way of expressing the view here criticised might be to say that what happens in dreams is that one has images or imagines that one sees the Hebrides or takes part in a fight. Professor Ryle seeks to assimilate 'having images' to imagining, fancying, pretending rather than to looking at pictures.[8] It seems plausible to apply this to dreams. But though Professor Ryle's interpretation may be correct for waking imaging and day dreaming it is, nevertheless, not applicable to dreams. A person who dreams that he is climbing a mountain or seeing the Hebrides is not properly described as fancying, pretending or imagining that he is climbing a mountain or seeing the Hebrides. For it always makes sense to say that fancying, pretending, imagining, like producing or contemplating works of art, can be controlled. One may choose to begin or end them. An artist, like Leonardo da Vinci, may abandon most

[8] *Loc. cit.*

of his works before completion. Likewise, a person may 'shake himself out of' a day dream and start to do something more useful. True, he may not always succeed. If he is insane, neurotically obsessed, hysterical or, perhaps, in some very peculiar circumstances, like dangling from a parachute over a raging sea, he may not, in fact, be able to control his imaginings any more than his terrors. But I think, though I am not absolutely certain of this, that it does make sense to say that he could control both, if he chose, and that it is *logically possible* that he should choose. Perhaps total insanity is an exception. But I am inclined to think that it is senseless to say that a person could choose to start or stop dreaming when he is asleep. My reason for this is the one which I have cited before, that once asleep, a dreamer can only dream that he makes such a choice. "I dreamed that I chose to dream or stop dreaming" does not, according to me, imply that I chose or that I did not choose but only that I *dreamed* that I chose, which is different. I admit that one sometimes dreams of saying "I will go on with this" and sometimes the dream continues or "I will stop this one" and the dream changes or one awakes. But these seem to me very different from deciding to continue or abandon a train of thought, a problem, a composition in waking life. No one is held responsible for dream choices, praised or blamed for them and their consequences. Suppose someone says, "I had a terrifying experience last night; I imagined (fancied) that I was falling (pretended to fall) down a precipice; it was horrible". One would be a little surprised, even contemptuous and might reply, "Well, why did you not stop fancying, imagining, pretending if it frightened you so much? Since you are not mad you were not obliged to continue." But he retorts, "You don't understand. I had a nightmare of falling." One would become much more sympathetic. "Why did you not say so at first? A nightmare is different. You can't help that and it may be terrifying. But you first said that you were only making believe." One normally thinks very differently of the day dreamer and the sufferer from 'bad dreams'. Not even a psycho-analyst expects a person wilfully to change or end his dreams. So far as is known, a dreamer will wake up when the dream has ceased to 'guard sleep' and that is not of his own free will. If this is so, it does indicate a fundamental logical difference between what can be said of dreams and of the fancies, imaginings and pretences which occur when awake. Moreover, "I imagined, fancied, pretended that *p*" implies that *p* either was or could have been discovered to be otherwise. But what is dreamed is not and cannot be later found otherwise than as dreamed. So on two counts, at least, dreaming must be distinguished from imagining, fancying and pretending.

To conclude. Philosophers have wrongly tried to assimilate dreaming to the waking perception of real and illusory physical objects; to the creation, construction and contemplation of pictures and other representations and to waking imaginative experience, though, perhaps, the last two are alternative expressions of the same state. All these identifications break down and lead to philosophical puzzles including that of scepticism of the senses which afflicted Descartes. What philosophers have overlooked is the peculiar significance of the verb 'to dream' which affects the logical status of all expressions used with it to describe what is dreamed. What is asserted by and is logically important in such statements as, "I dreamed that I perceived (did, chose, etc.) . . ." is not that I perceived, did, chose, etc. but that "I *dreamed* that . . .". Philosophers have tended to emphasise the subordinate clause at the expense of the rest of the sentence. To shift the emphasis to the main clause may help to show that what is asserted by the subordinate statement when used independently is quite different from what is asserted when it is subordinated to any part of the verb 'to dream' or is used with any cognate expression referring to a dream state. This is shown by differences in what is implied by each type of assertion. So that what can be significantly said of what is done outside dreams cannot be so said of what is dreamed even though similar expressions may be used of both. Having realised this, one may admit that dreams link up with waking states; that they occur to those who perceive physical objects and act and suffer in the external world, but their contents are not physical objects or states nor copies or reproductions of them nor anything else but *dreams*.

I have tried, then, to show some of the ways in which the

use of 'dream' differs from that of other words with which it has been confused. I suggest that these differences destroy the need for Descartes' lament that "there exist no certain marks by which the state of waking may be distinguished from sleep". For if what is said of one state is nonsensical when applied to the other, then this provides at least one certain mark by which to distinguish between them. I have not attempted to give an exhaustive account of the grammar of any of these words nor completely to unravel their entanglement by philosophers of perception.

THE CONCEPT OF DREAMING

Norman Malcolm

Where does the concept of dreaming come from? We are strongly inclined to think of dreaming as an inward state or process of the soul, and to suppose that each of us arrives at the concept of dreaming through taking note of the process in himself. But this idea gives rise to insoluble problems. For one thing, how could it be determined that the inner states of different people were the *same* and, therefore, that they meant the same thing by the word 'dreaming?' Even more serious, how could one know that the inner state one calls 'dreaming' is the same in oneself each time? Perhaps there is not enough regularity in one's application of the sound 'dreaming' for it to even qualify as a *word*! An appeal to one's own memory impression of its being the same state each time would be useless, because there would be no possibility of one's determining whether this impression was true or false. I am applying to dreaming the points made by Wittgenstein in his attack on the notion that one learns what thinking, remembering, mental images, sensations, and so on, are from 'one's own case'.[1]

One may think to overcome these difficulties by allowing that the *descriptions* that people give of their private states provides a determination of what those states are and whether

Norman Malcolm is Professor of Philosophy at Cornell University, and the author of *Dreaming* (New York, 1959), *Ludwig Wittgenstein: A Memoir* (New York, 1958), and *Knowledge and Certainty*) Englewood Cliffs, N.J., 1963).

[1] For an explanation of these points readers may care to refer to my review of the *Philosophical Investigations* (*Philosophical Review*, October, 1954) and to my article 'Knowledge of Other Minds' (*Journal of Philosophy*, November 6, 1958. Vol. LV, No. 23). [pp. 365–76].

they are the same. But if one takes this line (which is correct) one cannot then permit a question to be raised as to whether those descriptions are in error or not—for this would be to fall back into the original difficulty. One must treat the descriptions as the *criterion* of what the inner occurrences are. 'An "inner process" stands in need of outward criteria' (Wittgenstein, §580).

What we must say, although it seems paradoxical, is that the concept of dreaming is derived, not from dreaming, but from descriptions of dreams, i.e. from the familiar phenomenon that we call 'telling a dream'. If after waking from sleep a child tells us that he saw and did and thought various things, none of which could be true, and if his relation of these incidents has spontaneity and no appearance of invention, then we may say to him 'It was a dream'. We do not question whether he really had a dream or if it merely seems to him that he did.

> People who on waking tell us certain incidents (that they have been in such-and-such places, etc.). Then we teach them the expression 'I dreamt', which precedes the narrative. Afterwards I sometimes ask them 'did you dream anything last night?' and am answered yes or no, sometimes with an account of a dream, sometimes not. That is the language-game . . .
>
> Now must I make some assumption about whether people are deceived by their memories or not; whether they really had these images while they slept, or whether it merely seems so to them on waking? And what meaning has this question?—And what interest? Do we ever ask ourselves this when someone is telling us his dream? And if not—is it because we are sure his memory won't have deceived him? (And suppose it were a man with a quite specially bad memory?—) (Wittgenstein, p. 184).

That this question is not raised is not a mere matter of fact but is essential to our concept of dreaming. If someone questioned whether there really are dreams corresponding to peoples' reports of dreams presumably he would have some idea of what would settle the question. He would not be using the report of a dream as the criterion of what the dream was, and so he would have to mean something different by 'dreaming'.

> Assuming that dreams can yield important information about the dreamer, what yielded the information would be truthful accounts of dreams. The question whether the dreamer's memory deceives him when he reports the dream after waking cannot arise, unless indeed we introduce a completely new criterion for the report's 'agreeing' with the dream, a criterion which gives us a concept of 'truth' as distinct from 'truthfulness' here (*Ibid.*, pp. 222–223).

We speak of 'remembering' dreams, and if we consider this expression it can appear to us to be a misuse of language. When we think philosophically about memory the following sort of paradigm comes most naturally to our minds: I spoke certain words to you yesterday. Today I am requested to give an account of what those words were. The account I give is right or wrong. This is determined by whether it agrees with your account and that of other witnesses, perhaps also by whether it is plausible in the light of what is known about you and me and the circumstances yesterday, and perhaps by still other things. But when I speak of 'remembering' a dream there is nothing outside of my account of the dream (provided that I understand the words that compose it) to determine that my account is right or wrong. I may amend it slightly on a second telling—but only slightly. If I changed it very much or many times it would no longer be said that I was 'telling a dream'. My verbal behaviour would be too unlike the behaviour on which the concept of dreaming is founded.[2] That something is implausible or impossible does not go to show that I did not dream it. In a dream I can do the impossible in every sense of the word. I can climb Everest without oxygen and I can square the circle.[3] Since nothing

[2] We are told that a patient under psychoanalysis may radically revise his first account of a dream, after six months of treatment. Because this reaction is so dissimilar to the normal phenomenon of telling dreams it is better, I think, to say that in psychoanalysis there is a different concept of dreaming than to say that in psychoanalysis one finds out what one really dreamt.

[3] What would be more senseless than to suppose that someone should not be able to distinguish propositions from tables? But

counts as determining that my memory of my dream is right or wrong, what sense can the word 'memory' have here?

But of course it is no misuse of language to speak of 'remembering a dream'. We are taught this expression. Only we must be mindful of its actual *use* and of how sharply this differs from the use of 'remembering' that appeared in our paradigm. Failure to observe this results in such an argument as the following:

> Dreaming is a real experience. And since dreams can be remembered they must be conscious experiences. Just as it is correct to say that a dreamer really dreams and does not merely dream that he dreams, so it is correct to say that a dreamer is really aware of the contents of his dream and does not merely dream that he is aware of them.[4]

I do not understand what the first statement ('Dreaming is a real experience') could mean other than that people really do have dreams–which is undeniable. A philosopher has spoken of 'the theory that we don't dream, but only remember that we have dreamt'[5] but if there is this 'theory' it must result from confusion about the criterion of dreaming. The second statement in the argument above ('And since dreams can be remembered they must be conscious experiences') seems to embody the mistake of supposing that all uses of 'remembering' conform to the same paradigms. If I remember today how someone flapped his arms yesterday, then yesterday I must have been aware of the flapping arms. Does it follow that if I remember today a dream of last night, then last night I must have been aware of the dream or of its 'contents'? First, there is no warrant for thinking that 'remembering a dream' carries exactly the same implications as 'remembering a physical occurrence'. Next, considering the impossibility of establishing that someone was aware of anything at all while asleep and the possibility of establishing that he dreamt, how can it *follow* from his remembering a dream that he was

---

Moore had a dream in which he could not do this. See J. M. Keynes, *Two Memoirs* (London, 1949), p. 94.

[4] R. M. Yost, Jr. and D. Kalish, "Miss Macdonald on Sleeping and Waking," *Philosophical Quarterly*, April, 1955, p. 118.

[5] A. R. Manser, "Dreams," ASSV, XXX (1956), pp. 226–27.

aware of the dream when he dreamt it? Finally and most importantly, what is the *meaning* of this philosophical claim? (For it does not appear to be a mere decision to call dreams 'conscious experiences' because we speak of 'remembering' dreams). What would be one's criterion for saying that a sleeper is aware of his dream? I do not see what it could be other than his telling a dream on waking up. If that is what it is then the use of the philosopher's sentence, 'People are aware of their dreams', is the same as the use of the sentence, 'People have dreams'. Consequently the philosophical claim, 'When people dream they are aware of their dreams' (or: 'Dreams are conscious experiences'), says absolutely nothing.

I know one wishes to make this protest: 'To say that one dreamt is not just to say that, on waking, one has the impression of having dreamt. No: one means that, over and above the impression, a dream was really there!' One might add: 'The impression comes to one when awake but the dream occurred during sleep; therefore they cannot be the same'.

But I am not trying to maintain that a dream *is* the waking impression that one dreamt. This would be self-contradictory. Indeed I am not trying to say what dreaming *is*: I do not understand what it would mean to do that. I merely set forth the reminder that in our daily discourse about dreams what we take as determining beyond question that a man dreamt is that in sincerity he should tell a dream or say he had one.

It is not easy to understand the relation between dreams and waking convictions of having dreamt. The dream and the waking conviction are not one and the same thing, in the sense that the morning star and the evening star are one and the same. Are they *two* things, numerically different? Let us say so. Then the question is: How are these two things related? Can we say they are logically independent of each other in the sense that either could exist regardless of whether the other existed? Now it is possible to think of a case in which a man believes falsely that he did not dream: e.g. he woke up in the middle of the night and told a dream to someone, but on waking in the morning he has the impression of having had a dreamless sleep. The possibility of this case, however, does not prove the logical independence of dreams from waking impressions, because here we relied on his telling a dream in the night as establishing that he dreamt. If we try to suppose that mankind might have told dreams without ever having dreams, or might have had dreams without ever having told dreams, we are in an embarrassment as to what would establish the existence of a dream. We may say that dreams and waking impressions are two different things: but not—two logically independent things.

One cause of difficulty is a temptation to think that when one states the criterion for something one says what that something *is*—one *defines* it. But this is wrong. The criterion of someone's having a sore foot is what he does and says in certain circumstances: and *that* is not a sore foot. Considering this, one may be inclined to think that there cannot be a *criterion* (something that settles a question with certainty) of someone's having a sore foot or having dreamt, but merely various 'outer' phenomena that are empirically correlated with sore feet and dreams. This view, however, is self-contradictory: without criteria for the occurrence of these things the correlations could not be established. Without criteria the sentences 'His foot is sore', 'He had a dream', would have no use, either correct or incorrect. We must admit that there is a criterion for the use of 'He dreamt' and also admit that it does not tell us what a dream *is*, does not give the 'essence' of dreaming (whatever that might mean), but gives the conditions that determine whether the statement 'He dreamt' is true or false.

Our puzzlement over the criterion of dreaming is partly due to the fact that the sentence for which we want a criterion is in the *past* tense. How can a present occurrence, a person's telling a dream, be the criterion for something that happened previously, the dream? Well, why not? If we abandon the assumption that the criterion and the something of which it is the criterion must be identical, then why cannot a present occurrence be the criterion of a past occurrence? We feel a reluctance to admit that this can be so, and we incline towards the thought that the criterion of the occurrence of a dream is to be found in some behaviour, or in some physiological process, that is supposed to be simultaneous with the dream. This reluctance is largely due, I think, to the assumption just mentioned. But a contributing factor is a certain haziness that is present on the periphery of our ordinary discourse about dreams. I will explain this.

If a young man in love utters his sweetheart's name in his sleep and smiles and sighs, it would be natural for anyone to say 'He is dreaming about his sweetheart'. But how should we be using this sentence? I mean: should we be predicting that if he were awakened he would be able to relate a dream or at least say he had one? Is our criterion his testimony on waking or his present behaviour? We say of a dog, when he whines and twitches his feet in sleep, 'He must be having a dream': and here there is no question of what he will tell us when he wakes up. This use of language is not quite serious: one draws no practical consequences from the supposition that a dog is dreaming. But in the case of the young man who says 'Mabel' in his sleep we might draw important conclusions (e.g. that he should be introduced to some other girl). If on waking he does not recall a dream we may say 'You have forgotten it'. But how are we using *this* expression? Does it just mean 'So; you have no dream to tell?', or does it mean 'You had a dream all right but now it has slipped your mind?'

One might suppose that when we say 'He is dreaming', on the basis of his sighs and mutterings in sleep, that either we are using his behaviour as our *criterion* that he is dreaming or else as *evidence* that he will be able to relate a dream, the latter being our criterion. This would be so if our use of language was always clearly one thing or another, always had a definite purpose. I believe that here it is not so. When we say that someone is dreaming on the basis of his behaviour in sleep, our words do not fall definitely into either alternative, and indeed have no clear sense.

The case of nightmares is somewhat different. It is certain that there is *a* sense of 'nightmare' where the criterion is behaviour. When a man cries out, struggles, appears to be afraid, is difficult to arouse, and continues to exhibit traces of fear as he awakens, we call it a nightmare regardless of whether he can tell a dream. His state was, however, so unlike the paradigms of normal sleep that it is at least problematic whether it should be said that he was 'asleep' when those struggles were going on.

These odd phenomena and curious uncertainties in our use of language should not obscure the fact that our primary concept of dreaming has for its criterion, not the behaviour of a sleeping person but his subsequent testimony. If someone tells a dream we do not think of doubting its occurrence on the ground that his sleep was thoroughly quiet and relaxed. In this sense of 'dream' a dream has a *content* (a dog's dream has none) which is described when the dream is related. Dreaming in this primary sense is of great interest to people and also poses philosophical problems. Dreaming that has a purely behavioural criterion is of little interest.

Perhaps the greatest cause of perplexity about the telling of a dream as the criterion of the occurrence of a dream is the fact that one cannot apply this criterion to oneself. One does not find out that oneself had a dream by applying that criterion. One uses it only for 'He had a dream', not for 'I had a dream'. This asymmetry may lead one to deny that the third person sentence is governed by this criterion. 'I do not determine that *I* had a dream on the basis of my telling a dream. I use "I had a dream" and "He had a dream" in the *same* sense. Therefore, that another person tells a dream cannot be the thing that determines for me that he had a dream'. The trouble with this fallacious argument lies in the phrase 'the same sense'. One can rightly say that the two sentences are used in the same sense, as contrasted (for example) with the case in which the word 'dream' in one of them meant day-dream. But what *is* 'the same sense' here? To use the sentences of this asymmetrical pair in the same sense (in so far as they can be used in the same sense) is to use them in the normal way, where telling a dream serves as a criterion of verification for the one but not the other. To use the sentences 'I weigh 170 pounds' and 'He weighs 170 pounds' in the same sense, in contrast, is to use them in accordance with the same method of verification (same or similar methods of weighing). What it is to use the sentences of a first person third person pair 'in the same sense' depends on what their normal use is. One cannot deduce what their normal use is from the fact that they are used in the same sense.

From the fact that one does not use the above criterion for deciding that one dreamt does it follow that there is not such a thing as *knowing* one dreamt? No. One has grounds sometimes for concluding that one dreamt, and this is knowledge in a proper sense of the word. An example would be to wake up with the impression that one had just painted the bedroom walls blue, and then to note that the walls are still yesterday's yellow: 'So it was a dream'. To find out one dreamt the incident is to find out that the impression one had on waking is false. As one can know one dreamt, so can one be mistaken. You wake up, for example, with the impression that a policeman came into your room during the night; other people in the house *say* this did not occur; you conclude you dreamt it: but the event really happened and the others conspired to deceive you. Suppose you awoke with the impression that you had felt a pain in your leg during the night but you did not know whether this was dream or reality. Would it be impossible for this question to be settled? No, not impossible. Someone might have heard you cry out and seen you hold your leg at some time in the night. There is a temptation to think that with pain there is no difference between 'real' and 'dreamt'. But there is as much of a distinction here as between having quarrelled with someone and having dreamt that one quarrelled.

I am inclined to believe that statements of the form 'I dreamt so and so' are always inferential in nature. I do not mean that one always arrives at them by explicit processes of inference but rather that one might always defend them as conclusions from certain facts or supposed facts. If someone were to ask you how you knew that you dreamt so and so, you could always mention something that you supposed proved or made probable that the thing in question did not occur and that therefore you dreamt it.

What can have no justification and requires none is your statement that you have the *impression* that so and so occurred. (You may or may not believe that it did occur.) In this sense you cannot find out that you dreamt, although you can find out that someone else dreamt. What it does make sense to find out is whether your impression corresponds with reality, and to discover that it does not is to discover that you had a dream.

I said previously that in a dream anything is possible. We

can see why this is so. If we know that it is impossible for a certain thing to have occurred then the waking impression that it occurred is false, and we know therefore that one dreamt the impossible thing. Where the choice is between dream and reality the impossibility, in any sense, of a thing places it in a dream.

My assertion that the question 'How do you know you dreamt so and so?' can have the sense just described may appear to conflict with the claim at the beginning of this chapter that it is part of our concept of dreaming that we do not question whether someone had a dream or whether it merely seems to him that he did. But there is no conflict. What was meant there was that when someone on awaking 'remembers' certain incidents, and we know they did not occur, then we say he *dreamt* them, i.e. they 'occurred in a dream'. There is not a *further* question of whether a dream or the events of a dream really took place during sleep. If a man wakes up with the impression of having seen and done various things, and if it is known that he did not see and do those things, then it is known that he dreamt them. No problem remains of whether a dream really existed during his sleep, of whether anything *corresponds* to his memory of a dream.

It is to be noted that when someone says he dreamt so and so, he does not imply that while he was sleeping he was aware of being asleep or was aware of dreaming. When he says 'I dreamt so and so' he implies, first, that it seemed to him on waking up as if the so and so had occurred and, second, that the so and so did not occur. There is simply no place here for an implication or assumption that he was aware of anything at all while asleep. His testimony that he had a dream does not involve that nonsensical consequence.

I have said that the statement 'I dreamt such and such' implies that the such and such did not occur. Let us consider Pharaoh's dream, recorded in *Genesis* XLI, 17–24: (Revised Standard Version).

> Behold, in my dream I was standing on the banks of the Nile; and seven cows, fat and sleek, came up out of the Nile and fed in the reed grass; and seven other cows came

> up after them, poor and very gaunt and thin, such as I had never seen in all the land of Egypt. And the thin and gaunt cows ate up the first seven fat cows, but when they had eaten them no one would have known that they had eaten them, for they were still as gaunt as at the beginning. Then I awoke. I also saw in my dream seven ears growing on one stalk, full and good; and seven ears, withered, thin, and blighted by the east wind, sprouted after them, and the thin ears swallowed up the seven good ears.

It is plain enough that if Pharaoh had believed that during the night he had actually gone out and stood on the banks of the Nile and seen seven thin cows eat up seven fat ones, he would not have put into his narrative the phrase 'in my dream'. But suppose Pharaoh's tale had gone like this: 'Behold, in the night it seemed to me that I was standing on the banks of the Nile; and it seemed to me that seven cows, fat and sleek, came up out of the Nile and fed in the reed grass; . . . etc.'. Would his declaration that this was a dream have the force of implying that it did not *seem* to him that he stood on the banks of the Nile, and all the rest?[6] Yes. For suppose it was independently known that it had seemed to him, at some time during the night, that those things were occurring. Suppose that someone had observed him to sit up in bed and exclaim 'Behold, there is the Nile before me and, lo, here are seven cows, fat and sleek . . .' Let us suppose that he stared, gestured and pointed as a man might who was hallucinated. Then we should have corrected his morning's narrative, saying 'No, it was not a dream. You had an hallucination at about midnight last night, in which those things appeared to you'.[7]

There is a restriction that needs to be put on the principle

[6] Note Descartes' remark: '. . . in sleep we continually seem to feel or imagine innumerable things which have no existence' (*The Philosophical Works of Descartes*, E. Haldane and G. Ross, 2 vols. [Cambridge, 1934], I, p. 220).

[7] I am denying that a dream *qua* dream is a seeming, appearance or 'semblance of reality'. In telling a dream, however, one can say 'It seemed . . .', when this means that there was a vagueness or uncertainty in the dream. Otherwise it would be wrong to use this locution.

that 'I dreamt that *p*' implies 'not-*p*'. Someone in California might dream one night that Westminster Abbey was destroyed by fire and discover the next day that this had really happened. In this sense a dream could be 'veridical'. But if his dream narrative contained statements like 'I *saw* it burning', 'I *heard* the walls crashing'; or 'It *seemed to me* that I could see it burning and hear the walls crashing'—those statements, which ostensibly report experiences he had while asleep, would all be false. If we try to consider the statements composing the description of a dream in the normal use that they have outside of dream-telling discourse, then those among them that ostensibly report experiences of the speaker, are *necessarily* false—for if they were not false they could not properly be said to belong to the description of a *dream*. (Thus the claim is mistaken that it is merely a *contingent* matter that the visual, auditory and tactual contents of dreams are 'non-veridical'.[8]) There is however another way in which all the statements in a dream report, both those ostensibly reporting experiences and those ostensibly reporting physical events, may be taken, and when taken in this way 'I dreamt that *p*' entails '*p*'.[9]

[8] See N. Malcolm, *Dreaming*, p. 8.
[9] This is explained in *Dreaming*, Chapter 15.

DREAMING

D. F. Pears

The thesis of this monograph is that dreams are not identical with, or composed of thoughts, impressions, feelings, images or any other mental phenomena occurring during sleep (pp. 4, 45, 51).[1] This does not mean that dreams do not occur during sleep, nor that they cannot be classified as mental phenomena (52). The point is that, if they are so classified, they are a unique and peculiar exception. They are unique, because they are the only mental phenomena that do occur during sleep (50). They are peculiar, because the criterion of the truth of the statement that a person has had a certain dream is, essentially, his saying so (49).

The last contention is qualified in three ways. First, it is applied only to the primary concept of dreaming (62, 63, [271–2] 70). Secondly, the person's report might be untruthful (55) [266]. And thirdly, there is one way in which his report might be mistaken: what he reported might in fact be part of his waking life. This does not mean that, when he says that it was a dream, he has made an inference, but only that he might have defended what he said by pointing out that it was not part of his waking life (65) [273]. It is important that he could not make any other kind of mistake (66) [274]. For no sense can be made of the suggestion that his impression of memory might fail to correspond to his dream (56) [267]. If his report of his dream is false, and if this is not because it corresponds to something in his waking life, then the only possible explanation is that he is

D. F. Pears is a tutor of Christ Church and a University Lecturer at Oxford University.

[1] Page references in parentheses are to Norman Malcolm, *Dreaming,* New York, Humanities Press, 1959.

being untruthful. For, given that there is no correspondence with waking life, a truthful report of a dream simply is the criterion of the occurrence of that dream.

It would be too much to expect that this closely packed monograph should contain a full investigation of the concept of truthfulness. But there are certain difficulties in it. Of course, the person who reports the dream does not use his own report as the criterion of its occurrence: only his audience do that (63) [272]. But does he, therefore, as Professor Malcolm maintains, use no criterion? Suppose that it takes him some time to achieve a narrative that he really accepts. Perhaps he even experiments with slightly varying versions until he arrives at one which feels exactly right. Might he not then be said to be using a criterion? Maybe not. But the word "criterion" needs to have its own criterion fixed. Certainly the dreamer corrects himself in such cases, and he would not explain the rejected version by saying that it was the result of untruthfulness. Or, if he did say this, he would have to point out that his truthfulness sometimes cost him an effort, not because he knew what he ought to say but could not bring himself to say it, but because he had to work his way through various versions until he reached an acceptable one. Not that this process is typical. But it does occur sometimes, and its occurrence is important. For it suggests that there might sometimes be an alternative to the account according to which the dreamer simply wakes up with an impression of memory, and the only mistake that he might make is saying that it is a dream when in fact it is a piece of real life (57) [268]. Malcolm mentions these untypical cases but sees no need to modify his account in the light of them. This is probably because he is preoccupied with his main point, that no sense can be attached to the suggestion that the report might be mistaken because it did not correspond to the dream. For this point certainly makes the investigation of the exact process leading up to the report of the dream look rather small, since, if there is no question of correspondence between the report and the dream, the dreamer is the final arbiter, and his penultimate arbitrations do not seem to be very important. And, in any case, even if their importance is admitted, it may be that the concept of truthfulness can be made to cover this area. But with what modifications?

Another difficulty, of an entirely different kind, is that Malcolm's criterion of the truth of the statement that a person has had a certain dream does not seem to fit our concept of dreaming. It is, of course, not easy to decide whether it does or does not fit our concept, or, if it does not, how far it diverges. For the implications of his criterion are not quite clear, and it is a difficult matter to determine exactly what our concept is. In general, it is well known that supporters of this kind of reductive theory often attribute double vision to their critics, only to be met with the counter-charge of blindness either to the implications of the reduction or to certain aspects of the material. However, one thing is clear; we ordinarily think that a waking experience can be recapitulated in a subsequent dream. But the suggested criterion does not seem to allow for this possibility, since Malcolm appears to say that, given the impression of memory, absence of correspondence with anything in the person's waking life is not only a sufficient condition of his having dreamt it, but also a necessary condition (51, 68, [276] 80, 97). If he says this, it is probably a slip. But how should the criterion be amended? Is the occurrence of a recapitulating dream always to be left an open and undecidable possibility every time anyone remembers anything from his waking life? Certainly we do not ordinarily think that there is such a large area of undecidability here. But perhaps our ordinary thoughts on this matter are confused? Or is Malcolm's account of remembering too thin and Humean?

We might also raise the converse objection, that we ordinarily think that a sincere memory-claim might fail to correspond with anything, either in the person's waking life or in his dreams. For we do not think that all the sincere memory-claims of a person who had never slept in his life would be true. So it is unrealistic to suggest that, whenever a sleeper makes a sincere memory claim that does not correspond with anything in his waking life, it should be treated as the criterion that he has dreamt it. But Malcolm has a stronger defence against this objection. For he would argue that, since we could never establish that he has not dreamt it, the idea that this is an open possibility really is confused.

Problems of the same kind, but more complicated ones, are raised by the question whether dreams can be timed. What do we ordinarily think? And what does Malcolm's criterion allow? First, we certainly think that dreams can only occur during sleep; and he makes this a matter of definition (49, 83, 98). Secondly, we almost certainly think that dreams occur at particular times during periods of sleep; but he refuses to allow that any sense can be attached to this belief. Indeed, he even denies that dreams occur in physical time (43, 70). This denial appears to be incompatible with his concession that we do dream during sleep. But he claims that the appearance of incompatibility ought to vanish as soon as we whole-heartedly accept his criterion for the truth of the statement that a dream occurred during a period of sleep (77). If it lingers, spatial imagery must be exercising an undue influence.

This part of his thesis is not easy to understand. He is almost certainly offering a reductive analysis of the statement that dreams occur during periods of sleep, and so he is not rejecting this part of what we ordinarily think about the timing of dreams. But why, in that case, does he say that dreams do not occur in physical time? This is a very puzzling remark. Dr. Johnson would have tried to refute it by going off and having a dream. But, of course, it ought to mean that they do not occur in physical time in a sense that is governed by other criteria than Malcolm's. But, why, then, does he reject the second thing that we ordinarily think? That is, why does he refuse to allow that any sense can be attached to the belief that dreams occur at particular times during periods of sleep? The reason he gives is that, though indications of specific times are sometimes given in dreamers' reports, they are never precise enough to satisfy physical science (75, 76). But this does not seem to be a sufficient reason. These imprecise indications place dreams imprecisely in physical time. Moreover, it ought to make sense to say that, if the sleeper had awoken ten minutes earlier, he would not have had the dream, even if we cannot know whether this is so. For, if this did not make sense, why should it make sense to say that, if he had not slept at all that night, he would not have had the dream?

It looks as if Malcolm is offering a reductive analysis of part of what we ordinarily think, and rejecting the other part of what we ordinarily think. In general, this is a possible programme. But in this particular case, when one part is the thought that dreams occur during periods of sleep, and the other part is the thought that they occur at particular times during periods of sleep, it is hard to see how it could be carried out. If he really intended his thesis to be taken in this way, the explanation may be that he believed that, if he allowed that dreams occurred at particular times during periods of sleep, his reductive analysis would be unable to cover this possibility. But why should the exact timing of dreams escape his analysis if the inexact timing of them does not? Because exact timing would imply that what was timed was concrete and historical? But this suggestion, even if it were intelligible, would be irrelevant to the question of analysis. Then is the reason that counterfactual conditionals, like the one beginning "If he had awoken ten minutes earlier . . .", are unverifiable? But there could be indirect evidence for them.

However, suppose that he were to insist that sense should be given not only to the statement that a dream occurred at a particular time during sleep, but also to the further statement that it was composed of, say, images, on the ground that the first statement would have very little content unless the second statement, or something like it, were added. If he insisted on this, he could argue that, if the statement that dreams occur at particular times during periods of sleep is to have a substantial content, it cannot be analysed reductively in the way that he favours. For there would be nothing in the dreamer's subsequent report which could possibly give sense to the statement that a particular dream was composed of images rather than, say, unspoken words, and so the use of physiological evidence would seem to be unavoidable. But this would be contemporary. Therefore it would be impossible to carry out a reductive analysis that appealed to no contemporary facts except the bare fact that the dreamer slept.

This would provide him with a reason for thinking that at least such statements as "The dream was composed of images" cannot be given a reductive analysis of the kind that he favours, and therefore must be rejected by him. But it does not seem to have been his reason. For he never considers the possible difference in sense between the statement that a particular dream was composed of images, and the statement that it was composed of something else. He simply takes the statement that dreams, in general, are composed of images, thoughts, feelings, etc., and argues, in general, that the only sense that it could possibly have is that people dream that they have images, thoughts, feelings, etc.; and, if there are occasions when people would not actually call the thing a dream, this can only be because it is too brief; and this is unimportant, since it will still have the same logical status as a dream—i.e. the criterion of its occurrence will be, essentially, his subsequent report (42, 47, 84, 85). In any case, even if he had followed this line of thought, it would not have diminished the difficulty that has already been mentioned: *viz.* it is difficult to accept and reduce the statement that dreams occur during periods of sleep without giving the same treatment to the statement that dreams occur at particular times during periods of sleep. For the argument which shows that the reductive analysis would deprive the second statement of substantial content would also show that the reductive analysis deprives the first statement of substantial content.

Alternatively, it may be that he simply did not think of the possibility that the statement, that a particular dream was composed of, say, images, might be given a reductive analysis of the kind that he favours.

Finally, it is just possible that he is not offering a reductive analysis even of the statement that dreams occur during periods of sleep. For his puzzling remark, that dreams do not occur in physical time, may be intended quite generally. If so, his concept of dreaming really does diverge considerably from ours. But again what he rejects, if he is rejecting it, may seem to him to be confused.

It is important to try to determine the exact meaning of Malcolm's thesis, and its relation to our concept of dreaming. For, if it is felt to be paradoxical, it is necessary to decide whether this is because it rejects part of our concept, or because it accepts it all, but gives a new and strange reductive analysis of it. Now it is doubtful how the questions of detail that have just been raised ought to be answered. But there is no doubt that, in the main, he accepts and reduces. Nor is there much doubt that most people will find his reduction paradoxical. But some of the arguments for it are very strong. However, when a conclusion is felt to be paradoxical, and perhaps even fantastic, the very strength of the arguments is a source of irritation which could cause them to be neglected. This would be regrettable, since, even if they are not conclusive, they are important challenges. And even those of his arguments that are less strong are of great interest. For he raises difficult questions, which were almost totally neglected by philosophers until Wittgenstein wrote about dreams, and he pursues them with pertinacity.

His main argument is that there could be no criterion for the truth of the statement that a person had an image, thought, feeling, etc., in his sleep, unless it merely meant that he dreamed that he had one (10, 16, 35). For anything that tended to show that he was at that moment having one would necessarily show that he was at that moment not asleep, and it is no good appealing to his subsequent memory claims if there are no possible criteria for establishing the truth of their contents (11, 40). Our only resource is to interpret them as reports of dreams, and then, subject to the qualifications already given, they are the criteria of their own truth.

Unfortunately this argument does not always succeed in disentangling itself from a subsidiary argument, which looks like it, but is in fact different from it (7, 18). The subsidiary argument simply says that the hypothesis that a person might have an image, thought, feeling, etc. in his sleep is contradictory: for all these things entail that he was aware at the time, and awareness is incompatible with sleep. The difference between the two arguments is that, according to the subsidiary one, the hypothesis is contradictory; whereas, according to the main one what is contradictory is the hypothesis that we might verify the hypothesis.[2] The subsidiary argu-

[2] This distinction is clearly drawn on p. 36.

ment, of course, invites the retort that there might be another kind of awareness, and then the main argument would have to be invoked.

One reason why the main argument does not always succeed in disentangling itself from the subsidiary argument is that Malcolm's investigation of alleged mental phenomena during sleep develops out of a discussion of the statement "I am asleep". For it is very easy to assimilate this statement to the statements "I am dead", and "I do not exist", and in fact he makes both these assimilations. When he makes the first, he says that the assertion of both "I am asleep" and "I am dead" is incompatible with their truth (7). And this is clearly the subsidiary argument. When he makes the second assimilation, he says that I cannot wonder whether I am asleep any more than I can wonder whether I exist (18). And this too ought to be the subsidiary argument, since it seems to be too strong a statement for the main argument: but in fact it comes immediately after the first exposition of the main argument. The trouble is that the statement "I am asleep" looks very like a member of a class of statements that are perfect targets for the subsidiary argument, and so a general investigation, which happens to begin with it, but really relies on the main argument, naturally tends to neglect the distinction between the two arguments.

There are traces of the subsidiary argument at other points in the monograph. For example, Malcolm argues that my dreaming that I had thoughts and feelings does not establish that I had them while asleep any more than my dreaming that I climbed a mountain establishes that I climbed it while asleep (51, 52. Cf. pp. 65 [274] 95). Certainly. But I might retort that I could have a very quiet thought in my sleep, whereas even a small mountain would wake me up; so that, even if neither of these two things would be established, one of them could be true. And here again the main argument would have to be invoked.

This discussion of the difference between the two arguments might provoke the reply that it really does not matter. For if we find it contradictory to suppose that we could verify a hypothesis, this is just as bad as finding that the hypothesis itself is contradictory: in neither case does the hypothesis express a possibility. It is not certain that Malcolm would make this reply (37). It raises a profound question about sense. This question, and the problem of interpreting his views on this point may be postponed for the moment, until the main argument has been examined.

The main argument is directed against the very natural belief that, at the times during sleep when we dream, we enjoy another mode of consciousness. It is not clear exactly what this mode of consciousness is supposed to be, but at least it is not supposed to be the same as waking consciousness, so that the belief is immune to the subsidiary argument. Presumably it would be some trance-like state, like that of a person who has been drugged, or even of someone who is totally absorbed in a work of art. If people were asked to say more exactly what the stuff of dreams is, they would probably suggest images, and some kind of narrative or unspoken words. Against this belief the main argument simply says that it is contradictory to suppose that it might be verified. And, as has already been pointed out, the possibility that it might have a purely subsequent verification is not considered, perhaps for good reasons: the verification which is considered and rejected as impossible includes at least some contemporary things, and may even be purely contemporary.

Various doubts might be raised about the main argument. First, must every type of memory-claim be verified sometimes, or at least confirmed sometimes? If so, what counts as a type? And, if memory-claims that purport to transcend a plane of consciousness count as a type for this purpose, may they not be confirmed in cases where the sleeper exhibits some behaviour, or is subjected to some stimulus? And, if so, might not this type of confirmation be used to give sense to what appears to be our ordinary belief about dreams in the other cases where it is not available? Particularly if in all cases there is, or could be physiological confirmation as well?

It would be a lengthy matter to discuss these doubts properly, and to show how Malcolm tries to preserve the main argument against them. He has a strong position, built on three lines of defence. First, in his description of cases he tends to deny, but does not actually deny outright that there are grounds for saying that, when the sleeper exhibits behaviour or is subjected to a stimulus, he is aware in any special sense. Secondly, he denies that these cases are central cases of sleep, and implies that any attempt to extrapolate from them to the central cases would be illicit. His third, and most important line of defence is to maintain, at least about the physiological phenomena in central cases, and probably also about stimulus and behaviour in borderline cases, that we cannot give any separate sense to the hypothesis that these evidences are alleged to confirm, so that they are either irrelevant to dreaming, or else must be treated as a new criterion of dreaming, different from ours.

Let us begin with his first line of defence. Now the debate in the monograph starts from an examination of the statement "I am asleep", and some kind of behaviour on the sleeper's part might naturally be used as a ground for the belief that he made this statement; and later it passes on to a general discussion of all alleged mental phenomena during sleep, including things which would not be classified as activities, and for which, therefore, some kind of stimulus might be taken to be a plausible ground. So let us first concentrate on activities.

Now the making of statements is only one activity among many, but it is very important for this investigation, because it is closely related to one of the things which might be held to be the stuff of dreams–unspoken narration, so that its relevance is not restricted to the dreams inside which the dreamer makes a statement. This tends to be obscured in the monograph where it is assumed that the particular dreamer dreams that he makes a statement. Moreover, the statement which he dreams that he makes, "I am asleep", is a peculiar one. For, if he did make this statement in his sleep, it would be a reflection on the plane of consciousness on which it itself existed; or, on Malcolm's view, a reflection on the status of the memory-claim in which it was reported.

Suppose that this dreamer talked in his sleep, and "made" this peculiar statement. Then, as Malcolm observes, outside his dream he would not be making a claim, asserting or communicating, since all these performances require that the words should be deliberately addressed or at least sent off, and the dreamer does not, and perhaps could not even know that they are going out into the world (8). Nevertheless might they not be taken as providing ground for thinking that he is at that moment making this judgement during a dream? (9, 10). "Only if he is aware at that moment." But if a special kind of awareness is envisaged—as it must be, if this problem is going to be investigated—are his words not sufficient ground for thinking that he is aware at that moment, at least in those cases where he subsequently reports that he dreamt that he made the judgement? Malcolm considers talking in one's sleep, but, when he considers it, he does not ask himself this question (10, 62 [271]). So it is not quite certain how he would have answered it if he had asked it. In similar, but more extreme cases—*e.g.* where the person's behaviour shows that he is having a nightmare—he tends to say that he is not fully asleep (28, 100). Perhaps this means that he would allow that there is some ground for thinking, at least in extreme cases, that he is aware. If he did allow this, he would, of course, mean ordinary awareness. But, if it is admitted that there is ground for thinking that there is any sort of awareness in such cases, would it not be more plausible to say that it is the sort of awareness that most people believe themselves to have when they are dreaming? For a person in the throes of a nightmare is not like a person just waking up: perhaps neither is fully asleep, but the person in the throes of a nightmare is not faintly aware that he is doing things in the real world. However, in his description of this case, Malcolm does not concede this point. But he does concede more when he raises the question whether there are any grounds for thinking that things in which the mind is passive—*e.g.* images—occur during sleep.

If we now took up this question, the debate would follow a roughly parallel course. For suppose that the hypothesis were that dreams are composed partly of images. Then it would be important that these images would be thought to occur not only at those moments when the sleeper was dreaming that he was having an image (93). So, if he were subjected to a stimulus—*e.g.* if there were a loud noise in his vicinity—the idea would be that this noise might be woven into the images that composed his dream. And the same view would be taken of proprioceptive sensations. Now, if this hypothesis had a sense, it would not imply that the sleeper heard the noise in the full way: for he would not refer it to the world outside his dream, or, perhaps even think of that world. (This is parallel to the fact, already noted, that the person who talks in his sleep does not communicate, etc.) Malcolm suggests that, in order to make this clear, the sleeper should say, after waking up, "I *must* have heard the noise" (98, 99, cf. p. 32). This he might well do. But Malcolm then interprets this remark as a causal hypothesis, and not as a report of an actual experience. Obviously his theory necessitates this interpretation of the remark, but it is an unnatural one. And even he finds himself unable to extend this kind of treatment to the asthmatic sleeper, who both is, and dreams that he is suffocating (99). This man's feeling of suffocation is, he concedes, partly dreamt, and the context makes it fairly clear that he means that it is dreamt at the moment when he is actually suffocating. So this is a very important concession; it comes very close indeed to the admission that at that moment the sleeper is aware in a special sense. He seeks to neutralize it by observing that he is not fully asleep, and that, since his suffering and behaviour yield a criterion of the occurrence of his dream, it is not a dream in the primary sense–*i.e.* the sense that is governed by the recommended criterion. But, even if this were correct, it would still leave us with a borderline case where there is some contemporary ground for thinking that there is a special kind of awareness.

At several points in his discussion of things in which the mind is passive Malcolm is influenced by an argument which is connected with a point already made here, the point that his criterion of dreaming appears to rule out, probably by an oversight, dreams that recapitulate a past experience in waking life. According to this argument the following restriction must be put on the ways in which a dream can be true of the real world; if a person dreams that he saw something happen, or heard it, etc., then the content of his dream cannot correspond to the real world in his immediate vicinity at the time when the dream would ordinarily be taken to have occurred.[3] (There is, as has been noted, some doubt whether he would

[3] Pp. 68, [276], 98. *Cf.* p. 8 footnote.

extend this restriction to earlier times too, and thus rule out recapitulating dreams.) But why is contemporary correspondence impossible? Certainly the view that it did correspond would not normally be held by the person himself, either later, or in the dream (however that is to be analysed): nor, of course, would his statement that he dreamed that he had the experience imply that view. Nevertheless the view might be correct: the content of the dream might correspond to the contemporary events in his room; and, if it did, there would probably be a causal explanation of the correspondence. So any support that this argument might give to Malcolm's case must be subtracted.

There is also another point at which his first line of defence might be attacked. The phenomenology of going to sleep and waking up might be cited against it. For at those moments we sometimes find that dreaming and waking experience overlap. Admittedly, these are cases where the person is not fully asleep, so that we could not argue that, if he is aware at all, his awareness must be the special kind of awareness. But this does not matter, since this time he himself could testify that he was conscious on two different planes, or at least that he experienced the transition from one plane to the other.

If the attack on Malcolm's first line of defence had any effect he might make a stand on the second line that he has prepared, and say that we cannot understand awareness in deep sleep by extrapolating from cases of disturbed sleep (99, 100). But this would be a more difficult position to defend. For, once it is clearly understood that the kind of awareness that is meant is not ordinary awareness, it is hard to maintain the dilemma, that either reports of dreams in undisturbed sleep have a completely different sense, or else they are unintelligible. Must all extrapolation be disallowed? Must every type of statement get its sense entirely directly? If so, what counts as a type?

But his third line of defence is the most important one. For so far we have used the unanalysed notion of "a ground". But he would say that we must always ask whether a ground provides confirmation or verification: if it provides the latter, it is a criterion; while, if it provides the former, something else will have to provide the criterion of what is being confirmed, if it is going to have a definite sense (44). He would probably apply this dilemma to stimulus and behaviour, in order to defend his descriptions of cases which have just been challenged. But he certainly applies it to physiological phenomena (43, 76, 77, 81, 82). So let us first examine its application there.

Now it is very important that his thesis is reductive only in the sense that his criterion of the truth of the statement that a dream occurred is parsimonious. He carefully guards himself against the interpretation that would credit him with the unintelligible view that the dream is to be identified with his criterion of its occurrence (59, 60, 61) [269, 270, 271]. So, when he suggests the possibility that in central cases of sleep physiological phenomena, like rapid eye movements, might be taken as a new criterion of dreaming, he is not suggesting an absurd identification. But what is the justification of his dilemma, that such phenomena are either irrelevant to dreaming or else must be taken as a new criterion of dreaming, *i.e.* as a criterion of dreaming in a secondary sense? It is clear that, if the hypothesis, that in the central cases the sleeper is aware in a special way, could get its sense by extrapolation from the borderline cases, the dilemma would not be valid in the central cases. So let us go back to the borderline cases, and see how he applies the dilemma to them.

But the trouble is that it is not certain that he does apply the dilemma to borderline cases, where there is stimulus and behaviour. If he did apply it to borderline cases, he would not have the same reason for saying that the criterion would necessarily be a new one that he has for saying this in central cases. For if physiological phenomena were used as a criterion of dreaming, this would necessarily be a new criterion, since the phenomena have only been discovered recently and are not generally known. But this is not true of stimulus and behaviour in borderline cases.

Moreover, if he did apply the dilemma to borderline cases, he might find that it could be turned against himself. For, if he said that the physical state and behaviour of the asthmatic sleeper could provide only confirmation for the hypothesis that he had some special kind of awareness, on the ground that this awareness must amount to more than the observable phenomena, then the ordinary awareness of people who are awake will often be no more than confirmed. If, on the other hand, he says that it would provide verification, he will have to go on to establish that, if it is accepted as verification, a new criterion will, in fact, have been introduced. And this is never established in the monograph. It might look as if it is established, because he says that his criterion is the one that we use, and that it fixes the primary concept of dreaming (74, 79, 80, 81, 82). But the case for doubting whether it is the one that we use has already been sketched, and he never justifies his assertion that it fixes the primary concept, and not just part of the concept of dreaming.

There is, underlying this state of his main argument, the idea that every kind of statement must have a definite criterion whose fulfilment conclusively verifies it, and whose non-fulfilment conclusively falsifies it. Guided by this idea he goes to human behaviour in order to find out what the criterion for reports of dreams is. But perhaps the search is misguided. If dreaming really does involve a special kind of awareness at the time, why should we not think that we have two independent indications of this awareness, and therefore of dreams—subsequent memory-claims and contemporary behaviour? Given certain conditions, each could be taken as sufficient ground for saying that a dream occurred; and the absence of one of them would not be taken as sufficient ground for saying that a dream did not occur, so that, *e.g.* the fact that the dreamer had not behaved appropriately in his sleep would not show that his subsequent memory-claim was mistaken. And, if he objects that, in that case, we should never have anything more than contemporary confirmation for the hypothesis that a sleeper was aware in the special way and therefore dreaming, how could he avoid extending this objection to the hypothesis that people who are awake are aware in the ordinary way? Whatever the result of this debate, it ought to take place before the word "criterion" is used.

The main argument has been examined at length because the whole subject is difficult and uncertain, and because our ordinary beliefs in the matter are apt to exercise an undue influence, before their content has been exactly determined and before they have been shown to involve more than Malcolm's criterion allows in a reductive way. There is also a small group of auxiliary arguments which do not need much comment. According to one of these arguments, if the statement "I am asleep" came from the mouth of a sleeper, it could not be taken as reliable testimony (5). According to another, I could not verify the judgement "I am asleep": for I could not observe the state of my body, and I could not tell by noticing that I was having a certain experience, since there is no experience that is necessarily connected with sleep (12); and, if it were suggested that there was a contingent connection between being asleep and having a certain experience, how could this be verified? (40) Both these arguments would presumably be applied to the statement "I am dreaming", which entails the statement "I am asleep".

Now these arguments are directed against the man who refuses to accept a reductive analysis of the statement "I have visited the world of my dreams". They reply, in effect, that, if *per impossibile,* he were right, there would be no way in which he could then establish whether he was asleep and dreaming. But the reply is not convincing. For, whatever the correct analysis of the statement "I dreamed that I was having a dream", and whatever the status of the verdict that it reports, there is no doubt that both are often true. Now it is a very mysterious fact that the verdict is often true: for at least often I am totally unable to say what the basis of my verdict was. But this mysterious fact cannot be used as an objection against the man who rejects the reductive analysis. For any theory, including the reductive one, has to admit that it is a fact, and a mysterious one. So these arguments do not advance Malcolm's case beyond the point where the main argument left it. His contention, that the statement "I dreamed that I was having a dream" must be analysed reductively, may be right; and, if it is right, the verdict can be verified, but *not by my waiting to see.* But the contention gains no support from these arguments, and must, therefore, rest on the main argument.

Imagine a world in which things were made easier for the main argument, because in it there was no correlation between dreaming and stimulus, behaviour or physiological phenomena, and no overlapping of the two planes of consciousness. What exactly ought the conclusion to be? Ought it to be that, in this world, the hypothesis that the dreamer was aware in a special way during sleep had no sense, or that it did not have a sense that we could understand? The profound question that was postponed earlier was the question whether there is any difference between these two theses. Now to say that it would have no sense is ambiguous. It might mean that it was contradictory, so that what it expressed was not a possibility. But, as has been shown, one argument for this view, the subsidiary argument, is invalid. Nor is there any plausibility in arguing for it in the way in which some people have argued that the survival of death is contradictory: for there is no reason to think that all kinds of awareness are incompatible with sleep. Suppose, on the other hand, that the ambiguous thesis were taken to mean that it had not been given a sense, and so did not express an identifiable possibility. This, of course, might be for the uninteresting reason that nobody had tried to give it a sense. Alternatively, it might be because our best efforts to give it the sense that it seemed that it ought to have had always failed, so that the words were never connected with an identifiable possibility. This second alternative could be expressed by saying that the words did not have a sense that we could understand, and this, of course, is the second thesis. But, if the first thesis is interpreted in the first way, it differs from the second thesis.

Would either of them be a correct conclusion in the imagined world? Certainly it looks as if, even in the imagined world, we should have no reason to say that what was expressed by the hypothesis that the dreamer is aware in a special way during sleep was not a possibility. But would we have any reason to say that we could not connect it with an identifiable possibility? This is a more difficult question. First, suppose that we concede that reports of dreams are a type of memory-claim that needs to be verified, or at least confirmed sometimes, in order to avoid being treated as self-supporting in the way that Malcolm recommends. The reason for conceding this would be that, if the report of a dream were alleged to mean anything more than he allows, then in the imagined world nothing in waking life could count either in favour of or against the surplus possibility. Nevertheless it might still be a possibility, and, if it were, it is arguable that we could verify it while dreaming. For would we not then know that this was it, and do we not now understand what it would be like to know that then?

So we might argue. But would we be right? For verification involves the fitting together of a situation and a statement. And how could we understand now what it would be like to know then that we had remembered the right statement? How could we even understand now what it would be like for us to remember, at the moment in a dream when we judge that we are dreaming, that our judgement bears its usual sense? How could constancy of meaning be known to have been preserved across an impervious gap between two planes of consciousness? (54) [265] This is rather an abstruse question. If it is unanswerable, then in the imagined world the hypothesis that the dreamer is aware in a special way during sleep would not be connected with an identifiable possibility. However, it would not follow that this result applied to our world, in which dreaming is sometimes connected with stimulus, behaviour and physiological phenomena, and the two planes of consciousness do sometimes overlap. And, even if it did apply to our world, it would not follow that what the hypothesis expressed would not be a possibility.

The invalidity of this second step is extremely important, but it is not absolutely certain that it is recognized in the monograph. Two things suggest that it might not be recognized. Both happen because Malcolm approaches the problem by way of an examination of the statements "I am asleep", and "I am dreaming". The first thing, which has already been noted, is this: if it is possible for a sleeper to make either of these two judgements, it must be possible for him to be aware at the time; and, though the main argument shows, if it is successful, only that we cannot connect the hypothesis, that he is aware at the time, with an identifiable possibility, the subsidiary argument insinuates that what it is connected with is not a possibility. He probably did not intend this to happen. The second thing is that he argues that, because neither of the two statements has a correct use, neither of them expresses a possibility. At least these are the words that he sometimes employs (18). But he also sometimes phrases his conclusion in a different way, and says that neither of the two statements expresses a possibility that we can think (18, 114). Now this second version must be the one that he intends. For, while it is obvious that neither of the two statements can have a correct use in the way in which the statement "I am now approaching the target area" has a correct use, this shows, at the most, that the connection of each statement with a possibility is not that it expresses it, and not that what each is connected with is not a possibility. The second version, however, is still ambiguous. For when can I not think the possibilities? He makes it clear that he does not mean that I cannot think them in the past tense when awake; which would obviously be false. So he must mean that I cannot think them in the present tense when asleep. But what is the case for saying that I cannot think them when asleep? This time he seems to have avoided one categorical assertion of impossibility only by making another, which, like the first, gets no support from the main argument, and can only be treated as the untenable conclusion of the subsidiary argument.

This analysis of his remarks about possibility shows that it is not absolutely certain that he would disallow the inference from the premiss that the hypothesis cannot be connected with an identifiable possibility to the conclusion that what it is connected with is not a possibility. Yet he seems to disallow it in several passages, and, in the course of his discussion of the question[4] whether, perhaps, I might now be asleep and dreaming, he makes it very clear that he is not denying that this is a possibility. If we are going to understand that discussion it is of the utmost importance that we should understand what he really thinks about possibility.

What he says about the possibility that I might now be asleep and dreaming is succinct. First, he says that the classical way of answering the question by appealing to the coherence of my experiences is useless since I might only be dreaming that they cohered (108). Secondly he says that in any case the question is not about a possibility that I can

[4] Pp. 117–118. This passage is an answer to an objection raised by Mr. G. J. Warnock. It looks like a later addition to the original theory.

think (18, 109, 110, 118). But though this is succinct, it is not simple.

First, inside a dream–or perhaps we should say, alongside a dream–one seldom takes the dream for reality, if only because one seldom raises this question. This is a fact, and, of course, it remains a fact even when it is analysed in his reductive way. But now suppose that I say to myself that at this moment I might be dreaming. Does he think that if I immediately told myself that what my words were connected with was not a possibility, I would be right? No. For in the passage mentioned just now he explicitly says that a determined sceptic would realize that he might be dreaming that he was wondering whether he was dreaming (117, 118). And from this it follows that he thinks that what my original words were connected with was a possibility, since they might have been inside, or alongside a dream.

Now this passage confirms the interpretation of his views about possibility that was suggested above. But it also does much more than this. For, since his determined sceptic, or at least he himself is supposed to be awake, it implies that even for a man who is awake the possibility is identifiable: *i.e.* it implies that a man who is awake understands now what it would be like to verify the possibility then. But this is incompatible with the reductive analysis of reports of dreams. For, according to that analysis, the statement that a person is dreaming means, essentially, that, if he wakes up, he will say that he has dreamt, and means no more than this. Consequently, if anyone who accepted this analysis suggested, when he was awake, that he might at that moment be dreaming, and therefore only dreaming that he was suggesting it, he ought to be suggesting no more than that, at that moment, a certain future conditional statement might be true. But how could he avoid adding to what he meant the fact that he was doing something which, if he were right, would be dreaming that he was suggesting it? It would be relevant.

This objection does not owe its force to the assumption that the sceptic is in fact awake. It makes the general point that, if a philosopher maintains that the barrier between any two planes of consciousness is so impervious that on either of the two planes statements about the other must be analysed reductively, then he cannot consistently allow that a sceptic could understand the possibility that he might be on a different plane from the one on which he is in fact. Of course, the sceptic himself would specify the possibility that he believed himself to understand: just as a person who says "I thought your yacht was bigger than it is" has a specific size in mind. But the point made against the philosopher who maintains that the barrier is impervious is entirely general. It could also be made against a philosopher who maintained that inside a dream the meaning of the statement that an event occurred in waking life should be reduced, essentially, to the report of it in the dream. Now it so happens that Malcolm specifies the possibility that his determined sceptic wants to understand, and maintains that the plane of waking consciousness, on which the sceptic is, is the only one that really is a plane of consciousness. And against this position the objection too can be made specific; if the sceptic is awake, and if the barrier is so impervious that statements about dreams must be analysed reductively, then the sceptic cannot understand the possibility that he might at that moment be dreaming. Therefore, when Malcolm admits that he cannot refute the sceptic because the sceptic might suggest that he was at that moment dreaming that he was suggesting that he might be dreaming, he is abandoning his reductive analysis.

Malcolm, of course, never claimed to be able to refute the sceptic, but only to show that the possibility that he suggests is not a possibility that he can think. But this is still an exaggerated claim. For he specifies the possibility, which, according to him, the sceptic cannot think. But even if the sceptic had been convinced by the monograph that he could not understand the possibility that he might be on the other plane of consciousness, he would still be unable to specify what he did not understand, since he would not know which plane of consciousness he was, in fact, on.

If, in our world, the sceptic's question has a sense that he can understand, can he answer it? Malcolm says that he could not use coherence in order to establish his state, unless he already knew that he was not dreaming that he was establishing it in this way: and presumably he would say the same about the phenomenology of his experiences. But why should the nature of his experiences not tell him whether he was establishing it or dreaming that he was establishing it? Perhaps there is only the illusion of a circle here. But might the method not be unreliable? Certainly it might fail, and on rare occasions it does fail. But, if it were to become generally unreliable, dreams would have to become far less recessive in our lives, and this would involve radical changes. For example, when we entered the dream-world, it would always have to be at the place where we left it, unless someone had moved our dream-bodies while we were awake: after an absence from the dream-world we would find, on our return, that other people had kept their identities: logic would be generally respected: one thing would perplex us—the strange actions that we seemed to remember having performed in the waking life, and perhaps we should regard them as the expressions of wishes that we suppressed in dream life, etc.

Philosophers have always been fascinated by dreams, and rightly so. But they have not always seen the full range of problems that they raise. Many of these problems are profound, and many of them have analogues in other philosophical topics. Malcolm identifies and explores some of the neglected ones, and those who are not convinced by his solutions will find it easier to be under the impression that they have refuted his main argument than to refute it.

THE CRITERIA FOR A PSYCHO-ANALYTIC INTERPRETATION[1]

B. A. Farrell

I

Let us consider the following case.[2] An adolescent boy, whom I shall call John, was approaching seventeen years of age when he was sent to a clinical psychologist for vocational guidance. The difficulty was that he was quite uncertain what career to take up. His school reports stated that his work was uneven—sometimes he did good work and expressed himself well, on other occasions his spelling and expression were poor; and the reports stated repeatedly that he was disappointing in examinations. He was due to take eight "O" level subjects at the end of the academic year; but his showing at school suggested that entry to University would be difficult or late. He was the youngest child of a family of three, the others being sisters aged thirty and twenty-seven. These had university careers, and the father was a successful company executive. When the boy John was nine years old, the father was given an appointment abroad and the boy went to live as a boarder

B. A. Farrell is Wilde Reader in Mental Philosophy at Oxford University.

1 The symposiasts and the Aristotelian Society are grateful to the patient and his father for permission to reproduce extracts from the case notes contained in this symposium.

2 I wish at the outset to thank Dr. P. M. Turquet, Psychiatric Consultant at the Tavistock Clinic, London, for his great kindness and generosity in allowing, and arranging for, us to make use of this case material—thereby giving us a unique opportunity to get to closer quarters with psycho-analytic discourse and practice, and the problems they generate. I also wish to thank Mr. H. Phillipson, Senior Clinical Psychologist at the Tavistock Clinic, London, for his help in providing me with relevant material.

in a public school. It became apparent, both from the boy himself and from his elder sister, that he had found adjustment in his school very difficult in the first two terms and had missed his parents considerably. However, the parents thought that John had subsequently developed well at school. He was good at sport, and took part in the social life of the school. But he made less progress educationally, was late in attempting G.C.E., was in the second stream form, and the Headmaster had doubts about his capacity for sixth-form work. On psychological examination it was found that intellectually John had quite outstanding abilities—well up to good "A" level and University work—but that he was making use of them poorly and inefficiently, especially in any test requiring self-expression. The way he attempted the tests revealed a great fear of making mistakes and of things getting out of control. In short, the immediate problem John presented was one of intellectual under-functioning. In the light of the total picture he revealed, it was thought that he might benefit from analytic treatment. This was begun, when he was sixteen years ten months old, with three sessions a week. There were various interruptions, owing to illness and school holidays. By July 1961 he had had eighty sessions, of which seventy-seven are available in typescript records.

Now let us look at a tiny extract from these records. In session 16 John began by saying that he was quite looking forward to the holidays, for one thing because his father had arranged for him to have some car driving lessons. Session 18 (the first one after the holidays a few weeks later) opened and ran as follows for almost half of its length.

J 1. I found those driving lessons which I had were quite a —were quite a test really. H'm, I must say when I first started, I was extremely nervous and then after a couple of lessons I managed to settle down a bit and gradually I got more confident and now I am feeling quite O.K. about it, but right at the beginning—I was pretty nervous, really, I found, you know, I was sweating on the line all the time.

T 1. Any idea what about?

J 2. I don't know really. Just, I suppose, it was general nervousness, but it was—I found it a big jump from just cycling my bicycle around and then to start driving a car. I found really that–well–on a bicycle you can get into small places, but in a car, you know, you have to be far more careful about it and really, it was just being out on the roads with, well, loads of other people in cars and things, and I was a bit–a bit nervous about–well, just *being* there, the fact that I was unaccustomed to driving a car and being on a main road and just having to keep your end up and not making mistakes. The instructor was quite helpful, quite a nice chap, but it was the first few lessons, going through all the traffic, I found a bit hectic, but now I just find it a matter of course. I find it a lot easier and doing things without thinking about it. Before I had to think about everything before I actually did it and now it all comes quite naturally. (Pause)

T 2. Like coming here.

J 3. Well–(pause)

T 3. But it seems to me too that, when you start on something, some presumption comes up in your mind, makes you sweat along the line. I wonder what that presumption is.

J 4. Well, I have often been told, and it has been hinted at, and I thought about it that you start on something and you don't think that you are going to succeed in it and you haven't got confidence in yourself to–to do it and to finish the job.

T 4. To take it successfully to a conclusion.

J 5. Yes (pause). I think that could be applied to quite a number of things.

T 5. And in that sense also applied to coming here. Let me be more accurate, also coming here you are not sure that you can successfully take treatment through to a successful conclusion–something won't go wrong on the way.

J 6. I was afraid of that in the beginning and even now I am not absolutely positive.

T 6. This came out a moment ago when I suggested to you that reality was connected with coming here, and you were very doubtful. You said: Well, I am not really quite sure about "here" at the moment. You said: Well. You were not going to commit yourself.

J 7. Well, that is the sort of thing, where at that moment I'd rather–kind of–sit on the fence.

T 7. M'm, and you are not certain that you'll take this through. What's going to happen?

J 8. Well, it is determination that has got to see it through, but whether it will work or not–

T 8. Yes, I wonder what you picture is going to happen, because it seems that you feel that something will go wrong. In what way will it go wrong? How will it go wrong? What is going to come up, (*J*: Well) what's going to come up and prevent it from going right?

J 9. I don't know. I just got that feeling, it is just sort of there, you know. I suppose I am like that in quite lots of things. I don't believe it until it has been proved, until I have seen it–with quite a number of things and–it happens a lot at school–in a match, for instance. Somebody says: Oh, we will beat this team; and I say: Well, O.K., I believe it when we have done it, when it is over. Perhaps I never like to commit myself. (Pause)

T 9. You are having some anxiety about committing yourself afresh, as it were, to a term's work here.

J 10. Well, it's not really the same. I have been here before, so really it is a bit different and when, and when I was driving the car, I have never been driving a car before in my life, you see, but I have been here before, and I know what it is like.

T 10. And it is the thing father does, driving a car.

J 11. Yes he does. He–well–about before last Christmas, I think it was, he sort of tried to get me interested, but I wasn't really, and he said: All right, now, I'll show you how to work the gears; and he showed me, but I didn't take it in because I didn't bother. Partly because I just could not be fagged. Well, I just, well, I felt quite happy as I was with my bike at that time, and I think, was a bit scared to go on the roads by car. Well then, I think, he thought: right, well you have got to learn to drive some time or other, I might as well learn now and so my mother booked up the lessons at the school. Well, at first I wasn't–desperately keen. I only did it because, well, it had to be done some time and that was as good a time as any.

T 11. Yes, but I think our problem is to understand here a little bit more why you weren't keen, why you weren't interested when father showed you the gears, why you are still so unhappy on your luck. I think it is because you always feel frightened to do directly something that father does. It comes too near the sort of wishes to be like father, and yet dare you be father. I think you feel it is very frightening to be father (*J*: Yes) and in this sense it is easier for you then, I think, to be, I think, the little boy, and you yourself stressed the jump from riding a bike to driving a car. Whilst in one sense it is quite a big change, nevertheless you feel it is an enormous change, as if it was some sort of change from boyhood to adulthood.

J 12. There is that in it. There was also the fact that it was my bicycle, it didn't cost an awful lot of money compared with the car and the car was my father's. Well, if anything happened to the car, well, father would be pretty annoyed, I know. If I smashed my bike up, well, that is my look out, and I know if my father rode my bike and smashed it up, I would be pretty fed up about it and goodness knows what he would be about the car costing so much more. That was one side of it.

T 12. And father gets angry when you use his things?

J 13. No, he is not particularly worried. He—well, I have been out in his car and he sort of lets me know when he is not terribly pleased with something, and that was the only sort of thing that I was really scared about. I mean I use all his tools he has got, all that kind of thing and well—quite a lot of his bits and pieces that he has got around.

T 13. So that it is not quite true that in reality outside he gets very angry, but that your picture is that inside, the picture that you have of him inside you, is of his being very likely to turn into an angry person (*J*: Yes). And that this is a picture very much mirrored on how angry *you* get, it is *you* who will get very fed up, it is you who gets very angry, if something of yours is used and broken. Again, it is noticeable in this connexion how much you keep this anger within you, because when your bicycle was used by one of the people at school and there was difficulty in coming here, because the tyre was flat, your anger here was really very controlled, your anger was very muted. Yes, you said you were pretty fed up and what a nuisance it was, but this was not said I think, with the full force of the anger. [Here a few words are inaudible] you keep a great deal of this anger inside you, very bottled up, controlling it very hard, and are, I think, in a way, I think, rather frightened to show it, and I think at any moment you confuse your anger, which you have to control in this sort of way with this large, expensive object, a car, which you then picture as being angry at yourself, getting out of hand; and it is your own anger that you are afraid of, that you are afraid will get out of hand, and you have to, I think, quite carefully control it. You used the word 'fed up' rather than saying: I am angry. I am fed up, you said, as if you had to mute it, as if you had to diminish it, diminishing your feeling of anger, I think, because you were afraid of it getting out of control. (Pause)

J 14. I don't really know what to say to that. I can't really remember myself getting really angry with somebody, not really getting right out of hand, you know, completely losing yourself. (Pause)

I shall select an, or one, interpretative remark, or interpretation, by the analyst for examination. Consider the remark in T 11: "I think it is because you always feel frightened to do directly something that father does." Let me number it "T 11,2" for convenience of reference, the "2" standing for the second complete sentence in T 11. I shall pose the following question about this remark. By reference to what criteria or considerations can we determine, with a reasonable degree of assurance, whether it be true or false?

Let us note some preliminary difficulties that we meet when we try to answer this question.

(i) Just because an analytic session has been tape recorded and put into typescript, we must not assume that the typescript record is then automatically a complete and perfect record of what was said in the session. It may not be. When I carefully compared the first typescript draft of the part of session 18 quoted above with the tape record, I detected about seventy-five errors in it, some of which may not have been unimportant. I still doubt whether the record as I quote it above is free from error.

(ii) I have boldly picked out sentence T 11,2 as being "an or one interpretative remark or interpretation". But am I being fair or a bit arbitrary in doing this? For where does the interpretation the analyst is offering John at this point really end? Does it end with the sentence I picked out–T 11,2? This feels wrong because T 11,2 has very intimate links with what follows, whatever these links may be. But if we do include the following sentence (T 11,3) as part of this "one interpretation", where are we going to stop? It looks as if we might then be forced to include most, or even the whole, of T 11 as "one" interpretation. But this would make our example of "an interpretation" too unwieldly for us to investigate, and probably misrepresent the way analysts normally use the expression "an interpretation". This uncertainty simply draws our attention to the point that the criteria of an (or one) interpretation are far from clear. (What is the number of the interpretations offered in T 13, for instance?) I suggest that, having noted this difficulty, we keep it in mind and pass on.

(iii) It is characteristic of a number of interpretations in this whole record that they are far from clear. For example, just what is meant exactly by the remark in T 11,4: "I think you feel it very frightening to be father"? This point is important because uncertainty about the meaning of *p* may hold us up in our hunt for its truth criteria. Fortunately for us, however, interpretation T 11,2 *is* pretty clear (the word "directly" in it is perhaps the chief worry). So we can avoid getting bogged down at the outset by the need to clarify the remark we are proposing to examine. Should we feel irritated at what may seem to us the woolly obscurity that recurs in the analyst's remarks, we have to bear in mind that these remarks were made extempore for the benefit of a patient, not after reflection for a concentration of philosophers.

II

With these preliminaries out of the way, let us consider T 11,2. What are its truth criteria?

Consider the criterion of acceptance, or personal avowal. It may be suggested that it is necessary for John to accept T 11,2 before we can be reasonably sure that it is true.

Suppose we try to apply this criterion. Did John accept T 11,2 or not? What are we to say here? John did not do anything like explicitly avow in the course of this session that the remark T 11,2 is true. Nor have I been able to find that he did so in any of the other seventy-seven sessions that have been put into type. What is more, John could hardly be expected to accept T 11,2 or to react to it verbally in any way at all *at the time*, because to do so would be to interrupt the analyst in full flood; and this is something that a well-mannered adolescent like John does not often do. (Likewise, only more so, for the stream of interpretative remarks making up T 13. John can hardly be expected to accept or reject at once, or even at any later time, every one of the interpretative remarks in T 13. One is apt to sympathise with him reacting to T 13 with the remark (*J* 14): "I don't really know what to say to that"!) So it looks as if the criterion of acceptance does not apply to T 11,2.

But this may only be the case if we adopt the narrow use of the expressions "an (one) interpretation" which we mentioned above, and according to which the remark T 11,2 would constitute an (or one) interpretation. Suppose we widen the use of these expressions in some way or other that will allow us to take T 11,2 along with the next sentence and a half, with which it seems closely related, and to regard this whole sequence of remarks as an (or one) interpretation. (That is to say, the interpretation will now extend from the beginning of T 11,2 to the middle of T 11,4 (. . . very frightening to be father").) Did John accept *this* interpretation? The answer depends, in part, I suppose on what we make of the word "Yes" from John that follows this interpretation, and appears in the middle of T 11,4. Is this "Yes" a "Yes" of acceptance? Or is it a "Yes" with a query in it, a "Yes" of "Well-it's-possible-I'll-consider-that-but-let-me-hear-more-first"? Or what? This question seems to face one when one listens to the tape record, and compares the character of this "Yes" with the different and more clear-cut "Yes" in T 13. It appears, therefore, that we can only say John accepted the interpretation (T 11,2–middle 4) if we are prepared to *hear* his "Yes" in T 11 *as* the "Yes" of acceptance. Accordingly, when I take this "Yes" to be one of acceptance, I am making a judgment about this utterance of John's that is rather like the judgment I make about an ambiguous figure, or a picture in a Thematic Apperception Test. In other words, it would seem that I am reacting to the boy's utterance here rather in the way that I do to the material of a projective test, and am making something like a projective judgment about it. The same is true of the analyst. Should he, relying on this utterance alone, take it to be the "Yes" of acceptance, he would also seem to be making a projective judgment about it, or something akin to one. The upshot, then, appears to be as follows. We can only apply the criterion of acceptance in this instance by the aid of a projective judgment, or something like it. This means that we cannot use the criterion here as an "objective" standard to test, or help to determine, whether this interpretation is true or not. If it is necessary to obtain John's personal avowal, or acceptance, before we can be reasonably sure that this interpretation is true, then it is uncertain whether we have obtained an avowal here or not. In this instance the criterion seems to be inapplicable and hence unhelpful.

But surely the criterion of acceptance does not characteristically apply to single utterances in the yea or nay fashion I have suggested? No, it does not characteristically work in this fashion. An analyst will normally require more than a simple "Yes" from a patient before he is satisfied that the patient has come to see that the interpretation is true, and, therefore, has genuinely and insightfully accepted it. This is particularly so, perhaps, with a polite adolescent 'yes-sirring' patient like John. But precisely *what* more is normally required? And does the full record of the boy John supply it? These questions may or may not be fair ones to put to an analyst. But they serve to indicate that we are no longer concerned with a simple matter of avowal or non-avowal. We now seem to be concerned with a much more complex question, and one which the analyst answers by the aid of his clinical judgment. Such a judgment is not self-guaranteeing. On the contrary, it could be argued that it is partly projective in character and hence infected with uncertainty. If this is so, then it is again far from a straightforward, objective matter to determine whether any given interpretation is really accepted or not. Thus, with T 11,2, I find it difficult to discover anything in the record that suggests that John did accept it at the time, or later on in the analysis. About T 11,2–4, I can find material that suggests that John accepted it, or a view like it or containing it, at a later stage in the analysis.[3] But observe that I use the word "suggests". For if I am challenged to defend myself here on either count, I can only do so by saying: "Well, it looks to me if . . .", or "It seems to me that here John is saying . . .", and so on. I am inclined to believe that analysts would speak in the same sort of way as I do about this material. But this way of speaking is not the characteristic locution of, say, the experimental psychologist. It is more like the locution characteristic of the clinical worker—for ever putting an interpretation on his material in his constant striving to see significance in it.

I asked the question: Precisely what more than a mere yea or nay is normally required by an analyst before he will be satisfied that a patient has accepted an interpretation? This question may be an unfair or an unreasonable one to put. But it will obviously help us to obtain a better idea of what the analyst requires if we can find some negative examples. Can we find instances where an offered interpretation has been withdrawn in the light of non-acceptance by the patient? Well, I have not been able to find any in this record of the boy John. But before we start moving from this to any further conclusions, let us note that it is probably a complete mistake to suppose that the typescript record should necessarily reveal any such mistaken interpretations. For it is contrary to standard analytic practice for the analyst to say anything such as: "Ah! I see I am wrong about that interpreta-

[3] In sessions 32 and 33.

tion—I withdraw it!" At best, perhaps, one might find in the record that the analyst had given up pressing one line of interpretation, and suspect that he had done so in view of the negative responses from the patient. However, one could only tell whether it was these negative responses from the patient that had made him withdraw by inspecting, or otherwise discovering, what does not appear in the session records at all—namely, the analyst's views or opinions about the patient as the analysis continues. If these were recorded in sufficient detail at suitable intervals, one might be able to compare the session records with the analyst's opinion records about the patient, and note: (*a*) where the latter's negative responses were connected with the analyst's then withdrawing (or changing) some view of his about the patient; and (*b*) where he subsequently ceased offering an interpretation, or interpretations, related to this view. If we could find such examples we would have the negative instances we require, or something close to them. But analysts do not normally record their sessions, and, I gather, most of them do not keep full opinion records either.

In the case of John, I have only seen *one* such opinion record, and, to my knowledge, this is the only one that exists. It was composed very kindly at my request at about sessions 25 to 28. It was meant for my guidance and not for publication, and it was put together at great speed. Admittedly, therefore, it may not give an adequate view of the analyst's opinions at the time. However, I am forced to say that this opinion record does not appear to me to contain any example at all of an interpretation, or interpretative line, that was withdrawn in the light of John's own conduct in the sessions. The record does contain a description of John's attitude to his father, but this is not sufficiently detailed for us to be able to use it to find an example of an interpretation which concerned his attitudes to his father, and which was withdrawn.

I have been concerned with two interpretative remarks alone, T 11,2 and T 11,2–4; and I have exhibited some of the difficulties that arise when we try to apply the criterion of acceptance or avowal to them. How far do these or similar difficulties arise about *other* interpretative remarks made in the course of this analysis of John? The answer to this depends on a careful, objective study of the records to discover how far T 11,2 and T 11,2–4 are *representative* remarks in the relevant respects. Such a study has not been made. All I can do in its absence is to offer my impression–for the very little that this is worth. My impression is that T 11,2 and T 11,2–4 are *not* as *un*representative as we may be inclined to suppose at the outset. The reader can form his own impression by looking again at the extract from Session 18 quoted above. This session is, I think, a good example of the analysis in its early phase.

The conclusion about the criterion of acceptance seems to be this. It is difficult to apply the criterion to T 11,2 and T 11,2–4. When one does so, it is difficult to be reasonably sure that one has applied it correctly. So one is left uncertain whether these two remarks (T 11,2 and T 11,2–4) satisfy or fail to satisfy this truth condition that is alleged to be necessary. In so far as T 11,2 and T 11,2–4 are representative, the difficulty is a general one.

But, of course, this whole discussion leaves various questions untouched. For instance, the point could be made that what really shows whether an interpretation is true or false is not anything crude, such as whether John says "Yes" or "No". Such remarks may not mean much anyway in view of resistance difficulties and other defences he may be using. What matters is whether the interpretation elicits from the patient responses that can reasonably be explained as being associated with, and hence the outcome of, the offered interpretation. If an interpretation does have such a result–if it is, in this sense, "enactive"–then we have good grounds for supposing that the interpretation is on or near the mark, that it is true or getting near to the truth.

This is an important suggestion. But it runs into the usual snags. Is T 11,2 enactive or not? It seems doubtful whether it elicited anything from John. But this is not enough to oblige the analyst to withdraw T 11,2. Obviously not. So enactivity is not a necessary condition for the truth of T 11,2. What about T 11,2–4? Is this enactive? We may be able to point to certain supporting material in the record. But the criterion is so vague that if–on the strength of this material

—we go on to judge that the interpretation is enactive, we will produce a judgment that is probably clinical in character. Moreover, it is doubtful whether the criterion is open to much improvement. If we try to tighten it in a way sufficient to give us an agreed answer in every case, we will make it clinically useless. If it is to have clinical value, it will have to remain fairly loose. This means that if, and when, analysts do actually check an interpretation by reference to its enactivity, they are doing something very different, and far removed, from the ordinary attempts of a scientific worker to test an hypothesis.[4]

III

Let us consider a criterion of quite a different sort. Suppose we challenged an analyst to defend T 11,2. He might argue as follows. "Given the sort of person John is, and given the sort of material he produces here (in session 18) and in previous sessions, it is very likely that his fear of driving the car is a manifestation of his fear of doing what his father does. For this is what analytic experience with similar material would lead one to expect." We could now use this defence to say that, for us to be reasonably sure that T 11,2 is true, T 11,2 must be in accord with past analytic experience in the way just mentioned. I shall call this "the criterion of analogy". Will this criterion do?

Let us recognise at once that it has an air of artificiality about it. Part of the reason for this, I think, is that analysts do not make much *explicit* use of this criterion. For they do not find it easy or natural to exhibit their relevant past experience by, for example, running out a series of past cases which are similar to John in the relevant respects. They are somewhat inhibited from doing this, because they also look at any given case as being importantly different from every other. In this respect the practice of analysts is apt to differ from that of the main body of psychiatrists, for whom reference to series of similar cases is a standard form of argu-

[4] But *cf.* J. O. Wisdom, "Psycho-analytic Technology", *Brit. J. for the Phil. of Science* (1957), 7, 13–28.

ment.[5] Yet, if challenged to support T 11,2 an analyst might say, for example: "Well, it looked to me like a father-fear at work here." If we challenged him by pointing to material in John's record that he had apparently not noticed and which suggested, for example, that the car represented the breast and that the boy was afraid both of smashing it and of his wish to do so–if we took this line, the analyst might react in more than one way. For instance, he might agree that both interpretations may be correct about John, and that this is just a case of over-determination. Or he might accept that T 11,2 was perhaps not at work here, or not as important as he had originally supposed. But for the analyst to make either of these moves is to reveal that he makes *implicit* use of past material, and hence of the criterion of analogy.

However, let us waive the difficulty that this suggested criterion may be somewhat artificial. Let us suppose that John's fear is indeed analogous to previous cases, or past analytic experience, on which the analyst is relying here. The next question we have to ask is this. What reason have we to believe that the previous cases, in which fears resembling John's have been manifested, are cases in which these symptoms are manifestations of father-fears? If the answer consists in appealing to examples of analytic treatment of the sort we are examining with John, then the answer is not much help. For such an appeal assumes that psycho-analytic method is valid–that by means of it one can really arrive at, for example, the real character of peoples' fears and what they are manifestations of. But the offering and use of interpretations is an essential part of psycho-analytic method. To ask, therefore, for the criteria of a psycho-analytic interpretation, as we are doing, is in effect to question the validity of the method. It is to ask, *inter alia,* how we know that by means of this method we arrive at the truth about a patient. Hence, to defend T 11,2 by an appeal to past analytic experience is to beg the question. It is to assume the validity of the very technique whose validity we are investigating. Suppose, however, that the answer does not consist of point-

[5] *Cf. passim:* Mayer-Gross, Slater and Roth, *Clinical Psychiatry* (London, 1954). D. Russell Davis, *An Introduction to Psychopathology* (London, 1957).

ing to cases of a similar sort, but to evidence of quite a different type. What would this evidence be like? Clearly, as analytic experience is not self-supporting here, we require evidence from outside—external to and independent of the analytic session. But where is this evidence? We all know that appeals to "cures" or "improvement" are of little help. Appeals to the work of the experimental and objective psychologist are much more promising. But as yet, in spite of a large and growing body of knowledge coming from this work, what has been achieved in this quarter is still far removed from interpretations such as T 11,2 and not yet sufficient to underpin them securely.

The upshot, then, is this. It may be necessary that T 11,2 should satisfy the criterion of analogy for us to be reasonably assured that it is true. But the criterion seems too weak to give us the reasonable assurance we want.

IV

An analyst could also defend T 11,2 in the following way. "Part of my business is to try all the time to understand what is going on. Why does the patient offer this material now? What does it mean to him? And so on. When the patient John brought up the material about the car lessons, I offered T 11,2 in order, *inter alia,* to help him to face his fear of doing what father does. And I believe T 11,2 to be true because it helps to make John's fears about car driving intelligible—it makes sense out of them, it tells us what the car driving means to him. Moreover, T 11,2 does not stand alone. The analysis brought up a whole mass of material about John's attitudes towards his father—how he views him as a successful figure, whom he feels he must emulate but with whom he also feels he won't be able to compete. And so on. (The extract quoted above only gives us a small glimpse of all this further father-material). Part, also, of my business is to try to make the whole mass of father-material intelligible. But I obviously cannot do this in isolation, by itself alone. I must consider it in relation to the material as a whole, and I must try to form an intelligible view of the whole personality of the boy and his difficulties. Now my supposition in T 11,2 does not stand alone, but forms part of a comprehensive account, or narrative, that I could give about the boy as a whole, including his attitudes to his father. It is this fact that gives T 11,2 strong additional support, and really makes it worthy of serious consideration. For by means of this narrative we are able to explain the boy's response to his car driving lessons by showing how it is a manifestation of his general attitudes to his father and of his personality as a whole. T 11,2 enables us to fit an item in the material (namely, his fear about the car driving) into the jigsaw about his personality as a whole; and this is what really gives T 11,2 its strength."

Let us say that, in offering this defence of T 11,2, the analyst is appealing to "the criterion of intelligibility". It is very evident that this criterion, as stated, is extremely vague, and is far too large a topic to pursue adequately here. Accordingly, I shall only raise two difficulties about it.

(A). Let us agree to say that T 11,2 satisfies this criterion—that it makes sense out of the boy's fears, that it makes them intelligible. This fact would only give us reasonable assurance that T 11,2 was true if T 11,2 were the *only* interpretation that could be offered which satisfied this criterion, or which satisfied it anything like as well. We cannot be reasonably sure, therefore, that T 11,2 is true until we are reasonably sure that there is no alternative interpretation available of equal, or near equal, strength to explain the boy's fears, and so make them intelligible. But as soon as we try to satisfy ourselves on this question, we plunge at once into the endless sea of current, very technical dispute and discussion about the genesis of phobias and the conceptual schemes we ought to employ in dealing with personality. Thus, for example, it has been argued—with some clinical and experimental backing[6]—that the main contributory cause of a phobic response

[6] *Cf.* J. Woodward, "Emotional disturbances of burned children", *Brit. Med. J.* (1959), 1: 1009–13. R. R. Grinker and J. P. Spiegel, *Men under Stress*, Ch. 5, Case 13 (Philadelphia, 1945); J. H. Masserman, *Behaviour and Neurosis* (Chicago, 1943). For general discussions, see, for example: D. Russell Davis, *op. cit.* and H. Gwynne Jones in *Handbook of Abnormal Psychology*, H. J. Eysenck, ed. (1960), Ch. 13.

can be a single frightening occurrence. Consequently, it could also be argued that John's fears about car driving *may* have their main source in the acute fright that he might have given himself once, when, for example, as a small boy he released the brakes of the family car and made it run downhill. Of course, John's fear of driving may also be connected with his father. But if the *main* source springs from a traumatic incident of the sort indicated, then T 11,2 is at worst false, and at best only a small part of the truth. Consequently, we cannot be reasonably confident that T 11,2 is true of John unless we have good reason to think that there is no equally plausible alternative available to explain the boy's fears. I doubt whether the data and the analytic record about John enable us to decide this particular question about him. This difficulty about T 11,2 is likely to be a recurrent one–the present state of psychopathology and personality theory being what it is. So I doubt whether we can often apply the criterion of intelligibility with much confidence.

But what of the claim that T 11,2 gains great strength from the fact that it forms part of a comprehensive narrative about the boy's attitudes to his father and about his personality as a whole? Is this correct?

Let us answer this question by taking an interpretation which is not near to common-sense, such as T 11,2, and which may seem quite crazy. In session 66 John discussed waste and his attitude to money. The analyst ended the session with a long sequence of remarks in which he said that John seemed to have the very strong feeling that an object he might want might not always be there, that, for example, having spent some pocket money, he was then without it and this was to him "a very dreaded state". The analyst continued: "Somehow I think this must be linked very much to your relationship with mother . . . and essentially her breast"; and he then proceeded to develop this. Let us consider this last interpretation. We need not stay to ask what there was in the record to suggest and back it. Let us ask instead: how could this interpretation fit into and form part of a comprehensive narrative about John's difficulties and personality as a whole?

Suppose that I am an analyst and that the sort of narrative

I use about personality and its development is a Kleino-Freudian one. Suppose I am confronted with the boy John and his poor examination results, and general difficulties of intellectual under-functioning. I could then use the Kleino-Freudian scheme to produce a specific and comprehensive narrative about John to make these facts intelligible; and the gist of part of my explanation might be baldly expressed in the following form.

(i) When children suffer from loss of parental objects, they are liable to mislay objects in general.

John suffered in this way (*e.g.*, on being left at boarding school at nine).

We have reason, therefore, to believe that he, too, is liable to mislay objects in general.

(ii) When a person is liable to mislay objects in general, he will find it difficult to do well in examinations (*i.e.*, to lay his hands on the objects of his learning and to show, or express, the results of his search).

John is liable to mislay objects.

We have reason, therefore, to believe that John finds it difficult to learn and to show the results.

When I am now confronted, in session 66, with John's concern about being without money, etc., it is natural for me to offer the interpretation that this is connected with his mother and the breast that he has lost. It is natural for me to offer this "crazy" interpretation because it is the obvious way to apply a Kleino-Freudian scheme to this particular material in 66; and by so doing I can bring John's attitudes to money within the scope of a more comprehensive narrative about his learning difficulties and personality as a whole. So it is clear that this interpretation about the breast does not stand alone, but forms part of, or can be accommodated within, a more comprehensive narrative designed to give an intelligible picture of John and his problems.

But does this fact give the "breast" interpretation much added weight, and sufficient to entitle us to be reasonably assured of its truth? Hardly. For the weight that accrues in this way to an accommodated interpretation obviously depends on the strength of the comprehensive narrative which accommodates it. Now the specific narrative I have used about

John has a strained and far-fetched appearance; and it is very likely that there will be other competing narratives in the field, which seem, *prima facie*, just as, or even more, plausible and reasonable than my Kleino-Freudian story about John. So the fact that I can fit John's concern about waste and money into a comprehensive narrative about him by means of the "breast" interpretation does not, by itself, give this interpretation much support. Further discussion at this point is likely to shift, and indeed should shift, away from the interpretation itself and concentrate on the *sort* of comprehensive narrative we ought to use. If, therefore, we try to defend the "breast" interpretation in this way, we shall fail to obtain consensus and the reasonable assurance we want.

The same considerations apply, *mutatis mutandis*, to the "uncrazy" interpretation T 11,2. If T 11,2 can be fitted into a story about John's attitudes to his father, which in turn can be fitted into a comprehensive narrative about the boy as a whole, then this fact only gives T 11,2 great weight, or support, if we have reasonable assurance that this specific comprehensive narrative about John is itself true. In the absence of such assurance, T 11,2 will be left a bit in the air.

(B) The second difficulty about the criterion of intelligibility is quite a different one. It could be said that it is very doubtful whether the criterion functions typically in the way we have presented it, and that our way of presenting it just misrepresents what happens in psycho-analysis.

Suppose that I am an analyst working within the Kleino-Freudian tradition. It could be argued that, when a patient presents me with material, what I actually do is this. I try to make the material intelligible by fitting a specific Kleino-Freudian narrative to it; or, if you like, by bringing it within the scope of a narrative of this basic Kleino-Freudian sort or type. I do this quite naturally, because this basic type of narrative is the one that enables me to make what seems sense out of the data that come up in analysis. When, therefore, I offer an interpretation, I do not do so in a wholly *ad hoc*, or empirical way. On the contrary, I offer it in an attempt to fit the basic type of narrative I use in my work to the data. The interpretation represents such an attempted fit. If a certain interpretation does in fact help me to fit this basic Kleino-

Freudian story to the data, then it will go to form part of a specific, comprehensive narrative of this type; and I retain the interpretation. If, on the other hand, an offered interpretation does not help me to form a specific narrative of this type about a patient, if I find it getting in the way, then I drop the idea it contains and explore some other way of making sense out of the certain item in the data that the offered interpretation was meant to deal with. Such an interpretation, offered but then not pressed, represents an unsuccessful attempt to fit the basic type of narrative to the material. From this it is evident that I do allow the material, or data, presented by a patient to count for and against a particular *application* of the basic type of narrative. But I do not allow, or use, the material to count against the *basic type of narrative itself* that I employ.[7]

Now if this is a correct account of what I actually do, it follows that I cannot use the criterion of intelligibility to defend an interpretation in the way originally depicted. I cannot use it to show that we have reasonable assurance that an interpretation is true. At most I can use it to show that we have reasonable assurance that a certain interpretation represents the correct application of the basic type of Kleino-Freudian narrative I use to deal with psycho-analytic material. It could be argued, no doubt, that it is a necessary condition of the truth of an interpretation that it can be accommodated within a comprehensive narrative about a patient. If a particular interpretation, say, T 11,2, can be so accommodated, then this would count in favour of its truth. But the mere fact that an analyst can, and does, fit an interpretation into such a comprehensive narrative, whether of the Kleino-Freudian type or any other, does not in itself give us reasonable assurance that the interpretation is true. The way in which I–as a supposed analyst–actually use the Kleino-Freudian discourse may or may not be typical of analysts in this or any other tradition. But if my behaviour is typical, it follows that the criterion of intelligibility will fail generally to provide the reasonable guarantee that we want.

[7] On the general point raised here, *cf.* K. R. Popper, "Philosophy of Science: a Personal Report", in *British Philosophy in the Mid-Century*, C. A. Mace, ed. (London, 1957).

V

I end this paper by mentioning two further topics that suggest themselves at this point.

I. Let us assume that the criticisms I have brought against the suggested criteria either do not hold, or can be satisfactorily countered. Let us assume, that is to say, that the criteria we have discussed are all good necessary criteria. Let us assume, further, that they are satisfied by some interpretation, such as T 11,2 or T 13,1, and satisfied in a way that is as convincing as we could hope for. Is this fact *sufficient* to give us reasonable assurance that the interpretation is true?

It seems doubtful. The doubt stems from the relation between analyst and patient. This is admittedly a very special relation, and one which is markedly different from the normal relation between two conversationalists in ordinary life. Now it has been maintained that this special relation lays the patient open to suggestion from the analyst, and, more important, renders him highly suggestible. Accordingly, if an analyst starts fitting a certain basic type of narrative to the patient, the latter is liable to come to accept the interpretations that are offered him as being true of himself. Hence, the fact that an interpretation of, say, a Kleino-Freudian type convincingly satisfies the criteria we have discussed is not sufficient to show that this interpretation is really true of the patient. The most this fact does show is that the analyst is being very successful in transforming the patient into a "Kleino-Freudian type" of person—one whom a Kleino-Freudian narrative obviously fits, and hence of whom the interpretations appear to be true both to patient and analyst.[8]

The strength of this objection depends largely on the hypothesis that the special relation in analysis opens wide the door to suggestion and suggestibility in the way indicated. This is clearly a matter which requires scientific investigation. To the best of my knowledge, no adequate investigation of this hypothesis and its related problems has yet been made. It is not much, if any, use for analysts to repudiate the hypothesis on the strength of convictions derived from their

[8] *Cf.* Popper's reference to the "Oedipus effect", *loc. cit.*

own experience as analysts. For the validity of psycho-analytic method, and hence of their own experience as analysts, is precisely what is in question here. Nor is the mere impression of the outsider of much, if any, use either. Thus, it is very tempting to point to the fact that in session 18 the analyst seems to be doing as much talking as the boy John, and seems very obviously to be exerting enormous pressure on this tight, polite and withdrawn adolescent. But something much more, or other, than the mere quantity of speech and a sense of pressure is required to substantiate the hypothesis that psycho-analytic method works in the way alleged. However, though we cannot appeal to a definitive scientific answer, we are confronted by the fact that quite a good case can be made out in support of this hypothesis. The case rests on general considerations of a technical character, considerations which draw attention to the similarity between psycho-analytic method and other techniques of human transformation, such as religious conversion and brain-washing. As long as we are confronted by this reasonable objection to psycho-analytic method, it is doubtful whether the criteria we have considered are sufficient to give us reasonable assurance that an interpretation is true.

II. Why is our search for criteria so difficult and frustrating? Is there, perhaps, any general reason that helps us to account for this? I am inclined to think there may be.

When I set out, near the beginning of this paper, in search of the truth criteria for an interpretation, I took over the general, if not universal, assumption about interpretations. This is the assumption that when an analyst offers an interpretation, he is uttering a statement that is primarily declaratory in character, and which, therefore, serves primarily to express an hypothesis about the patient. If this assumption were true, then it would be quite in order and natural to search for truth criteria; and one might expect, perhaps, that it would be a relatively straightforward matter to discover them. But it is doubtful whether this general assumption is true. Thus, when a statement such as T 11,2 is offered to the patient, its primary function does not seem to be declaratory and hypothesis-stating at all. Its chief point seems to be an instrumental one. For the analyst is primarily interested: (*a*) in disturbing, goading and impelling John into recognising and talking about his own feelings, attitudes, etc., at the time, quite ignoring whether and to what extend John's feelings, etc., are an artefact of the analysis itself; and (*b*) in changing John from a tight, withdrawn adolescent, who is intellectually under-functioning, into a more relaxed outgoing individual, who is no longer so anxiety-bound that he is unable to show his examiners what he can do. T 11,2 is uttered as part of a long, persistent, and many-sided attempt to change the boy in this way. Moreover as we have already noted, the utterance of T 11,2 may indeed be artefact producing, and thereby help to change the patient so as to make the interpretation seem to be true of him. It could be argued, therefore, that T 11,2 is primarily a transforming statement, and in this respect is characteristic of interpretations offered by analysts.

What follows from this contention? One possible consequence is that it is illegitimate, and therefore absurd, to suppose that an interpretative utterance can be true or false at all. From this it follows that an interpretation has no truth criteria. It is quite understandable, therefore, that our search for such criteria has been difficult and frustrating; for there are none to be found. Another possible but weaker consequence is this. Though an interpretation is primarily a transforming statement, it nevertheless retains hypothesis-stating, and hence declaratory, features. But these are apt to be overlaid by, and lost in, the complicated instrumental context in which this sort of statement functions. Consequently, even though such a statement has declaratory features, it may be difficult on many occasions to discover from its context just what its truth criteria are. Indeed, it may be so difficult as to make the search for truth criteria hardly worth while. For even when one tries to state and use the obvious candidates, one is likely to find that actually they cannot be applied at all, or applied to much effect. This is just what we discovered with T 11,2; and it is the natural outcome of the fact that T 11,2 is primarily a transforming statement. However, on either view, the stronger or the weaker, we can still ask certain, very important questions about T 11,2. These are questions about its appropriateness and effectiveness—the point and value of offering it when and how the analyst did.[9]

But this conclusion—in either its stronger or its weaker form—seems to be rather small and uninteresting beer. For all it seems to amount to is that it is logically impossible or practically difficult to find the truth criteria of an interpretation when this is uttered *within* the context of the analytic session. This conclusion does not say that an interpretation has no truth criteria when uttered *outside* this context. Moreover, it is clear that, even if we accept the conclusion in its stronger form (in which an interpretation-in-session is not an hypothesis at all and hence uncheckable and unfalsifiable), we cannot go on to say that the *generalisations* of psycho-analytic theory are uncheckable and unfalsifiable. The inference does not follow at all.[10] However this conclusion is not quite as small and trivial as it may seem. It has important implications for psycho-analytic theory and method. For one thing, it would appear to loosen the connexion traditionally supposed to exist between psycho-analytic theory and the clinical data. We may now have to rethink the evidential relation between the theory and the interpretations used in applying it therapeutically. For another, the conclusion may serve to alter the character of analytic practice. At present interpretations are offered in the guise of hypotheses. But it may not be helpful to offer them in this form to a patient who happens to have read this paper and accepted the conclusion we have just discussed! Freud once wrote as follows:

> It is true that during the analysis Hans had to be told many things that he could not say himself, that he had to

[9] *Cf.* P. Alexander, and A. MacIntyre, "Cause and Cure in Psychotherapy", Aristotelian Society, *Supplementary Volume*, 1955. It is interesting to record that a very good case can be made for the view that John did change in the desired direction during the period of the analysis. His improvement is shown in his examination results, in his performance when re-tested psychologically, and it is suggested by his way of talking in later sessions, as a tape recording can reveal. Of course, such evidence by itself does not show what contribution, if any, the analysis made to this happy transformation.

[10] *Cf.* B. A. Farrell, "Can Psychoanalysis be refuted?", *Inquiry*, Vol. I (1961), 16–36.

> be presented with thoughts which he had so far shown no sign of possessing, and that his attention had to be turned in the direction from which his father was expecting something to come. This detracts from the evidental value of the analysis; but the procedure is the same in every case. For a psycho-analysis is not an impartial scientific investigation, but a therapeutic measure. Its essence is not to prove anything, but merely to alter something. In a psycho-analysis the physician always gives his patient (sometimes to a greater and sometimes to a lesser extent) the conscious anticipatory image by the help of which he is put in a position to recognise and to grasp the unconscious material.[11]

It is a pity that Freud does not appear to have followed up the insights contained in this passage, and, in particular, to have asked how far the acceptance of psycho-analytic method as a therapeutic and transforming procedure is compatible with the claim that the method enables the patient "to recognise and to grasp the unconscious material", and thus to discover the truth about himself. However, I confess that I am unclear about the implications of all this for psycho-analysis. I have not yet been able to carry my personal analysis beyond this point.

[11] S. Freud, "Analysis of a Phobia in a five-year-old boy" (1909), *Coll. Papers,* Vol. III.

PERSONAL IDENTITY AND INDIVIDUATION

B. A. O. Williams

There is a special problem about personal identity for two reasons. The first is self-consciousness—the fact that there seems to be a peculiar sense in which a man is conscious of his own identity. This I shall consider in Section 3 of this paper. The second reason is that a question of personal identity is evidently not answered merely by deciding the identity of a certain physical body. If I am asked whether the person in front of me is the same person as one uniquely present at place *a* at time *t*, I shall not necessarily be justified in answering 'yes' merely because I am justified in saying that this human body is the same as that present at *a* at *t*. Identity of body is at least not a sufficient condition of personal identity, and other considerations, of personal characteristics and, above all, memory, must be invoked.

Some have held, further, that bodily identity is not a necessary condition of personal identity. This, however, is ambiguous, and yields either a weak or a strong thesis, depending on one's view of the necessity and sufficiency of the other conditions. The weaker thesis asserts merely that at least one case can be consistently constructed in which bodily identity fails, but in which the other conditions will be sufficient for an assertion of personal identity; even though there may be some other imaginable case in which, some other condition failing, bodily identity *is* a necessary condition of personal identity. The stronger thesis asserts that there is no conceiva-

B. A. O. Williams is Lecturer in Philosophy at University College, London, and has contributed to *The Nature of Metaphysics* (London, 1957), *Freedom and the Will* (London, 1963), and many journals.

ble situation in which bodily identity would be necessary, some other conditions being always both necessary and sufficient. I take it that Locke's theory[1] is an example of this latter type.

I shall try to show that bodily identity is always a necessary condition of personal identity, and hence that both theses fail. In this connexion I shall discuss in detail a case apparently favourable to the weaker thesis (Section 1). I shall also be concerned with the stronger thesis, or rather with something that follows from it–the idea that we can give a sense to the concept of *a particular personality* without reference to a body. This I shall consider chiefly in Section 4, where the individuation of personalities will be discussed; the notion occurs, however, at various other places in the paper. The criterion of bodily identity itself I take for granted. I assume that it includes the notion of spatio-temporal continuity, however that notion is to be explained.

In discussions of this subject, it is easy to fall into ways of speaking that suggest that "bodily" and other considerations are easily divorced. I have regrettably succumbed to this at some points, but I certainly do not believe that this easy divorce is possible; I hope that both the general tenor of my thesis and some more direct remarks on the subject (Section 2) will show why.

1. *Deciding another's identity*. Suppose someone undergoes a sudden and violent change of character. Formerly quiet, deferential, church-going and home-loving, he wakes up one morning and has become, and continues to be, loud-mouthed, blasphemous and bullying. Here we might ask the question

(*a*) Is he the same person as he used to be?

There seem to be two troubles with the formulation of this question, at least as an *identity* question. The first is a doubt about the reference of the second 'he' if asked the question "as *who* used to be?", we may well want to say "this person", which answers the original question (*a*) for us. This is not a serious difficulty, and we can easily avoid it by rephrasing the question in some such way as

(*b*) Is this person the same as the person who went to sleep here last night?

[1] *Essay Concerning Human Understanding*, II, 27.

We do not, however, *have* to rephrase the question in any such way; we can understand (*a*) perfectly well, and avoid paradox, because our use of personal pronouns and people's names is malleable. It is a reflection of our concept of 'a person' that some references to *him* cannot be understood as references to *his body* or to parts of it, and that others can; and that these two sorts of reference can readily occur in one statement ("He was embarrassed and went red."). In the case of (*a*), the continuity of reference for 'he' can be supplied by the admitted continuity of reference of 'his body', and the more fundamental identity question can be discussed in these terms without any serious puzzlement.

The second difficulty with (*a*) is that it is too readily translated into

(*c*) Is he the same sort of person as he used to be? or possibly

(*d*) Has he the same personality as he used to have?

But (*c*) and (*d*) are not identity questions in the required sense. For on any interpretation, 'sort of person', and on one interpretation, 'personality', are quality-terms, and we are merely asking whether the same subject now has different qualities, which is too easy to answer.

But this is only one interpretation of 'personality'. It corresponds interestingly to a loose sense of 'identity', which is found for instance in Mr. Nigel Dennis' novel *Cards of Identity*. There 'identity' is often used to mean 'a set of characteristics', and 'giving someone an identity' means 'convincing someone that he is a certain sort of person'. It does not, however, only mean this; for Mr. Dennis' Identity Club do not stop at giving someone a new character—they give him a new background as well, and a local sponger is made by their persuasive methods not just into a submissive old-style butler, but into such a butler who used to be at sea and has deserted his wife.

We might feel that this was the point at which something specially uncanny was beginning to happen, and that this was the kind of anomalous example we were really looking for—the uncanniness of someone's acquiring a new past is connected with our increasing reluctance to describe the situation as one in which the same man has acquired a new set of qualities. Here we have one powerful motive for the introduction of memory. It can be put by saying that there are, or we can imagine, cases where we want to use some term like 'personality' in such a way that it is not a type-expression, meaning 'set of characteristics', but is a particular term meaning something like *individual* personality. It may seem that this particularity is attained by reference to memory —the possession of a particular past. Thus we are concerned here with cases more drastic than those in which for instance people say "it has made a new man of him", or even "he is not the same person as he used to be" in the sense suggested by a change of character; these cases we can too readily re-describe. Thus we may put our question in the barbarous form

(*e*) Is the (particular) personality he has now the same as the one he had before?

We must now see whether we can make sense, in terms of memory, of the idea of a particular personality; and whether there can be personal identity without bodily identity.

In doing this, two obvious but important features of memory have to be borne in mind.

(I) To say "A remembers x", without irony or inverted commas, is to imply that x really happened; in this respect 'remember' is parallel to 'know'.

(II) It does not follow from this, nor is it true, that all claims to remember, any more than all claims to know, are veridical; or, not everything one seems to remember is something one really remembers.

So much is obvious, although Locke[2] was forced to invoke the providence of God to deny the latter. These points have been emphasised by Prof. A. G. N. Flew in his discussion of Locke's views on personal identity.[3] In formulating Locke's thesis, however, Prof. Flew makes a mistake; for he offers Locke's thesis in the form "if X can remember Y's doing such-and-such, then X and Y are the same person." But this obviously will not do, even for Locke, for we constantly say

[2] *Loc. cit.* §13 He is speaking, however, only of the memories of actions.

[3] *Philosophy*, 1951.

things like "I remember my brother joining the army" without implying that I and my brother are the same person. So if we are to formulate such a criterion, it looks as though we have to say something like "if X remembers doing such-and-such, then he is the person who did that thing." But since "remembers doing" means "remembers himself doing", this is trivially tautologous, and moreover lends colour to Butler's famous objection that memory, so far from constituting personal identity, presupposed it. Hence the criterion should rather run: "if X claims to remember doing such-and-such. . . ." We must now ask how such a criterion might be used.

Suppose the man who underwent the radical change of character—let us call him Charles—claimed, when he woke up, to remember witnessing certain events and doing certain actions which earlier he did not claim to remember; and that under questioning he could not remember witnessing other events and doing other actions which earlier he did remember. Would this give us grounds for saying that he now was or had, in some particular sense, a different personality? An argument to show that it did gives us such grounds might be constructed on the following lines.

Any token event E, and any token action A, are by definition particulars. Moreover, the description "the man who did the action A" necessarily individuates some one person; for it is logically impossible that two persons should do the same *token* action.[4] In the case of events, it is possible that two persons should witness the same token event; but nevertheless the description "the man who witnessed E" may happen to individuate some one person, and "the man who witnessed $E_1, E_2 \ldots E_n$" has a proportionately greater chance of so

[4] This is to ignore the case of joint or co-operative actions. Thus when three persons A, B and C jointly fell a tree, it might be said that each of them has done the same action, that of felling the particular tree. But this would not be quite accurate. They have *all* felled the tree; what *each* of them has done is to share in the felling of the tree, or to have felled the tree with the help of the other two. When the variables implicit in this last expression are replaced with names, we obtain descriptions of token actions which indeed individuate; thus it is true of A, but not of B or C, that he is the man who felled the tree *with the help of B and C*.

doing. Thus if our subject Charles now claims to remember doing certain actions A_1, A_2, etc., and witnessing certain events E_1, E_2, etc., which are themselves suitably identified, we have good grounds for saying that he is some particular person or has some particular personality.

Now by principle (II), we have no reason without corroborative evidence of some kind to believe Charles when he now claims to remember A or E; so we must set about checking. How are we to do this in the present case? Ordinarily if some person X claims to have witnessed E, and we wish to check this, we must find out whether there is any record, or anyone has any memory, of X's witnessing E. This is evidently inapplicable to the present case. For either the evidence shows that Charles was *bodily* present at E, or it does not. If it does, then Charles is remembering in the ordinary way, which is contrary to the hypothesis. If it does not, then there is no corroboration. Here we have a first important step. We are trying to prise apart "bodily" and "mental" criteria; but we find that the normal operation of one "mental" criterion involves the "bodily" one.

However, the situation may not be quite as desperate as this makes it appear. We can examine Charles' putative memories, and we may find that he can offer detailed information which there is no reason to believe he would ordinarily have known, and which strongly suggests the reports of an eye-witness of some particular events. What we can do with this information in the present case depends on a number of considerations. I shall now examine these, first in connexion with events, and then with actions. Events can in principle be witnessed by any number of persons, or by none. Some of the events which Charles claims to remember witnessing may be events of which we have other eye-witness accounts; others may be events which we believe to have occurred, though we do not know whether or not anyone witnessed them; others again may be events which we believe to have occurred, but which we believe no-one to have witnessed.

For all these, there is an hypothesis about—or, perhaps, description of—Charles' present condition which has nothing to do with a change of personality: the hypothesis of clairvoyance.[5] To describe Charles as clairvoyant is certainly not to advance very far towards an *explanation* of his condition; it amounts to little more than saying that he has come to know, by no means, what other people know by evidence. But so long as Charles claimed to remember events which were supposedly or certainly unwitnessed, such a description might be the best we could offer. We might do better than this, however, if the events Charles claimed to remember were witnessed; in this case we could begin to advance to the idea that Charles had a new identity, because we would have the chance of finding someone for him to be identical *with*. Thus if the events were witnessed, we might say that Charles was (now) identical with a witness of these events. This is ambiguous; it might mean that he was identical with anyone who witnessed the events, or with some particular person who witnessed the events. The former of these is no advance, since it comes to a roundabout way of saying that he claims to have witnessed the events, *i.e.* is possibly clairvoyant. The situation is different, however, if we can identify some one person who, it is plausible to suppose, witnessed all the events that Charles now claims to remember. That this should be possible is, indeed, a necessary condition of describing what has happened to Charles as *a change of identity*; I shall return to this point a little later.

If we now turn to actions, it looks as though we can find even better grounds for describing the case in terms of a change of identity. While there can be unwitnessed token events, there can be no unwitnessed token actions; moreover, as we noticed above, each token action can be performed by only one person. So if we can find out who performed the actions that Charles now claims to remember performing, it looks as if we can find out who he now is. These supposed advantages, however, are largely illusory. We may say, crudely, that there are many features of actions in which they are just like events—which, from another point of view, they indeed are. What differentiates actions from events are rather certain features of the agent, such as his intentions. In a particular case, some of these latter features may be known to, or in-

[5] Together, of course, with the loss of his real memories.

ferred by, observers, while others may remain private to the agent. In neither case, however, do these special features of actions much help our investigation of Charles' identity. In so far as these special features may be known to observers, they are still, for the purposes of the investigation, in the class of events, and Charles' claim to remember them may still be plausibly described as clairvoyance; and in so far as these features remain private to the performer of the actions in question, we can have no ground for saying whether Charles' claims to remember them are even correct.

Again, the logical truth that a description of the form "the person who did the (token) action A" individuates some one person, does not give unfailing help. How much help it gives depends on how effectively, and by what means, we can identify the action in question. Suppose that several men at a certain time and place are each sharpening a pencil. In these circumstances the description "the man sharpening a pencil" fails to individuate: the action of sharpening a pencil is common to them all. If, however, the pencils were of different colours, I might be able to identify a particular pencil, and through this a token action of sharpening; thus "the man sharpening the red pencil" may individuate. But such methods of identifying token actions are not always available. In particular, there are some cases in which a token action can be effectively identified only through a reference to the agent. Thus if several men were all dancing the czardas, I might be able to identify a token dancing only as *e.g.* "*Josef's* dancing of the czardas". In such a case reference to a token action cannot help in identifying its agent, since I must identify him in order to identify it.

However, we often can effectively identify actions without actually identifying the agents, and so have a use for descriptions like "the person who murdered the Duchess, whoever it was". It is obvious that such descriptions can play a peculiarly useful rôle in an enquiry into identity; and this rôle may, for several reasons, be more useful than that played by descriptions like "the man who witnessed the event E". For, first, granted that I have identified *an action*, the description cannot fail of reference because there is no such agent; while the mere fact that I have identified a certain event E of course does not guarantee the description "the man who *witnessed* the event E" against failure of reference. Secondly, it is inherently less likely that the description referring to an action should fail of unique reference because of multiplicity, than it is that the description referring to an event should so fail. For it is in general less probable that a certain action should have been co-operatively undertaken than that a certain event should have been multiply witnessed; and, as we noticed above, for every description of a co-operative action, we can produce a series of descriptions of constituent actions which have progressively greater chance of unique reference. Last, knowledge of a particular action can give one knowledge not only of the location, but of the character, of its agent, but knowledge of a particular event will standardly give one knowledge only of the location of its witnesses.

Let us now go back to the case of Charles. We may suppose that our enquiry has turned out in the most favourable possible way, and that all the events he claims to have witnessed and all the actions he claims to have done point unanimously to the life-history of some one person in the past—for instance, Guy Fawkes. Not only do all Charles' memory-claims that can be checked fit the pattern of Fawkes' life as known to historians, but others that cannot be checked are plausible, provide explanations of unexplained facts, and so on. Are we to say that Charles is now Guy Fawkes, that Guy Fawkes has come to life again in Charles' body, or some such thing?

Certainly the temptation to say something on this pattern is very strong. It is difficult to insist that we *couldn't* say that Charles (or sometime Charles) had become Guy Fawkes; this is certainly what the newspapers would say if they heard of it. But newspapers are prone to exaggeration, and this might be an exaggeration. For why shouldn't we say that Charles had, except for his body, become just like Guy Fawkes used to be; or perhaps that Charles clairvoyantly—*i.e.* mysteriously—knows all about Guy Fawkes and his *ambiance*? In answer to this, it will be argued that this is just what memory was introduced to rule out; granted that we need similar personal characteristics, skills, and so on as necessary conditions of the identification, the final—and, granted these others, sufficient—condition is provided by memories of seeing just *this*, and doing just *that*, and it is these that pick out a particular man. But perhaps this point is fundamentally a logical trick. Granted that in a certain context the expressions "the man who did A", "the man who saw E", do effectively individuate, it is logically impossible that two different persons should (correctly) remember being the man who did A or saw E; but it is not logically impossible that two different persons should *claim* to remember being this man, and this is the most we can get.

This last argument is meant to show only that we are not forced to accept the description of Charles' condition as his being identical with Guy Fawkes. I shall now put forward an argument to strengthen this contention and to suggest that we should not be justified in accepting this description. If it is logically possible that Charles should undergo the changes described, then it is logically possible that some other man should simultaneously undergo the same changes; *e.g.* that both Charles and his brother Robert should be found in this condition. What should we say in that case? They cannot both be Guy Fawkes; if they were, Guy Fawkes would be in two places at once, which is absurd. Moreover, if they were both identical with Guy Fawkes, they would be identical with each other, which is also absurd. Hence we could not say that they were both identical with Guy Fawkes. We might instead say that one of them was identical with Guy Fawkes, and that the other was just like him; but this would be an utterly vacuous manœuvre, since there would be *ex hypothesi* no principle determining which description was to apply to which. So it would be best, if anything, to say that both had mysteriously become like Guy Fawkes, clairvoyantly knew about him, or something like this. If this would be the best description of each of the two, why would it not be the best description of Charles if Charles alone were changed?

Perhaps this last rhetorical question too readily invites an answer. It might be said that there is a relevant difference between the case in which two persons are changed and the case in which only one is changed, the difference being just this difference in numbers; and that there is no guarantee that what we would say in one of these situations would be the same as what we would say in the other. In the more complicated situation our linguistic and conceptual resources would be taxed even more severely than in the simpler one, and we might not react to the demands in the same way. Moreover, there is a reason why we should not react in the same way. The standard form of an identity question is "Is this x the same x as that x which . . . ?", and in the simpler situation we are at least presented with just the materials for constructing such a question; but in the more complicated situation we are baffled even in asking the question, since both the transformed persons are equally good candidates for being its subject, and the question "Are these two x's the same (x?) as the x which . . . ?" is not a recognizable form of identity question. Thus, it might be argued, the fact that we could not speak of identity in the latter situation is no kind of proof that we could not do so in the former.

Certainly it is not a proof.[6] Yet the argument does indicate that to speak of identity in the simpler case would be at least quite vacuous. The point can be made clearer in the following way. In the case of material objects, we can draw a distinction between identity and exact similarity; it is clearly not the same to say that two men live in the same house, and that they live in exactly similar houses. This notion of identity is given to us primarily, though not completely, by the notion of spatio-temporal continuity. In the case of character, however, this distinction cannot be drawn, for to say that A and B have the same character is just to say that A's character is exactly similar to B's. Nor can this distinction be drawn in the case of memories–if you could say that two men had the same memories, this would be to say that their memories were exactly similar. There is, however, an extreme difficulty in saying these things about memories at all; it is unclear what it would mean to say that there were *two* men who had exactly similar, or the same, memories, since to call them real memories is to imply their correctness. Thus if we are to describe Charles' relations to Guy Fawkes in terms of *exact similarity* of everything except the body, we are going to have difficulty in finding a suitable description in these terms of his memory claims. We cannot say that he has the same mem-

[6] I am grateful to Mr. P. F. Strawson for making this clear to me.

ories as Guy Fawkes, as this is to imply, what we want to deny, that he really is Guy Fawkes; nor can we say that the memory claims he makes are the same as those made by Guy Fawkes, as we have little idea of what memory claims Fawkes in fact made, or indeed of how much he at various times remembered. All we actually know is that Charles' claims fit Fawkes' life.

These difficulties, in applying the concept of exact similarity in the matter of the supposed memories, are (I suspect) a motive for the thought that we *must* describe the situation in terms of identity. This is where the reduplicated situation of Charles and Robert gives some help. In that situation it is quite obvious that the idea of identity cannot be applied, and that we must fall back on similarity; and that one respect in which the trio are similar is—however we are to express it—that of "memory". (If the situation sometimes occurred, we might find an expression; we might speak of "similarity of one's supposed past".) This eases the way for doing the same thing in the case of Charles alone, whose relation to Fawkes in his unique case is exactly the same as both his and Robert's in the reduplicated one. We can then say that Charles has the same character, and the same supposed past, as Fawkes; which is just the same as to say that they are in these respects exactly similar. This is not to say that they are identical at all. The only case in which identity and exact similarity could be distinguished, as we have just seen, is that of the body—"same body" and "exactly similar body" really do mark a difference. Thus I should claim that the omission of the body takes away all content from the idea of personal *identity*.[7]

I should like to make one last point about this example. This turns on the fact, mentioned before, that in order to describe Charles' change as a change of identity, we must be able to identify some one person who might plausibly be supposed to have seen and done all the things that Charles now claims to remember having seen and done; otherwise there would be nothing to pin down Charles' memory claims as other than random feats of clairvoyance. We succeeded in

[7] I am indebted here, and elsewhere in this paper, to Mr. D. F. Pears.

doing this, just by discovering that Charles' memory claims fitted Fawkes' life. This could be done only by knowing what Fawkes did, and what Fawkes did could be known only by reference to witnesses of Fawkes' activities, and these witnesses must have seen Fawkes' *body*. In order for their accounts to be connected into the history of one person, it is necessary to rely on the continuity of this body.

Now the fact that Fawkes is in this sense identified through his body does not rule out the possibility that Charles should later be identified with Fawkes without reference to a body; *i.e.* this fact does not rule out the weaker thesis about the non-necessity of bodies. To illustrate this, one might compare the case of someone's going to a crowded party, where he sees a girl who is very like all the other girls at the party except that she has red hair. This girl sings various songs and quarrels with the band; she is easily identified on each occasion by the colour of the hair. The man later meets a platinum blonde who recalls singing songs at a party and quarrelling with the band. He can identify her as the red-haired girl at the party, even though she has changed the colour of her hair in the meantime. There is an important difference, however, between this case and that of Fawkes. If the girl had remarkably changed the colour of her hair between songs and before the quarrel, identifying her at the various stages of the party would have been more difficult, but not in principle impossible; but if the Fawkes-personality changed bodies frequently, identification would become not just difficult but impossible. For the only other resource would be the memory criterion, and the operation of this would once more make exactly the same requirements. Hence it is a necessary condition of making the supposed identification on non-bodily grounds that at some stage identifications should be made on bodily grounds. Hence any claim that bodily considerations can be absolutely omitted from the criteria of personal identity must fail; *i.e.* these facts do rule out the stronger thesis.

2. *Some remarks on bodily interchange.* Anyone who believed that personalities could be identified without reference to bodies might be expected to make sense of the idea of bodily interchange; and anyone who thought that they might

always be identified in this way would presumably require that for any two contemporaneous persons we should be able to make sense of the idea that their bodies should be interchanged. It is worth considering how far we can make sense of it, if we look at it closely.

Suppose a magician is hired to perform the old trick of making the emperor and the peasant become each other. He gets the emperor and the peasant in one room, with the emperor on his throne and the peasant in the corner, and then casts the spell. What will count as success? Clearly not that after the smoke has cleared the old emperor should be in the corner and the old peasant on the throne. That would be a rather boring trick. The requirement is presumably that the emperor's body, with the peasant's personality, should be on the throne, and the peasant's body, with the emperor's personality, in the corner. What does this mean? In particular, what has happened to the voices? The voice presumably ought to count as a bodily function; yet how would the peasant's gruff blasphemies be uttered in the emperor's cultivated tones, or the emperor's witticisms in the peasant's growl? A similar point holds for the features; the emperor's body might include the sort of face that just *could not* express the peasant's morose suspiciousness, the peasant's a face no expression of which could be taken for one of fastidious arrogance. These "could's" are not just empirical—such expressions on these features might be unthinkable.

The point need not be elaborated; I hope I have said enough to suggest that the concept of bodily interchange cannot be taken for granted, and that there are even logical limits to what we should be prepared to say in this direction. What these limits are, cannot be foreseen—one has to consider the cases, and for this one has to see the cases. The converse is also true, that it is difficult to tell in advance how far certain features may suddenly seem to express something quite unexpected. But there are limits, and when this is recognized, the idea of the interchange of personalities seems very odd. There might be something like a logical impossibility of the magician's trick's succeeding. However much of the emperor's past the sometime peasant now claimed to remember, the trick would not have succeeded if he could not satisfy the simpler requirement of being the same *sort* of person as the sometime emperor. Could he do this, if he could not smile royally? Still less, could he be the same person, if he could not smile the characteristic smile of the emperor?

These considerations are relevant to the present question in two ways. First, the stronger view about the identification implies that an interchange is always conceivable; but there are many cases in which it does not seem to be conceivable at all. Secondly, there is connected with this the deeper point, that when we are asked to distinguish a man's personality from his body, we do not really know what to distinguish from what. I take it that this was part of what Wittgenstein meant when he said that the best picture of the human soul was the human body.[8]

3. *A criterion for oneself?* I now turn to a different supposed use of a criterion of identity for persons. It may be objected that I have been discussing all the time the use of memory and other criteria of personal identity as applied to one man by others; but that the real rôle of memory is to be seen in the way it reveals a man *to himself*. Thus Locke speaks of "consciousness" (and by this he means here memory) as "what makes a man be himself to himself."[9]

It is difficult to see what this can mean. If we take it to mean that a man could use memory as a criterion in deciding whether he was the same person, in the particular sense, as he used to be, the suggestion is demonstrably absurd. I hope that a short and schematized argument will be enough to show this point. Suppose a man to have had previously some set of memories S, and now a different set S_1. This should presumably be the situation in which he should set about using the criterion to decide the question of his identity. But this cannot be so, for when he has memories S, and again when he has memories S_1, he is in no doubt about his identity, and so the question does not even occur to him. For it to occur to him, he would have to have S and S_1 at the same time, and so S would be included in S_1, which is contrary to the hypothesis that they are, in the relevant sense, different.

[8] *Philosophical Investigations*, II, iv.
[9] *Loc. cit.*, §10.

Alternatively, let S_1 include a general memory to the effect that he used to remember things that he no longer remembers. This would again present no question to him, for it is the condition of most of us. So let us strengthen this into the requirement that S_1 include a general memory Σ to the effect that he used to remember things empirically incompatible with memories in S_1. In this situation he might set about trying to find out what kind of illusion he was under. His most economical hypothesis would be that Σ itself was an illusion. If he were not satisfied with this, or if some parts of S *were* left over in S_1, so that he seemed to have definitely incompatible "memories", there would be nothing he could do with the help of his own memory; he would have to ask others about his past. In doing this, he would be relying on other people's memories of his past; but this is certainly not what was meant by the suggestion of memory as a criterion for the man himself. It is just a reversion to the case of such a criterion being used by some persons about another. Thus there is no way in which memory could be used by a man as a criterion of his own identity.

A criterion, however, must be used by someone. This is a point that has been notably and unhappily neglected by theorists of personal identity. Thus Hume, for instance, in the course of his account revealingly says[10] "Suppose we could see clearly into the breast of another, and observe that succession of perceptions, which constitutes his mind or thinking principle, and suppose that he always preserves the memory of a considerable part of past perceptions . . ." Others, in criticising or expanding Hume's account, have written in terms that similarly require an externalized view of the contents of a man's mind, a view obtainable from no conceivable vantage-point. Theorising which is in this sense abstract must be vacuous, because this privileged but positionless point of view can mean nothing to us.

At this point it might be objected that if what has been said is true about a criterion of identity, then it was not a *criterion* that memory was supposed uniquely to provide. "You have argued", it might be said, "that no man can use

[10] Hume, *Treatise of Human Nature,* Bk. I, Pt. IV, Sec. VI.

memory as a criterion of his own identity. But this is just what shows that memory is the essence of personal identity; figuratively speaking, memory is so much what makes him a certain person that when provided with certain memories, he cannot doubt who he is. This is just the heart of the thesis." Or the objection might be put by saying that a man might conceivably have occasion to look into a mirror and say "this is not my body", but could never have occasion to say "these are not my memories." Or, again, a man who has lost his memory cannot say who he is.

If this is what the thesis asserts, however, it comes to little. A man who has lost his memory cannot say who anyone else is, either, nor whether any object is the same as one previously presented, since he will not remember the previous presentation. So the last argument shows nothing about personal identity as such; it just shows that identifying anything is a process that involves memory. Nor is the first argument more illuminating. It comes really to no more than the trivialities that in order to remember, you have to have something to remember, and that if you are remembering everything you can remember, there is nothing else you can remember. Again, the example of the man looking into the mirror does not do what is required. In order to sustain the objection it would be necessary to show not just that a man might say "this is not my body", but that if he said it, he would necessarily be right; or at least that the question whether he was right or not did not involve any reference to other people's memories. It is obvious that neither is the case, because the situation of the example *might* be best described by saying that this was a man who misremembered what he looked like, and the question whether this was the best description of the situation would have to be decided by other people conducting the kind of enquiry into identity that was earlier discussed at length.

It is not part of my aim to discuss in general consciousness of self. I have tried in this section to show in a limited way that although we may have the feeling that, by consideration of it alone, we may be given the clue to personal identity, this is in fact an illusion. That it is an illusion is disguised by those theories of personal identity which, by assuming no particular point of view, try to get the best of both worlds, the inner and the outer. If we abandon this for a more realistic approach, the facts of self-consciousness prove incapable of yielding the secret of personal identity, and we are forced back into the world of public criteria.

If we accept these conclusions, together with the earlier ones, it may seem that the attempt to give a sense to 'particular personality' that omits reference to the body has failed. However, there is another and familiar class of cases that seems to provide strong independent grounds for the view that such a sense can be given: these are the cases in which more than one personality is associated with one body. I shall end by discussing this type of case and some related questions.

4. *Multiple personality and individuation.* Examples of multiple personality, such as the notorious case of Miss Beauchamp,[11] raise identity questions interestingly different from those that arose in the case of Charles. In that case, we identified, by means that turned out to involve the body, what would normally, if tendentiously, be called a different person, and asked whether the person in front of us was identical with him. In the cases of multiple personality, we are in a sense more directly confronted with personalities, and naturally make direct reference to them in order to ask our identity questions at all. The standard type of identity question about Miss Beauchamp is whether the personality that is now being manifested in her behaviour (or some such description) is the same as that which was being manifested two hours ago. In asking a question of this type, we may in fact feel a doubt about the reference of descriptions like "the personality now manifesting itself", because the principal question here just is what personalities there are to be referred to—how many personalities there are, and how the subject's behaviour is to be "sorted out" into the manifestations of different personalities.

For this reason, there is a strong motive for not putting our questions about Miss Beauchamp in the form of identity questions at all. Instead of asking something of the form

[11] See Morton Prince, *The Dissociation of a Personality* (1905), *passim.*

"Is this personality the same as that?" we may prefer to ask, "Do these two pieces of behaviour belong to one personality or to two?"; that is, instead of referring to personalities *through* their manifestations and asking whether they are identical, we may refer *to* manifestations and ask how they are to be allocated to personalities. A parallel to this would be the case of a tangled skein of wool, where, catching hold of a piece at each end, we might ask either "Is this thread the same as that?" or "Are these pieces parts of one thread?" The second formulation in each case might seem to be strictly preferable to the first, because the references that are being made are more determinate; I can tell you exactly which *part* or which *manifestation* I am referring to in the second formulation, but can tell you much less exactly which *thread* or which *personality* I am referring to in the first. It is useful to distinguish these sorts of questions, and I shall call the first, questions of identity, and the second, questions of individuation. I shall also in this section speak of our having individuated a personality when, roughly, we have answered enough questions of this type for us to have picked out a certain personality from the pattern of manifestations. I shall not here examine the complexities involved in a proper formulation of these concepts.

We have just seen that it might be preferable to put our questions about Miss Beauchamp in the form of individuation, and not of identity, questions. It might seem, indeed, that it is essential to do this. Because asking an identity question about personalities involves referring to personalities, and this involves knowing what personalities one is referring to, it is tempting to think that we could not use the identity form in a case where our problem was just what, and how many, personalities there were. This, however, would be an exaggeration. I do not have to be able to answer the question "which personality are you referring to?" in the thoroughgoing way suggested by this argument. I may do enough to establish the reference by saying "I just mean the personality now being manifested, whichever that is", without committing myself thereby to more than the belief that there is at least one personality to be referred to, and possibly more. I should be *debarred* from using the identity form only in a situation where I was in doubt whether there was even one personality to be referred to.

The case of Miss Beauchamp is more relevant to the discussion of the rôle of the body in the individuation of personalities than it is to the straightforward question whether bodily identity is a necessary condition of personal identity; since bodily identity is granted, this case can have no tendency to show that bodily identity is not a necessary condition (though it will of course tend to show that it is not a sufficient condition). It will, however, lend colour to the idea that we can individuate particular personalities, and not through bodies; if there are here four different particular personalities, and only one body, it is clear that there can be some principle for distinguishing personalities without at least *distinguishing* bodies. There is such a principle; but it does not yield as exciting a result from this case as might be hoped.

Miss Beauchamp's strikingly different personalities were individuated in the first place by reference to personal characteristics, in which they were largely opposed; also by tastes and preferences (B1 and B4 hated smoking, for instance, and B3 loved it); and by skills (B3, unlike the others, knew no French or shorthand). Memory did not serve straightforwardly to individuate them, because their memories were asymmetrical. B1 and B4, for instance, knew only what they were told by the investigator about the others, but B3 knew, without being told, everything that B4 did, and in the case of B1 knew all her thoughts as well; she referred to them both in the third person.[12] These remarkable and systematic discontinuities in Miss Beauchamp's behaviour, together with the violent and active conflict between her various selves, who abused and tricked each other, make the reference to different particular personalities completely natural. Thus we have individuated various personalities by reference to character, attainments and (up to a point) memories, and without reference to bodies.

This claim, however, is liable to serious misinterpretation. There has been no reference to bodies only in the sense that

[12] Prince, *op. cit.*, p. 181. The extent of memory discontinuity in such cases varies: *cf.*, *e.g.*, William James, *Principles of Psychology*, Vol. I, pp. 379 *seq.*

no such reference came into the principles used; but it does not follow from this that there was no reference to a body in starting to individuate at all. Obviously there was, because the problem arose only in connexion with the fact that too many and too various things were going on in connexion with one body; if Miss Beauchamp had been four sisters, there would have been no problem. Thus the individuation by reference to character and so on alone, was individuation in the context of the continuity of a certain body; and the fact that these principles were successful in individuating in this case does not show that they would be successful in so doing generally. The point may be put by saying that what we have succeeded in doing on these principles is individuating particular personalities *of Miss Beauchamp*, who is bodily identified; this is not to say that they provide us with a principle for individuating particular personalities without any reference to bodies at all.

This is quite obvious if we look at the principles themselves. Leaving aside memory, which only partially applies to the case, character and attainments are quite clearly general things. *Jones'* character is, in a sense, a particular; just because "Jones' character" refers to the instantiation of certain properties by a particular (and bodily) man.[13] Even so, the sense in which it is a particular is peculiar and limited. This can be seen from the odd workings of its criterion of identity. Consider the statement

(i) He has the same character as his father (*or* he has his father's character)

and compare the two statements

(ii) He wears the same clothes as his father
(iii) He has his father's watch.

Of these, (ii) is ambiguous, the expression "his father's clothes" see-sawing over the line between particular and general (though its companion "he wears his father's clothes" seems to allow only the particular interpretation). Neither (i) nor (iii) is ambiguous in this way; and in (iii) "his father's watch" obviously refers to a particular. But (i) is quite

[13] *Cf.* P. F. Strawson, "Particular and General," *Proceedings of the Aristotelian Society*, Vol. LIV (1953–4), pp. 250 *al.*

different from (iii). If (iii) is true, then if the watch he has is going to be pawned tomorrow, his father's watch is going to be pawned; but it does not similarly follow from (i) that if his character is going to be ruined by the Army, his father's character is going to be ruined. This illustrates how little weight can be laid on the idea of Jones' character being a particular, and throws us back on the familiar point that to talk of Jones' character is a way of talking about what Jones is like.

Miss Beauchamp's various personalities are particulars only in the weak sense that Jones' character is a particular, a sense which is grounded in the particular body. In using character and attainments to individuate them, I am telling the difference between them in just the sense that I tell the difference between sets of characteristics; Miss Beauchamp was peculiar in having more than one set of characteristics. Her personalities, like more normal people's, each had *peculiarities*, the combination of which might well have been, as a matter of fact, uniquely instantiated; but this does not affect the fundamental logical issue. About her memories, it need only be said that if different personalities have the same memories, memory is not being used to individuate; if they have different memories, the bodily identity connecting the various remembered occasions makes it easy to describe the situation as one of Miss Beauchamp's sometimes being able to remember what at other times she could not.

When Miss Beauchamp was nearly cured, and only occasionally lapsed into dissociation, she spoke freely of herself as having been B1 or B4. "These different states seem to her very largely differences of moods. She regrets them, but does not attempt to excuse them, because, as she says, 'After all, it is always myself.'"[14]

[14] Prince, *op. cit.*, p. 525.

ONE'S KNOWLEDGE OF OTHER MINDS

A. J. Ayer

Let us see how there comes to be a problem about one's knowledge of other minds. Consider the following propositions:

1) When someone, other than myself, says that he is thinking about a philosophical problem, or that he has a headache, or that he has seen a ghost, what he is saying about himself is the same as what I should be saying about myself if I were to say that I was thinking about a philosophical problem, or that I had a headache, or that I had seen a ghost.

2) When I say of someone other than myself that he is thinking about a philosophical problem, or that he has a headache, or that he has seen a ghost, what I am saying about him is the same as what I should be saying about myself if I were to say that I was thinking about a philosophical problem, or that I had a headache, or that I had seen a ghost.

3) When I say that I am thinking about a philosophical problem, or that I have a headache, or that I have seen a ghost, my statement is not equivalent to any statement, or set of statements, however complicated, about my overt behaviour.

4) I have direct knowledge of my own experiences.

5) I cannot have direct knowledge of anyone else's experiences.

6) Consequently, the only ground that I can have for believing that other people have experiences, and that some at least of their experiences are of the same character as my

A. J. Ayer is a Fellow of New College and Wykeham Professor of Logic at Oxford University. His books include *The Foundations of Empirical Knowledge* (London, 1940), *The Problem of Knowledge* (London, 1956), *Philosophical Essays* (London, 1959), and *The Concept of a Person* (London, 1963).

own, is that their overt behaviour is similar to mine. I know that certain features of my own behaviour are associated with certain experiences, and when I observe other people behaving in similar ways I am entitled to infer, by analogy, that they are having similar experiences.

There are philosophers who accept all these propositions, and to them the question how one is to justify one's belief in the existence of other minds presents no special difficulty. If they are concerned with it at all, they are interested only in the choice of premises for the argument from analogy. Thus they may maintain that the basis of the argument is not so much that there is a physical resemblance between other people's behaviour and one's own as that other people also use language or that they behave purposefully. But none of this raises any serious question of principle.

To many philosophers, however, this argument from analogy appears too weak for its purpose; some of them indeed, for reasons into which we shall enter later on, maintain that it is altogether invalid, or at least that it cannot be valid if the other propositions which I have listed are true. But this leaves them rather at a loss to justify their belief in the existence of minds other than their own. Some take the view that the sixth proposition is incompatible with the fifth. They hold that the argument from analogy can be valid only if it is possible, at least in principle, for one person to have direct knowledge of the experiences of another. Others, who will not allow this to be possible, try to resolve the difficulty by denying the second proposition on my list. Their contention is that while the statements that one makes about one's own experiences need not be equivalent to statements about one's overt behaviour, this does not apply *mutatis mutandis* to the statements that one makes about the experiences of others; to say of someone other than oneself that he is having such and such an experience is, on this view, always to describe his actual, or potential, behaviour. But this asymmetry in the analysis of statements which appear so very similar arouses objections on the score of common sense. A way of removing it is to deny my third and fourth propositions, with the result that all statements about experiences, whether one's own or anybody else's, are interpreted as statements about behaviour;

and there are philosophers who take this heroic course. Finally, there are those who, rejecting the sixth proposition but accepting the other five, find themselves inadequately defended against solipsism. Let us try to see where the truth lies.

We may take as our starting point the propositions that I can have direct knowledge of my own experiences and that I cannot have direct knowledge of anyone else's. What does it mean to say that I have direct knowledge of my own experiences? Presumably the knowledge claimed is knowledge that something or other is the case, that I have a headache, or that I am thinking about a philosophical problem: and the point is that if the statement which expresses what I claim to know refers only to my present experience, I am in the best possible position to decide its truth. If I judge it to be true, it is on the basis of an experience which conclusively verifies it, inasmuch as it is the experience which the statement describes. Let it be granted that others besides myself can come to know that such a statement is true. Even so their knowledge will not be direct. For it can be founded only upon experiences of their own, and however strongly these experiences favour the truth of the statement about my experience, they do not establish it conclusively. It remains at least conceivable that these experiences should occur and the statement in question be false. But no such possibility of error arises when an experience testifies only to itself. Thus the warrant for saying that I can have direct knowledge of my own experiences but not of anybody else's is just that my experiences are exclusively my own. The reason why I cannot directly know the experiences of another person is simply that I cannot have them.

But is it true that I cannot? There is a good and familiar sense in which two different people may be said to perceive the same object, hear the same sound, feel the same feeling, and from this it follows that they do have the same experiences. But, it will be answered, even though they may perceive the same objects or hear the same sounds, they do not sense the same sense-data: the sense-data which they respectively sense may be qualitatively similar but they cannot be numerically the same. And if it be asked why they cannot, the answer is that sense-data are made private by definition;

they are characterized in such a way that the statement that one person has another's sense-data describes no possible situation. Similarly, if one person is afraid and another shares his feeling, it will still be said that there are two feelings of fear and not one. To say that the feeling is shared is to say that the two feelings are qualitatively similar and that they have the same ostensible object: it is not to say that they are numerically identical. But how are they differentiated? It is not to be supposed that one can number people's feelings as one can number the things that they may carry in their pockets. The answer is that we are to say that there are two feelings and not one, just because there are two persons. It is made a convention that any feeling that one has is an experience which is private to oneself. And so it becomes a necessary truth that one person cannot have, and therefore cannot strictly know, the experiences of another.

In this sense, then, to wish that one directly knew the thoughts and feelings of others is to demand a logical impossibility. It is not surprising therefore, nor should it be a matter of dissatisfaction, that the wish cannot be gratified. The situation, however, is normally not so simple as this. In the end one may be in the ridiculous position of deploring a necessary truth; but at the outset the complaint that one does not know what others are thinking or feeling may very well have its source in empirical fact. It may in fact be the case that other people baffle or deceive me. I have some evidence to show what they are really like, but it is not sufficient for me. Even though they tell me, with every appearance of honesty, what is going on in their minds, I may still doubt whether they are telling me the truth. How can I ever be sure, in such a case, that I am not mistaken? A question of this sort frequently expresses a felt anxiety.

But how is this anxiety to be allayed? If someone finds himself in this position, what can be required to reassure him? Perhaps only that he should get to know other people better, and this he may achieve; it is at all events a practical problem. Perhaps he needs something out of the ordinary, like telepathy, which he may not in fact be able to achieve. But even if he were to achieve it he would be doing no more than add to his current methods of communication. What is strange about telepathy is that a message is transmitted apparently without the employment of any physical means. But to be informed of another's feeling telepathically is not to share it; and even if it were to share it there would be exactly the same grounds here as in the case of any other shared feelings for saying that there were two feelings and not one. There is the experience of the person who makes the communication and the experience of the person who receives it. These experiences are necessarily different, since they are the experiences of different persons, and this remains true no matter how the communication is made. In this respect telepathy is no better than the telephone.

The reason why telepathy is apt to be appealed to in this context is that it is regarded as a possible means of bridging the gap between one person and another. But if the gap is empirical in character, if it is a question of practical ignorance or misunderstanding, then there are surer ways of bridging it than by telepathy. And if the gap is logical, nothing can bridge it. It is suggested that in order really to know what another person is thinking or feeling, I have literally to share his experiences; and then it turns out that to share his experiences, in the sense required, is to have his experiences and that in order to have his experiences I have to be that person, so that what is demanded of me is that I become another person while remaining myself, which is a contradiction. The contradiction is masked when the requirement is put in the form of my needing to know another person's experiences in the way that I know my own. For this may not seem too much to expect until it is realized that the way in which I am supposed to know my own experiences is by actually having them, and that the reason why I cannot in this way know the experiences of others is that my literally having their experiences has been made a logical impossibility.

Just as the factual complaint that other people are opaque is carried to the point where the knowledge sought is made logically unobtainable, so there is a tendency to try to overcome this logical impossibility by making it only factual. No doubt telepathy is not enough, but if I were co-conscious with another person, then perhaps I should really know his experiences in the way that I know my own: I should really then succeed in being two persons at once. Now there is no reason why we should not describe certain paranormal phenomena by speaking of co-consciousness: and if someone who complains that other minds are closed to him is complaining only that he does not have such unusual experiences, his problem is still practical; he may hope to find some means of acquiring them. But even in an instance of co-consciousness it may still be argued that the gulf between persons remains. For either there is only one person involved, in which case all that is in question is his knowledge of himself, or there are two or more, and in that case there are as many sets of experiences as there are people. Each person has his own experiences, and no one can have those of any other person. The gap is not bridged, and never can be bridged, because, for someone who argues in this way, nothing is ever going to count as one person's having the experiences of another.

It is the crossing and recrossing of the line between the empirical and the logical that makes this a text-book problem in the theory of knowledge. The undoubted fact that one sometimes does not know what other people are thinking and feeling gives rise to the suspicion that one never really does know; the next step is to pass from saying that one never does in fact know what goes on in another person's mind to saying that one never can know, and interpreting this statement in such a way that it is necessarily true. But this appears to concede too much to scepticism, and so a move is made in the reverse direction. It is suggested that even if we never do in fact know what goes on in the minds of others there might be circumstances in which we should. The assertion of our ignorance is thus reconstrued as empirical but, like an alien without a valid passport, it is constantly liable to deportation. As soon as an attempt is made to treat it seriously as an empirical statement, it tends to change back into a necessary truth. At this point it is tempting to lose one's patience with the problem. It is simply, one may say, a matter of what one chooses to understand by knowledge. If in order to know what another person is thinking or feeling I have literally to share his experiences and if at the same time nothing is going to count as my literally sharing his experiences, then plainly nothing is going to count as my knowing, really knowing, what he thinks or feels. But the moral of this is just that if we interpret »knowing» in so strict a fashion we deprive ourselves of the right to use it in this context. All that one has to do to defeat the sceptic is to give up the stipulation that in order to know what goes on in another's mind one must literally share his experiences; or, if the stipulation is to be retained, we must interpret it in such a way that it is at least theoretically capable of being met; one must allow it to be possible that experiences should, in the relevant sense, be common to different persons. In either case the question whether we can know what goes on in the minds of others becomes, what it ought to be, a question of empirical fact.

But this solution of the problem is too simple. The philosopher who raises doubts about our knowledge of other minds is not primarily concerned with questions of linguistic usage. He may readily admit that there is a sense in which different people can be said to share the same experiences: he may admit even that, as words are ordinarily used, it is perfectly legitimate to speak of a person's knowing what goes on in someone else's mind. Nevertheless he will insist that there must still remain a sense in which it is necessarily true that experiences are private, and necessarily true also that one cannot know the thoughts and feelings of others in the way that one knows one's own. Consequently, he will maintain, the statements that one makes about the experiences of others stand in need of justification in a way in which the statements that one makes about one's own experiences do not. The fact, if it be a fact, that it is socially correct in certain circumstances to speak of knowing such statements to be true is beside the point. The question at issue is what such claims to knowledge can be worth.

Even so, it may be said, the sceptic's difficulties are illusory. Let us allow it to be necessarily true that I cannot know the experiences of others in the way that I know my own. It by no means follows that I cannot have good reasons to believe in their existence. Such reasons will indeed be supplied to me by experiences of my own, just as the reasons which someone else may have for believing in the existence of my experiences must ultimately be supplied to him by experiences of his own. But they may be good reasons none the less. Even if knowledge is defined so strictly that one can never rightly claim to know what others think or feel, it will still be true that we can attain to states of highly probable opinion. It may well be thought perverse to insist on speaking of highly probable opinion in cases where attention to ordinary usage should lead us to speak of knowledge; but this is not a point of any great importance. What is important is that many of the statements which one makes about the experiences of others are fully justifiable on the basis of one's own.

But once again this manner of disposing of the problem is too simple. We are still left with the question how these statements can be justified and how the insistence that they shall be justifiable conditions their interpretation. There is here an instructive parallel to be drawn with the case of statements about the past. Thus, just as it is necessarily true that I cannot have the experiences of another person, so is it necessarily true that I cannot now experience a past event. Accordingly, if I am asked what reason I have to believe in the truth of any statement which refers to the past, the best answer that I can make is to produce a record, whether in the form of memory or some other. And with this most people would be satisfied. Even though no form of record be infallible, when different records agree they are willing to rely upon them. But philosophers are not so easily satisfied. They point out that it is logically possible that all the records should be false and, what is more, that it is logically impossible to test them, since that would require returning to the past. Then some attempt to elude the logical necessity by claiming that in remembering an event we actually return to the past, a view which they express less crudely by saying that memory is, or may be, a form of direct knowledge, that when an event is remembered it may be literally re-experienced. And others argue that since our reasons for believing a proposition about the past always come down to our having some experiences in the present, or expecting to have some experiences in the future, propositions about the past are really propositions about the present or the future in disguise. But both are mistaken. Propositions about the past are not about the present or future: they are about the past.

And if an event is past in the sense which is here in question, its occurrence is logically independent of any present experience, even if the present experience is a memory of it and the memory is veridical. In the same way my knowing, or believing, that some other person is having an experience of a certain sort is not my having his experience; and in saying, on the basis of certain evidence, that he is having this experience, I am not merely giving a redescription of the evidence.

But if my statement is not just a redescription of the evidence, then one is inclined to say that it must be an inference from it. And this brings back the question whether, and how, the inference is justified. To which as we have seen, the usual answer is that it is justified by an argument from analogy. But here we come upon the difficulty that the argument, at least as it is commonly presented, is not like any ordinary argument of this type. In the ordinary way, an argument from analogy is a substitute for direct observation. Suppose that the symptoms of two diseases are similar in certain respects and that I have discovered that one of the diseases is caused by a microbe of a certain sort; I may infer by analogy that the other disease also is caused by a microbe which I have not so far observed, and I may then set about trying to detect it. Had I already detected it I should not need the argument from analogy to establish its existence. But what is the direct observation for which the argument from analogy is a substitute in the case of other minds? There is nothing describable as detecting the thoughts and feelings of another apart from adding to the premises of the argument, that is, collecting further information about his behaviour. And it is for this reason that many philosophers hold that the argument from analogy is invalid in this case. Yet surely part at least of my reason for ascribing thoughts and feelings and sensations to others is that I have them myself. Suppose that someone tells me that he has had a tooth extracted without an anaesthetic, and I express my sympathy and suppose that I am then asked »How do you know that it hurt him?» I might reasonably reply: »Well, I know that it would hurt me. I have been to the dentist and know how painful it is to have a tooth stopped without an anaesthetic, let alone taken out. And he has the same sort of nervous system as I have. I infer therefore that in these conditions he felt considerable pain, just as I should myself.»

Now here I do argue by analogy and up to a point the argument proceeds like any other. By analogy with what I have observed of other people and what I have learned about myself, I infer that someone with the relevant sort of nervous system, when operated on in such and such conditions, will show signs of pain, signs that I may well be able to detect if I watch him closely enough. But then I want to go further and argue from the existence of these signs to the existence of his actual feeling of pain, which *ex hypothesi*, since it is not my feeling, I cannot detect. And at this point some philosophers will object. »You want to infer from the shadows on the blind to the existence of the people inside the room; but the parallel does not hold. For there is nothing which corresponds in this case to going into the room and meeting the people. It is rather as if you were to look for the invisible fairy that you supposed to animate your watch. You are succumbing to the myth of the ghost in the machine.» Nevertheless I maintain that my feeling pain when the dentist operates on me does supply me with a reason for believing that my friend feels pain when the dentist operates on him; and that when I say that my friend feels pain, I do not mean merely that he shows signs of pain. I mean to ascribe to him a feeling of the same sort as I have myself. But what, it may be asked, are we to understand by this?

This question takes us back to the first of the propositions which I began by listing. »When someone other than myself says that he has a headache what he is saying about himself is the same as what I should be saying about myself if I were to say that I had a headache». A shorter and more familiar form of this proposition is: »When someone other than myself says 'I have a headache' what he means is the same as what I mean when I say 'I have a headache'». But when it is put in this way, there is clearly a sense in which the proposition is false. For when he says 'I have a headache' he means that he has a headache, and when I say 'I have a headache' I mean that I have a headache, and since we are two different persons our meanings are not the same. There is, however, a sense in which they are the same. For if he is using the English language correctly, he uses the words 'I have a headache' to state that he has a headache and not, for example, to state that he has a toothache or that he has seen a ghost; and I too, if I am using the English language correctly, use the words 'I have a headache' to state that I have a headache, and not that I have a toothache or that I have seen a ghost. Rules can be given for the correct use in English of expressions like 'I have a headache' and these rules are intersubjective in the sense that not only I but anyone can follow them. Thus the reason for saying that what my friend means when he says that he has a headache is the same as what I mean when I say that I have a headache is that our use of the expression 'I have a headache' conforms to the same rules.

The next question to consider is whether, when I say of him that he has a headache, what I am saying about him is the same as what I say about myself when I say that I have a headache. And here again the answer is that it is the same in so far as the use of the expression 'he has a headache' is governed by the same rules as the use of the expression 'I have a headache'. There are indeed peculiarities about the use of personal pronouns, especially in the first person, which make these two expressions function somewhat discrepantly; but there is still a sense in which they may properly be said to conform to the same rules. Thus, the statement that he has a headache is not entailed by 'he says he has a headache' or by 'he groans and clutches his head' or by any combination of such statements, any more than the statement that I have a headache is entailed by any statements about what I say, or about my overt behaviour, or by any combination of such statements. And just as my saying that I have a headache and my behaving in certain ways is good evidence in favour of my having a headache, and none the less good because I myself do not require it, so his saying that he has a headache and his behaving in certain ways is good evidence in favour of his having a headache, and none the less good because he does not require it. But the evidence, though good, is not conclusive. It does not constitute the meaning of the statement whose truth it supports. What it means to say of any person, whether myself or any other, that he has a headache is that he has a headache, that his head is hurting him, that he feels pain in his head. It does not mean that he says he has a headache, or that he gives any outward signs of pain. But his saying that he has a headache, or his showing signs of pain, may be the best evidence that those who are not the person in question ever in fact have for concluding that he really is in pain.

But now some philosopher may say: »Is it really good evidence? Prove to me that it is good evidence.» To which one might answer: »He is a truthful sort of person, and people do commonly tell the truth in these circumstances unless they have special reason not to, and he seems to have no motive for lying to us in this instance.»: or »When people behave in this sort of way they generally do have headaches». »But how do you know that they do?» »Well I do for one and so and so says that he has a headache when he behaves in this way, and he usually tells the truth.» »But how do you know that he is truthful?» And then I give the evidence. »But perhaps he is truthful about the things that you can test, but not about his own thoughts or feelings. How do you know that this is not so? Can one ever really know anything about the thoughts and feelings of another?»

This threatens to bring us back to the point from which we started. Let us see if we cannot now find a way of escaping from the circle. It would seem that this is one of the cases in which the denial that knowledge is attainable has its source in the fact that those to whom it is denied are regarded as being in some way underprivileged. We cannot really know what happened in the past because we cannot go back and look. The best evidence that we can now obtain is not the best conceivable; this follows simply from the fact that we are not contemporary with the events in question. So, if really knowing is to be equated with having the best evidence conceivable, it becomes, as I have said, a necessary fact that one cannot really know the truth of any statement about the past. In the same way, we cannot really know what is going on in some other part of space. This seems a smaller deprivation than the other because of the possibility of visiting the place in question. If we cannot visit it, it is for a practical and not a logical reason. Even so it takes time for us to travel, and by the time we get to the distant place the event will be past.

Our evidence for its occurrence will not be so good as it could be, as it might have been if we had been at the right place when the event was still present. But it is impossible, logically impossible, that, being where we are, we should also be somewhere else. Once more we are necessarily underprivileged, given our actual situation. It is not necessary that we should be in this situation, but it is necessary that if we are in this situation, then we are not also in some other which is incompatible with it. One might have lived at a different time, though it is arguable that this is not to be admitted without qualification. To say of someone living now that he might have lived many million years ago provokes at least the query whether he could, in that case, still be the same person: on the other hand, it appears to make quite good sense to say that one might be a few years older or younger than one is. And clearly one might at any given moment be in a different place from that in which one happens then to be. A statement which misdescribes a person's spatial position is false but not self-contradictory. But if the best possible evidence for the truth of a statement is to be obtained only by those who are in a spatio-temporal situation which happens not to be ours, it does follow necessarily that we cannot obtain it. And if it is, by definition, only the privileged, the eyewitnesses, who can really know the fact in question, then, given that we are not among them, it is necessarily true that we can never really know it.

It does not follow, however, that we are reduced to scepticism. So long as we hold it to be theoretically conceivable that we should be in the privileged situation, the fact that we are not is not regarded as condemning us to utter ignorance. We are not inclined to say that the evidence we can obtain is good for nothing at all just because it is not, and in the circumstances cannot be, the best possible. Thus, when it is a question of knowing about events which are remote from us in space, we are quite ready to accept inductive arguments. For, in such cases, the handicap from which we suffer, though logically insuperable, is easily overcome in our imagination. It seems to us that we might very well be privileged, even though we are not; that in some straightforward sense we could be there among the eyewitnesses, rather than here where we are in fact. And this assumption that direct evidence is theoretically accessible to us is all that we require to make us content with indirect evidence, provided of course that this is good of its kind. When the handicap is due to our position in time it does indeed appear more serious. We find it less easy to conceive of ourselves as occupying a different position in time than as occupying a different position in space; and this difficulty, as I have remarked, increases as the time envisaged is more remote. The doubt arises whether events occurring at a distant time are even theoretically accessible to us, whether there is any sense in saying that we might have been in the best possible position to observe them; and this in its turn throws doubt upon the validity of the evidence that we are in fact in a position to obtain, however, good of its kind it may appear to be. Nevertheless this doubt does not as a rule take serious hold even upon philosophers. The fact that some at least of the events which are now remote from us in time have been, or will be, offered to our observation secures them admission into the category of those that are theoretically accessible, and the warrant is then extended to the other members of the class. In this way we credit ourselves with having the required support for our inductive arguments.

When it comes, however, to the case of other minds, the fact of our being underprivileged appears, at first sight, very much more serious. For here it might seem not only that we were necessarily handicapped given our actual situation, but that the handicap itself was necessary. To be privileged is to be the other person. Only he really knows when he thinks and feels. I do not and cannot because I am myself and not he. But is it even conceivable that I should be he? It is plainly a contradiction that I should both remain myself and be someone other than myself: yet this is exactly what here seems to be required. In the other cases which we have considered, the fact that one was underprivileged was the outcome of one's situation, the position that one happened to occupy in space and time; and it could be remedied, at least in theory, by the situation's being changed. But how could a change in my situation make me someone else? Unless I keep something of myself, that is, some characteristic which is peculiar to me, I have not just changed my situation, I am abolished altogether. But if I do keep something of myself, I have not attained the privileged position, I am not identified with the other person. Thus it seems that the thoughts and feelings of others are inaccessible to us, not merely because we happen to occupy the relatively unfavourable position that we do, but because we are respectively the persons that we are. The privileged position, in any given instance, which is that of being the person who has the thoughts and feelings in question, is one that only he could occupy. It would appear, therefore, that we are debarred from »really knowing» one another's inner experiences in a more radical way than we are debarred from »really knowing» events which are remote from us in space or time. For while we are underprivileged in these cases also it is at least conceivable that we should not have been.

This reasoning is plausible but I do not think that it is sound. Admittedly, to say that an experience is not one's own but someone else's is to imply that one is not, and could not be, in the best possible position to know that it exists. But equally, to say of an event that it is remote in time or space is to imply that one is not, and could not be, in the best possible position to know that it exists: for the description of the event as occurring somewhere else, or as being future or past, already carries the implication that one is underprivileged. This does not follow from a mere description of the event, or even from a description of its place and date, so long as it contains no reference to the position of the speaker; and it is for this reason that it can be held to be contingent that the speaker's actual position is not the best possible. But equally, the implication that one is underprivileged is not contained in any mere description of an experience, or even in a description of the person whose experience it is, so long as no reference is made to the identity of the speaker. The use of pronouns like 'he' and 'they' and 'you' shows that the speaker is not himself the person whose experiences are in question and consequently not in the most favourable position to know about them, just as the use of tenses or of words like 'miles away' shows that the speaker's spatio-temporal position is not privileged. But the implied, or explicit, reference to the situation, or identity, of the speaker is logically irrelevant to the facts which he describes. When these demonstratives are replaced by descriptions it becomes an open question whether the speaker is, or is not, in the best possible position to verify his statement. Suppose that the statement does in fact refer to the experience of some other person. Even so, what is stated is just that someone who answers to a given description is having such and such an experience, and from this it does not follow, with regard to any person who is not actually identified as one who does not answer to the description or is not having the experience, that he is not the person in question. It does not follow, therefore, that the description is not satisfied by the speaker himself. Once it is stated that an experience is the experience of someone other than myself, the possibility of its also being my experience is indeed ruled out. But so long as the statement contains no explicit or implicit reference to me, it can be no part of its descriptive content that I am relatively ill-equipped to verify it. In a sense, therefore, there are no such things as statements about other minds. There are many statements which do in fact refer to the experiences of persons other than the speaker. But they do not themselves state that this is so. Considered only with respect to its descriptive content, no statement says anything about the point of view from which it is made.

What is asserted, then, by a statement which in fact refers to the experience of someone other than myself is that the experience in question is the experience of someone who satisfies a certain description: a description which as a matter of fact I do not satisfy. And then the question arises whether it is logically conceivable that I should satisfy it. But the difficulty here is that there are no fixed rules for determining what properties are essential to a person's being the person that he is. My answer to the question whether it is conceivable that I should satisfy some description which I actually do not, or that I should be in some other situation than that in which I am, will depend upon what properties I choose, for the occasion, to regard as constitutive of myself. Ordinarily one does not regard one's spatial position as constitutive of oneself and so can readily conceive that, apart from causal obstacles, one might at any given moment be in a different place from that in which one is. Neither does one regard as constitutive the property of living at the precise time at which one does. On the other hand, the property of living at about that time does tend to be regarded as constitutive of the person: and this is the explanation of the fact, which we have already noticed, that while one can easily imagine oneself to be a year or two older or younger that one is, the picture of oneself as living many million years ago has about it an air of contradiction. But it is contradictory only if one chooses to make it so. It is logically, although not causally, possible that having the moral character I have, nothing else being regarded as essential, I should have lived in the ice age. It is logically possible even that I should under this condition have had my actual memories, though of course they would in that case all have been delusive. In general, it would appear that one can imaginatively deprive a person of any particular property that he possesses without falling into contradiction, but that as this procedure is continued there comes a point where he ceases to be the same person. But the determination of this point, that is, the decision to regard a certain set of properties as being indispensable, is very largely arbitrary. So long as some are kept constant, all the others can be varied, and with the choice of a new set of constants the ones that were previously held constant can be varied in their turn.

Let us now see what bearing this has upon our present problem. The analogy between two persons is never perfect: this follows simply from the fact that they are two different persons. Neither can one suppose it to be perfect; for to suppose it perfect would be to merge the two persons into one. At the same time, it may be very extensive, and it can always be conceived as being more extensive than it is. Now when one ascribes some inner experience, some thought or feeling, to another, the rational ground for this ascription consists in one's knowing him to possess some further properties. The assumption is that there is a uniform connection between the possession of these properties and the undergoing of an experience of the sort in question. I infer that my friend is in pain, because of the condition of his tooth, because of his nervous system, because of his wincing, and so forth; and the connection of these properties with a feeling of pain is one that I can, in principle, test, one that I may in fact have tested in my own experience. But, it may be objected, the connection may not hold good in his case. How can you tell? But if it does not hold good in his case, this must be because of some other property that he possesses, the addition of which creates a counter-example to the rule. It would not hold good, for instance, if the additional property were that of his having been hypnotized to feel no pain. But with regard to any further property that he possesses it is conceivable at least that I should test the rule so as to find out whether the addition of this property does make a difference. Sometimes I can carry out the test directly by myself acquiring the properties concerned. Of course there are many properties that I cannot acquire. If I happen, for example, to have been born on a Thursday, I cannot directly test the hypothesis that people who were born on a Wednesday do not in these circumstances feel pain. But I have no reason to suppose that this is a relevant factor, and good indirect evidence that it is not. And, if our argument is correct, there will be no properties that I am in principle debarred from testing, however, many there may be that I cannot test in fact. But even if my friend has no properties which make him an exception to the rule about feeling pain, may he not still be an exception just as being the person that he is? And in that case how can the rest of us ever know whether or not he really does feel pain? But the answer to this is that nothing is described by his being the person that he is except the possession of certain properties. If, *per impossibile*, we could test for all the properties that he possesses, and found that they did not produce a counterexample to our general hypothesis about the conditions in which pain is felt, our knowledge would be in this respect as good as his: there would be nothing further left for us to discover.

To sum up, it is necessarily true that, being the person that I am, I am not also someone else. It is necessarily true that I could not conceivably satisfy all the descriptions that some other person satisfies, and still remain a distinct person. And if this is made the requirement for my really knowing what he thinks or feels, then it is necessarily true that this is something that I can never really know. On the other hand, with regard to any given property, which I may or may not myself in fact possess, there seems to be no logical reason why I should not test the degree of its connection with some other properties: and what I am asserting when I ascribe an experience to some other person is just that the property of having it is co-instantiated with certain others. The inference is not from my experience as such to his experience as such but from the fact that certain properties have been found to be conjoined in various contexts to the conclusion that in a further context the conjunction will still hold. This is a normal type of inductive argument; and I cannot see that it is in any degree invalidated by the fact that however far one is able to extend the positive analogy, it always remains within the compass of one's own experience.

KNOWLEDGE OF OTHER MINDS

Norman Malcolm

I

I believe that the argument from analogy for the existence of other minds still enjoys more credit than it deserves, and my first aim in this paper will be to show that it leads nowhere. J. S. Mill is one of many who have accepted the argument and I take his statement of it as representative. He puts to himself the question, "By what evidence do I know, or by what considerations am I led to believe, that there exist other sentient creatures; that the walking and speaking figures which I see and hear, have sensations and thoughts, or in other words, possess Minds?" His answer is the following:

> I conclude that other human beings have feelings like me, because, first, they have bodies like me, which I know, in my own case, to be the antecedent condition of feelings; and because, secondly, they exhibit the acts, and other outward signs, which in my own case I know by experience to be caused by feelings. I am conscious in myself of a series of facts connected by an uniform sequence, of which the beginning is modifications of my body, the middle is feelings, the end is outward demeanor. In the case of other human beings I have the evidence of my senses for the first and last links of the series, but not for the intermediate link. I find, however, that the sequence between the first and last is as regular and constant in those other cases as it is in mine. In my own case I know that the first link produces the last through the intermediate link, and could not produce it without. Experience, therefore, obliges me to conclude that there must be an intermediate link; which must either be the same in others as in myself, or a differ-

> ent one: I must either believe them to be alive, or to be automatons: and by believing them to be alive, that is, by supposing the link to be of the same nature as in the case of which I have experience, and which is in all other respects similar, I bring other human beings, as phenomena, under the same generalizations which I know by experience to be the true theory of my own existence.[1]

I shall pass by the possible objection that this would be very *weak* inductive reasoning, based as it is on the observation of a single instance. More interesting is the following point: suppose this reasoning could yield a conclusion of the sort "It is probable that that human figure (pointing at some person other than oneself) has thoughts and feelings." Then there is a question as to whether this conclusion can *mean* anything to the philosopher who draws it, because there is a question as to whether the sentence "That human figure has thoughts and feelings" can mean anything to him. Why should this be a question? Because the assumption from which Mill starts is that he has *no criterion* for determining whether another "walking and speaking figure" does or does not have thoughts and feelings. If he had a criterion he could apply it, establishing with certainty that this or that human figure does or does not have feelings (for the only plausible criterion would lie in behavior and circumstances that are open to view), and there would be no call to resort to tenuous analogical reasoning that yields at best a probability. If Mill has no criterion for the existence of feelings other than his own then in that sense he does not understand the sentence "That human figure has feelings" and therefore does not understand the sentence "It is *probable* that that human figure has feelings."

There is a familiar inclination to make the following reply: "Although I have no criterion of verification still I *understand*, for example, the sentence 'He has a pain.' For I understand the meaning of 'I have a pain,' and 'He has a pain' means that he has the *same* thing I have when I have a pain." But this is a fruitless maneuver. If I do not know how

[1] J. S. Mill, *An Examination of Sir William Hamilton's Philosophy*, 6th ed. (London, 1889), pp. 243–44.

to establish that someone has a pain then I do not know how to establish that he has the *same* as I have when I have a pain.[2] You cannot improve my understanding of "He has a pain" by this recourse to the notion of "the same," unless you give me a criterion for saying that someone *has* the same as I have. If you can do this you will have no use for the argument from analogy: and if you cannot then you do not understand the supposed conclusion of that argument. A philosopher who purports to rely on the analogical argument cannot, I think, escape this dilemma.

There have been various attempts to repair the argument from analogy. Mr. Stuart Hampshire has argued[3] that its validity as a method of inference can be established in the following way: others sometimes infer that I am feeling giddy from my behavior. Now I have direct, non-inferential knowledge, says Hampshire, of my own feelings. So I can check inferences made about me against the facts, checking thereby the accuracy of the "methods" of inference.

> All that is required for testing the validity of any method of factual inference is that each one of us should sometimes be in a position to confront the conclusions of the doubtful method of inference with what is known by him to be true independently of the method of inference in question. Each one of us is certainly in this position in respect of our common methods of inference about the feelings of persons other than ourselves, in virtue of the fact that each one of us is constantly able to compare the results of this type of inference with what he knows to be true directly and non-inferentially; each one of us is in the position to make this testing comparison, whenever he is the designated subject of a statement about feelings and sensations. I, Hampshire, know by what sort of signs I may be misled in inferring Jones' and Smith's feelings, because

[2] "It is no explanation to say: the supposition that he has a pain is simply the supposition that he has the same as I. For *that* part of the grammar is quite clear to me: that is, that one will say that the stove has the same experience as I, *if* one says: it is in pain and I am in pain" (Wittgenstein, *Philosophical Investigations* [Oxford, 1953], §350).

[3] "The Analogy of Feeling," *Mind*, LXI (1952), 1–12.

I have implicitly noticed (though probably not formulated) where Jones, Smith and others generally go wrong in inferring my feelings (pp. 4–5).

Presumably I can also note when the inferences of others about my feelings do not go wrong. Having ascertained the reliability of some inference-procedures I can use them myself, in a guarded way, to draw conclusions about the feelings of others, with a modest but justified confidence in the truth of those conclusions.

My first comment is that Hampshire has apparently forgotten the purpose of the argument from analogy, which is to provide some probability that "the walking and speaking figures which I see and hear, have sensations and thoughts" (Mill). For the reasoning that he describes involves the assumption that other human figures *do* have thoughts and sensations: for they are assumed to *make inferences* about me from *observations* of my behavior. But the philosophical problem of the existence of other minds *is* the problem of whether human figures other than oneself do, among other things, make observations, inferences, and assertions. Hampshire's supposed defense of the argument from analogy is an *ignoratio elenchi.*

If we struck from the reasoning described by Hampshire all assumption of thoughts and sensations in others we should be left with something roughly like this: "When my behavior is such-and-such there come from nearby human figures the sounds 'He feels giddy.' And generally I do feel giddy at the time. Therefore when another human figure exhibits the same behavior and I say 'He feels giddy,' it is probable that he does feel giddy." But the reference here to the sentence-like sounds coming from other human bodies is irrelevant, since I must not assume that those sounds express inferences. Thus the reasoning becomes simply the classical argument from analogy: "When my behavior is such-and-such I feel giddy; so probably when another human figure behaves the same way he feels the same way." This argument, again, is caught in the dilemma about the criterion of the *same.*

The version of analogical reasoning offered by Professor

H. H. Price[4] is more interesting. He suggests that "one's evidence for the existence of other minds is derived primarily from the understanding of language" (p. 429). His idea is that if another body gives forth noises one understands, like "There's the bus," and if these noises give one new information, this "provides some evidence that the foreign body which uttered the noises is animated by a mind like one's own. . . . Suppose I am often in its neighborhood, and it repeatedly produces utterances which I can understand, and which I then proceed to verify for myself. And suppose that this happens in many different kinds of situation. I think that my evidence for believing that this body is animated by a mind like my own would then become very strong" (p. 430). The body from which these informative sounds proceed need not be a human body. "If the rustling of the leaves of an oak formed intelligible words conveying new information to me, and if gorse bushes made intelligible gestures, I should have evidence that the oak or the gorse bush was animated by an intelligence like my own" (p. 436). Even if the intelligible and informative sounds did not proceed from a body they would provide evidence for the existence of a (disembodied) mind (p. 435).

Although differing sharply from the classical analogical argument, the reasoning presented by Price is still analogical in form: I know by introspection that when certain combinations of sounds come from me they are "symbols in acts of spontaneous thinking"; therefore similar combinations of sounds, not produced by me, "probably function as instruments to an act of spontaneous thinking, which in this case is not my own" (p. 446). Price says that the reasoning also provides an *explanation* of the otherwise mysterious occurrence of sounds which I understand but did not produce. He anticipates the objection that the hypothesis is nonsensical because unverifiable. "The hypothesis is a perfectly conceivable one," he says, "in the sense that I know very well what the world would have to be like if the hypothesis were true—what sorts of entities there must be in it, and what sorts of events must occur in them. I know from introspec-

[4] "Our Evidence for the Existence of Other Minds," *Philosophy*, XIII (1938), 425–56.

tion what acts of thinking and perceiving are, and I know what it is for such acts to be combined into the unity of a single mind . . ." (pp. 446–47).

I wish to argue against Price that no amount of intelligible sounds coming from an oak tree or a kitchen table could create any probability that it has sensations and thoughts. The question to be asked is: What would show that a tree or table *understands* the sounds that come from it? We can imagine that useful warnings, true descriptions and predictions, even "replies" to questions, should emanate from a tree, so that it came to be of enormous value to its owner. How should we establish that it understood those sentences? Should we "question" it? Suppose that the tree "said" that there was a vixen in the neighborhood, and we "asked" it "What is a vixen?" and it "replied," "A vixen is a female fox." It might go on to do as well for "female" and "fox." This performance might incline us to say that the tree understood the words, in contrast to the possible case in which it answered "I don't know" or did not answer at all. But would it show that the tree understood the words in the same sense that a person could understand them? With a person such a performance would create a presumption that he could make correct *applications* of the word in question: but not so with a tree. To see this point think of the normal teaching of words (e.g., "spoon," "dog," "red") to a child and how one decides whether he understands them. At a primitive stage of teaching one does not require or expect definitions, but rather that the child should *pick out* reds from blues, dogs from cats, spoons from forks. This involves his looking, pointing, reaching for and going to the right things and not the wrong ones. That a child says "red" when a red thing and "blue" when a blue thing is put before him, is indicative of a mastery of those words *only* in conjunction with the other activities of looking, pointing, trying to get, fetching and carrying. Try to suppose that he says the right words but looks at and reaches for the wrong things. Should we be tempted to say that he has mastered the use of those words? No, indeed. The disparity between words and behavior would make us say that he does not understand the words. In the case of a tree there could be no disparity between its words and its "behavior" because it is logically incapable of behavior of the relevant kind.

Since it has nothing like the human face and body it makes no sense to say of a tree, or an electronic computer, that it is looking or pointing at or fetching something. (Of course one can always *invent* a sense for these expressions.) Therefore it would make no sense to say that it did or did not understand the above words. Trees and computers cannot either pass or fail the tests that a child is put through. They cannot even take them. That an object was a source of intelligible sounds or other signs (no matter how sequential) would not be enough by itself to establish that it had thoughts or sensations. How informative sentences and valuable predictions could emanate from a gorse bush might be a grave scientific problem, but the explanation could never be that the gorse bush has a mind. Better no explanation than nonsense!

It might be thought that the above difficulty holds only for words whose meaning has a "perceptual content" and that if we imagined, for example, that our gorse bush produced nothing but pure mathematical propositions we should be justified in attributing thought to it, although not sensation. But suppose there was a remarkable "calculating boy" who could give right answers to arithmetical problems but could not apply numerals to reality in empirical propositions, i.e., he could not *count* any objects. I believe that everyone would be reluctant to say that he *understood* the mathematical signs and truths that he produced. If he could count in the normal way there would not be this reluctance. And "counting in the normal way" involves looking, pointing, reaching, fetching, and so on. That is, it requires the human face and body, and human behavior—or something similar. Things which do not have the human form, or anything like it, not merely do not but *cannot* satisfy the criteria for thinking. I am trying to bring out part of what Wittgenstein meant when he said, "We only say of a human being and what is like one that it thinks" (*Investigations*, §360), and "The human body is the best picture of the human soul" (*ibid.*, p. 178).

I have not yet gone into the most fundamental error of

the argument from analogy. It is present whether the argument is the classical one (the analogy between my body and other bodies) or Price's version (the analogy between my language and the noises and signs produced by other things). It is the mistaken assumption that *one learns from one's own case* what thinking, feeling, sensation are. Price gives expression to this assumption when he says: "I know from introspection what acts of thinking and perceiving are . . ." (*op. cit.*, p. 447). It is the most natural assumption for a philosopher to make and indeed seems at first to be the only possibility. Yet Wittgenstein has made us see that it leads first to solipsism and then to nonsense. I shall try to state as briefly as possible how it produces those results.

A philosopher who believes that one must learn what thinking, fear, or pain is "from one's own case," does not believe that the thing to be observed is one's behavior, but rather something "inward." He considers behavior to be related to the inward states and occurrences merely as an accompaniment or possibly an effect. He cannot regard behavior as a *criterion* of psychological phenomena: for if he did he would have no use for the analogical argument (as was said before) and also the priority given to "one's own case" would be pointless. He believes that he notes something in himself that he calls "thinking" or "fear" or "pain," and then he tries to infer the presence of the *same* in others. He should then deal with the question of what his criterion of the *same* in others is. This he cannot do because it is of the essence of his viewpoint to reject circumstances and behavior as a criterion of mental phenomena in others. And what else could serve as a criterion? He ought, therefore, to draw the conclusion that the notion of thinking, fear, or pain in others is in an important sense meaningless. He has no idea of what would count for or against it.[5] "That there should be thinking or pain other than my own is unintelligible," he ought to hold. This would be a rigorous solipsism, and a correct outcome of the assumption that one can know

[5] One reason why philosophers have not commonly drawn this conclusion may be, as Wittgenstein acutely suggests, that they assume that they have "an infallible paradigm of identity in the identity of a thing with itself" (*Investigations*, §215).

only from one's own case what the mental phenomena are. An equivalent way of putting it would be: "When I say 'I am in pain,' by 'pain' I mean a certain inward state. When I say 'He is in pain,' by 'pain' I mean *behavior*. I cannot attribute pain to others *in the same sense* that I attribute it to myself."

Some philosophers before Wittgenstein may have seen the solipsistic result of starting from "one's own case." But I believe he is the first to have shown how that starting point destroys itself. This may be presented as follows: one supposes that one inwardly picks out something as thinking or pain and thereafter identifies it whenever it presents itself in the soul. But the question to be pressed is, Does one make *correct* identifications? The proponent of these "private" identifications has nothing to say here. He feels sure that he identifies correctly the occurrences in his soul; but feeling sure is no guarantee of being right. Indeed he has no idea of what being *right* could mean. He does not know how to distinguish between actually making correct identifications and being under the impression that he does. (See *Investigations*, §§258–59.) Suppose that he identified the emotion of anxiety as the sensation of pain? Neither he nor anyone else could know about this "mistake." Perhaps he makes a mistake *every* time! Perhaps all of us do! We ought to see now that we are talking nonsense. We do not know what a *mistake* would be. We have no standard, no examples, no customary practice, with which to compare our inner recognitions. The inward identification cannot hit the bull's-eye, or miss it either, because there is no bull's-eye. When we see that the ideas of correct and incorrect have no application to the supposed inner identification, the latter notion loses its appearance of sense. Its collapse brings down both solipsism and the argument from analogy.

II

This destruction of the argument from analogy also destroys the *problem* for which it was supposed to provide a solution. A philosopher feels himself in a difficulty about other minds because he assumes that first of all he is acquainted with mental phenomena "from his own case." What troubles him is how to make the transition from his own case to the case of others. When his thinking is freed of the illusion of the priority of his own case, then he is able to look at the familiar facts and to acknowledge that the circumstances, behavior, and utterances of others actually are his *criteria* (not merely his evidence) for the existence of their mental states. Previously this had seemed impossible.

But now he is in danger of flying to the opposite extreme of behaviorism, which errs by believing that through observation of one's own circumstances, behavior, and utterances one can find out that one is thinking or angry. The philosophy of "from one's own case" and behaviorism, though in a sense opposites, make the common assumption that the first-person, present-tense psychological statements are verified by self-observation. According to the "one's own case" philosophy the self-observation cannot be checked by others; according to behaviorism the self-observation would be by means of outward criteria that are available to all. The first position becomes unintelligible; the second is false for at least many kinds of psychological statements. We are forced to conclude that the first-person psychological statements are not (or hardly ever) verified by self-observation. It follows that they have no verification at all; for if they had a verification it would have to be by self-observation.

But if sentences like "My head aches" or "I wonder where she is" do not express observations then what do they do? What is the relation between my declaration that my head aches and the fact that my head aches, if the former is not the report of an observation? The perplexity about the existence of *other* minds has, as the result of criticism, turned into a perplexity about the meaning of one's own psychological sentences about oneself. At our starting point it was the sentence "*His* head aches" that posed a problem; but now it is the sentence "*My* head aches" that puzzles us.

One way in which this problem can be put is by the question, "How does *one know when to say* the words 'My head aches'?" The inclination to ask this question can be made acute by imagining a fantastic but not impossible case of a person who has survived to adult years without ever experiencing pain. He is given various sorts of injections to correct this condition, and on receiving one of these one day, he jumps and exclaims, "Now I feel pain!" One wants to ask, "How did he *recognize* the new sensation as a pain?"

Let us note that if the man gives an answer (e.g., "I knew it must be pain because of the way I jumped") then he proves by that very fact that he has not mastered the correct use of the words "I feel pain." They cannot be used to state a *conclusion*. In telling us *how* he did it he will convict himself of a misuse. Therefore the question "How did he recognize his sensation?" requests the impossible. The inclination to ask it is evidence of our inability to grasp the fact that the use of this psychological sentence has nothing to do with recognizing or identifying or observing a state of oneself.

The fact that this imagined case produces an especially strong temptation to ask the "How?" question shows that we have the idea that it must be more difficult to give the right name of one's sensation *the first time*. The implication would be that it is not so difficult *after* the first time. Why should this be? Are we thinking that then the man would have a paradigm of pain with which he could compare his sensations and so be in a position to know right off whether a certain sensation was or was not a pain? But the paradigm would be either something "outer" (behavior) or something "inner" (perhaps a memory impression of the sensation). If the former then he is misusing the first-person sentence. If the latter then the question of whether he compared *correctly* the present sensation with the inner paradigm of pain would be without sense. Thus the idea that the use of the first-person sentences can be governed by paradigms must be abandoned. It is another form of our insistent misconception of the first-person sentence as resting somehow on the identification of a psychological state.

These absurdities prove that we must conceive of the first-person psychological sentences in some entirely different light. Wittgenstein presents us with the suggestion (to which philosophers have not been sufficiently attentive) that the first-person sentences are to be thought of as similar to the natural nonverbal, behavioral expressions of psychological states. "My leg hurts," for example, is to be assimilated to crying, limping, holding one's leg. This is a bewildering comparison and one's first thought is that two sorts of things could not be more unlike. By saying the sentence one can make a *statement*; it has a *contradictory*; it is *true* or *false*; in saying it one *lies* or *tells the truth*; and so on. None of these things, exactly, can be said of crying, limping, holding one's leg. So how can there be any resemblance? But Wittgenstein knew this when he deliberately likened such a sentence to "the primitive, the natural, expressions" of pain, and said that it is "new pain-behavior" (*ibid.*, §244). Although my limits prevent my attempting it here, I think this analogy ought to be explored. For it has at least two important merits: first, it breaks the hold on us of the question "How does one *know when to say* 'My leg hurts'?" for in the light of the analogy this will be as nonsensical as the question "How does one know when to cry, limp, or hold one's leg?"; second, it explains how the utterance of a first-person psychological sentence by another person can have *importance* for us, although not as an identification—for in the light of the analogy it will have the same importance as the natural behavior which serves as our preverbal criterion of the psychological states of others.

PERSONS

P. F. Strawson

I

In the *Tractatus* (5.631-5.641), Wittgenstein writes of the I which occurs in philosophy, of the philosophical idea of the subject of experiences. He says first: "The thinking, presenting subject–there is no such thing." Then, a little later: "*In an important sense* there is no subject." This is followed by: "The subject does not belong to the world, but is a limit of the world." And a little later comes the following paragraph: "There is [therefore] really a sense in which in philosophy we can talk nonpsychologically of the I. The I occurs in philosophy through the fact that the 'world is my world.' The philosophical I is not the man, not the human body, or the human soul of which psychology treats, but the metaphysical subject, the limit–not a part of the world." These remarks are impressive, but also puzzling and obscure. Reading them, one might think: Well, let's settle for the human body and the human soul of which psychology treats, and which is a part of the world, and let the metaphysical subject go. But again we might think: No, when I talk of myself, I do after all talk of that which has all of my experiences, I do talk of the subject of my experiences–and yet also of something that is part of the world in that it, but not the world, comes to an end when I die. The limit of *my* world is not–and is not so thought of by me–the limit of *the* world. It may be difficult to explain the idea of something which is both a subject of experiences and a part of the world. But it is an idea we have: it should be an idea we can explain.

P. F. Strawson is a Fellow of University College, Oxford. He is the author of *Introduction to Logical Theory* (London, 1952), and *Individuals* (1959).

Let us think of some of the ways in which we ordinarily talk of ourselves, of some of the things which we ordinarily ascribe to ourselves. They are of many kinds. We ascribe to ourselves *actions* and *intentions* (I am doing, did, shall do this); *sensations* (I am warm, in pain); *thoughts* and *feelings* (I think, wonder, want this, am angry, disappointed, contented); *perceptions* and *memories* (I see this, hear the other, remember that). We ascribe to ourselves, in two senses, position: *location* (I am on the sofa) and *attitude* (I am lying down). And of course we ascribe to ourselves not only temporary conditions, states, and situations, like most of these, but also enduring characteristics, including such physical characteristics as height, coloring, shape, and weight. That is to say, among the things we ascribe to ourselves are things of a kind that we also ascribe to material bodies to which we would not dream of ascribing others of the things that we ascribe to ourselves. Now there seems nothing needing explanation in the fact that the particular height, coloring, and physical position which we ascribe to ourselves, should be ascribed to *something or other*; for that which one calls one's body is, at least, a body, a material thing. It can be picked out from others, identified by ordinary physical criteria and described in ordinary physical terms. But it can seem, and has seemed, to need explanation that one's states of consciousness, one's thoughts and sensations, are ascribed *to the very same thing* as that to which these physical characteristics, this physical situation, is ascribed. Why are one's states of consciousness ascribed to the very same thing as certain corporeal characteristics, a certain physical situation, etc.? And once this question is raised, another question follows it, viz.: Why are one's states of consciousness ascribed to (said to be of, or to belong to) anything at all? It is not to be supposed that the answers to these questions will be independent of one another.

It might indeed be thought that an answer to both of them could be found in the unique role which each person's body plays in his experience, particularly his perceptual experience. All philosophers who have concerned themselves with these questions have referred to the uniqueness of this role. (Descartes was well enough aware of its uniqueness: "I am *not* lodged in my body like a pilot in a vessel.") In what does this uniqueness consist? Well, of course, in a great many facts. We may summarize some of these facts by saying that for each person there is one body which occupies a certain *causal* position in relation to that person's perceptual experience, a causal position which is in various ways unique in relation to each of the various kinds of perceptual experience he has; and—as a further consequence—that this body is also unique for him as an *object* of the various kinds of perceptual experience which he has. This complex uniqueness of the single body appears, moreover, to be a contingent matter, or rather a cluster of contingent matters; we can, or it seems that we can, imagine many peculiar combinations of dependence and independence of aspects of our perceptual experience on the physical states or situation of more than one body.

Now I must say, straightaway, that this cluster of apparently contingent facts about the unique role which each person's body plays in his experience does not seem to me to provide, *by itself*, an answer to our questions. Of course these facts explain *something*. They provide a very good reason why a subject of experience should have a very *special regard* for just one body, why he should think of it as unique and perhaps more important than any other. They explain—if I may be permitted to put it so—why I feel *peculiarly attached* to what in fact I call my own body; they even might be said to explain why, granted that I am going to speak of one body as *mine*, I should speak of this body (the body that I do speak of as mine) as mine. But they do not explain why I should have the concept of *myself* at all, why I should ascribe my thoughts and experiences to *anything*. Moreover, even if we were satisfied with some other explanation of why one's states of consciousness (thoughts and feelings and perceptions) were ascribed to *something*, and satisfied that the facts in question sufficed to explain why the "possession" of a particular body should be ascribed to the *same* thing (i.e., to explain why a particular body should be spoken of as standing in some special relation, called "being possessed by" to that thing), yet the facts in question still do not explain why we should, as we do, ascribe certain corporeal characteristics not simply to the body standing in this special relation to the thing to which we ascribe thoughts, feelings, etc., but to the thing itself to which we ascribe those thoughts and feelings. (For we say "I am bald" as well as "I am cold," "I am lying on the hearthrug" as well as "I see a spider on the ceiling.") Briefly, the facts in question explain why a subject of experience should pick out one body from others, give it, perhaps, an honored name and ascribe to it whatever characteristics it has; but they do not explain why the experiences should be ascribed to any subject at all; and they do not explain why, if the experiences are to be ascribed to something, they *and* the corporeal characteristics which might be truly ascribed to the favored body, should be ascribed to the same thing. So the facts in question do not explain the use that we make of the word "I," or how any word has the use that word has. They do not explain the concept we have of a person.

II

A possible reaction at this point is to say that the concept we have is wrong or confused, or, if we make it a rule not to say that the concepts we have are confused, that the usage we have, whereby we ascribe, or seem to ascribe, such different kinds of predicate to one and the same thing, is confusing, that it conceals the true nature of the concepts involved, or something of this sort. This reaction can be found in two very important types of view about these matters. The first type of view is Cartesian, the view of Descartes and of others who think like him. Over the attribution of the second type of view I am more hesitant; but there is some evidence that it was held, at one period, by Wittgenstein and possibly also by Schlick. On both of these views, one of the questions we are considering, namely "Why do we ascribe our states of consciousness to the very same thing as certain corporeal characteristics, etc.?" is a question which does not arise; for on both views it is only a linguistic illusion that both kinds of predicate are properly ascribed to one and the same thing, that there is a common owner, or subject, of both types of predicate. And on the second of these views, the other question we are considering, namely "Why do we ascribe our states of consciousness to anything at all?" is also a question which does not arise; for on this view, it is only a linguistic illusion that one ascribes one's states of consciousness at all, that there is any proper subject of these apparent ascriptions, that states of consciousness belong to, or are states of, anything.

That Descartes held the first of these views is well enough known. When we speak of a person, we are really referring to one or both of two distinct substances (two substances of different types), each of which has its own appropriate type of states and properties; and none of the properties or states of either can be a property or state of the other. States of consciousness belong to one of these substances, and not to the other. I shall say no more about the Cartesian view at the moment—what I have to say about it will emerge later on —except to note again that while it escapes one of our questions, it does not escape, but indeed invites, the other: "Why are one's states of consciousness *ascribed* at all, to *any* subject?"

The second of these views I shall call the "no-ownership" or "no-subject" doctrine of the self. Whether or not anyone has explicitly held this view, it is worth reconstructing, or constructing, in outline.[1] For the errors into which it falls

[1] The evidence that Wittgenstein at one time held such a view is to be found in the third of Moore's articles in *Mind* on "Wittgenstein's Lectures in 1930–33" (*Mind*, LXIV [1955], especially 13–14). He is reported to have held that the use of "I" was utterly different in the case of "I have a toothache" or "I see a red patch" from its use in the case of "I've got a bad tooth" or "I've got a matchbox." He thought that there were two uses of "I" and that in one of them "I" was replaceable by "this body." So far the view might be Cartesian. But he also said that in the other use (the use exemplified by "I have a toothache" as opposed to "I have a bad tooth"), the "I" *does not denote a possessor*, and that no ego is involved in thinking or in having toothache; and referred with apparent approval to Lichtenberg's dictum that, instead of saying "I think," we (or Descartes!) ought to say "There is a thought" (i.e., "Es denkt").

The attribution of such a view to Schlick would have to rest on his article "Meaning and Verification," Pt. V (in *Readings in Philosophical Analysis*, ed. H. Feigl and W. Sellars [New York, 1949]). Like Wittgenstein, Schlick quotes Lichtenberg, and then goes on to

are instructive. The "no-ownership" theorist may be presumed to start his explanations with facts of the sort which illustrate the unique causal position of a certain material body in a person's experience. The theorist maintains that the uniqueness of this body is sufficient to give rise to the idea that one's experiences can be ascribed to some particular individual thing, can be said to be possessed by, or owned by, that thing. This idea, he thinks, though infelicitously and misleadingly expressed in terms of ownership, would have some validity, would make some sort of sense, so long as we thought of this individual thing, the possessor of the experiences, as the body itself. So long as we thought in this way, then to ascribe a particular state of consciousness to this body, this individual thing, would at least be to say something contingent, something that might be, or might have been, false. It might have been a misascription; for the experience in question might be, or might have been, causally dependent on the state of some other body; in the present admissible, though infelicitous, sense of "belong," it might have belonged to some other individual thing. But now, the theorist suggests, one becomes confused: one slides from this admissible, though infelicitous, sense in which one's experiences may be said to belong to, or be possessed by, some particular thing, to a wholly inadmissible and empty sense of these expressions; and in this new and inadmissible sense, the par-

say: "Thus we see that unless we choose to call our body the owner or bearer of the data [the data of immediate experience]—which seems to be a rather misleading expression—we have to say that the data have no owner or bearer." The full import of Schlick's article is, however, obscure to me, and it is quite likely that a false impression is given by the quotation of a single sentence. I shall say merely that I have drawn on Schlick's article in constructing the case of my hypothetical "no-subject" theorist; but shall not claim to be representing his views.

Lichtenberg's anti-Cartesian dictum is, as the subsequent argument will show, one that I endorse, if properly used. But it seems to have been repeated, without being understood, by many of Descartes' critics.

The evidence that Wittgenstein and Schlick ever held a "no-subject" view seems indecisive, since it is possible that the relevant remarks are intended as criticisms of a Cartesian view rather than as expositions of the true view.

ticular thing which is supposed to possess the experiences is not thought of as a body, but as something else, say an ego.

Suppose we call the first type of possession, which is really a certain kind of causal dependence, "having$_1$," and the second type of possession, "having$_2$"; and call the individual of the first type "B" and the supposed individual of the second type "E." Then the difference is that while it is genuinely a contingent matter that *all my experiences are had$_1$ by B*, it appears as a necessary truth that *all my experiences are had$_2$ by E*. But the belief in E and in having$_2$ is an illusion. Only those things whose ownership is logically transferable can be owned at all. So experiences are not owned by anything except in the dubious sense of being causally dependent on the state of a particular body. This is at least a genuine relationship to a thing, in that they might have stood in it to another thing. Since the whole function of E was to own experiences in a logically non-transferable sense of "own," and since experiences are not owned by anything in this sense, for there is no such sense of "own," E must be eliminated from the picture altogether. It only came in because of a confusion.

I think it must be clear that this account of the matter, though it contains *some* of the facts, is not coherent. It is not coherent, in that one who holds it is forced to make use of that sense of possession of which he denies the existence, in presenting his case for the denial. When he tries to state the contingent fact, which he thinks gives rise to the illusion of the "ego," he has to state it in some such form as "All *my* experiences are had$_1$ by (uniquely dependent on the state of) body B." For any attempt to eliminate the "my," or some other expression with a similar possessive force, would yield something that was not a contingent fact at all. The proposition that *all* experiences are causally dependent on the state of a single body B, for example, is just false. The theorist means to speak of all the experiences *had by a certain person* being contingently so dependent. And the theorist cannot consistently argue that "all the experiences of person P" *means the same thing* as "all experiences contingently dependent on a certain body B"; for then his proposition would not be contingent, as his theory requires, but analytic. He must mean to be speaking of some class of experiences of the members of which it is in fact contingently true that they are all dependent on body B. And the defining characteristic of this class is in fact that they are "*my* experiences" or "the experiences *of* some person," where the sense of "possession" is the one he calls into question.

This internal incoherence is a serious matter when it is a question of denying what prima facie is the case: that is, that one does genuinely ascribe one's states of consciousness to something, viz., oneself, and that this kind of ascription is precisely such as the theorist finds unsatisfactory, i.e., is such that it does not seem to make sense to suggest, for example, that the identical pain which was in fact one's own might have been another's. We do not have to seek far in order to understand the place of this logically non-transferable kind of ownership in our general scheme of thought. For if we think of the requirements of identifying reference, in speech, to *particular* states of consciousness, or private experiences, we see that such particulars cannot be thus identifyingly referred to except as the states or experiences *of* some identified *person*. States, or experiences, one might say, *owe* their identity as particulars to the identity of the person whose states or experiences they are. And from this it follows immediately that if they can be identified as particular states or experiences at all, they must be possessed or ascribable in just that way which the no-ownership theorist ridicules, i.e., in such a way that it is logically impossible that a particular state or experience in fact possessed by someone should have been possessed by anyone else. The requirements of identity rule out logical transferability of ownership. So the theorist could maintain his position only by denying that we could ever refer to particular states or experiences at all. And *this* position is ridiculous.

We may notice, even now, a possible connection between the no-ownership doctrine and the Cartesian position. The latter is, straightforwardly enough, a dualism of two subjects (two types of subject). The former could, a little paradoxically, be called a dualism too: a dualism of one subject (the body) and one non-subject. We might surmise that the second dualism, paradoxically so called, arises out of the first dualism, nonparadoxically so called; in other words, that if we try to think of that to which one's states of consciousness are ascribed as something utterly different from that to which certain corporeal characteristics are ascribed, then indeed it becomes difficult to see why states of consciousness should be ascribed, thought of as belonging to, anything at all. And when we think of this possibility, we may also think of another: viz., that both the Cartesian and the no-ownership theorist are profoundly wrong in holding, as each must, that there are two uses of "I" in one of which it denotes something which it does not denote in the other.

III

The no-ownership theorist fails to take account of all the facts. He takes account of some of them. He implies, correctly, that the unique position or role of a single body in one's experience is not a sufficient explanation of the fact that one's experiences, or states of consciousness, are ascribed to something which *has* them, with that peculiar non-transferable kind of possession which is here in question. It may be a necessary part of the explanation, but it is not, by itself, a sufficient explanation. The theorist, as we have seen, goes on to suggest that it is perhaps a sufficient explanation of something else: viz., of our confusedly and mistakenly *thinking* that states of consciousness are to be ascribed to something in this special way. And this suggestion, as we have seen, is incoherent: for it involves the denial that someone's states of consciousness are anyone's. We avoid the incoherence of this denial, while agreeing that the special role of a single body in someone's experience does not suffice to explain why that experience should be ascribed to anybody. The fact that there is this special role does not, by itself, give a sufficient reason why what we think of as a subject of experience should have any use for the conception of himself as such a subject.

When I say that the no-ownership theorist's account fails through not reckoning with all the facts, I have in mind a very simple but, in this question, a very central, thought: viz., that it is a necessary condition of one's ascribing states of consciousness, experiences, to oneself, in the way one does, that one should also ascribe them (or be prepared to ascribe them) to others who are not oneself.[2] This means not less than it says. It means, for example, that the ascribing phrases should be used in just the same sense when the subject is another, as when the subject is oneself. Of course the thought that this is so gives no trouble to the non-philosopher: the thought, for example, that "in pain" means the same whether one says "I am in pain" or "He is in pain." The dictionaries do not give two sets of meanings for every expression which describes a state of consciousness: a first-person meaning, and a second- and third-person meaning. But to the philosopher this thought has given trouble; indeed it has. How could the sense be the same when the method of verification was so different in the two cases—or, rather, when there *was* a method of verification in the one case (the case of others) and not, properly speaking, in the other case (the case of one-

[2] I can imagine an objection to the unqualified form of this statement, an objection which might be put as follows. Surely the idea of a uniquely applicable predicate (a predicate which in *fact* belongs to only one individual) is not absurd. And, if it is not, then surely the most that can be claimed is that a necessary condition of one's ascribing predicates of a certain class to one individual (oneself) is that one should be prepared, or ready, on appropriate occasions, to ascribe them to other individuals, and hence that one should have a conception of what those appropriate occasions for ascribing them would be; but not, necessarily, that one should actually do so on any occasion.

The shortest way with the objection is to admit it, or at least to refrain from disputing it; for the lesser claim is all that the argument strictly requires, though it is *slightly* simpler to conduct it on the basis of the larger claim. But it is well to point out further that we are not speaking of a single predicate, or merely of some group or other of predicates, but of the whole of an enormous class of predicates such that the applicability of those predicates or their negations determines a major logical type or category of individuals. To insist, at this level, on the distinction between the lesser and the larger claims is to carry the distinction over from a level at which it is clearly correct to a level at which it may well appear idle or, possibly, senseless.

The main point here is a purely logical one: the idea of a predicate is correlative with that of a range of distinguishable individuals of which the predicate can be significantly, though not necessarily truly, affirmed.

self)? Or, again, how can it be right to talk of *ascribing* in the case of oneself? For surely there can be a question of ascribing only if there is or could be a question of identifying that to which the ascription is made? And though there may be a question of identifying the one who is in pain when that one is another, how can there be such a question when that one is oneself? But this last query answers itself as soon as we remember that we speak primarily to others, for the information of others. In one sense, indeed, there is no question of my having to *tell who it is* who is in pain, when I am. In another sense I may have to *tell who it is*, i.e., to let others know who it is.

What I have just said explains, perhaps, how one may properly be said to ascribe states of consciousness to oneself, given that one ascribes them to others. But how is it that one can ascribe them to others? Well, *one* thing is certain: that *if* the things one ascribes states of consciousness to, in ascribing them to others, are thought of as a set of Cartesian egos to which *only* private experiences can, in correct logical grammar, be ascribed, *then* this question is unanswerable and this problem insoluble. If, in identifying the things to which states of consciousness are to be ascribed, private experiences are to be all one has to go on, then, just for the very same reason as that for which there is, from one's own point of view, no question of telling that a private experience is one's own, there is also no question of telling that a private experience is another's. All private experiences, all states of consciousness, will be mine, i.e., no one's. To put it briefly: one can ascribe states of consciousness to oneself only if one can ascribe them to others; one can ascribe them to others only if one can identify other subjects of experience; and one cannot identify others if one can identify them *only* as subjects of experience, possessors of states of consciousness.

It might be objected that this way with Cartesianism is too short. After all, there is no difficulty about distinguishing bodies from one another, no difficulty about identifying bodies. And does not this give us an indirect way of identifying subjects of experience, while preserving the Cartesian mode? Can we not identify such a subject as, for example, "the subject that stands to that body in the same special relation as I stand to this one"; or, in other words, "the subject of those experiences which stand in the same unique causal relation to body N as *my* experiences stand to body M?" But this suggestion is useless. It requires me to have noted that *my* experiences stand in a special relation to body M, when it is just the right to speak of *my* experiences at all that is in question. (It requires me to have noted that *my* experiences stand in a special relation to body M; but it requires me to have noted this as a condition of being able to identify other subjects of experience, i.e., as a condition of having the idea of myself as a subject of experience, i.e., as a condition of thinking of any experience as *mine*.) So long as we persist in talking, in the mode of this explanation, of experiences on the one hand, and bodies on the other, the most I may be allowed to have noted is that experiences, *all* experiences, stand in a special relation to body M, that body M is unique in just this way, that this is what makes body M unique among bodies. (This "most" is, perhaps, too much–because of the presence of the word "experiences.") The proffered explanation runs: "Another subject of experience is distinguished and identified as the subject of those experiences which stand in the same unique causal relationship to body N as *my* experiences stand to body M." And the objection is: "But what is the word 'my' doing in this explanation? (It could not get on without it.)"

What we have to acknowledge, in order to begin to free ourselves from these difficulties, is the *primitiveness* of the concept of a person. What I mean by the concept of a person is the concept of a type of entity such that *both* predicates ascribing states of consciousness *and* predicates ascribing corporeal characteristics, a physical situation, etc. are equally applicable to a single individual of that single type. And what I mean by saying that this concept is primitive can be put in a number of ways. One way is to return to those two questions I asked earlier: viz., (1) why are states of consciousness ascribed to anything at all? and (2) why are they ascribed to the very same thing as certain corporeal characteristics, a certain physical situation, etc.? I remarked at the beginning that it was not to be supposed that the answers to these questions were independent of each other. And now

I shall say that they are connected in this way: that a necessary condition of states of consciousness being ascribed at all is that they should be ascribed to the *very same things* as certain corporeal characteristics, a certain physical situation, etc. That is to say, states of consciousness could not be ascribed at all, *unless* they were ascribed to persons, in the sense I have claimed for this word. We are tempted to think of a person as a sort of compound of two kinds of subject—a subject of experiences (a pure consciousness, an ego), on the one hand, and a subject of corporeal attributes on the other.

Many questions arise when we think in this way. But, in particular, when we ask ourselves how we come to frame, to get a use for, the concept of this compound of two subjects, the picture—if we are honest and careful—is apt to change from the picture of two subjects to the picture of one subject and one nonsubject. For it becomes impossible to see how we could come by the idea of different, distinguishable, identifiable subjects of experiences—different consciousnesses —*if this idea is thought of as logically primitive*, as a logical ingredient in the compound idea of a person, the latter being composed of two subjects. For there could never be any question of assigning an experience, as such, to any subject other than oneself; and therefore never any question of assigning it to oneself either, never any question of ascribing it to a subject at all. So the concept of the pure individual consciousness—the pure ego—is a concept that cannot exist; or, at least, cannot exist as a primary concept in terms of which the concept of a person can be explained or analyzed. It can only exist, if at all, as a secondary, nonprimitive concept, which itself is to be explained, analyzed, in terms of the concept of a person. It was the entity corresponding to this illusory primary concept of the pure consciousness, the ego-substance, for which Hume was seeking, or ironically pretending to seek, when he looked into himself, and complained that he could never discover himself without a perception and could never discover anything but the perception. More seriously—and this time there was no irony, but a confusion, a Nemesis of confusion for Hume—it was this entity of which Hume vainly sought for the principle of unity, confessing himself perplexed and defeated; sought vainly because there is no principle of unity where there is no principle of differentiation. It was this, too, to which Kant, more perspicacious here than Hume, accorded a purely formal ("analytic") unity: the unity of the "I think" that accompanies all my perceptions and therefore might just as well accompany none. And finally it is this, perhaps, of which Wittgenstein spoke when he said of the subject, first, that there is no such thing, and, second, that it is not a part of the world, but its limit.

So, then, the word "I" never refers to this, the pure subject. But this does not mean, as the no-ownership theorist must think and as Wittgenstein, at least at one period, seemed to think, that "I" in some cases does not refer at all. It refers, because I am a person among others. And the predicates which would, *per impossibile*, belong to the pure subject if it could be referred to, belong properly to the person to which "I" does refer.

The concept of a person is logically prior to that of an individual consciousness. The concept of a person is not to be analyzed as that of an animated body or of an embodied anima. This is not to say that the concept of a pure individual consciousness might not have a logically secondary existence, if one thinks, or finds, it desirable. We speak of a dead person—a body—and in the same secondary way we might at least think of a disembodied person, retaining the logical benefit of individuality from having been a person.[3]

IV

It is important to realize the full extent of the acknowledgment one is making in acknowledging the logical primitiveness of the concept of a person. Let me rehearse briefly the stages of the argument. There would be no question of ascribing one's own states of consciousness, or experiences, to anything, unless one also ascribed states of consciousness, or experiences, to other individual entities of the same logical type as that thing to which one ascribes one's own states of

[3] A little further thought will show how limited this concession is. But I shall not discuss the question now.

consciousness. The condition of reckoning oneself as a subject of such predicates is that one should also reckon others as subjects of such predicates. The condition, in turn, of this being possible, is that one should be able to distinguish from one another (pick out, identify) different subjects of such predicates, i.e., different individuals of the type concerned. And the condition, in turn, of this being possible is that the individuals concerned, including oneself, should be of a certain unique type: of a type, namely, such that to each individual of that type there *must* be ascribed, or ascribable, *both* states of consciousness *and* corporeal characteristics. But this characterization of the type is still very opaque and does not at all clearly bring out what is involved. To bring this out, I must make a rough division, into two, of the kinds of predicates properly applied to individuals of this type. The first kind of predicate consists of those which are also properly applied to material bodies to which we would not dream of applying predicates ascribing states of consciousness. I will call this first kind M-predicates: and they include things like "weighs 10 stone," "is in the drawing room," and so on. The second kind consists of all the other predicates we apply to persons. These I shall call P-predicates. And P-predicates, of course, will be very various. They will include things like "is smiling," "is going for a walk," as well as things like "is in pain," "is thinking hard," "believes in God," and so on.

So far I have said that the concept of a person is to be understood as the concept of a type of entity such that *both* predicates ascribing states of consciousness *and* predicates ascribing corporeal characteristics, a physical situation, etc., are equally applicable to an individual entity of that type. And all I have said about the meaning of saying that this concept is primitive is that it is not to be analyzed in a certain way or ways. We are not, for example, to think of it as a secondary kind of entity in relation to two primary kinds, viz., a particular consciousness and a particular human body. I implied also that the Cartesian error is just a special case of a more general error, present in a different form in theories of the no-ownership type, of thinking of the designations, or apparent designations, of persons as *not* denoting precisely the same thing, or entity, for all kinds of predicate ascribed to the entity designated. That is, if we are to avoid the general form of this error we must *not* think of "I" or "Smith" as suffering from type-ambiguity. (If we want to locate type-ambiguity somewhere, we would do better to locate it in certain predicates like "is in the drawing room," "was hit by a stone," etc., and say they mean one thing when applied to material objects and another when applied to persons.)

This is all I have so far said or implied about the meaning of saying that the concept of a person is primitive. What has to be brought out further is what the implications of saying this are as regards the logical character of those predicates in which we ascribe states of consciousness. And for this purpose we may well consider P-predicates in general. For though not all P-predicates are what we should call "predicates ascribing states of consciousness" (for example, "going for a walk" is not), they may be said to have this in common, that they imply the possession of consciousness on the part of that to which they are ascribed.

What then are the consequences of this view as regards the character of P-predicates? I think they are these. Clearly there is no sense in talking of identifiable individuals of a special type, a type, namely, such that they possess both M-predicates and P-predicates, unless there is in principle some way of telling, with regard to any individual of that type, and any P-predicate, whether that individual possesses that P-predicate. And, in the case of at least some P-predicates, the ways of telling must constitute in some sense logically adequate kinds of criteria for the ascription of the P-predicate. For suppose in no case did these ways of telling constitute logically adequate kinds of criteria. Then we should have to think of the relation between the ways of telling and what the P-predicate ascribes (or a part of what it ascribes) always in the following way: we should have to think of the ways of telling as *signs* of the presence, in the individual concerned, of this different thing (the state of consciousness). But then we could only know that the way of telling was a sign of the presence of the different thing ascribed by the P-predicate, by the observation of correlations between the two. But this observation we could each make only in one case, namely, our own. And now we are back in the position of the defender of Cartesianism, who thought our way with it was too short. For what, now, does "our own case" mean? There is no sense in the idea of ascribing states of consciousness to oneself, or at all, unless the ascriber already knows how to ascribe at least some states of consciousness to others. So he cannot (or cannot generally) argue "from his own case" to conclusions about how to do this; for unless he already knows how to do this, he has no conception of *his own case*, or any *case* (i.e., any subject of experiences). Instead, he just has evidence that pain, etc., may be expected when a certain body is affected in certain ways and not when others are.

The conclusion here is, of course, not new. What I have said is that one ascribes P-predicates to others on the strength of observation of their behavior; and that the behavior criteria one goes on are not just signs of the presence of what is meant by the P-predicate, but are criteria of a logically adequate kind for the ascription of the P-predicate. On behalf of this conclusion, however, I am claiming that it follows from a consideration of the conditions necessary for any ascription of states of consciousness to anything. The point is not that we must accept this conclusion in order to avoid skepticism, but that we must accept it in order to explain the existence of the conceptual scheme in terms of which the skeptical problem is stated. But once the conclusion is accepted, the skeptical problem does not arise. (And so with the generality of skeptical problems: their statement involves the pretended acceptance of a conceptual scheme and at the same time the silent repudiation of one of the conditions of its existence. This is why they are, in the terms in which they are stated, insoluble.) But this is only half the picture about P-predicates.

Now let us turn to the other half. For of course it is true, at least of some important classes of P-predicates, that when one ascribes them to oneself, one does not do so on the strength of observation of those behavior criteria on the strength of which one ascribes them to others. This is not true of all P-predicates. It is not, in general, true of those which carry assessments of character and capability: these, when self-ascribed, are in general ascribed on the same kind of basis as that on which they are ascribed to others. And of those P-predicates of which it is true that one does not generally ascribe them to oneself on the basis of the criteria on the strength of which one ascribes them to others, there are many of which it is also true that their ascription is liable to correction by the self-ascriber on this basis. But there remain many cases in which one has an entirely adequate basis for ascribing a P-predicate to oneself, and yet in which this basis is quite distinct from those on which one ascribes the predicate to another. (Thus one says, reporting a present state of mind or feeling: "I feel tired, am depressed, am in pain.") How can this fact be reconciled with the doctrine that the criteria on the strength of which one ascribes P-predicates to others are criteria of a logically adequate kind for this ascription?

The apparent difficulty of bringing about this reconciliation may tempt us in many directions. It may tempt us, for example, to deny that these self-ascriptions are really ascriptions at all; to *assimilate* first-person ascriptions of states of consciousness to those other forms of behavior which constitute criteria on the basis of which one person ascribes P-predicates to another. This device seems to avoid the difficulty; it is not, in all cases, entirely inappropriate. But it obscures the facts, and is needless. It is merely a sophisticated form of failure to recognize the special character of P-predicates (or at least of a crucial class of P-predicates). For just as there is not (in general) one primary process of learning, or teaching oneself, an inner private meaning for predicates of this class, then another process of learning to apply such predicates to others on the strength of a correlation, noted in one's own case, with certain forms of behavior, so—and equally—there is not (in general) one primary process of learning to apply such predicates to others on the strength of behavior criteria, and then another process of acquiring the secondary technique of exhibiting a new form of behavior, viz., first-person P-utterances. Both these pictures are refusals to acknowledge the unique logical character of the predicates concerned.

Suppose we write "Px" as the general form of propositional function of such a predicate. Then according to the first picture, the expression which primarily replaces "x" in this form is "I," the first-person singular pronoun; its uses with other replacements are secondary, derivative, and shaky. According to the second picture, on the other hand, the primary replacements of "x" in this form are "he," "that person," etc., and its use with "I" is secondary, peculiar, not a true ascriptive use. But it is essential to the character of these predicates that they have both first- and third-person ascriptive uses, that they are both self-ascribable otherwise than on the basis of observation of the behavior of the subject of them, and other-ascribable on the basis of behavior criteria. To learn their use is to learn both aspects of their use. In order to *have* this type of concept, one must be both a self-ascriber and an other-ascriber of such predicates, and must see every other as a self-ascriber. And in order to *understand* this type of concept, one must acknowledge that there is a kind of predicate which is unambiguously and adequately ascribable *both* on the basis of observation of the subject of the predicate *and* not on this basis (independently of observation of the subject): the second case is the case where the ascriber is also the subject. If there were no concepts answering to the characterization I have just given, we should indeed have no philosophical problem about the soul; but equally we should not have *our* concept of a person.

To put the point—with a certain unavoidable crudity—in terms of one particular concept of this class, say, that of depression, we speak of behaving in a depressed way (of depressed behavior) and also of feeling depressed (of a feeling of depression). One is inclined to argue that feelings can be felt, but not observed, and behavior can be observed, but not felt, and that therefore there must be room here to drive in a logical wedge. But the concept of depression spans the place where one wants to drive it in. We might say, in order for there to be such a concept as that of X's depression, the depression which X has, the concept must cover both what is felt, but not observed, by X and what may be observed, but not felt, by others than X (for all values of X). But it is perhaps better to say: X's depression *is* something, one and the same thing, which is felt but not observed by X and observed but not felt by others than X. (And, of course, what can be observed can also be faked or disguised.) To refuse to accept this is to refuse to accept the structure of the language in which we talk about depression. That is, in a sense, all right. One might give up talking; or devise, perhaps, a different structure in terms of which to soliloquize. What is not all right is simultaneously to pretend to accept that structure and to refuse to accept it; i.e., to couch one's rejection in the language of that structure.

It is in this light that we must see some of the familiar philosophical difficulties in the topic of the mind. For some of them spring from just such a failure to admit, or fully appreciate, the character which I have been claiming for at least some P-predicates. It is not seen that these predicates could not have either aspect of their use (the self-ascriptive and the non-self-ascriptive) without having the other aspect. Instead, one aspect of their use is taken as self-sufficient, which it could not be, and then the other aspect appears as problematical. And so we oscillate between philosophical skepticism and philosophical behaviorism. When we take the self-ascriptive aspect of the use of some P-predicate (say, "depressed") as primary, then a logical gap seems to open between the criteria on the strength of which we say that another is depressed, and the actual state of depression. What we do not realize is that if this logical gap is allowed to open, then it swallows not only his depression, but our depression as well. For if the logical gap exists, then depressed behavior, however much there is of it, is no more than a sign of depression. And it can become a sign of depression only because of an observed correlation between it and depression. But whose depression? Only mine, one is tempted to say. But if *only* mine, then *not* mine at all. The skeptical position customarily represents the crossing of the logical gap as at best a shaky inference. But the point is that not even the syntax of the premises of the inference exists if the gap exists.

If, on the other hand, we take the other-ascriptive uses of these predicates as self-sufficient, we may come to think that all there is in the meaning of these predicates, as predicates, is the criteria on the strength of which we ascribe them to others. Does this not follow from the denial of the logical gap? It does not follow. To think that it does is to forget the self-ascriptive use of these predicates, to forget that we have to do with a class of predicates to the meaning of which it is essential that they should be both self-ascribable and other-ascribable to the same individual, when self-ascriptions are not made on the observational basis on which other-ascriptions are made, but on another basis. It is not that these predicates have two kinds of meaning. Rather, it is essential to the single kind of meaning that they do have that both ways of ascribing them should be perfectly in order.

If one is playing a game of cards, the distinctive markings of a certain card constitute a logically adequate criterion for calling it, say, the Queen of Hearts; but, in calling it this, in the context of the game, one is also ascribing to it properties over and above the possession of those markings. The predicate gets its meaning from the whole structure of the game. So it is with the language which ascribes P-predicates. To say that the criteria on the strength of which we ascribe P-predicates to others are of a logically adequate kind for this ascription is not to say that all there is to the ascriptive meaning of these predicates is these criteria. To say this is to forget that they are P-predicates, to forget the rest of the language-structure to which they belong.

V

Now our perplexities may take a different form, the form of the question "But how can one ascribe to oneself, not on the basis of observation, *the very same thing* that others may have, on the basis of observation, a logically adequate reason for ascribing to one?" And this question may be absorbed in a wider one, which might be phrased: "How are P-predicates possible?" or "How is the concept of a person possible?" This is the question by which we replace those two earlier questions, viz.: "Why are states of consciousness ascribed at all, ascribed to anything?" and "Why are they ascribed to the very same thing as certain corporeal characteristics, etc.?" For the answer to these two initial questions is to be found nowhere else but in the admission of the primitiveness of the concept of a person, and hence of the unique character of P-predicates. So residual perplexities have to frame themselves in this new way. For when we have acknowledged the primitiveness of the concept of a person and, with it, the unique character of P-predicates, we may still want to ask what it is in the natural facts that makes it intelligible that we should have this concept, and to ask this in the hope of a non-trivial answer.[4] I do not pretend to be able to satisfy this demand at all fully. But I may mention two very different things which might count as beginnings or fragments of an answer.

And, first, I think a beginning can be made by moving a certain class of P-predicates to a central position in the picture. They are predicates, roughly, which involve doing something, which clearly imply intention or a state of mind or at least consciousness in general, and which indicate a characteristic pattern, or range of patterns, of bodily movement, while not indicating at all precisely any very definite sensation or experience. I mean such things as "going for a walk," "furling a rope," "playing ball," "writing a letter." Such predicates have the interesting characteristic of many P-predicates that one does not, in general, ascribe them to oneself on the strength of observation, whereas one does ascribe them to others on the strength of observation. But, in the case of these predicates, one feels minimal reluctance to concede that what is ascribed in these two different ways is the same. And this is because of the marked dominance of a fairly definite pattern of bodily movement in what they ascribe, and the marked absence of any distinctive experience. They release us from the idea that the only things we can know about without observation, or inference, or both, are private experiences; we can know also, without telling by either of these means, about the present and future movements of a body. Yet bodily movements are certainly also things we can know about by observation and inference.

Among the things that we observe, as opposed to the things we know without observation, are the movements of bodies similar to that about which we have knowledge not based on observation. It is important that we understand such ob-

[4] I mean, in the hope of an answer which does not *merely* say: Well, there are people in the world.

served movements; they bear on and condition our own. And in fact we understand them, we interpret them, only by seeing them as elements in just such plans or schemes of action as those of which we know the present course and future development without observation of the relevant present movements. But this is to say that we see such movements (the observed movements of others) as *actions*, that we interpret them in terms of intention, that we see them as movements of individuals of a type to which also belongs that individual whose present and future movements we know about without observation; that we see others, as self-ascribers, not on the basis of observations, of what we ascribe to them on this basis.

Of course these remarks are not intended to suggest how the "problem of other minds" could be solved, or our beliefs about others given a general philosophical "justification." I have already argued that such a "solution" or "justification" is impossible, that the demand for it cannot be coherently stated. Nor are these remarks intended as a priori genetic psychology. They are simply intended to help to make it seem intelligible to us, at this stage in the history of the philosophy of this subject, that we have the conceptual scheme we have. What I am suggesting is that it is easier to understand how we can see each other (and ourselves) as persons, if we think first of the fact that we act, and act on each other, and act in accordance with a common human nature. "To see each other as persons" is a lot of things; but not a lot of separate and unconnected things. The class of P-predicates that I have moved into the center of the picture are not unconnectedly there, detached from others irrelevant to them. On the contrary, they are inextricably bound up with the others, interwoven with them. The topic of the mind does not divide into unconnected subjects.

I spoke just now of a common human nature. But there is also a sense in which a condition of the existence of the conceptual scheme we have is that human nature should not be common, should not be, that is, a community nature. Philosophers used to discuss the question of whether there was, or could be, such a thing as a "group mind." And for some the idea had a peculiar fascination, while to others it seemed utterly absurd and nonsensical and at the same time, curiously enough, pernicious. It is easy to see why these last found it pernicious: they found something horrible in the thought that people should cease to have toward individual persons the kind of attitudes that they did have, and instead have attitudes in some way analogous to those toward groups; and that they might cease to decide individual courses of action for themselves and instead merely participate in corporate activities. But their finding it pernicious showed that they understood the idea they claimed to be absurd only too well. The fact that we find it natural to individuate as persons the members of a certain class of what might also be individuated as organic bodies does not mean that such a conceptual scheme is inevitable for any class of beings not utterly unlike ourselves.

Might we not construct the idea of a special kind of social world in which the concept of an individual person has no employment, whereas an analogous concept for groups does have employment? Think, to begin with, of certain aspects of actual human existence. Think, for example, of two groups of human beings engaged in some competitive but corporate activity, such as battle, for which they have been exceedingly well trained. We may even suppose that orders are superfluous, though information is passed. It is easy to imagine that, while absorbed in such activity, the members of the groups make no references to individual persons at all, have no use for personal names or pronouns. They do, however, refer to the groups and apply to them predicates analogous to those predicates ascribing purposive activity which we normally apply to individual persons. They may, *in fact*, use in such circumstances the plural forms "we" and "they"; but these are not genuine plurals, they are plurals without a singular, such as we use in sentences like these: "We have taken the citadel," "We have lost the game." They may also refer to elements in the group, to members of the group, but exclusively in terms which get their sense from the parts played by these elements in the corporate activity. (Thus we sometimes refer to what are in fact persons as "stroke" or "tackle.")

When we think of such cases, we see that we ourselves,

over a part of our social lives—not, I am thankful to say, a very large part—do operate conceptual schemes in which the idea of the individual person has no place, in which its place is taken, so to speak, by that of a group. But might we not think of communities or groups such that this part of the lives of their members was the dominant part—or was the whole? It sometimes happens, with groups of human beings, that, as we say, their members think, feel, and act "as one." The point I wish to make is that a condition for the existence, the use, of the concept of an individual person is that this should happen *only sometimes*.

It is absolutely useless to say, at this point: But all the same, even if this happened all the time, every member of the group would have an individual consciousness, would be an individual subject of experience. The point is, once more, that there is no sense in speaking of the individual consciousness just as such, of the individual subject of experience just as such: for there is no way of identifying such pure entities.[5] It is true, of course, that in suggesting this fantasy, I have taken our concept of an individual person as a starting point. It is this fact which makes the useless reaction a natural one. But suppose, instead, I had made the following suggestion: that each part of the human body, each organ and each member, had an individual consciousness, was a separate center of experiences. This, in the same way, but more obviously, would be a useless suggestion. Then imagine all the intermediate cases, for instance these. There is a class of moving natural objects, divided into groups, each group exhibiting the same characteristic pattern of activity. Within each group there are certain differentiations of appearance accompanying differentiations of function, and in particular there is one member of each group with a distinctive appearance. Cannot one imagine different sets of observations which might lead us, in the one case, to think of the particular member as the spokesman of the group, as its mouthpiece; and in the other case to think of him as its mouth, to think of the group as a single *scattered* body? The point is that as soon as we adopt the latter way of thinking then

[5] More accurately: their identification is necessarily secondary to the identification of persons.

we want to drop the former; we are no longer influenced by the human analogy in its first form, but only in its second; and we no longer want to say: "Perhaps the members have consciousness." To understand the movement of our thought here, we need only remember the startling ambiguity of the phrase "a body and its members."

VI

I shall not pursue this attempt at explanation any further. What I have been mainly arguing for is that we should acknowledge the logical primitiveness of the concept of a person and, with this, the unique logical character of certain predicates. Once this is acknowledged, certain traditional philosophical problems are seen not to be problems at all. In particular, the problem that seems to have perplexed Hume[6] does not exist—the problem of the principle of unity, of identity, of the particular consciousness, of the particular subject of "perceptions" (experiences) considered as a primary particular. There is no such problem and no such principle. If there were such a principle, then each of us would have to apply it in order to decide whether any contemporary experience of his was his or someone else's; and there is no sense in this suggestion. (This is not to deny, of course, that one *person* may be unsure of his own identity in some way, may be unsure, for example, whether some particular action, or series of actions, had been performed by him. Then he uses the same methods (the same in principle) to resolve the doubt about himself as anyone else uses to resolve the same doubt about him. And these methods simply involve the application of the ordinary criteria for *personal* identity. There remains the question of what exactly these criteria are, what their relative weights are, etc.; but, once disentangled from spurious questions, this is one of the easier problems in philosophy.)

Where Hume erred, or seems to have erred, both Kant and Wittgenstein had the better insight. Perhaps neither always expressed it in the happiest way. For Kant's doctrine

[6] *Cf.* the Appendix to the *Treatise of Human Nature.*

that the "analytic unity of consciousness" neither requires nor entails any principle of unity is not as clear as one could wish. And Wittgenstein's remarks (at one time) to the effect that the data of consciousness are not owned, that "I" as used by Jones, in speaking of his own feelings, etc., does not refer to what "Jones" as used by another refers to, seem needlessly to flout the conceptual scheme we actually employ. It is needlessly paradoxical to deny, or seem to deny, that when Smith says "Jones has a pain" and Jones says "I have a pain," they are talking about the same entity and saying the same thing about it, needlessly paradoxical to deny that Jones can *confirm* that he has a pain. Instead of denying that self-ascribed states of consciousness are really ascribed at all, it is more in harmony with our actual ways of talking to say: For each user of the language, there is just one person in ascribing to whom states of consciousness he does not need to use the criteria of the observed behavior of that person (though he does not necessarily not do so); and that person is himself. This remark at least respects the structure of the conceptual scheme we employ, without precluding further examination of it.

SELECTED BIBLIOGRAPHY

This bibliography, with the exception of a very few notable articles, is comprised of philosophical literature which appeared in periodicals between the years 1945–63. In gathering this bibliography, only articles dealing explicitly with the philosophy of mind were included. Many articles dealing with auxiliary problems can be found in the anthologies listed below. An asterisk indicates that the anthology contains a bibliography.

ANTHOLOGIES

ANDERSON, ALAN ROSS, ed.: *Minds and Machines*, Englewood Cliffs, N.J.: Prentice-Hall, 1964.

*AYER, A. J., ed.: *Logical Positivism*, Glencoe, Ill.: Free Press, 1959.

*BLACK, MAX, ed.: *Philosophical Analysis*, Ithaca, N.Y.: Cornell University Press, 1950.

———, ed.: *Philosophy in Ameica*, Ithaca, N.Y.: Cornell University Press, 1965.

BUTLER, R. J., ed.: *Analytical Philosophy*, Oxford: Blackwell, 1963.

———, ed.: *Analytical Philosophy*, Second Series, Oxford: Blackwell, 1965.

*CHAPPELL, V. C., ed.: *The Philosophy of Mind*, Englewood Cliffs, N.J.: Prentice-Hall, 1962.

COLODNY, R. G., ed.: *Frontiers of Science and Philosophy*, Pittsburgh: University of Pittsburgh Press, 1962.

FEIGL, HERBERT, ed.: *Minnesota Studies in the Philosophy of Science*, Vol. I, The Foundations of Science and the Concepts of Psychology and Psychoanalysis, eds. Herbert Feigl and Michael Scriven; Vol. II, Concepts, Theories, and the Mind-Body Problem, eds. Herbert Feigl, Michael Scriven, and Grover Maxwell; Vol. III, Scientific Explanation, Space, and Time, eds. Herbert Feigl and Grover Maxwell. Minneapolis: University of Minnesota Press, 1956–62.

*———, and WILFRED SELLARS, eds.: *Readings in Philosophical Analysis*, N.Y.: Appleton, 1949.

FLEW, ANTONY, ed.: *Logic and Language*, First Series, Oxford: Blackwell, 1951.

———, ed.: *Logic and Language*, Second Series, Oxford: Blackwell, 1953.

———, ed.: *Essays in Conceptual Analysis*, London: Macmillan, 1956.

———, ed.: *Body, Mind and Death*, New York: Macmillan, 1964.

HOOK, SIDNEY, ed.: *Dimensions of Mind; a Symposium*, New York: New York University Press, 1960.

LEWIS, H. D., ed.: *Contemporary British Philosophy*, Third Series, London: George Allen & Unwin, 1956.

MACDONALD, MARGARET, ed.: *Philosophy and Analysis*, Oxford: Blackwell, 1954.

MACE, C. A., ed.: *British Philosophy in the Mid-Century*, London: George Allen & Unwin, 1957.

VESEY, G. N. A., ed.: *Body and Mind*, London: George Allen & Unwin, 1964.

ARTICLES

Journals frequently cited are abbreviated as follows:

A	*Analysis*
ASP	*Aristotelian Society Proceedings*
ASSV	*Aristotelian Society Supplementary Volume*
JP	*Journal of Philosophy*
M	*Mind*
P	*Philosophy*
PQ	*Philosophical Quarterly*
PR	*Philosophical Review*

AARON, R. I., "Dispensing with Mind," ASP, LII (1951–52), 225–42.

ABELSON, R., "'Because I want to'," M, LXXIV (1965), 540–53.

ALBRITTON, R., "On Wittgenstein's Use of the Term 'Criterion,'" JP, LVI (1959), 845–57.

ALDRICH, V. C., "Reflections on Ayer's *Concept of a Person*," JP, LXII (1965), 111–28.

ALEXANDER, P., "Other People's Experiences," ASP, LI (1950–51), 25–46.

———, "Cause and Cure in Psychotherapy," ASSV, XXIX (1955), 25–42.

———, "Rational Behavior and Psychoanalytic Explanation," M, LXXI (1962), 326–41.

ANSCOMBE, G. E. M., "Pretending," ASSV, XXXII (1958), 279–94.

———, "The Two Kinds of Error in Action," JP, LX (1963), 393–400.

AUNE, BRUCE, "The Problem of Other Minds," PR, LXX (1961), 320–39.

———, "Feelings, Moods, and Introspection," M, LXXII (1963), 187–208.

AUSTIN, J. L., "Other Minds," ASSV, XX (1946), 148–87.

———, "Ifs and Cans," *Proceedings of the British Academy*, XLII (1956), 109–32.

AYER, A. J., "Can There Be a Private Language?" ASSV, XXVIII (1954), 63–78.

———, "Professor Malcolm on Dreams," JP, LVII (1960), 517–35.

BAIER, K., "Decisions and Descriptions," M, LX (1951), 181–204.

———, "Pains," *Australasian Journal of Philosophy*, XL (1962), 1–23.

———, "The Place of a Pain," PQ, XIV (1964), 138–50.

———, "Action and Agent," *The Monist*, XLIX (1965), 183–95.

BARNES, W. H. F., "Talking about Sensations," ASP, LIV (1953–54), 261–78.

———, "Knowing," PR, LXII (1963), 3–16.

BEDFORD, ERROL, "Pleasure and Belief," ASSV, XXXIII (1959), 73–92.

BENNETT, D., "Action, Reason and Purpose," JP, LXII (1965), 85–96.

BRADLEY, R. D., "Avowals of Immediate Experience," M, LXIII (1964), 186–203.

BRANDT, RICHARD and JAEGWON KIM, "Wants as Explanations of Actions," JP, LX (1963), 425–34.

BRITTON, KARL, "Seeming," ASSV, XXVI (1952), 195–214.

———, "Feelings and Their Expression," P, XXXII (1957), 97–111.

CANFIELD, JOHN V., "Judgements in Sleep," PR, LXX (1961), 224–30.

——— and DON F. GUSTAFSON, "Self-Deception," A, XXXIII (1962), 32–36.

CASTAÑEDA, HECTOR-NERI, "Criteria, Analogy, and Knowledge of Other Minds," JP, LIX (1962), 533–46.

CHAPPELL, V. C., "The Concept of Dreaming," PQ, XIII (1963), 193–213.

———, "Myself and Others," *Analysis Supplement*, 23 (1963), 50–57.

CHISHOLM, RODERICK M., "Sentences about Believing," ASP, LVI (1955–56), 125–48.

COOK, J. W., "Wittgenstein on Privacy," PR, LXXIV (1965), 281–314.

DANTO, ARTHUR C., "Concerning Mental Pictures," JP, LV (1958), 12–20.

———, "What Can We Do," JP, LX (1963), 435–45.

DAVENEY, T. F., "Wanting," PQ, XI (1961), 135–44.

———, "Choosing," M, LXXIII (1964), 515–26.

DAY, J. P., "Unconscious Perception," ASSV, XXXIV (1960), 47–66.

DILMAN, ILHAM, "The Unconscious," M, LXVIII (1959), 446–73.

DODWELL, P. C., "Causes of Behavior and Explanation in Psychology," M, LXIX (1960), 1–13.

DONNELLAN, KEITH S., "Knowing What I Am Doing," JP, LX (1963), 401–9.

EBERSOLE, FRANK B., "De Somniis," M, LXVIII (1959), 336–49.

EVANS, J. L., "Knowledge and Behavior," ASP, LIV (1953–54), 27–48.

———, "Choice," PQ, V (1955), 301–15.

EWING, A. C., "The Justification of Emotions," ASSV, XXXI (1957), 59–74.

FARRELL, B. A., "Can Psychoanalysis be Refuted?" *Inquiry*, IV (1961), 16–36.

FEIGL, HERBERT, "Other Minds and the Egocentric Predicament," JP, LV (1958), 978–87.

FINDLAY, J. N., "Linguistic Approach to Psycho-Physics," ASP, L (1949–50), 43–64.

———, "Is There Knowledge by Acquaintance?" ASSV, XXIII (1949), 111–28.

———, "The Justification of Attitudes," M, LXIII (1954), 145–61.

FLEMING, BRICE NOEL, "On Avowals," PR, LXIV (1955), 614–25.

———, "On Intention," PR, LXXIII (1964), 301–20.

FLEW, ANNIS, "Images, Supposing and Imagining," P, XXVIII (1953), 246–54.

FLEW, ANTONY, "Psycho-Analytic Explanation," A, X (1949–50), 8–15.

FURLONG, E. J., "Memory," M, LVII (1948), 16–44.

GALLAGHER, K. T., "On Choosing to Choose," M, LXXIII (1964), 480–95.

GALLIE, W. B., "Pleasure," ASSV, XXVIII (1954), 147–64.

GINNANE, W. J., "Thoughts," M, LXIX (1960), 372–90.

GOSLING, J., "Mental Causes and Fear," M, LXXI (1962), 289–306.

———, "Emotion and Object," PR, LXXIV (1965), 486–503.

GRANT, C. K., "Good At," ASSV, XXXII (1958), 173–94.

GRIFFITHS, A. P. and R. S. PETERS, "The Autonomy of Prudence," M, LXXI (1962), 161–80.

GUSTAFSON, DON F., "On the Identity Theory," A, XXIV (1963), 30–32.

———, "Voluntary and Involuntary," *Philosophy and Phenomenological Research*, XXIV (1964), 493–501.

———, "Privacy," *The Southern Journal of Philosophy*, III (1965), 140–46.

——— and JOHN V. CANFIELD, "Self-Deception," A, XXIII (1962), 32–36.

HALL, ROLAND, "Presuming," PQ, XI (1961), 10–22.

HAMLYN, D. W., "Behaviour," P, XXVIII (1953), 132–45.

———, "The Stream of Thought," ASP, LVI (1955–56), 63–82.

HAMPSHIRE, STUART, "The Concept of Mind. By Gilbert Ryle," M, LIX (1950), 237–55.

———, "The Analogy of Feeling," M, LXI (1952), 1–12.

———, "Self-Knowledge and the Will," *Revue Internationale de Philosophie*, VII (1953), 230–45.

———, "Dispositions," A, XIV (1953–54), 5–11.

———, "On Referring and Intending," PR, LXV (1956), 1–13.

——— and H. L. A. HART, "Decision, Intention and Certainty," M, LXVII (1958), 1–12.

HARRISON, JONATHAN, "Does Knowing Imply Believing?" PQ, XIII (1963), 322–32.

HART, H. L. A., "The Ascription of Responsibility and Rights," ASP, XLIX (1948–49), 171–94.

———, "Is There Knowledge by Acquaintance?" ASSV, XXIII (1949), 69–90.

——— and STUART HAMPSHIRE, "Decision, Intention and Certainty," M, LXVII (1958), 1–12.

HEATH, P. L., "Intentions," ASSV, XXIX (1955), 147–64.

HOLLAND, R. F., "The Empiricist Theory of Memory," M, LXIII (1954), 464–86.

HORSBURGH, H. J. N., "Prudence," ASSV, XXXVI (1962), 65–76.

HUDSON, H., "Why We Cannot Witness or Observe What Goes On 'In Our Heads,'" M, LXV (1956), 218–30.

———, "Why Are Our Feelings of Pain Perceptually Unobservable?" A, XXI (1960–61), 97–100.

HUGHES, G. E., "Is There Knowledge by Acquaintance?" ASSV, XXIII (1949), 91–110.

HUNTER, J. F. M., "Conscience," M, LXXII (1963), 309–34.

JONES, J. R., "Self-Knowledge," ASSV, XXX (1956), 120–42.

———, "The Two Contexts of Mental Concepts," ASP, LIX (1958–59), 105–24.

JONES, O. R., "Things Known Without Observation," ASP, LXI (1960–61), 129–50.

KAUFMAN, ARNOLD S., "Ability," JP, LX (1963), 537–51.
KIM, JAEGWON and RICHARD BRANDT, "Wants as Explanations of Actions," JP, LX (1963), 425–34.
KNEALE, M., "What Is the Mind-Body Problem?" ASP, L (1949–50), 105–22.
KNEALE, W., "Experience and Introspection," ASP, L (1949–50), 1–28.
KOURANY, JANET, "Memory," JP, LXII (1965), 387–98.
LANDESMAN, CHARLES, "Philosophical Problems of Memory," JP, LVIV (1962), 57–65.
———, "The New Dualism in the Philosophy of Mind," *Review of Metaphysics*, XIX (1965).
LINSKY, L., "Illusions and Dreams," M, LXXI (1962), 364–71.
———, "Deception," *Inquiry*, VI (1963), 157–69.
LLOYD, A. C., "Thinking and Language," ASSV, XXV (1951), 35–64.
LONG, D. C., "The Philosophical Concept of a Human Body," PR, LXXIII (1964), 321–37.
LOUCH, A. R., "Privileged Access," M, LXXIV (1965), 155–73.
MABBOTT, J. D., "Prudence," ASSV, XXXVI (1962), 51–64.
MC CRACKEN, D. L., "Motives and Causes," ASSV, XXVI (1952), 163–78.
MACE, C. A., "Abstract Ideas and Images," ASSV, XXVII (1953), 137–48.
——— and R. S. PETERS, "Emotions and the Category of Passivity," PAS, LXII (1961–62), 117–42.
MC GUINNESS, B. F., "'I Know What I Want,'" ASP, LVII (1956–57), 305–20.
MAC INTYRE, A. C., "Cause and Cure in Psychotherapy," ASSV, XXIX (1955), 43–58.
———, "Purpose and Intelligent Action," ASSV, XXXIV (1960), 79–96.
———, "Pleasure as a Reason for Action," *The Monist*, XLIX (1965), 215–33.
MALCOLM, NORMAN, "Knowledge and Belief," M, LXI (1952), 178–89.
———, "Direct Perception," PQ, III (1953), 301–16.
———, "Wittgenstein's *Philosophical Investigations*," PR, LXIII (1954), 530–59.
———, "Memory and the Past," *Monist*, XLVII (1963), 247–66.
MANSER, A. R., "Dreams," ASSV, XXX (1956), 208–28.
———, "Pleasure," ASP, LXI (1960–61), 223–38.
MARTIN, MICHAEL, "The Scientific Status of Psychoanalytic Clinical Evidence," *Inquiry*, VII (1964), 13–36.

MEILAND, J. W., "Are There Unintentional Actions?" PR, LXXII (1963), 377–81.

MELDEN, A. I., "Willing," PR, 69 (1960), 475–84.

MILES, T. R., "Self-Knowledge," ASSV, XXX (1956), 143–56.

———, "The 'Mental'-'Physical' Dichotomy," ASP, LXIV (1964), 71–84.

MITCHELL, D., "Privileged Utterances," M, LXII (1953), 355–66.

MURDOCH, IRIS, "Thinking and Language," ASSV, XXV (1951), 25–34.

MYERS, G. E., "Motives and Wants," M, LXXIII (1964), 173–85.

NAGEL, THOMAS, "Physicalism," PR, LXXIV (1965), 339–56.

NELSON, JOHN O., "The Validation of Memory and Our Conception of a Past," PR, LXXII (1963), 35–47.

———, "An Inconsistency in *Dreaming*," *Philosophical Studies*, XV (1964), 33–35.

NOWELL-SMITH, P. H., "Choosing, Deciding and Doing," A, XVIII (1957–58), 63–69.

———, "Purpose and Intelligent Action," ASSV, XXXIV (1960), 97–112.

O'SHAUGHNESSY, B., "The Origin of Pain," A, XV (1954–55), 121–30.

———, "The Limits of the Will," PR, LXV (1956), 443–90.

PASSMORE, J. A., "Intentions," ASSV, XXIX (1955), 131–46.

PEARS, D. F., "The Logical Status of Supposition," ASSV, XXV (1951), 83–98.

PENELHUM, TERENCE, "Personal Identity, Memory, and Survival," JP, LVI (1959), 882–903.

PERKINS, MORELAND, "Two Arguments Against a Private Language," JP, LXII (1965), 443–59.

PETERS, R. S., "Cause, Cure and Motive," A, X (1949–50), 103–9.

———, "Observationalism in Psychology," M, LX (1951), 43–61.

———, "Motives and Causes," ASSV, XXVI (1952), 139–62.

———, "Motives and Motivation," P, XXXI (1956), 117–30.

——— and A. P. GRIFFITHS, "The Autonomy of Prudence," M, LXXI (1962), 161–80.

——— and C. A. MACE, "Emotions and the Category of Passivity," PAS, LXII (1961–62), 117–42.

PITCHER, G., "Emotion," M, LXXIV (1965), 326–46.

PLACE, U. T., "Is Consciousness a Brain Process," *The British Journal of Psychology*, XLVII (1956), 44–50.

POLE, DAVID, "Understanding—a Psychical Process," ASP, LX (1959–60), 253–68.

POWELL, BETTY, "Uncharacteristic Actions," M, LXVIII (1959), 492–509.

PRICE, H. H., "Belief and Will," ASSV, XXVIII (1954), 1–26.
PUTNAM, HILARY, "Psychological Concepts, Explication, and Ordinary Language," JP, LIV (1957), 94–100.
QUINTON, A. M., "Seeming," ASSV, XXVI (1952), 235–52.
———, "The Problem of Perception," M, LXIV (1955), 28–51.
———, "The Soul," JP, LIX (1962), 393–409.
REES, W. J., "Continuous States," ASP, LVIII (1957–58), 223–44.
RESCHER, NICHOLAS, "Belief–Contravening Suppositions," PR, LXX (1961), 176–96.
RHEES, R., "Can There Be a Private Language?" ASSV, XXVIII (1954), 77–94.
RITCHIE, A. D., "Agent and Act in Theory of Mind," ASP, LII (1951–52), 1–22.
ROLLINS, C. D., "Personal Predicates," PQ, X (1960), 1–11.
RORTY, R., "Mind-Body Identity, Privacy, and Categories," *Review of Metaphysics*, XIX (1965), 24–54.
RYLE, GILBERT, "Feelings," PQ, I (1950–51), 193–205.
———, "Thinking and Language," ASSV, XXV (1951), 65–82.
SAUNDERS, JOHN T., "Skepticism and Memory," PR, LXXII (1963), 487–96.
SCRIVEN, MICHAEL, "The Mechanical Concept of Mind," M, LXII (1953), 230–40.
———, "Modern Experiments in Telepathy," PR, LXV (1956), 231–53.
SELLARS, WILFRED, "Mind, Meaning and Behavior," *Philosophical Studies*, III (1953), 45–82.
SEVERENS, RICHARD, "Psychological Contexts," JP, LIV (1962), 95–100.
SHAFFER, JEROME, "Could Mental States Be Brain Processes?" JP, LVIII (1961), 813–22.
———, "Recent Work on the Mind-Body Problem," *American Philosophical Quarterly*, II (1965), 81–104.
SHOEMAKER, SYDNEY S., "Personal Identity and Memory," JP, LVI (1959), 868–82.
SIBLEY, FRANK, "Seeking, Scrutinizing and Seeing," M, LXIV (1955), 455–78.
SIEGLER, F. A., "Self-deception," *Australasian Journal of Philosophy*, XLI (1963), 29–43.
SILBER, J. R., "Human Action and the Language of Volitions," ASP, LXIV (1964), 199–220.
SMITH, BRIAN, "Dreaming," *Australasian Journal of Philosophy*, XLIII (1965), 48–57.
SPARSHOTT, F. E., "Avouls and Their Uses," PAS, LXII (1961–62), 63–76.

STRAWSON, P. F., "Philosophical Investigations. By Ludwig Wittgenstein," M, LXIII (1954), 70–99.

SUTHERLAND, N. S., "Motives as Explanations," M, LXVIII (1959), 145–59.

TAYLOR, C. C. W., "Pleasure," *Analysis Supplement* 23 (1963), 2–19.

TAYLOR, D., "Thinking," M, LXV (1956), 246–51.

TAYLOR, JAMES G., "Towards a Science of Mind," M, LXVI (1957), 434–52.

TAYLOR, PAUL W., "Need 'Statements,'" A, XIX (1958–59), 106–11.

TAYLOR, RICHARD, "'I Can,'" PR, LXIX (1958), 78–89.

———, "Deliberation and Foreknowledge," *American Philosophical Quarterly*, I (1964), 73–80.

TEICHMANN, J., "Mental Cause and Effect," M, LXX (1961), 36–52.

THALBERG, I., "False Pleasures," JP, LVIX (1962), 65–74.

———, "Remorse," M, LXXII (1963), 545–55.

———, "Emotion and Thought," *American Philosophical Quarterly*, I (1964), 45–55.

THOMSON, J. F., "The Argument from Analogy and Our Knowledge of Other Minds," M, LX (1951), 336–50.

———, "Private Languages," *American Philosophical Quarterly*, I (1964), 20–31.

TOULMIN, STEPHEN, "The Logical Status of Psychoanalysis," A, IX (1948–49), 23–29.

TURQUET, P. M., "The Criteria for a Psycho-Analytic Interpretation," ASSV, XXXVI (1962), 121–44.

URMSON, J. O., "Motives and Causes," ASSV, XXVI (1952), 179–94.

———, "Recognition," ASP, LVI (1955–56), 259–80.

VENDLER, ZENO, "Verbs and Times," PR, LXVI (1957), 143–60.

VESEY, G. N. A., "Unconscious Perception," ASSV, XXXIV (1960), 67–78.

———, "Bodily Sensations," *Australasian Journal of Philosophy*, XLII (1964), 232–47.

WARNOCK, G. J., "Seeing," ASP, LV (1954–55), 201–18.

WARNOCK, MARY, "The Justification of Emotions," ASSV, XXI (1957), 43–58.

WELLMAN, CARL, "Our Criteria for Third Person Psychological Sentences," JP, LVIII (1961), 281–93.

WHEATLEY, J. M. O., "Wishing and Hoping," A, XVIII (1957–58), 121–31.

WHITE, ALAN R., "'Good At,'" ASSV, XXXII (1958), 195–206.

———, "The Language of Motives," M, LXVII (1958), 258–63.

———, "Different Kinds of Heed Concepts," A, XX (1959–60), 112–16.

———, "The Concept of Care," PQ, X (1960), 271–74.

———, "Inclination," A, XXI (1960–61), 40–42.

WHITELEY, C. H., "Behaviorism," M, LXX (1961), 164–74.

WILLIAMS, B. A. O., "Pleasure and Belief," ASSV, XXXIII (1959), 57–72.

WISDOM, JOHN, "Other Minds I–VIII," M, XLIX–LII (1940, 1941, 1942, 1943).

———, "Other Minds," ASSV, XX (1946), 122–47.

———, "The Concept of Mind," ASP, L (1950), 189–204.

WISDOM, J. O., "Mentality in Machines," ASSV, XXVI (1952), 1–26.

———, "The Criteria for a Psycho-Analytic Interpretation," ASSV, XXXVI (1962), 101–20.

WOLGAST, ELIZABETH, "Wittgenstein and Criteria," *Inquiry*, VII (1964), 348–66.

WOLLHEIM, RICHARD, "Privacy," ASP, LI (1950–51), 83–104.

———, "The Difference Between Sensing and Observing," ASSV, XXVIII (1954), 219–40.